CLASS ACT

To my son Bill and my daughter Jill for their love and devotion.

Class Act
An International Legal Perspective on Class Discrimination

ANNE-MARIE MOONEY COTTER
The Social Security Disability Law Firm, USA

Routledge
Taylor & Francis Group
LONDON AND NEW YORK

First published in paperback 2024

First published 2011 by Ashgate Publishing

Published 2016
by Routledge
4 Park Square, Milton Park, Abingdon, Oxon OX14 4RN

and by Routledge
605 Third Avenue, New York, NY 10158

Routledge is an imprint of the Taylor & Francis Group, an informa business

Publisher's Note
The publisher has gone to great lengths to ensure the quality of this reprint but points out that some imperfections in the original copies may be apparent.

British Library Cataloguing in Publication Data
Cotter, Anne-Marie Mooney.
Class act : an international legal perspective on class discrimination.
1. Equality before the law. 2. Discrimination – Law and legislation. 3. Educational mobility. 4. Educational equalization.
I. Title
342'.085–dc22

Library of Congress Cataloging-in-Publication Data
Cotter, Anne-Marie Mooney.
Class act : an international legal perspective on class discrimination / by Anne-Marie Mooney Cotter.
p. cm.
Includes bibliographical references and index.
ISBN 978–1–4094–1934–1 (hardback : alk. paper)
1. Discrimination – Law and legislation. 2. Equality before the law.
I. Title.
K3242.C676 2010
342.08'5–dc22 2010040018

ISBN: 978-1-4094-1934-1 (hbk)
ISBN: 978-1-03-292097-9 (pbk)
ISBN: 978-1-315-57235-2 (ebk)

DOI: 10.4324/9781315572352

Contents

List of Tables

Biography

Dr. Anne-Marie Mooney Cotter, Esq. is a Montrealer, fluent in both English and French. She earned her Bachelor's degree from McGill University at age 18, her Juris Doctor law degree from one of the leading civil rights institutions, Howard University School of Law, and her Doctorate degree (Ph.D.) from Concordia University, where she specialized in Political Economy International Law, particularly on the issue of equality. Her work experience has been extensive: Chief Advisor and later Administrative Law Judge appointed by the Prime Minister to the Veterans Review and Appeals Tribunal in Canada; Supervising Attorney and later Executive Director for the Legal Services Corporation in the United States; National Director for an environmental network in Canada; Faculty for Business Law at the Law School, Law Society of Ireland; Associate at the law firm of Blake Cassels and Graydon L.L.P. with a secondment as in-house counsel with Agrium Inc. in Canada; Attorney with the Disability Law Center of Alaska; and Solo Practitioner of the Social Security Disability Law Firm. She is also a gold medallist in figure skating. Dr. Cotter is the wife of Mark Badger and the proud mother of Bill and Jill.

Biography

Chapter 1
Introduction to Class Act

> So we come here today to dramatize a shameful condition. In a sense we've come to our nation's capital to cash a check. When the architects of our republic wrote the magnificent words of the Constitution and the Declaration of Independence, they were signing a promissory note to which every (human) was to fall heir. This note was the promise that all ... would be guaranteed the unalienable rights of life, liberty, and the pursuit of happiness … A check which has come back marked insufficient funds. We refuse to believe that there are insufficient funds in the great vaults of opportunity of this nation. And so we've come to cash this check, a check that will give us upon demand the riches of freedom and the security of justice.[1]

In our universal quest for justice in general, and tolerance for class distinctions in *Class Act*, we may learn from the immortal words of one of the greatest civil rights leaders and human rights activists Dr. Martin Luther King Jr. This book, *Class Act*, focuses on the goal of class equality, and the importance of the law and legislation to combat class discrimination in these troubling times. The aim of this book is to better understand the issue of inequality and to improve the likelihood of achieving class equality in the future and ending class inequality, using education levels as the determining factor for class differentiations. *Class Act* examines the primary role of legislation, which has an impact on the court process, as well as the primary role of the judicial system, which has an impact on the fight for class tolerance. This is the ninth book in a series of books on discrimination law. Other titles in the series are *Gender Injustice* dealing with gender discrimination, *Race Matters* dealing with race discrimination, *This Ability* dealing with disability discrimination, *Just A Number* dealing with age discrimination, *Heaven Forbid* dealing with religious discrimination, *Ask No Questions* dealing with sexual orientation discrimination, *Pregnant Pause* dealing with maternity discrimination and *Culture Clash* dealing with ethnic discrimination. A similar approach and structure is used throughout the series to illustrate comparisons and contradictions in discrimination law.

Fundamental rights are rights which either are inherent in a person by natural law or are instituted in the citizen by the State. The ascending view of the natural law of divine origin over human law involves moral expectations in human beings through a social contract, which includes minimum moral rights of which one may not be deprived by government or society. The competing view is that courts operating under the Constitution can enforce only those guarantees which are

---

1 King Jr., Martin Luther, *March on Washington*, 28 August, 1963.

expressed. Thus, legislation has an impact on the court system and on society as a whole. Internationally and nationally, attempts have been made to improve the situation of those who are members of all classes and outlaw class discrimination through acceptance and accommodation.

In looking at the relationship between "Class Act" and the law, the book deals comprehensively with the issue of class discrimination throughout its chapters by outlining important legislation in the area, with no particular position argued necessarily but with the intent to give the reader the knowledge to make up their own mind; also, for the most part, the countries examined were chosen because of their predominant common law background, because of their predominant use of the English language in legislation and case law, and because of their predominant role in the fight against discrimination: Chapter 1 introduces the reader to the core area of class inequality; Chapter 2 covers class inequality in human relations around the world; Chapter 3 looks at the United Nations; Chapters 4 and 5 examine class inequality in Australia and New Zealand, and Africa and South Africa, respectively; Chapters 6 and 7 examine class inequality in Canada, Mexico and the United States, and the North American situation with the North American Free Trade Agreement regarding class discrimination, respectively; Chapters 8 and 9 examine class inequality in the United Kingdom and Ireland, and the European situation with the European Union Treaty regarding class discrimination, respectively; and Chapter 10 concludes this overview of class inequality.

The globalization process and the various economic agreements have a direct impact on people's lives as key players in the labor market today. This study seeks to comparatively analyze legislation impacting class equality in various countries internationally. It also examines the two most important trade agreements of our day, namely the North American Free Trade Agreement and the European Union Treaty in a historical and compelling analysis of equality. Although an important trade agreement with implications for labor, the North American Free Trade Agreement has a different system from the European system in that it has no overseeing court with jurisdiction over the respective countries. Further, the provisions for non-discrimination in the labor process are contained in a separate document, the North American Agreement on Labor Cooperation. On the other hand, the European Union Treaty takes a different approach, by directly providing for non-discrimination, as well as an overseeing court, the European Court of Justice, and the treaty is made part of the domestic law of every Member State, weakening past discriminatory laws and judgments. Further, the European process actively implements equality by way of European Union legislation.

North America, as the new world with its image of freedom and equality, is considered to have made great strides in civil rights. However, the American philosophy of survival of the fittest, the pursuit of materialism and the search for the fountain of youth have slowed down the process. With the advent of the European Union, the coming together of nations has had a very positive influence on the enforcement of human rights, much more so than that of North America, because of the unique European approach.

All parties must cooperate, and governments need to work with businesses, trade unions and society as a whole, so together they can create an environment where all humans can participate at all levels of political life and decision-making. Indeed, combating class inequality and achieving class equality requires a strong "Class Act" focus on class neutrality in constitutional, legal, judicial and electoral frameworks for all humans to be actively involved at the national and international levels.

According to liberal democracy, the rule of law is the foundation stone for the conduct of institutions. *Class Act* offers a defense of the notion that social reform is possible and plausible through key institutions, which include the legal system and its use of the law. For liberal democracy, the legislative system is the core for the governance of society in the way it functions toward social equality of opportunity. It is clear that if we initially reform our legislation and our laws and in the end our way of thinking, then there will be a change in the institutions of society and their functioning, which will be a major step forward in societal reform.

The law is of central importance in the debate for change from class inequality to class equality. Actionable and enforceable rights are legal norms, which represent social facts demarcating areas of action linked with universalized freedom.[2] Law is a powerful tool, which can and must be used to better society. Associated with command, duty and sanction, and emanating from a determined source, law is a rule of conduct enforced by sanctions, and administered by a determinate locus of power concentrated in a sovereign or a surrogate, the court. Therefore, the justice system and the courts play a vital role in enforcing the law.

Legitimacy has subjective guarantees of internalization with the acceptance and belief in authority, and objective guarantees of enforcement with the expectation of reactions to the behavior.[3] Therefore, the law must recognize equally all members of society, in order for it to be effective. Further, in order for a law to be seen as legitimate from society's point of view and accepted by the people, in general to be followed, a process of inclusive interaction by all affected must first be realized. When creating laws, this means that input from various groups, including all humans regardless of class, is critical.

Thus, laws have two components: namely, facts, which stabilize expectations and sustain the order of freedom, and norms, which provide a claim of approval by everyone. Law makes possible highly artificial communities whose integration is based simultaneously on the threat of internal sanctions and the supposition of a rationally motivated agreement.[4] Class discrimination and injustice can be undercut through the effective use of both the law and the courts.

The facticity of the enforcement of law is intertwined with the legitimacy of a genesis of law that claims to be rational, because it guarantees liberty. Laws can go a long way in forbidding inequality and providing for equality; where one ends

---

2 Habermas, Jürgen, *Between Facts and Norms*, Massachusetts, 1998, p. xii.

3 Fried, Morton, *The Evolution of Political Society*, New York, 1967, p. 23.

4 Habermas, Jürgen, *Between Facts and Norms*, Massachusetts, 1998, p. 8.

the other begins. There are two ranks of law, namely ordinary law of legislation, administration and adjudication, and higher constitutional law affecting rights and liberties, which government must respect and protect. The latter encompasses the constitutions of the various nations as interpreted by the supreme courts. Law holds its legitimacy and validity by virtue of its coercive potential, its rational claim of acceptance as right. It is procedurally constructed to claim agreement by all citizens in a discursive process purported to be open to all equally for legitimacy with a presumption of fair results. The legitimate legal order is found in its reflexive process. Therefore, we must all believe that equality is a good and necessary thing, which is essential to the very growth of society and to the ending of **class** discrimination.

Thus, conflict resolution is a process of reasoned agreement where, firstly, members assume the same meanings by the same words; secondly, members are rationally accountable for their actions; and thirdly, mutually acceptable resolutions can be reached so that supporting arguments justify the confidence in the notion that the truth in justice will not be proven false.[5] Disenchantment with the law and the legal process only serves to undermine the stabilization of communities. By legitimizing the legal process and holding up the ideals of equality in the fight against class discrimination, the law and the courts can bring about change.

All humans have had to fight in the formulation of laws and in the enforcement of equality in the courts. Human differences rest on economic determination and historical change. Inequality in the distribution of private property among different classes of people has been a characteristic of society. The ruling class loathes that which it is not, that which is foreign to it. The patriarchal system has freely fashioned laws and adjusted society to suit those in power, and this has traditionally been young white Anglo-Saxon Protestant men.

Relationships, opportunities, attributes and preconceived notions are socially constructed and are learned through socialization processes. They are context and time-specific but changeable, since the physical and the mental determine what is expected, allowed and valued in a given situation. In most societies, there are differences and inequalities between humans in the decision-making opportunities, assignment of responsibilities, undertaking of activities, and access to and control over resources with class part of the broader sociocultural context. There are important criteria for analysis, including class, poverty, gender, race, ethnicity, disability, age, religion and sexual orientation, and hence all these can, alone or combined, amount to discrimination.

The concept of equality is the ignoring of difference between individuals for a particular purpose in a particular context, or the deliberate indifference to specified differences in the acknowledgement of the existence of difference. It is important to note that assimilation is not equality. The notion of rights and of equality should be bound to the notion of justice and fairness. Legal freedom and rights must be seen as relationships not possessions, as doing, not having.

5 Ibid., p. xv.

While injustice involves a constraint of freedom and a violation of human dignity through a process of oppression and domination, justice involves the institutional conditions necessary for the development and exercise of individual capacities for collective communication and cooperation.[6] Discrimination is the withholding from the oppressed and subordinated what enables them to exercise private and public autonomy. The struggle must be continued to bring about psychological, sociological and institutional changes to allow all members of the human race, regardless of class, to feel equal and to recognize all as being so. Solidarity and cooperation are required for universal and global equality.

Though humans are mortal and civilizations come and go, from biblical times to our days, there has been a fixed pivot for the thoughts of all generations and for humans of all continents, namely the equal dignity inherent in the human personality.[7] Even Pope John XXIII described the United Nations Declaration of Human Rights in his 1963 Encyclical *Pacem in Terris*, as "one of the most important acts of the United Nations" and as "a step towards the politico-judicial organization of the world community"; "In social life, every right conferred on man by nature creates in others (individuals and collectivities) a duty, that of recognizing and respecting that right."[8] Further, Pope John Paul II described the importance of work and of just remuneration in his 1981 Encyclical *Laborem Exercens*:

> Work bears a particular mark of … humanity, the mark of a person operating within a community of persons … While work, in all its many senses, is an obligation, that is to say a duty, it is also a source of rights on the part of the worker. These rights must be examined in the broad context of human rights as a whole, which are connatural with man, and many of which are proclaimed by various international organisations and increasingly guaranteed by the individual States for their citizens. Respect for this broad range of human rights constitutes the fundamental condition for peace in the modern world: peace both within individual countries and societies and in international relations … The human rights that flow from work are part of the broader context of those fundamental rights of the person … The key problem of social ethics … is that of just remuneration for work done … Hence, in every case, a just wage is the concrete means of verifying the justice of the whole socio-economic system and, in any case, of checking that it is functioning justly.[9]

An improvement in equality of opportunity is sought for all rather than a utopian state of equality. No one should misunderstand this. Clearly, oppression exists. Rather, this book *Class Act* seeks to add to the list of inequalities to be considered, in this context class discrimination, and does not rule out other forms of injustices.

---

6 Ibid., p. 419.

7 Cassin, René, *From the Ten Commandments to the Rights of Man*, France, 1969.

8 Pope John XXIII, *Pacem in Terris*, Rome, 1963.

9 Pope John Paul II, *Laborem Exercens*, Rome, 1981.

Generalities are not presumed nor are they made here, for this would detract from the very purpose of this book, to bring to the forefront of discussion the reality of injustice, not to create further injustice, in the pursuit of "Class Act".

Chapter 2
Class Act in Class Discrimination

Introduction

In the quest for tolerance of class distinctions in *Class Act*, this chapter will examine discrimination, including the World Summit and Declaration on Social Development, and the World Summit and Declaration on Education for All: Meeting Basic Learning Needs. All human, civil, cultural, economic, political and social rights, including the right to development, are universal, indivisible, interdependent and interrelated. Governments and others must not only refrain from violating human rights, but must work actively to promote and protect these rights.

The word "discrimination" comes from the Latin *discriminare*, which means to "distinguish between". Discrimination is action based on prejudice resulting in unfair treatment of people. Social theories of egalitarianism claim that social equality regardless of class issues should prevail. Unlawful discrimination can be characterized as direct or indirect: direct discrimination involves treating someone less favorably, because of the possession of a prohibited attribute such as class than they would treat someone without the prohibited attribute who was in the same circumstances; and indirect discrimination involves setting a condition or requirement that a smaller proportion of those with the prohibited attribute can comply with than those who do not have the prohibited attribute without reasonable justification. Forms of invidious discrimination include distinctions based on class, gender, race, ethnicity, disability, age, religion and sexual orientation. If the justification is rational, then the discrimination is not invidious. Many governments have attempted to control discrimination through civil rights legislation, equal opportunity laws and institutionalized policies of affirmative action. Within the equal opportunities/individual merit approach can be found a spectrum of tests for discrimination: at one end of the spectrum there is the "equality as mere rationality", where arbitrary and unreasonable behavior is deemed discriminatory, but justifications for discrimination are accepted at face value; at the other end of the spectrum there is the "equality as fairness", where justifications are examined critically, the possibility of indirect discrimination is recognized, and burdens of proof may be shifted; and a third conception of equality is the "equality of opportunity", which argues for institutional and structural changes to remove the barriers to equal participation of people belonging to different groups. Further, prejudice is the process of pre-judging something, and refers to existing biases toward the members of certain groups, based on social stereotypes. Many prejudicial behaviors are picked up at a young age by children emulating their elders' way of thinking and speaking. Overall, equal opportunity refers to the idea that all people should start out in life from the same platform, in that all should have equal opportunities in life, regardless of where they were born or who their parents were. Egalitarianism is the moral doctrine that equality ought to prevail throughout society, and according to legal egalitarianism, everyone ought to be considered equal under the law. Tokenism occurs when a small group is invited to participate in an initiative to demonstrate that a program is progressive or to show someone has consulted the constituency, but in fact has ignored their views, which is discriminatory in itself.

Standards or rules of behavior are norms, which help us to predict the behavior of others and, in turn, allow others to know what to expect of us, with our culture defining what is proper and improper behavior, what is right and wrong, and what we are expected to do and not to do.[1] The concept of minority group has long provided a valuable frame of reference for understanding the experiences of groups of people in society who are singled out, based on some cultural or physical characteristic, for discriminatory treatment.[2] In terms of class and culture, they are a cross-cutting determinant, since cultural values and traditions determine to a large extent how a given society views class.[3] Culture is a key factor in whether or not co-residency with others is the preferred way of living. There is cultural diversity and complexity within countries, and among countries and regions of the world. Policies and programs need to respect current cultures and traditions, while de-bunking outdated stereotypes and misinformation. Moreover, there are critical universal values that transcend culture, such as ethics and human rights. While the significance of national and regional particularities, and various historical, cultural and religious backgrounds must be borne in mind, it is the duty of States, regardless of their political, economic and cultural systems, to promote and protect human rights and fundamental freedoms of all people. The implementation of these principles of equality, including through national laws, strategies, policies, programs and development priorities, is the sovereign responsibility of each State, in conformity with human rights and fundamental freedoms.

There must be immediate and concerted action by all to create a peaceful, just and humane world based on human rights and fundamental freedoms, including the principle of equality for people and from all walks of life, and to this end, broad-based and sustained economic growth in the context of sustainable development is necessary to sustain social development and social justice. Success will require a strong commitment on the part of governments, international organizations and institutions at all levels, and will also require adequate mobilization of resources from multilateral, bilateral and private sources for the advancement of all humans for strengthening the capacity of national, sub-regional, regional and

---

1 Harris, Diana K., "Age Norms", in Erdman B. Palmore, Laurence Branch and Diana K. Harris, *Encyclopedia of Ageism*, New York, 2005.

2 Wirth, L., "The Problem of Minority Groups", in R. Linton (ed.), *The Science of Man in the World Crisis*, New York, 1945, pp. 347–72.

3 United Nations, Beijing Platform for Action.

international institutions; a commitment to equal rights, equal responsibilities and equal opportunities for the equal participation of all regardless of class issues in all national, regional and international bodies in the policy-making processes; and the establishing or strengthening of mechanisms at all levels for accountability to the world's population in general. As globalization continues to influence economic opportunities worldwide, its effects remain uneven, creating both risks and opportunities for different groups. For many, globalization has intensified existing inequalities and insecurities, often translating into the loss of livelihoods, labor rights and social benefits. Organizations and networks are taking on issues of social justice and equal rights to influence economic policies and decisions at the micro, meso and macro levels.

Even with economic growth, conditions can arise which can aggravate social inequality and marginalization. Hence, it is indispensable to search for new alternatives that ensure that all members of society benefit from economic growth based on a holistic approach to all aspects of development: equality between people, social justice, conservation and protection of the environment, sustainability, solidarity, participation and cooperation, peace and respect for human rights. The rapid process of adjustment due to downsizing in sectors has led to increased unemployment and underemployment. Only a new era of international cooperation among peoples based on a spirit of partnership within an equitable international social and economic environment, along with a radical transformation of the relationship to one of full and equal partnership will enable the world to meet the challenges of the twenty-first century. Non-governmental organizations (NGOs) have played an important advocacy role in advancing legislation or mechanisms to ensure the promotion of all people, and have become catalysts for new approaches to development.

Actions to be taken at the national and international levels by all governments, the United Nations' system, international and regional organizations, including international financial institutions, the private sector, non-governmental organizations (NGOs) and other actors of civil society, include the creation and maintenance of a non-discriminatory as well as class-sensitive legal environment through review of legislation with a view to striving to remove discriminatory provisions. Problems continue to persist in addressing the challenges of equalities, empowerment, poverty eradication, and advancement of all. Political, economic and ecological crises, systematic or *de facto* discrimination, violations of and failure to protect human rights and fundamental freedoms, and ingrained prejudicial attitudes towards different groups are impediments to equality. It will be critical for the international community to demonstrate a new commitment for the future to inspire a new generation to work together for a more just society.

Class mobility is the movement of people between social classes, and mobility can be upward or downward. A number of things, such as wealth and money, education and occupation, can influence one's social class. Other factors such as race, ethnicity, gender, disability, age and language, can be a hindrance or a help for class mobility. Many societies are loosely divided into a lower, middle, and upper class: the lower classes are typically laborers of low income with limited education and few opportunities for educational or economic advancement; the middle classes are more economically stable, with more education and many more social opportunities as a result of their elevated class status; and the upper class, usually the smallest group, includes people with established social positions which include great prestige, along with economic security.

More than 1 billion people in the world today, the great majority of whom are women, live in unacceptable conditions of poverty, mostly in the developing countries. Poverty has various causes, including structural ones, and is often related to class issues. Poverty is a complex, multidimensional problem, with origins in both the national and international domains. The globalization of the world's economy and the deepening interdependence among nations present challenges and opportunities for sustained economic growth and development, as well as risks and uncertainties for the future of the world economy. The uncertain global economic climate has been accompanied by economic restructuring as well as, in a certain number of countries, persistent, unmanageable levels of external debt and structural adjustment programs. In addition, all types of conflict, displacement of people and environmental degradation have undermined the capacity of governments to meet the basic needs of their populations. Transformations in the world economy are profoundly changing the parameters of social development in all countries. Macroeconomic policies need rethinking and reformulation to address such trends.

Poverty has various manifestations, including lack of income and productive resources sufficient to ensure a sustainable livelihood; hunger and malnutrition; ill health; limited or lack of access to education and other basic services; increasing morbidity and mortality from illness; homelessness and inadequate housing; unsafe environments; and social discrimination and exclusion. It is also characterized by lack of participation in decision-making and in civil, social and cultural life. It occurs in all countries, as mass poverty in many developing countries and as pockets of poverty amidst wealth in developed countries. Poverty may be caused by an economic recession that results in loss of livelihood or by disaster or conflict. There is also the poverty of low-wage workers and the utter destitution of people who fall outside family support systems, social institutions and safety nets. Poverty is directly related to the absence of economic opportunities and autonomy, lack of access to economic resources, including credit, land ownership and inheritance, lack of access to education and support services and the minimal participation in the decision-making process of those affected by poverty. In countries with a high level of school enrolment of girls, those who leave the educational system the earliest, without any qualification, are among the most vulnerable in the labor market. Sustainable development and economic growth that is both sustained and sustainable are possible only through improving the economic, social, political, legal and cultural status of all human beings. Equitable social development that recognizes empowering the poor to utilize environmental resources sustainably is a necessary foundation for sustainable development.

In terms of the economy, there are considerable differences in women's and men's access to and opportunities to exert power over economic structures in their societies. In most parts of the world, women are virtually absent from or are poorly represented in economic decision-making, including the formulation of financial, monetary, commercial and other economic policies, as well as tax systems and rules governing pay. Since it is often within the framework of such policies that individual men and women make their decisions, inter alia, on how to divide their time between remunerated and unremunerated work, the actual development of these economic structures and policies has a direct impact on a person's access to economic resources, their economic power and consequently the extent of equality between them at the individual and family levels as well as in society as a whole.

Therefore, governments should enact and enforce laws and introduce implementing measures, including means of redress and access to justice in cases of non-compliance, to prohibit direct and indirect discrimination on grounds of class or social origin, in relation to access to employment, conditions of employment, including training, promotion, health and safety, as well as termination of employment and social security of workers; and enact and enforce laws and develop workplace policies against class or social origin discrimination in the labor market, in hiring and promotion, and in the extension of employment benefits and social security, as well as regarding discriminatory working conditions. Further, governments and Corporations should develop leadership training and opportunities to encourage all to take leadership roles both as students and as adults in civil society; develop appropriate education and information programs with due respect for multilingualism, particularly in conjunction with the mass media, that make the public, particularly parents, aware of the importance of non-discriminatory education for children and the equal sharing of family responsibilities by girls and boys; promote life-long education and training to ensure the availability of a broad range of educational and training programs that lead to ongoing acquisition by women and girls of the knowledge and skills required for living in, contributing to and benefiting from their communities and nations; and finally, create flexible education, training and retraining programs for life-long learning that facilitate transitions between women's activities at all stages of their lives.[4]

Overall, the promotion and protection of all human rights and fundamental freedoms is essential for the creation of an inclusive society for all. Specifically, tolerance toward class and social origin requires a political, economic, ethical and spiritual vision for social development based on human dignity, human rights, equality, respect, peace, democracy, mutual responsibility and cooperation, and full respect for the various religious and ethical values, and cultural backgrounds of people. On the national level, innovation, mobilization of financial resources and the development of necessary human resources should be undertaken simultaneously. Progress should be contingent upon effective partnership among governments, all parts of civil society and the private sector, as well as an enabling

4 Ibid.

environment based on democracy, the rule of law, respect for all human rights, fundamental freedoms and good governance at all levels, including national and international levels. Other crucial elements include: effective organizations of all people; educational, training and research activities on tolerance; and national data collection and analysis, such as the compilation of specific information for policy planning, monitoring and evaluation. Independent impartial monitoring of progress in implementation is valuable. Governments, as well as civil society, can facilitate the mobilization of resources by organizations representing and supporting all people by increasing incentives. On the international level, globalization and interdependence are opening new opportunities through trade, investment and capital flows, and advances in technology, including information technology, for the growth of the world economy and the development.

However, there remain serious challenges, including serious financial crises, insecurity, poverty, exclusion and inequality within and among societies. Considerable obstacles to further integration and full participation in the global economy remain. Unless the benefits of social and economic development are extended to all countries, a growing number of people in all countries and even entire regions will remain marginalized from the global economy. Obstacles affecting peoples and countries must be overcome in order to realize the full potential of opportunities presented for the benefit of all. Thus, globalization offers opportunities and challenges, but the developing countries and countries with economies in transition face special difficulties in responding to those challenges and opportunities. Globalization should be fully inclusive and equitable, with a strong need for policies and measures at the national and international levels, formulated and implemented with the full and effective participation of developing countries and countries with economies in transition to help them respond effectively to those challenges and opportunities.[5]

World Summit and Declaration on Social Development

At the World Summit on Social Development, held in March 1995 in Copenhagen, governments reached a new consensus on the need to put people at the centre of development, adopting the Copenhagen Declaration and Programme of Action which represent a new consensus on the need to put people at the centre of development. The largest gathering yet of world leaders, 117 heads of State or Government, pledged to make the conquest of poverty, the goal of full employment and the fostering of stable, safe and just societies their overriding objectives. The Copenhagen Declaration on Social Development states:

> 1. For the first time in history, at the invitation of the United Nations, we gather as heads of State and Government to recognize the significance of social

5 Ibid.

development and human well-being for all and to give to these goals the highest priority both now and into the twenty-first century.
2. We acknowledge that the people of the world have shown in different ways an urgent need to address profound social problems, especially poverty, unemployment and social exclusion, that affect every country. It is our task to address both their underlying and structural causes and their distressing consequences in order to reduce uncertainty and insecurity in the life of people.
3. We acknowledge that our societies must respond more effectively to the material and spiritual needs of individuals, their families and the communities in which they live throughout our diverse countries and regions. We must do so not only as a matter of urgency but also as a matter of sustained and unshakeable commitment through the years ahead.
4. We are convinced that democracy and transparent and accountable governance and administration in all sectors of society are indispensable foundations for the realization of social and people-centred sustainable development.
5. We share the conviction that social development and social justice are indispensable for the achievement and maintenance of peace and security within and among our nations. In turn, social development and social justice cannot be attained in the absence of peace and security or in the absence of respect for all human rights and fundamental freedoms. This essential interdependence was recognized 50 years ago in the Charter of the United Nations and has since grown ever stronger.
6. We are deeply convinced that economic development, social development and environmental protection are interdependent and mutually reinforcing components of sustainable development, which is the framework for our efforts to achieve a higher quality of life for all people. Equitable social development that recognizes empowering the poor to utilize environmental resources sustainably is a necessary foundation for sustainable development. We also recognize that broad-based and sustained economic growth in the context of sustainable development is necessary to sustain social development and social justice.
7. We recognize, therefore, that social development is central to the needs and aspirations of people throughout the world and to the responsibilities of Governments and all sectors of civil society. We affirm that, in both economic and social terms, the most productive policies and investments are those that empower people to maximize their capacities, resources and opportunities. We acknowledge that social and economic development cannot be secured in a sustainable way without the full participation of women and that equality and equity between women and men is a priority for the international community and as such must be at the centre of economic and social development.
8. We acknowledge that people are at the centre of our concerns for sustainable development and that they are entitled to a healthy and productive life in harmony with the environment.
9. We gather here to commit ourselves, our Governments and our nations to enhancing social development throughout the world so that all men and

> women, especially those living in poverty, may exercise the rights, utilize the resources and share the responsibilities that enable them to lead satisfying lives and to contribute to the well-being of their families, their communities and humankind. To support and promote these efforts must be the overriding goals of the international community, especially with respect to people suffering from poverty, unemployment and social exclusion.
>
> 10. We make this solemn commitment on the eve of the fiftieth anniversary of the United Nations, with a determination to capture the unique possibilities offered by the end of the cold war to promote social development and social justice. We reaffirm and are guided by the principles of the Charter of the United Nations and by agreements reached at relevant international conferences, including the World Summit for Children, held at New York in 1990; the United Nations Conference on Environment and Development, held at Rio de Janeiro in 1992; the World Conference on Human Rights, held at Vienna in 1993; the Global Conference on the Sustainable Development of Small Island Developing States, held at Bridgetown, Barbados in 1994; and the International Conference on Population and Development, held at Cairo in 1994. By this Summit we launch a new commitment to social development in each of our countries and a new era of international cooperation between Governments and peoples based on a spirit of partnership that puts the needs, rights and aspirations of people at the centre of our decisions and joint actions.
>
> 11. We gather here in Copenhagen in a Summit of hope, commitment and action. We gather with full awareness of the difficulty of the tasks that lie ahead but with a conviction that major progress can be achieved, must be achieved and will be achieved.
>
> 12. We commit ourselves to this Declaration and Programme of Action for enhancing social development and ensuring human well-being for all throughout the world now and into the twenty-first century. We invite all people in all countries and in all walks of life, as well as the international community, to join us in our common cause.[6]

Section A outlines the current social situation and reasons for convening the Summit:

> 13. We are witnessing in countries throughout the world the expansion of prosperity for some, unfortunately accompanied by an expansion of unspeakable poverty for others. This glaring contradiction is unacceptable and needs to be corrected through urgent actions.
>
> 14. Globalization, which is a consequence of increased human mobility, enhanced communications, greatly increased trade and capital flows, and technological developments, opens new opportunities for sustained economic growth and development of the world economy, particularly in developing

6 Copenhagen Declaration on Social Development.

countries. Globalization also permits countries to share experiences and to learn from one another's achievements and difficulties, and promotes a cross-fertilization of ideals, cultural values and aspirations. At the same time, the rapid processes of change and adjustment have been accompanied by intensified poverty, unemployment and social disintegration. Threats to human well-being, such as environmental risks, have also been globalized. Furthermore, the global transformations of the world economy are profoundly changing the parameters of social development in all countries. The challenge is how to manage these processes and threats so as to enhance their benefits and mitigate their negative effects upon people.

15. There has been progress in some areas of social and economic development:

(a) The global wealth of nations has multiplied sevenfold in the past 50 years and international trade has grown even more dramatically;

(b) Life expectancy, literacy and primary education, and access to basic health care, including family planning, have increased in the majority of countries and average infant mortality has been reduced, including in developing countries;

(c) Democratic pluralism, democratic institutions and fundamental civil liberties have expanded. Decolonization efforts have achieved much progress, while the elimination of apartheid is a historic achievement.

16. Yet we recognize that far too many people, particularly women and children, are vulnerable to stress and deprivation. Poverty, unemployment and social disintegration too often result in isolation, marginalization and violence. The insecurity that many people, in particular vulnerable people, face about the future – their own and their children's – is intensifying:

(a) Within many societies, both in developed and developing countries, the gap between rich and poor has increased. Furthermore, despite the fact that some developing countries are growing rapidly the gap between developed and many developing countries, particularly the least developed countries, has widened;

(b) More than one billion people in the world live in abject poverty, most of whom go hungry every day. A large proportion, the majority of whom are women, have very limited access to income, resources, education, health care or nutrition, particularly in Africa and the least developed countries;

(c) There are also serious social problems of a different nature and magnitude in countries with economies in transition and countries experiencing fundamental political, economic and social transformations;

(d) The major cause of the continued deterioration of the global environment is the unsustainable pattern of consumption and production, particularly in industrialized countries, which is a matter of grave concern, aggravating poverty and imbalances;

(e) Continued growth in the world's population, its structure and distribution, and its relationship with poverty and social and gender inequality challenge the adaptive capacities of Governments, individuals, social institutions and the natural environment;

(f) Over 120 million people world wide are officially unemployed and many more are underemployed. Too many young people, including those with formal education, have little hope of finding productive work;

(g) More women than men live in absolute poverty and the imbalance continues to grow, with serious consequences for women and their children. Women carry a disproportionate share of the problems of coping with poverty, social disintegration, unemployment, environmental degradation and the effects of war;

(h) One of the world's largest minorities, more than 1 in 10, are people with disabilities, who are too often forced into poverty, unemployment and social isolation. In addition, in all countries older persons may be particularly vulnerable to social exclusion, poverty and marginalization;

(i) Millions of people world wide are refugees or internally displaced persons. The tragic social consequences have a critical effect on the social stability and development of their home countries, their host countries and their respective regions.

17. While these problems are global in character and affect all countries, we clearly acknowledge that the situation of most developing countries, and particularly of Africa and the least developed countries, is critical and requires special attention and action. We also acknowledge that these countries, which are undergoing fundamental political, economic and social transformation, including countries in the process of consolidating peace and democracy, require the support of the international community.

18. Countries with economies in transition, which are also undergoing fundamental political, economic and social transformation, require the support of the international community as well.

19. Other countries that are undergoing fundamental political, economic and social transformation require the support of the international community as well.

20. The goals and objectives of social development require continuous efforts to reduce and eliminate major sources of social distress and instability for the family and for society. We pledge to place particular focus on and give priority attention to the fight against the world-wide conditions that pose severe threats to the health, safety, peace, security and well-being of our people. Among these conditions are chronic hunger; malnutrition; illicit drug problems; organized crime; corruption; foreign occupation; armed conflicts; illicit arms trafficking, terrorism, intolerance and incitement to racial, ethnic, religious and other hatreds; xenophobia; and endemic, communicable and chronic diseases. To this end, coordination and cooperation at the national level and especially at the regional and international levels should be further strengthened.

21. In this context, the negative impact on development of excessive military expenditures, the arms trade, and investment for arms production and acquisition must be addressed.
22. Communicable diseases constitute a serious health problem in all countries and are a major cause of death globally; in many cases, their incidence is increasing. These diseases are a hindrance to social development and are often the cause of poverty and social exclusion. The prevention, treatment and control of these diseases, covering a spectrum from tuberculosis and malaria to the human immunodeficiency virus / acquired immunodeficiency syndrome (HIV/AIDS), must be given the highest priority.
23. We can continue to hold the trust of the people of the world only if we make their needs our priority. We know that poverty, lack of productive employment and social disintegration are an offence to human dignity. We also know that they are negatively reinforcing and represent a waste of human resources and a manifestation of ineffectiveness in the functioning of markets and economic and social institutions and processes.
24. Our challenge is to establish a people-centred framework for social development to guide us now and in the future, to build a culture of cooperation and partnership, and to respond to the immediate needs of those who are most affected by human distress. We are determined to meet this challenge and promote social development throughout the world.[7]

Section C outlines the various commitments, most notably:
Commitment 1 deals generally with social development:

We commit ourselves to creating an economic, political, social, cultural and legal environment that will enable people to achieve social development.
To this end, at the national level, we will:
(a) Provide a stable legal framework, in accordance with our constitutions, laws and procedures, and consistent with international law and obligations, which includes and promotes equality and equity between women and men, full respect for all human rights and fundamental freedoms and the rule of law, access to justice, the elimination of all forms of discrimination, transparent and accountable governance and administration and the encouragement of partnership with free and representative organizations of civil society;
(b) Create an enabling economic environment aimed at promoting more equitable access for all to income, resources and social services;
(c) Reinforce, as appropriate, the means and capacities for people to participate in the formulation and implementation of social and economic policies and programmes through decentralization, open management of public institutions and strengthening the abilities and opportunities of civil society and local communities to develop their own organizations, resources and activities;

---

7 Ibid., at Section A.

(d) Reinforce peace by promoting tolerance, non-violence and respect for diversity, and by settling disputes by peaceful means;

(e) Promote dynamic, open, free markets, while recognizing the need to intervene in markets, to the extent necessary, to prevent or counteract market failure, promote stability and long-term investment, ensure fair competition and ethical conduct, and harmonize economic and social development, including the development and implementation of appropriate programmes that would entitle and enable people living in poverty and the disadvantaged, especially women, to participate fully and productively in the economy and society;

(f) Reaffirm, promote and strive to ensure the realization of the rights set out in relevant international instruments and declarations, such as the Universal Declaration of Human Rights, the Covenant on Economic, Social and Cultural Rights and the Declaration on the Right to Development, including those relating to education, food, shelter, employment, health and information, particularly in order to assist people living in poverty;

(g) Create the comprehensive conditions to allow for the voluntary repatriation of refugees in safety and dignity to their countries of origin, and the voluntary and safe return of internally displaced persons to their places of origin and their smooth reintegration into their societies.

At the international level, we will:

(h) Promote international peace and security and make and support all efforts to settle international disputes by peaceful means in accordance with the Charter of the United Nations;

(i) Strengthen international cooperation for achieving social development;

(j) Promote and implement policies to create a supportive external economic environment, through, inter alia, cooperation in the formulation and implementation of macroeconomic policies, trade liberalization, mobilization and/or provision of new and additional financial resources that are both adequate and predictable and mobilized in a way that maximizes the availability of such resources for sustainable development, using all available funding sources and mechanisms, enhanced financial stability, and more equitable access of developing countries to global markets, productive investments and technologies and appropriate knowledge, with due consideration to the needs of countries with economies in transition;

(k) Strive to ensure that international agreements relating to trade, investment, technology, debt and official development assistance are implemented in a manner that promotes social development;

(l) Support, particularly through technical and financial cooperation, the efforts of developing countries to achieve rapid, broadly based sustainable development. Particular consideration should be given to the special needs of small island and land-locked developing countries and the least developed countries;

(m) Support, through appropriate international cooperation, the efforts of countries with economies in transition to achieve rapid broadly based sustainable development;

(n) Reaffirm and promote all human rights, which are universal, indivisible, interdependent and interrelated, including the right to development as a universal and inalienable right and an integral part of fundamental human rights, and strive to ensure that they are respected, protected and observed.[8]

Commitment 2 deals with the issue of poverty and its eradication:

We commit ourselves to the goal of eradicating poverty in the world, through decisive national actions and international cooperation, as an ethical, social, political and economic imperative of humankind.
To this end, at the national level, in partnership with all actors of civil society and in the context of a multidimensional and integrated approach, we will:
(a) Formulate or strengthen, as a matter of urgency, and preferably by the year 1996, the International Year for the Eradication of Poverty, national policies and strategies geared to substantially reducing overall poverty in the shortest possible time, reducing inequalities and eradicating absolute poverty by a target date to be specified by each country in its national context;
(b) Focus our efforts and policies to address the root causes of poverty and to provide for the basic needs of all. These efforts should include the elimination of hunger and malnutrition; the provision of food security, education, employment and livelihood, primary health-care services including reproductive health care, safe drinking water and sanitation, and adequate shelter; and participation in social and cultural life. Special priority will be given to the needs and rights of women and children, who often bear the greatest burden of poverty, and to the needs of vulnerable and disadvantaged groups and persons;
(c) Ensure that people living in poverty have access to productive resources, including credit, land, education and training, technology, knowledge and information, as well as to public services, and participate in decision-making on a policy and regulatory environment that would enable them to benefit from expanding employment and economic opportunities;
(d) Develop and implement policies to ensure that all people have adequate economic and social protection during unemployment, ill health, maternity, child-rearing, widowhood, disability and old age;
(e) Ensure that national budgets and policies are oriented, as necessary, to meeting basic needs, reducing inequalities and targeting poverty, as a strategic objective;
(f) Seek to reduce inequalities, increase opportunities and access to resources and income, and remove any political, legal, economic and social factors and constraints that foster and sustain inequality.
At the international level, we will:
(g) Strive to ensure that the international community and international organizations, particularly the multilateral financial institutions, assist developing

8 Ibid., at Commitment 1.

> countries and all countries in need in their efforts to achieve our overall goal of eradicating poverty and ensuring basic social protection;
> (h) Encourage all international donors and multilateral development banks to support policies and programmes for the attainment, in a sustained manner, of the specific efforts of the developing countries and all countries in need relating to people-centred sustainable development and to meeting basic needs for all; to assess their existing programmes in consultation with the concerned developing countries to ensure the achievement of the agreed programme objectives; and to seek to ensure that their own policies and programmes will advance the attainment of agreed development goals that focus on meeting basic needs for all and eradicating absolute poverty. Efforts should be made to ensure that participation by the people concerned is an integral part of such programmes;
> (i) Focus attention on and support the special needs of countries and regions in which there are substantial concentrations of people living in poverty, in particular in South Asia, and which therefore face serious difficulties in achieving social and economic development.[9]

Commitment 3 deals with full-employment and its promotion:

> We commit ourselves to promoting the goal of full employment as a basic priority of our economic and social policies, and to enabling all men and women to attain secure and sustainable livelihoods through freely chosen productive employment and work.
> To this end, at the national level, we will:
> (a) Put the creation of employment, the reduction of unemployment and the promotion of appropriately and adequately remunerated employment at the centre of strategies and policies of Governments, with full respect for workers' rights and with the participation of employers, workers and their respective organizations, giving special attention to the problems of structural, long-term unemployment and underemployment of youth, women, people with disabilities, and all other disadvantaged groups and individuals;
> (b) Develop policies to expand work opportunities and productivity in both rural and urban sectors by achieving economic growth, investing in human resource development, promoting technologies that generate productive employment, and encouraging self-employment, entrepreneurship, and small and medium-sized enterprises;
> (c) Improve access to land, credit, information, infrastructure and other productive resources for small and micro-enterprises, including those in the informal sector, with particular emphasis on the disadvantaged sectors of society;

9 Ibid., at Commitment 2.

(d) Develop policies to ensure that workers and employers have the education, information and training needed to adapt to changing economic conditions, technologies and labour markets;
(e) Explore innovative options for employment creation and seek new approaches to generating income and purchasing power;
(f) Foster policies that enable people to combine their paid work with their family responsibilities;
(g) Pay particular attention to women's access to employment, the protection of their position in the labour market and the promotion of equal treatment of women and men, in particular with respect to pay;
(h) Take due account of the importance of the informal sector in our employment development strategies with a view to increasing its contribution to the eradication of poverty and to social integration in developing countries, and to strengthening its linkages with the formal economy;
(i) Pursue the goal of ensuring quality jobs, and safeguard the basic rights and interests of workers and to this end, freely promote respect for relevant International Labour Organization conventions, including those on the prohibition of forced and child labour, the freedom of association, the right to organize and bargain collectively, and the principle of non-discrimination.
At the international level, we will:
(j) Ensure that migrant workers benefit from the protections provided by relevant national and international instruments, take concrete and effective measures against the exploitation of migrant workers, and encourage all countries to consider the ratification and full implementation of the relevant international instruments on migrant workers;
(k) Foster international cooperation in macroeconomic policies, liberalization of trade and investment so as to promote sustained economic growth and the creation of employment, and exchange experiences on successful policies and programmes aimed at increasing employment and reducing unemployment.[10]

Commitment 4 deals with human rights and its protection:

We commit ourselves to promoting social integration by fostering societies that are stable, safe and just and that are based on the promotion and protection of all human rights, as well as on non-discrimination, tolerance, respect for diversity, equality of opportunity, solidarity, security, and participation of all people, including disadvantaged and vulnerable groups and persons.
To this end, at the national level, we will:
(a) Promote respect for democracy, the rule of law, pluralism and diversity, tolerance and responsibility, non-violence and solidarity by encouraging educational systems, communication media and local communities and

10 Ibid., at Commitment 3.

organizations to raise people's understanding and awareness of all aspects of social integration;

(b) Formulate or strengthen policies and strategies geared to the elimination of discrimination in all its forms and the achievement of social integration based on equality and respect for human dignity;

(c) Promote access for all to education, information, technology and know-how as essential means for enhancing communication and participation in civil, political, economic, social and cultural life, and ensure respect for civil, political, economic, social and cultural rights;

(d) Ensure the protection and full integration into the economy and society of disadvantaged and vulnerable groups and persons;

(e) Formulate or strengthen measures to ensure respect for and protection of the human rights of migrants, migrant workers and their families, to eliminate the increasing acts of racism and xenophobia in sectors of many societies, and to promote greater harmony and tolerance in all societies;

(f) Recognize and respect the right of indigenous people to maintain and develop their identity, culture and interests, support their aspirations for social justice and provide an environment that enables them to participate in the social, economic and political life of their country;

(g) Foster the social protection and full integration into the economy and society of veterans, including veterans and victims of the Second World War and other wars;

(h) Acknowledge and encourage the contribution of people of all age groups as equally and vitally important for the building of a harmonious society, and foster dialogue between generations in all parts of society;

(i) Recognize and respect cultural, ethnic and religious diversity, promote and protect the rights of persons belonging to national, ethnic, religious or linguistic minorities, and take measures to facilitate their full participation in all aspects of the political, economic, social, religious and cultural life of their societies and in the economic progress and social development of their countries;

(j) Strengthen the ability of local communities and groups with common concerns to develop their own organizations and resources and to propose policies relating to social development, including through the activities of non-governmental organizations;

(k) Strengthen institutions that enhance social integration, recognizing the central role of the family and providing it with an environment that assures its protection and support. In different cultural, political and social systems, various forms of the family exist;

(l) Address the problems of crime, violence and illicit drugs as factors of social disintegration.

At the international level, we will:

(m) Encourage the ratification of, the avoidance as far as possible of the resort to reservations to, and the implementation of international instruments and

adherence to internationally recognized declarations relevant to the elimination of discrimination and the promotion and protection of all human rights;
(n) Further enhance international mechanisms for the provision of humanitarian and financial assistance to refugees and host countries and promote appropriate shared responsibility;
(o) Promote international cooperation and partnership on the basis of equality, mutual respect and mutual benefit.[11]

Commitment 6 deals with the important issue of education:

> We commit ourselves to promoting and attaining the goals of universal and equitable access to quality education, the highest attainable standard of physical and mental health, and the access of all to primary health care, making particular efforts to rectify inequalities relating to social conditions and without distinction as to race, national origin, gender, age or disability; respecting and promoting our common and particular cultures; striving to strengthen the role of culture in development; preserving the essential bases of people-centred sustainable development; and contributing to the full development of human resources and to social development. The purpose of these activities is to eradicate poverty, promote full and productive employment and foster social integration.
> To this end, at the national level, we will:
> (a) Formulate and strengthen time-bound national strategies for the eradication of illiteracy and universalization of basic education, which includes early childhood education, primary education and education for the illiterate, in all communities, in particular for the introduction, if possible, of national languages in the educational system and by support of the various means of non-formal education, striving to attain the highest possible standard of learning;
> (b) Emphasize lifelong learning by seeking to improve the quality of education to ensure that people of all ages are provided with useful knowledge, reasoning ability, skills, and the ethical and social values required to develop their full capacities in health and dignity and to participate fully in the social, economic and political process of development. In this regard, women and girls should be considered a priority group;
> (c) Ensure that children, particularly girls, enjoy their rights and promote the exercise of those rights by making education, adequate nutrition and health care accessible to them, consistent with the Convention on the Rights of the Child, and recognizing the rights, duties and responsibilities of parents and other persons legally responsible for children;
> (d) Take appropriate and affirmative steps to enable all children and adolescents to attend and complete school and to close the gender gap in primary, secondary, vocational and higher education;

11 Ibid., at Commitment 4.

(e) Ensure full and equal access to education for girls and women, recognizing that investing in women's education is the key element in achieving social equality, higher productivity and social returns in terms of health, lower infant mortality and the reduced need for high fertility;
(f) Ensure equal educational opportunities at all levels for children, youth and adults with disabilities, in integrated settings, taking full account of individual differences and situations;
(g) Recognize and support the right of indigenous people to education in a manner that is responsive to their specific needs, aspirations and cultures, and ensure their full access to health care;
(h) Develop specific educational policies, with gender perspective, and design appropriate mechanisms at all levels of society in order to accelerate the conversion of general and specific information available world wide into knowledge, and the conversion of that knowledge into creativity, increased productive capacity and active participation in society;
(i) Strengthen the links between labour market and education policies, realizing that education and vocational training are vital elements in job creation and in combating unemployment and social exclusion in our societies, and emphasize the role of higher education and scientific research in all plans of social development;
(j) Develop broad-based education programmes that promote and strengthen respect for all human rights and fundamental freedoms, including the right to development, promote the values of tolerance, responsibility and respect for the diversity and rights of others, and provide training in peaceful conflict resolution, in recognition of the United Nations Decade for Human Rights Education (1995–2005);
(k) Focus on learning acquisition and outcome, broaden the means and scope of basic education, enhance the environment for learning and strengthen partnerships among Governments, non-governmental organizations, the private sector, local communities, religious groups and families to achieve the goal of education for all.[12]

World Summit and Declaration on Education for All: Meeting Basic Learning Needs

The World Conference on Education for All was held in Jomtien, Thailand in 1990, and adopted the World Declaration on Education for All and the Framework for Action to Meet Basic Learning Needs. The Preamble of the World Declaration on Education for All states:

> More than 40 years ago, the nations of the world, speaking through the Universal Declaration of Human Rights, asserted that 'everyone has a right to education'.

12 Ibid., at Commitment 6.

Despite notable efforts by countries around the globe to ensure the right to education for all, the following realities persist:

– More than 100 million children, including at least 60 million girls, have no access to primary schooling;

– More than 960 million adults, two-thirds of whom are women, are illiterate, and functional illiteracy is a significant problem in all countries, industrialized and developing;

– More than one-third of the world's adults have no access to the printed knowledge, new skills and technologies that could improve the quality of their lives and help them shape, and adapt to, social and cultural change; and

– More than 100 million children and countless adults fail to complete basic education programmes; millions more satisfy the attendance requirements but do not acquire essential knowledge and skills;

At the same time, the world faces daunting problems: notably mounting debt burdens, the threat of economic stagnation and decline, rapid population growth, widening economic disparities among and within nations, war, occupation, civil strife, violent crime, the preventable deaths of millions of children and widespread environmental degradation. These problems constrain efforts to meet basic learning needs, while the lack of basic education among a significant proportion of the population prevents societies from addressing such problems with strength and purpose.

These problems have led to major setbacks in basic education in the 1980s in many of the least developed countries. In some other countries, economic growth has been available to finance education expansion, but even so, many millions remain in poverty and unschooled or illiterate. In certain industrialized countries too, cutbacks in government expenditure over the 1980s have led to the deterioration of education.

Yet the world is also at the threshold of a new century, with all its promise and possibilities. Today, there is genuine progress toward peaceful detente and greater cooperation among nations. Today, the essential rights and capacities of women are being realized. Today, there are many useful scientific and cultural developments. Today, the sheer quantity of information available in the world – much of it relevant to survival and basic well-being – is exponentially greater than that available only a few years ago, and the rate of its growth is accelerating. This includes information about obtaining more life-enhancing knowledge – or learning how to learn. A synergistic effect occurs when important information is coupled with another modern advance – our new capacity to communicate.

These new forces, when combined with the cumulative experience of reform, innovation, research and the remarkable educational progress of many countries, make the goal of basic education for all – for the first time in history – an attainable goal.

Therefore, we participants in the World Conference on Education for All, assembled in Jomtien, Thailand, from 5 to 9 March, 1990:

Recalling that education is a fundamental right for all people, women and men, of all ages, throughout our world;

Understanding that education can help ensure a safer, healthier, more prosperous and environmentally sound world, while simultaneously contributing to social, economic, and cultural progress, tolerance, and international cooperation;

Knowing that education is an indispensable key to, though not a sufficient condition for, personal and social improvement;

Recognizing that traditional knowledge and indigenous cultural heritage have a value and validity in their own right and a capacity to both define and promote development;

Acknowledging that, overall, the current provision of education is seriously deficient and that it must be made more relevant and qualitatively improved, and made universally available;

Recognizing that sound basic education is fundamental to the strengthening of higher levels of education and of scientific and technological literacy and capacity and thus to self-reliant development; and

Recognizing the necessity to give to present and coming generations an expanded vision of, and a renewed commitment to, basic education to address the scale and complexity of the challenge; proclaim the following.[13]

Article 1 covers the need to meet basic learning needs:

1(1) Every person – child, youth and adult – shall be able to benefit from educational opportunities designed to meet their basic learning needs. These needs comprise both essential learning tools (such as literacy, oral expression, numeracy, and problem solving) and the basic learning content (such as knowledge, skills, values, and attitudes) required by human beings to be able to survive, to develop their full capacities, to live and work in dignity, to participate fully in development, to improve the quality of their lives, to make informed decisions, and to continue learning. The scope of basic learning needs and how they should be met varies with individual countries and cultures, and inevitably, changes with the passage of time.
(2) The satisfaction of these needs empowers individuals in any society and confers upon them a responsibility to respect and build upon their collective cultural, linguistic and spiritual heritage, to promote the education of others, to

13 World Summit and Declaration on Education for All: Meeting Basic Learning Needs, at the Preamble.

further the cause of social justice, to achieve environmental protection, to be tolerant towards social, political and religious systems which differ from their own, ensuring that commonly accepted humanistic values and human rights are upheld, and to work for international peace and solidarity in an interdependent world.

(3) Another and no less fundamental aim of educational development is the transmission and enrichment of common cultural and moral values. It is in these values that the individual and society find their identity and worth.

(4) Basic education is more than an end in itself. It is the foundation for lifelong learning and human development on which countries may build, systematically, further levels and types of education and training.[14]

Article 2 deals with shaping the vision of education for all:

2. To serve the basic learning needs of all requires more than a recommitment to basic education as it now exists. What is needed is an 'expanded vision' that surpasses present resource levels, institutional structures, curricula, and conventional delivery systems while building on the best in current practices. New possibilities exist today which result from the convergence of the increase in information and the unprecedented capacity to communicate. We must seize them with creativity and a determination for increased effectiveness.

As elaborated in Articles 3–7, the expanded vision encompasses:

- Universalizing access and promoting equity;
- Focussing on learning;
- Broadening the means and scope of basic education;
- Enhancing the environment for learning;
- Strengthening partnerships.

The realization of an enormous potential for human progress and empowerment is contingent upon whether people can be enabled to acquire the education and the start needed to tap into the ever-expanding pool of relevant knowledge and the new means for sharing this knowledge.[15]

Article 3 encourages universalizing access and promoting equity:

3(1) Basic education should be provided to all children, youth and adults. To this end, basic education services of quality should be expanded and consistent measures must be taken to reduce disparities.

(2) For basic education to be equitable, all children, youth and adults must be given the opportunity to achieve and maintain an acceptable level of learning.

---

14 Ibid., at Article 1.

15 Ibid., at Article 2.

> (3) The most urgent priority is to ensure access to, and improve the quality of, education for girls and women, and to remove every obstacle that hampers their active participation. All gender stereotyping in education should be eliminated.
> (4) An active commitment must be made to removing educational disparities. Underserved groups: the poor; street and working children; rural and remote populations; nomads and migrant workers; indigenous peoples; ethnic, racial, and linguistic minorities; refugees; those displaced by war; and people under occupation, should not suffer any discrimination in access to learning opportunities.
> (5) The learning needs of the disabled demand special attention. Steps need to be taken to provide equal access to education to every category of disabled persons as an integral part of the education system.[16]

Article 4 focusses on learning:

> 4. Whether or not expanded educational opportunities will translate into meaningful development – for an individual or for society – depends ultimately on whether people actually learn as a result of those opportunities, i.e., whether they incorporate useful knowledge, reasoning ability, skills, and values. The focus of basic education must, therefore, be on actual learning acquisition and outcome, rather than exclusively upon enrolment, continued participation in organized programmes and completion of certification requirements. Active and participatory approaches are particularly valuable in assuring learning acquisition and allowing learners to reach their fullest potential. It is, therefore, necessary to define acceptable levels of learning acquisition for educational programmes and to improve and apply systems of assessing learning achievement.[17]

Article 5 encourages the broadening of the means and scope of basic education:

> 5. The diversity, complexity, and changing nature of basic learning needs of children, youth and adults necessitates broadening and constantly redefining the scope of basic education to include the following components:
> – *Learning begins at birth.* This calls for early childhood care and initial education. These can be provided through arrangements involving families, communities, or institutional programmes, as appropriate.
> – *The main delivery system for the basic education of children outside the family is primary schooling.* Primary education must be universal, ensure that the basic learning needs of all children are satisfied, and take into account the culture, needs, and opportunities of the community. Supplementary alternative programmes can help meet the basic learning needs of children with limited or

16 Ibid., at Article 3.
17 Ibid., at Article 4.

no access to formal schooling, provided that they share the same standards of learning applied to schools, and are adequately supported.
– *The basic learning needs of youth and adults are diverse and should be met through a variety of delivery systems.* Literacy programmes are indispensable because literacy is a necessary skill in itself and the foundation of other life skills. Literacy in the mother-tongue strengthens cultural identity and heritage. Other needs can be served by: skills training, apprenticeships, and formal and non-formal education programmes in health, nutrition, population, agricultural techniques, the environment, science, technology, family life, including fertility awareness, and other societal issues.
– *All available instruments and channels of information, communications, and social action could be used to help convey essential knowledge and inform and educate people on social issues.* In addition to the traditional means, libraries, television, radio and other media can be mobilized to realize their potential towards meeting basic education needs of all.
These components should constitute an integrated system – complementary, mutually reinforcing, and of comparable standards, and they should contribute to creating and developing possibilities for lifelong learning.[18]

Article 6 deals with enhancing the environment for learning:

6. Learning does not take place in isolation. Societies, therefore, must ensure that all learners receive the nutrition, health care, and general physical and emotional support they need in order to participate actively in and benefit from their education. Knowledge and skills that will enhance the learning environment of children should be integrated into community learning programmes for adults. The education of children and their parents or other caretakers is mutually supportive and this interaction should be used to create, for all, a learning environment of vibrancy and warmth.[19]

Article 7 encourages the covers strengthening of partnerships:

7. National, regional, and local educational authorities have a unique obligation to provide basic education for all, but they cannot be expected to supply every human, financial or organizational requirement for this task. New and revitalized partnerships at all levels will be necessary: partnerships among all sub-sectors and forms of education, recognizing the special role of teachers and that of administrators and other educational personnel; partnerships between education and other government departments, including planning, finance, labour, communications, and other social sectors; partnerships between government and non-governmental organizations, the private sector, local communities,

18 Ibid., at Article 5.
19 Ibid., at Article 6.

> religious groups, and families. The recognition of the vital role of both families and teachers is particularly important. In this context, the terms and conditions of service of teachers and their status, which constitute a determining factor in the implementation of education for all, must be urgently improved in all countries in line with the joint ILO / UNESCO Recommendation Concerning the Status of Teachers (1966). Genuine partnerships contribute to the planning, implementing, managing and evaluating of basic education programmes. When we speak of 'an expanded vision and a renewed commitment', partnerships are at the heart of it.[20]

Article 8 deals with developing a supportive policy context:

> 8(1) Supportive policies in the social, cultural, and economic sectors are required in order to realize the full provision and utilization of basic education for individual and societal improvement. The provision of basic education for all depends on political commitment and political will backed by appropriate fiscal measures and reinforced by educational policy reforms and institutional strengthening. Suitable economic, trade, labour, employment and health policies will enhance learners' incentives and contributions to societal development.
> (2) Societies should also insure a strong intellectual and scientific environment for basic education. This implies improving higher education and developing scientific research. Close contact with contemporary technological and scientific knowledge should be possible at every level of education.[21]

Article 9 covers mobilizing resources:

> 9(1) If the basic learning needs of all are to be met through a much broader scope of action than in the past, it will be essential to mobilize existing and new financial and human resources, public, private and voluntary. All of society has a contribution to make, recognizing that time, energy and funding directed to basic education are perhaps the most profound investment in people and in the future of a country which can be made.
> (2) Enlarged public-sector support means drawing on the resources of all the government agencies responsible for human development, through increased absolute and proportional allocations to basic education services with the clear recognition of competing claims on national resources of which education is an important one, but not the only one. Serious attention to improving the efficiency of existing educational resources and programmes will not only produce more, it can also be expected to attract new resources. The urgent task of meeting basic learning needs may require a reallocation between sectors, as, for example, a transfer from military to educational expenditure. Above all,

20 Ibid., at Article 7.
21 Ibid., at Article 8.

> special protection for basic education will be required in countries undergoing structural adjustment and facing severe external debt burdens. Today, more than ever, education must be seen as a fundamental dimension of any social, cultural, and economic design.[22]

Finally, Article 10 looks at the importance of strengthening international solidarity:

> 10(1) Meeting basic learning needs constitutes a common and universal human responsibility. It requires international solidarity and equitable and fair economic relations in order to redress existing economic disparities. All nations have valuable knowledge and experiences to share for designing effective educational policies and programmes.
> (2) Substantial and long-term increases in resources for basic education will be needed. The world community, including intergovernmental agencies and institutions, has an urgent responsibility to alleviate the constraints that prevent some countries from achieving the goal of education for all. It will mean the adoption of measures that augment the national budgets of the poorest countries or serve to relieve heavy debt burdens. Creditors and debtors must seek innovative and equitable formulae to resolve these burdens, since the capacity of many developing countries to respond effectively to education and other basic needs will be greatly helped by finding solutions to the debt problem.
> (3) Basic learning needs of adults and children must be addressed wherever they exist. Least developed and low-income countries have special needs which require priority in international support for basic education in the 1990s.
> (4) All nations must also work together to resolve conflicts and strife, to end military occupations, and to settle displaced populations, or to facilitate their return to their countries of origin, and ensure that their basic learning needs are met. Only a stable and peaceful environment can create the conditions in which every human being, child and adult alike, may benefit from the goals of this Declaration.[23]

The World Declaration on Education for All: Meeting Basic Learning Needs concludes by stating:

> We, the participants in the World Conference on Education for All, reaffirm the right of all people to education. This is the foundation of our determination, singly and together, to ensure education for all. We commit ourselves to act cooperatively through our own spheres of responsibility, taking all necessary steps to achieve the goals of education for all. Together we call on governments, concerned organizations and individuals to join in this urgent undertaking. The basic learning needs of all can and must be met … There has never been a more

22 Ibid., at Article 9.
23 Ibid., at Article 10.

> propitious time to commit ourselves to providing basic learning opportunities for all the people of the world … .[24]

Further, the Framework for Action to Meet Basic Learning Needs espouses:

1. Expansion of early childhood care and developmental activities, including family and community interventions, especially for poor, disadvantaged and disabled children;
2. Universal access to, and completion of, primary or basic education;
3. Improvement in learning achievement such that an agreed percentage attains or surpasses a defined level of necessary learning achievement;
4. Reduction of the adult illiteracy rate, with sufficient emphasis on female literacy to significantly reduce the current disparity between male and female illiteracy rates;
5. Expansion of provisions of basic education and training in other essential skills required by youth and adults, with programme effectiveness assessed in terms of behavioural changes and impacts on health, employment and productivity;
6. Increased acquisition by individuals and families of the knowledge, skills and values required for better living and sound and sustainable development, made available through all education channels, with effectiveness assessed in terms of behavioural change.[25]

The preconditions for educational quality, equity and efficiency, are set in the early childhood years, making attention to care and development essential to the achievement of basic education goals throughout life. Expanding access to basic education of satisfactory quality is an effective way to improve equity and stop class discrimination.[26]

However, since the World Conference on Education for All, approximately 100 million children, including at least 60 million girls, are without access to primary schooling and more than two-thirds of the world's 960 million illiterate adults are women. The high rate of illiteracy prevailing in most developing countries, in particular in sub-Saharan Africa and some Arab States, remains a severe impediment to the advancement of women and to development. Discrimination in girls' access to education persists in many areas, owing to customary attitudes, early marriages and pregnancies, inadequate and gender-biased teaching and educational materials, sexual harassment and lack of adequate and physically and otherwise accessible schooling facilities. Everyone should be enabled to benefit from an ongoing acquisition of knowledge and skills beyond those acquired during

---

24 Ibid.

25 World Declaration on Education for All: Meeting Basic Learning Needs, The Framework for Action to Meet Basic Learning Needs.

26 Ibid.

youth. This concept of lifelong learning includes knowledge and skills gained in formal education and training, as well as learning that occurs in informal ways, including volunteer activity, unremunerated work and traditional knowledge.

Education is a human right and an essential tool for achieving the goals of equality, development and peace. Non-discriminatory education benefits both girls and boys, and thus ultimately contributes to more equal relationships between women and men. Equality of access to and attainment of educational qualifications is necessary if more people are to become agents of change. Investing in formal and non-formal education and training for girls and women, with its exceptionally high social and economic return, has proved to be one of the best means of achieving sustainable development and economic growth that is both sustained and sustainable. Discrimination in education and training, hiring and remuneration, promotion and horizontal mobility practices, as well as inflexible working conditions, lack of access to productive resources and inadequate sharing of family responsibilities, combined with insufficient services such as child care, continue to restrict employment, economic, professional and other opportunities and mobility for women and make their involvement stressful. Moreover, attitudinal obstacles inhibit women's participation in developing economic policy, and restrict the access of women and girls to education and training for economic management.

Governments should advance the goal of equal access to education by taking measures to eliminate discrimination in education at all levels on the basis of class, gender, race, language, religion, national origin, age or disability, or any other form of discrimination and, as appropriate, consider establishing procedures to address grievances. This means eradicating illiteracy and providing universal access to quality education, including at the university level. Further training should also be available to provide for skills to meet the needs of a changing socio-economic context for improving their employment opportunities.

In looking at the level of educational attainment (Table 2.1), the counties in column two are the leading countries.

More people around the world are completing university courses and other forms of tertiary education than ever before. However, progress has been uneven across countries and some have significantly fallen behind, potentially compromising their future ability to keep up with economic and social progress. Almost all Organization for Economic Co-operation and Development (OECD) countries have seen a rise in the education levels of their citizens over the past decade, and in some countries the increase has been spectacular. On average across OECD countries, half of today's young adults now enter universities or other institutions during their life. An average 32% complete a first university-level degree, but this ranges from less than 20% in Austria, the Czech Republic, Germany and Switzerland to 45% in Australia and Finland. Enrolment in tertiary education, which covers both university-level education and high-level vocational programs, increased by more than 50% in the Czech Republic, Greece, Hungary, Iceland, Korea and Poland, and by more than 20% in Australia, Finland,

Table 2.1 Educational Attainment – Percentage of adults (aged 25–64) obtaining a tertiary education by country

Rank	Countries	Amount
1	Canada	42%
2	United States	37%
3	Ireland	36%
4	Japan	34%
5	Finland	32%
5	Sweden	32%
7	Australia	29%
7	New Zealand	29%
9	Norway	28%
10	Belgium	27%
10	Denmark	27%
12	United Kingdom	26%
13	Switzerland	25%
14	Germany	23%
14	France	23%
16	Netherlands	22%
17	Austria	14%
18	Italy	10%
Weighted Average		**27.6%**

Source: OECD Education at a Glance: OECD Indicators 2003

Ireland, Mexico, Portugal, Spain, Sweden and the United Kingdom. Austria, France and Germany are the only countries which did not see increases, mainly because rising enrolment rates could not make up for the demographic decline in these countries.[27]

However, in eight OECD countries, 20% or more of 20–24 year-olds have at most only lower secondary school qualifications and are not in education. Mexico is in the least favorable position, with 70% of people in this age group having

27 OECD, Education at a Glance., 2004

lower secondary education or less, followed by Turkey (56%), Portugal (47%), Spain (32%), Iceland (29%), Italy (25%), the Netherlands (21%) and Luxembourg (20%). Low educational attainment concerns more young males than females in 19 out of the 27 countries for which statistics are available, and particularly in Greece, Iceland, Ireland, Italy, Portugal and Spain.

In general, people with tertiary qualifications command significantly higher salaries than those with only secondary education. In the United States, earnings for tertiary graduates are 86% higher on average than those for people with only secondary education and in Hungary, they are more than double; at the other end of the scale, the difference is smallest in Denmark, where graduates earn on average 25% more than non-graduates, and Spain, where they earn 29% more. They also stand a stronger chance of finding jobs: around 89% of men and 78% of women with university degrees are in employment, compared with around 84% of men and 63% of women who ended their education at secondary level.

Improved education also contributes to a country's overall prosperity, helping to raise labor productivity and technological progress and thereby boosting economic growth. The long-run impact in the OECD area of one additional year of education is estimated to increase economic output by between 3% and 6%. Tertiary education is rapidly becoming an international domain. In 2002, 1.9 million students were enrolled in the OECD area outside their country of origin, with nearly three-quarters of them choosing Australia, France, Germany, the United Kingdom and the United States as their destination.

Significant progress has also been achieved in reducing the gender gap in educational qualifications. Younger women today are far more likely to have completed a tertiary qualification than women 30 years ago: in 19 of the 30 OECD countries, more than twice as many women aged 25 to 34 have completed tertiary education than women aged 55 to 64 do. As well, 15-year-old girls tend to show much higher expectations for their careers than boys of the same age. What has remained broadly unchanged, though, is that women still earn less on average than men in all countries, whatever their level of education: on average, women without upper secondary education obtain 60% of the earnings of men with the same level of education, and women with upper secondary and tertiary qualifications average 65% of equivalent male earnings.[28]

Overall, education is seen as a tool for advancement and in the fight against class discrimination. Parents with higher education levels, it is argued, have children with higher education levels.[29] There are several explanations: the selection explanation is that the type of parent who has more education and earns a higher salary has the type of child who will do so as well; the causation explanation is that obtaining more education makes for a different type of parent leading to the children having

---

28 Ibid.

29 Black, Sandra, Devereux, Paul and Salvanes, Kjell, "Why the Apple Doesn't Fall Far: Understanding Intergenerational Transmission of Human Capital", *American Economic Review*, Vol. 95, No. 1 (Mar. 2005), pp. 437–49.

higher educational outcomes. There is a direct impact on a parent's education on a child's schooling. An interesting study of the Norway education system showed little causal relationship between a father's education and children's education, and no causal relationship between a mother's education and her daughter's education, but a significant causal relationship between a mother's education and her son's education, suggesting a high correlation between parental and children's education due primarily to selection not causation.[30]

Further, women's intergenerational occupational mobility is an important factor in childrens' educations and occupations.[31] Major differences between male and female roles exist in the family and occupational systems.[32] Females have a double responsibility strain with regard to the economic and family spheres. This leads to a role conflict for women, which may result in females working at lower occupational levels than would warrant their educational levels in order to accommodate their dual role as mother and professional.[33]

Interestingly, the relationship between mothers and daughters can play an important role in the career choices of women.[34] Mothers can often have a strong influence on daughters, which far exceeds the influence that fathers may have on daughters and sons. A mother's occupational attainment has been found to have some impact in predicting a daughter's occupational inheritance and destiny. A mother is a strong gender role model, and her occupation is a significant dimension in intergenerational occupational mobility. Mothers, who worked in a field classified as professional or non-manual workers, had a positive effect on their daughter's achievement of professional work. However, mothers who were classified as semi-skilled/unskilled manual workers or housewives, had a negative effect on their daughter's chances for professional work, since daughters often significantly inherit the occupational status of their mothers.[35] This reinforces gender disparity and inequality of opportunities, and class discrimination.

---

30 Ibid.

31 Rosenfeld, Rachel, "Women's Intergenerational Occupational Mobility", *American Sociological Review*, Vol. 43, No. 1 (Feb. 1978), pp. 36–46.

32 DeJong, Peter, Brawer, Milton and Robin, Stanley, "Patterns of Female Intergenerational Occupational Mobility: A Comparison with Male Patterns of Intergenerational Occupational Mobility", *American Sociological Review*, Vol. 36, No. 6 (Dec. 1971), pp. 1033–42.

33 Ibid.

34 Hayes, Bernadette, "Female Intergenerational Occupational Mobility Within Northern Ireland and the Republic of Ireland", *British Journal of Sociology*, Vol. 38, May 1987, p. 66.

35 Ibid.

Conclusion

Eliminating discrimination helps everyone to have an equal opportunity to work and to develop their skills. In order to protect human rights, it is necessary for States to avoid, as far as possible, resorting to reservations of international agreements, and to ensure that no reservation is incompatible with the object and purpose of the Convention or is otherwise incompatible with international treaty law. The full enjoyment of equal rights is undermined by the discrepancies between some national legislation, and international law and international instruments on human rights. Overly complex administrative procedures, lack of awareness within the judicial process and inadequate monitoring of the violation of human rights, coupled with the underrepresentation of disabled groups in justice systems, insufficient information on existing rights, and persistent attitudes and practices perpetuate de facto and de jure inequality, which is also exacerbated by the lack of enforcement of civil, penal, labor and commercial laws or codes, or administrative rules and regulations intended to ensure the full enjoyment of human rights and fundamental freedoms, in the pursuit of "Class Act".

Chapter 3
Class Act in the United Nations

Introduction

In the quest for tolerance of class distinctions in *Class Act*, this chapter will examine efforts against class discrimination in the United Nations. It will look at the important United Nations' legislation dealing with class discrimination in the fight for class equality and educational advancement to combat inequality, namely the Charter of the United Nations; the Statute of the International Court of Justice; the Universal Declaration of Human Rights; the International Covenant on Civil and Political Rights; the Optional Protocol to the International Covenant on Civil and Political Rights; the International Covenant on Economic, Social and Cultural Rights; for minorities, the International Convention on the Elimination of All Forms of Racial Discrimination; for women, the Convention on the Elimination of All Forms of Discrimination against Women and the Optional Protocol to the Convention on the Elimination of All Forms of Discrimination against Women; United Nations Principles for Older Persons; the Equal Remuneration Convention (ILO No. 100); the Discrimination (Employment and Occupation) Convention (ILO No. 111); the Employment Policy Convention (ILO No. 122); and the Convention against Discrimination in Education.

Through the work of the United Nations, international laws, called treaties or conventions, have been developed that require countries to work towards the elimination of all forms of discrimination, and they operate like a contract, as they apply throughout the world. When a country becomes a Party to a convention, it is bound to act in accordance with the rules contained in that convention. In addition to international treaties and conventions, there are several international declarations. The declarations are statements of principles, which are developed through the United Nations or other international bodies, and express the international community's aspirations to eliminate discrimination. These international declarations differ from treaties, because they do not always impose binding international legal obligations, but they are morally binding and have much influence over countries in setting acceptable standards of human rights protections. Internationally, the fundamental concept of human rights is one which human beings have striven both to suppress and promote.

Charter of the United Nations

The Preamble of the Charter of the United Nations, signed on 26 June 1945, states:

WE THE PEOPLES OF THE UNITED NATIONS DETERMINED

to save succeeding generations from the scourge of war, which twice in our lifetime has brought untold sorrow to mankind, and
to reaffirm faith in fundamental human rights, in the dignity and worth of the human person, in the equal rights of men and women and of nations large and small, and
to establish conditions under which justice and respect for the obligations arising from treaties and other sources of international law can be maintained, and
to promote social progress and better standards of life in larger freedom,

AND FOR THESE ENDS

to practice tolerance and live together in peace with one another as good neighbours, and
to unite our strength to maintain international peace and security, and
to ensure, by the acceptance of principles and the institution of methods, that armed force shall not be used, save in the common interest, and
to employ international machinery for the promotion of the economic and social advancement of all peoples,

HAVE RESOLVED TO COMBINE OUR EFFORTS TO ACCOMPLISH THESE AIMS

Accordingly, our respective Governments, through representatives assembled in the city of San Francisco, who have exhibited their full powers found to be in good and due form, have agreed to the present Charter of the United Nations and do hereby establish an international organization to be known as the United Nations.[1]

The purposes of the United Nations as outlined in Article 1 are to maintain international peace and security, and to that end to take effective collective measures for the prevention and removal of threats to the peace, and for the suppression of acts of aggression or other breaches of the peace, and to bring about by peaceful means, and in conformity with the principles of justice and international law, adjustment or settlement of international disputes or situations which might lead to a breach of the peace; to develop friendly relations among nations based on respect for the principle of equal rights and self-determination of peoples, and to take other appropriate measures to strengthen universal peace; to achieve international cooperation in solving international problems of an economic, social, cultural or humanitarian character, and in promoting and encouraging respect for human

1 United Nations, Charter of the United Nations, at the Preamble.

rights and for fundamental freedoms for all without distinction; and to be a center for harmonizing the actions of nations in the attainment of these common ends. [2]

In terms of international economic and social cooperation, Article 55 guarantees equal rights in employment without distinction, impacting class discrimination:

> 55. With a view to the creation of conditions of stability and well-being which are necessary for peaceful and friendly relations among nations based on respect for the principle of equal rights and self-determination of peoples, the United Nations shall promote:
>
> (a) higher standards of living, full employment, and conditions of economic and social progress and development;
>
> (b) solutions of international economic, social, health, and related problems; and international cultural and educational cooperation; and
>
> (c) universal respect for, and observance of, human rights and fundamental freedoms for all without distinction as to race, sex, language, or religion.[3]

Importantly, the International Court of Justice is established under Article 92 as the principal judicial organ of the United Nations, functioning in accordance with the Statute of the Permanent Court of International Justice.[4] By virtue of Article 96, the General Assembly, the Security Council, and other organs of the United Nations and specialized agencies may request the International Court of Justice to give an advisory opinion on any legal question.[5] Further, Article 94 binds Member States in their compliance with the decisions of the International Court of Justice in that each Member of the United Nations undertakes to comply with the decision of the International Court of Justice in any case to which it is a party; and if any party to a case fails to perform the obligations incumbent upon it under a judgment rendered by the Court, the other party may have recourse to the Security Council, which may, if it deems necessary, make recommendations or decide upon measures to be taken to give effect to the judgment.[6] In addition, Article 95 holds that nothing in the present Charter shall prevent Members of the United Nations from entrusting the solution of their differences to other tribunals by virtue of agreements already in existence or which may be concluded in the future.[7]

---

2 Ibid., at Article 1.
3 Ibid., at Article 55.
4 Ibid., at Article 92.
5 Ibid., at Article 96.
6 Ibid., at Article 94.
7 Ibid., at Article 95.

Statute of the International Court of Justice

Article 1 of the Statute of the International Court of Justice, signed on 26 June 1945, holds that the International Court of Justice, established by the Charter of the United Nations as the principal judicial organ of the United Nations, shall be constituted and shall function in accordance with the provisions of the present Statute.[8] By virtue of Article 34, only States may be parties in cases before the Court which, subject to and in conformity with its Rules, may request of public international organizations information relevant to cases before it, and shall receive such information presented by such organizations on their own initiative.[9]

Jurisdiction of the Court is established under Article 36 as comprising all cases which the parties refer to it and all matters specially provided for in the Charter of the United Nations or in treaties and conventions in force. Further, the States Parties to the present Statute may at any time declare that they recognize as compulsory *ipso facto* and without special agreement, in relation to any other State accepting the same obligation, the jurisdiction of the Court in all legal disputes concerning the interpretation of a treaty; any question of international law; the existence of any fact which, if established, would constitute a breach of an international obligation; and the nature or extent of the reparation to be made for the breach of an international obligation.[10] As to the application of choice of law, Article 38 maintains that the Court, whose function is to decide in accordance with international law such disputes as are submitted to it, shall apply international conventions, whether general or particular, establishing rules expressly recognized by the contesting States; international custom, as evidence of a general practice accepted as law; the general principles of law recognized by civilized nations; and judicial decisions and the teachings of the most highly qualified publicists of the various nations, as subsidiary means for the determination of rules of law.[11]

Universal Declaration of Human Rights

The Universal Declaration of Human Rights was adopted by the United Nations on 10 December 1948 and is an important legal document for combating discrimination, including class. The Preamble of the Universal Declaration of Human Rights states:

> Whereas recognition of the inherent dignity and of the equal and inalienable rights of all members of the human family is the foundation of freedom, justice and peace in the world,

---

8 United Nations, Statute of the International Court of Justice, at Article 1.

9 Ibid., at Article 34.

10 Ibid., at Article 36.

11 Ibid., at Article 38.

Whereas disregard and contempt for human rights have resulted in barbarous acts which have outraged the conscience of mankind, and the advent of a world in which human beings shall enjoy freedom of speech and belief and freedom from fear and want has been proclaimed as the highest aspiration of the common people,

Whereas it is essential, if man is not to be compelled to have recourse, as a last resort, to rebellion against tyranny and oppression, that human rights should be protected by the rule of law,

Whereas it is essential to promote the development of friendly relations between nations,

Whereas the peoples of the United Nations have in the Charter reaffirmed their faith in fundamental human rights, in the dignity and worth of the human person and in the equal rights of men and women and have determined to promote social progress and better standards of life in larger freedom,

Whereas Member States have pledged themselves to achieve, in co-operation with the United Nations, the promotion of universal respect for and observance of human rights and fundamental freedoms,

Whereas a common understanding of these rights and freedoms is of the greatest importance for the full realization of this pledge.

The General Assembly of the United Nations proclaims:

THIS UNIVERSAL DECLARATION OF HUMAN RIGHTS as a common standard of achievement for all peoples and all nations, to the end that every individual and every organ of society, keeping this Declaration constantly in mind, shall strive by teaching and education to promote respect for these rights and freedoms and by progressive measures, national and international, to secure their universal and effective recognition and observance, both among the peoples of Member States themselves and among the peoples of territories under their jurisdiction.[12]

Article 1 recognizes human beings as free and equal:

1. All human beings are born free and equal in dignity and rights. They are endowed with reason and conscience and should act towards one another in a spirit of brotherhood.[13]

---

12 United Nations, Universal Declaration of Human Rights, at the Preamble.

13 Ibid., at Article 1.

In the fight for equality, Article 2, which includes 'other status', is a helpful tool, since it holds that:

> 2. Everyone is entitled to all the rights and freedoms set forth in this Declaration, without distinction of any kind, such as race, colour, sex, language, religion, political or other opinion, national or social origin, property, birth or other status.[14]

Equality before the law without discrimination, important for **class** discrimination cases, is guaranteed in Article 7:

> 7. All are equal before the law and are entitled without any discrimination to equal protection of the law. All are entitled to equal protection against any discrimination in violation of this Declaration and against any incitement to such discrimination.[15]

In the effort to redress discriminatory action, Article 8 establishes that everyone has the right to an effective remedy by competent national tribunals for acts violating the fundamental rights granted him by the constitution or by law.[16]

Employment rights, including equal pay for equal work, are protected under Article 23:

> 23(1) Everyone has the right to work, to free choice of employment, to just and favorable conditions of work and to protection against unemployment.
> (2) Everyone, without any discrimination, has the right to equal pay for equal work.
> (3) Everyone who works has the right to just and favorable remuneration ensuring for himself and his family an existence worthy of human dignity, and supplemented, if necessary, by other means of social protection.
> (4) Everyone has the right to form and to join trade unions for the protection of his interests.[17]

Importantly, the right to education as a means of enhancement and advancement, and as a tool for combating class discrimination, is established in Article 26:

> 26(1) Everyone has the right to education. Education shall be free, at least in the elementary and fundamental stages. Elementary education shall be compulsory. Technical and professional education shall be made generally available and higher education shall be equally accessible to all on the basis of merit.

---

14 Ibid., at Article 2.
15 Ibid., at Article 7.
16 Ibid., at Article 8.
17 Ibid., at Article 23.

(2) Education shall be directed to the full development of the human personality and to the strengthening of respect for human rights and fundamental freedoms. It shall promote understanding, tolerance and friendship among all nations, racial or religious groups, and shall further the activities of the United Nations for the maintenance of peace.
(3) Parents have a prior right to choose the kind of education that shall be given to their children.[18]

The Universal Declaration of Human Rights was codified into two Covenants, which the General Assembly adopted on 16 December 1966; these are the International Covenant on Civil and Political Rights and the International Covenant on Economic, Social and Cultural Rights. Described as the "International Bill of Human Rights", the Covenants along with the Optional Protocols are landmarks in the efforts of the international community to promote human rights.

International Covenant on Civil and Political Rights (ICCPR)

The International Covenant on Civil and Political Rights was adopted and opened for signature, ratification and accession by the United Nations General Assembly in Resolution 2200A (XXI) of 16 December 1966, and entered into force on 23 March 1976, and is an important legal document for combating discrimination, including that based on class and social origin. The Covenant is divided into six parts: Part I reaffirms the right of self-determination; Part II formulates general obligations by States Parties, notably to implement the Covenant through legislative and other measures, to provide effective remedies to victims and to ensure equality, and it restricts the possibility of derogation; Part III outlines the general civil and political rights, including the right to life, the prohibition of torture, the right to liberty and security of person, the right to freedom of movement, the right to a fair hearing, the right to privacy, the right to freedom of religion, freedom of expression, freedom of peaceful assembly, the right to family life, the rights of children to special protection, the right to participate in the conduct of public affairs, the overarching right to equal treatment, and the special rights of persons belonging to ethnic, religious and linguistic minorities; Part IV regulates the election of members of the Human Rights Committee, the State reporting procedure and the interstate complaints mechanism; Part V stipulates that nothing in the Covenant shall be interpreted as impairing the inherent right of all peoples to fully enjoy and to utilize their natural resources; and Part VI provides that the Covenant shall extend to all parts of federal States and sets out the amendment procedure. It prohibits discrimination in law or in fact in any field regulated by public authorities and its scope is not limited to civil and political rights, so that it

18 Ibid., at Article 26.

can be used to challenge discriminatory laws whether or not they relate to civil and political rights. Importantly, the Covenant is not subject to denunciation.

In the Preamble of the Covenant on Civil and Political Rights, which specifically protects human beings' social rights, the States Parties to the present Covenant undertake the agreement:

> Considering that, in accordance with the principles proclaimed in the Charter of the United Nations, recognition of the inherent dignity and of the equal and inalienable rights of all members of the human family is the foundation of freedom, justice and peace in the world,
>
> Recognizing that these rights derive from the inherent dignity of the human person,
>
> Recognizing that, in accordance with the Universal Declaration of Human Rights, the ideal of free human beings enjoying civil and political freedom and freedom from fear and want can only be achieved if conditions are created whereby everyone may enjoy his civil and political rights, as well as his economic, social and cultural rights,
>
> Considering the obligation of States under the Charter of the United Nations to promote universal respect for, and observance of, human rights and freedoms,
>
> Realizing that the individual, having duties to other individuals and to the community to which he belongs, is under a responsibility to strive for the promotion and observance of the rights recognized in the present Covenant.[19]

The right to social development and subsistence are guaranteed in Article 1:

> 1(1) All peoples have the right of self-determination. By virtue of that right they freely determine their political status and freely pursue their economic, social and cultural development.
> (2) All peoples may, for their own ends, freely dispose of their natural wealth and resources without prejudice to any obligations arising out of international economic co-operation, based upon the principle of mutual benefit, and international law. In no case may a people be deprived of its own means of subsistence.
> (3) The States Parties to the present Covenant, including those having responsibility for the administration of Non-Self-Governing and Trust Territories, shall promote the realization of the right of self-determination, and

19 United Nations, International Covenant on Civil and Political Rights, at the Preamble.

> shall respect that right, in conformity with the provisions of the Charter of the United Nations.[20]

Further, the obligations of Member States are established in Article 2, which enumerates 'other status' in Article 2(1), which should include class distinctions:

> 2(1) Each State Party to the present Covenant undertakes to respect and to ensure to all individuals within its territory and subject to its jurisdiction the rights recognized in the present Covenant, without distinction of any kind, such as race, colour, sex, language, religion, political or other opinion, national or social origin, property, birth or other status.
> (2) Where not already provided for by existing legislative or other measures, each State Party to the present Covenant undertakes to take the necessary steps, in accordance with its constitutional processes and with the provisions of the present Covenant, to adopt such laws or other measures as may be necessary to give effect to the rights recognized in the present Covenant.
> (3) Each State Party to the present Covenant undertakes:
> (a) To ensure that any person whose rights or freedoms as herein recognized are violated shall have an effective remedy, notwithstanding that the violation has been committed by persons acting in an official capacity;
> (b) To ensure that any person claiming such a remedy shall have his right thereto determined by competent judicial, administrative or legislative authorities, or by any other competent authority provided for by the legal system of the State, and to develop the possibilities of judicial remedy;
> (c) To ensure that the competent authorities shall enforce such remedies when granted.[21]

Equality before the law, which is essential for class discrimination cases, is guaranteed under Article 26, which includes 'social origin':

> 26. All persons are equal before the law and are entitled without any discrimination to the equal protection of the law. In this respect, the law shall prohibit any discrimination and guarantee to all persons equal and effective protection against discrimination on any ground such as race, colour, sex, language, religion, political or other opinion, national or social origin, property, birth or other status.[22]

Finally, Article 4 guarantees protection from discrimination, including that based on social origin, even in time of public emergencies:

20 Ibid., at Article 1.
21 Ibid., at Article 2.
22 Ibid., at Article 26.

> 4(1) In time of public emergency which threatens the life of the nation and the existence of which is officially proclaimed, the States Parties to the present Covenant may take measures derogating from their obligations under the present Covenant to the extent strictly required by the exigencies of the situation, provided that such measures are not inconsistent with their other obligations under international law and do not involve discrimination solely on the ground of race, colour, sex, language, religion or social origin.[23]

Children are afforded special protection under Article 24, including freedom from class discrimination as relating to social origin:

> 24(1) Every child shall have, without any discrimination as to race, colour, sex, language, religion, national or social origin, property or birth, the right to such measures of protection as are required by his status as a minor, on the part of his family, society and the State.[24]

Further, Article 18 ensures the rights of parents to the moral education of their children:

> 18(4) The States Parties to the present Covenant undertake to have respect for the liberty of parents and, when applicable, legal guardians to ensure the religious and moral education of their children in conformity with their own convictions.[25]

Importantly, the Human Rights Committee is established under Article 28 and consists of 18 members, carrying out the functions provided.[26] Additionally, the submission of reports in compliance with the Covenant is required in Article 40 and Article 45. Under Article 40, the States Parties to the present Covenant undertake to submit reports on the measures they have adopted which give effect to the rights recognized herein and on the progress made in the enjoyment of those rights within one year of the entry into force of the present Covenant for the States Parties concerned; and thereafter whenever the Committee so requests. Reports shall indicate the factors and difficulties, if any, affecting the implementation of the present Covenant. The Committee shall study the reports submitted by the States Parties to the present Covenant, and shall transmit its reports, and such general comments as it may consider appropriate, to the States Parties.[27] Under Article 45, the Committee shall submit to the General Assembly of the United Nations,

---

23 Ibid., at Article 4(1).
24 Ibid., at Article 24(1).
25 Ibid., at Article 18(4).
26 Ibid., at Article 28.
27 Ibid., at Article 40.

through the Economic and Social council, an annual report on its activities.[28] The Human Rights Committee monitors implementation by States Parties in a variety of ways, and initial and periodic reports are examined by the plenary, which formulates concluding observations with concrete recommendations.

Other procedures of recourse are permitted under Article 44, which states that the provisions for the implementation of the present Covenant shall apply without prejudice to the procedures prescribed in the field of human rights by or under the constituent instruments and the conventions of the United Nations and of the specialized agencies and shall not prevent the States Parties to the present Covenant from having recourse to other procedures for settling a dispute in accordance with general or special international agreements in force between them.[29]

Optional Protocol to the International Covenant on Civil and Political Rights

The Optional Protocol to the International Covenant on Civil and Political Rights (ICCPR) of 16 December 1966 allows individuals, whose countries are party to the ICCPR and the protocol, who claim their rights under the ICCPR have been violated, and who have exhausted all domestic remedies, to submit written communications to the United Nations Human Rights Committee. States Parties to the ICCPR undertake to ensure that all enjoy all the civil and political rights in the Covenant on a basis of equality.

The Preamble of the Optional Protocol to the International Covenant on Civil and Political Rights states:

> The States Parties to the present Protocol,
>
> Considering that in order further to achieve the purposes of the International Covenant on Civil and Political Rights (hereinafter referred to as the Covenant) and the implementation of its provisions it would be appropriate to enable the Human Rights Committee set up in part IV of the Covenant (hereinafter referred to as the Committee) to receive and consider, as provided in the present Protocol, communications from individuals claiming to be victims of violations of any of the rights set forth in the Covenant.[30]

Article 1 empowers the Committee to hear claims of violations:

---

28 Ibid., at Article 45.

29 Ibid., at Article 44.

30 United Nations, Optional Protocol to the International Covenant on Civil and Political Rights, at the Preamble.

> 1. A State Party to the Covenant that becomes a Party to the present Protocol recognizes the competence of the Committee to receive and consider communications from individuals subject to its jurisdiction who claim to be victims of a violation by that State Party of any of the rights set forth in the Covenant. No communication shall be received by the Committee if it concerns a State Party to the Covenant which is not a Party to the present Protocol.[31]

Finally, Article 2 preserves a person's right to redress:

> 2. Subject to the provisions of article 1, individuals who claim that any of their rights enumerated in the Covenant have been violated and who have exhausted all available domestic remedies may submit a written communication to the Committee for consideration.[32]

International Covenant on Economic, Social and Cultural Rights (ICESCR)

The International Covenant on Economic, Social and Cultural Rights was adopted and opened for signature, ratification and accession by General Assembly resolution 2200A (XXI) of 16 December 1966, and entered into force 16 January 1976, is an important legal document for combating discrimination, including **class**.[33] In a world where, according to the United Nations Development Programme (UNDP), "a fifth of the developing world's population goes hungry every night, a quarter lacks access to even a basic necessity like safe drinking water, and a third lives in a state of abject poverty at such a margin of human existence that words simply fail to describe it",[34] the importance of renewed attention and commitment to the full realization of economic, social and cultural rights is self-evident with such marginalization. Despite significant progress since the establishment of the United Nations in addressing problems of human deprivation, well over 1 billion people live in circumstances of extreme poverty, homelessness, hunger and malnutrition, unemployment, illiteracy and chronic ill-health. More than 1.5 billion people lack access to clean drinking water and sanitation, and some 500 million children do not have access to even primary education, with more than 1 billion adults not able to read and write. Economic, social and cultural rights are designed to ensure the protection of people as full persons, based on a perspective in which people can enjoy rights, freedoms and social justice.

---

31 Ibid., at Article 1.

32 Ibid., at Article 2.

33 United Nations, International Covenant on Economic, Social and Cultural Rights.

34 United Nations Development Programme, *Human Development Report*, Oxford, 1994, p. 2.

In the Preamble of the International Covenant on Economic, Social and Cultural Rights, the States Parties to the present Covenant undertake the agreement, implicitly recognizing social rights:

> Considering that, in accordance with the principles proclaimed in the Charter of the United Nations, recognition of the inherent dignity and of the equal and inalienable rights of all the members of the human family is the foundation of freedom, justice and peace in the world,
>
> Recognizing that these rights derive from the inherent dignity of the human person,
>
> Recognizing that, in accordance with the Universal Declaration of Human Rights, the ideal of free human beings enjoying freedom from fear and want can only be achieved if conditions are created whereby everyone may enjoy his economic, social and cultural rights, as well as his civil and political rights and freedom,
>
> Realizing that the individual, having duties to other individuals and to the community to which he belongs, is under a responsibility to strive for the promotion and observance of the rights recognized in the present Covenant.[35]

Article 2 specifically guarantees the right to be free from discrimination, which includes discrimination based on social origin and other status under Article 2(2):

> 2(1) Each State Party to the present Covenant undertakes to take steps, individually and through international assistance and co-operation, especially economic and technical, to the maximum of its available resources, with a view to achieving progressively the full realization of the rights recognized in the present Covenant by all appropriate means, including particularly the adoption of legislative measures.
> (2) The States Parties to the present Covenant undertake to guarantee that the rights enunciated in the present Covenant will be exercised without discrimination of any kind as to race, colour, sex, language, religion, political or other opinion, national or social origin, property, birth or other status.
> (3) Developing countries, with due regard to human rights and their national economy, may determine to what extent they would guarantee the economic rights recognized in the present Covenant to non-nationals.[36]

Article 3 guarantees social rights to men and women:

---

35 United Nations, International Covenant on Economic, Social and Cultural Rights, at the Preamble.

36 Ibid., at Article 2.

> 3. The States Parties to the present Covenant undertake to ensure the equal right of men and women to the enjoyment of all economic, social and cultural rights set forth in the present Covenant.[37]

Importantly, employment rights are outlined under Article 6, which protects educational programmes for social development under Article 6(2):

> 6(1) The States Parties to the present Covenant recognize the right to work, which includes the right of everyone to the opportunity to gain his living by work which he freely chooses or accepts, and will take appropriate steps to safeguard this right.
> (2) The steps to be taken by a State Party to the present Covenant to achieve the full realization of this right shall include technical and vocational guidance and training programmes, policies and techniques to achieve steady economic, social and cultural development and full and productive employment under conditions safeguarding fundamental political and economic freedoms to the individual.[38]

Further, Article 7 is a guarantee for equal rights in terms of equal pay and access to employment:

> 7. The States to the present Covenant recognize the right of everyone to the enjoyment of just and favorable conditions of work which ensure, in particular:
> (1) Remuneration which provides all workers, as a minimum, with:
> 1. Fair wages and equal remuneration for work of equal value without distinction of any kind, … with equal pay for equal work;
> 2. A decent living for themselves and their families in accordance with the provisions of the present Covenant;
> (2) Safe and healthy working conditions;
> (3) Equal opportunity for everyone to be promoted in his employment to an appropriate higher level, subject to no considerations other than those of seniority and competence;
> (4) Rest, leisure and reasonable limitation of working hours and periodic holidays with pay, as well as remuneration for public holidays.[39]

The right to be unionized is protected under Article 8:

> 8(1) The States Parties to the present Covenant undertake to ensure:
> (a) The right of everyone to form trade unions and join the trade union of his choice, subject only to the rules of the organization concerned, for the promotion and protection of his economic and social interests. No restrictions

37 Ibid, at Article 3.
38 Ibid., at Article 6.
39 Ibid., at Article 7.

> may be placed on the exercise of this right other than those prescribed by law and which are necessary in a democratic society in the interests of national security or public order or for the protection of the rights and freedoms of others;
> (b) The right of trade unions to establish national federations or confederations and the right of the latter to form or join international trade-union organizations;
> (c) The right of trade unions to function freely subject to no limitations other than those prescribed by law and which are necessary in a democratic society in the interests of national security or public order or for the protection of the rights and freedoms of others;
> (d) The right to strike, provided that it is exercised in conformity with the laws of the particular country.[40]

The protection of the family unit is guaranteed under Article 10:

> 10. The States Parties to the present Covenant recognize that:
> (1) The widest possible protection and assistance should be accorded to the family, which is the natural and fundamental group unit of society, particularly for its establishment and while it is responsible for the care and education of dependent children. Marriage must be entered into with the free consent of the intending spouses.[41]

The paramount importance of education is recognized as an important tool for social and economic development under Article 13:

> 13(1) The States Parties to the present Covenant recognize the right of everyone to education. They agree that education shall be directed to the full development of the human personality and the sense of its dignity, and shall strengthen the respect for human rights and fundamental freedoms. They further agree that education shall enable all persons to participate effectively in a free society, promote understanding, tolerance and friendship among all nations and all racial, ethnic or religious groups, and further the activities of the United Nations for the maintenance of peace.
> (2) The States Parties to the present Covenant recognize that, with a view to achieving the full realization of this right:
> (a) Primary education shall be compulsory and available free to all;
> (b) Secondary education in its different forms, including technical and vocational secondary education, shall be made generally available and accessible to all by every appropriate means, and in particular by the progressive introduction of free education;

40 Ibid., at Article 8.
41 Ibid., at Article 10.

> (c) Higher education shall be made equally accessible to all, on the basis of capacity, by every appropriate means, and in particular by the progressive introduction of free education;
> (d) Fundamental education shall be encouraged or intensified as far as possible for those persons who have not received or completed the whole period of their primary education;
> (e) The development of a system of schools at all levels shall be actively pursued, an adequate fellowship system shall be established, and the material conditions of teaching staff shall be continuously improved.
>
> (3) The States Parties to the present Covenant undertake to have respect for the liberty of parents and, when applicable, legal guardians to choose for their children schools, other than those established by the public authorities, which conform to such minimum educational standards as may be laid down or approved by the State and to ensure the religious and moral education of their children in conformity with their own convictions.
>
> (4) No part of this article shall be construed so as to interfere with the liberty of individuals and bodies to establish and direct educational institutions, subject always to the observance of the principles set forth in paragraph I of this article and to the requirement that the education given in such institutions shall conform to such minimum standards as may be laid down by the State.[42]

Compliance by States Parties with their obligations under the Covenant and the level of implementation of the rights and duties in question is monitored by the Committee on Economic, Social and Cultural Rights, which submits annual reports on its activities to the Economic and Social Council. The Committee works on the basis of many sources of information, including reports submitted by States Parties and information from United Nations specialized agencies, including the International Labour Organization, the United Nations Educational, Scientific and Cultural Organization, the World Health Organization, the Food and Agriculture Organization of the United Nations, the World Bank and the International Monetary Fund, as well as the United Nations Development Programme, the Office of the United Nations High Commissioner for Refugees and the United Nations Centre for Human Settlements (Habitat). It also makes use of information from other United Nations treaty bodies, from national non-governmental and community-based organizations working in States which have ratified the Covenant, and from international human rights organizations.

Of all the basic human rights standards, the International Covenant on Economic, Social and Cultural Rights provides one of the most important international legal frameworks for protecting basic human rights. The Covenant contains significant international legal provisions establishing economic, social and cultural rights, including rights relating to work in just and favorable conditions, social protection, an adequate standard of living, the highest attainable standards of physical and

42 Ibid., at Article 13.

mental health, education, and enjoyment of the benefits of cultural freedom and scientific progress. In the fight against discrimination, it also provides for the right of self-determination; the right to work; the right to just and favorable conditions of work; the right to form and join trade unions; the right to social security and social insurance; protection and assistance to the family; the right to adequate standard of living; the right to the highest attainable standard of physical and mental health; the right to education; the right to take part in cultural life; and the right to enjoy the benefits of scientific progress.

International Convention on the Elimination of All Forms of Racial Discrimination (ICEAFRD)

The International Convention on the Elimination of All Forms of Racial Discrimination was adopted on 21 December 1965.[43] The Convention was the first human rights instrument to establish an international monitoring system and was also revolutionary in its provision of national measures toward the advancement of specific racial or ethnic groups. The Convention defines and condemns racial discrimination, and commits States to change national laws and policies, which create or perpetuate racial discrimination. One of the main objectives of the Convention is to promote racial equality, and as such, the Convention not only aims to achieve *de jure* racial equality but also *de facto* equality, which allows the various ethnic, racial and national groups to enjoy the same social development. Furthermore, the Convention recognizes that certain racial or ethnic groups may need special protection or may need to be assisted by special measures in order to achieve adequate development, and the Convention provides that such special measures shall not be considered racial discrimination as long as they are not continued after the objectives for which they were taken have been achieved.

The Preamble of the International Covenant on the Elimination of All Forms of Racial Discrimination states:

> The States Parties to this Convention,
>
> Considering that the Charter of the United Nations is based on the principles of the dignity and equality inherent in all human beings, and that all Member States have pledged themselves to take joint and separate action, in co-operation with the Organization, for the achievement of one of the purposes of the United Nations which is to promote and encourage universal respect for and observance of human rights and fundamental freedoms for all, without distinction as to race, sex, language or religion,

43 United Nations, International Convention on the Elimination of All Forms of Racial Discrimination.

Considering that the Universal Declaration of Human Rights proclaims that all human beings are born free and equal in dignity and rights and that everyone is entitled to all the rights and freedoms set out therein, without distinction of any kind, in particular as to race, colour or national origin,

Considering that all human beings are equal before the law and are entitled to equal protection of the law against any discrimination and against any incitement to discrimination,

Considering that the United Nations has condemned colonialism and all practices of segregation and discrimination associated therewith, in whatever form and wherever they exist, and that the Declaration on the Granting of Independence to Colonial Countries and Peoples of 14 December 1960 (General Assembly resolution 1514 (XV)) has affirmed and solemnly proclaimed the necessity of bringing them to a speedy and unconditional end,

Considering that the United Nations Declaration on the Elimination of All Forms of Racial Discrimination of 20 November 1963 (General Assembly resolution 1904 (XVIII)) solemnly affirms the necessity of speedily eliminating racial discrimination throughout the world in all its forms and manifestations and of securing understanding of and respect for the dignity of the human person,

Convinced that any doctrine of superiority based on racial differentiation is scientifically false, morally condemnable, socially unjust and dangerous, and that there is no justification for racial discrimination, in theory or in practice, anywhere,

Reaffirming that discrimination between human beings on the grounds of race, colour or ethnic origin in an obstacle to friendly and peaceful relations among nations and is capable of disturbing peace and security among peoples and the harmony of persons living side by side even within one and the same State,

Convinced that the existence of racial barriers is repugnant to the ideals of any human society,

Alarmed by manifestations of racial discrimination still in evidence in some areas of the world and by governmental policies based on racial superiority or hatred, such as policies of apartheid, segregation or separation,

Resolved to adopt all necessary measures for speedily eliminating racial discrimination in all its forms and manifestations, and to prevent and combat racist doctrines and practices in order to promote understanding between races and to build an international community free from all forms of racial segregation and racial discrimination,

Bearing in mind the Convention concerning Discrimination in respect of Employment and Occupation adopted by the International Labour Organisation in 1958, and the Convention against Discrimination in Education adopted by the United Nations Educational, Scientific and Cultural Organization in 1960,

Desiring to implement the principles embodied in the United Nations Declaration on the Elimination of All Forms of Racial Discrimination and to secure the earliest adoption of practical measures to that end,

Have agreed as follows.[44]

Importantly, Article 5 guarantees certain freedoms, including the social right to education and training as a toll for advancement under Article 5(e)(v):

5. In compliance with the fundamental obligations laid down in article 2 of this Convention, States Parties undertake to prohibit and to eliminate racial discrimination in all its forms and to guarantee the right of everyone, without distinction as to race, colour, or national or ethnic origin, to equality before the law, notably in the enjoyment of the following rights:

(a) The right to equal treatment before the tribunals and all other organs administering justice;

(b) The right to security of person and protection by the State against violence or bodily harm, whether inflicted by government officials or by any individual, group or institution;

(c) Political rights, in particular the rights to participate in elections to vote and to stand for election on the basis of universal and equal suffrage, to take part in the Government as well as in the conduct of public affairs at any level and to have equal access to public service;

(d) Other civil rights, in particular:

(i) The right to freedom of movement and residence within the border of the State;

(ii) The right to leave any country, including one's own, and to return to one's country;

(iii) The right to nationality;

(iv) The right to marriage and choice of spouse;

(v) The right to own property alone as well as in association with others;

(vi) The right to inherit;

(vii) The right to freedom of thought, conscience and religion;

(viii) The right to freedom of opinion and expression;

(ix) The right to freedom of peaceful assembly and association;

(e) Economic, social and cultural rights, in particular:

---

44 Ibid., at the Preamble.

> (i) The rights to work, to free choice of employment, to just and favourable conditions of work, to protection against unemployment, to equal pay for equal work, to just and favourable remuneration;
> (ii) The right to form and join trade unions;
> (iii) The right to housing;
> (iv) The right to public health, medical care, social security and social services;
> (v) The right to education and training;
> (vi) The right to equal participation in cultural activities;
> (f) The right of access to any place or service intended for use by the general public, such as transport, hotels, restaurants, cafes, theatres and parks.[45]

Article 1(1) defines racial discrimination:

> 1(1) In this Convention, the term 'racial discrimination' shall mean any distinction, exclusion, restriction or preference based on race, colour, descent, or national or ethnic origin which has the purpose or effect of nullifying or impairing the recognition, enjoyment or exercise, on an equal footing, of human rights and fundamental freedoms in the political, economic, social, cultural or any other field of public life.[46]

Affirmative action programs by way of special measures are covered under Article 1(3):

> 1(3) Special measures taken for the sole purpose of securing adequate advancement of certain racial or ethnic groups or individuals requiring such protection as may be necessary in order to ensure such groups or individuals equal enjoyment or exercise of human rights and fundamental freedoms shall not be deemed racial discrimination, provided, however, that such measures do not, as a consequence, lead to the maintenance of separate rights for different racial groups and that they shall not be continued after the objectives for which they were taken have been achieved.[47]

Finally, Article 7 outlines the importance of education to combat discrimination and prejudices to promote tolerance:

> 7. States Parties undertake to adopt immediate and effective measures, particularly in the fields of teaching, education, culture and information, with a view to combating prejudices which lead to racial discrimination and to promoting understanding, tolerance and friendship among nations and racial or

45 Ibid., at Article 5.
46 Ibid., at Article 1(1).
47 Ibid., at Article 1(3).

> ethnical groups, as well as to propagating the purposes and principles of the Charter of the United Nations, the Universal Declaration of Human Rights, the United Nations Declaration on the Elimination of All Forms of Racial Discrimination, and this Convention.[48]

Convention on the Elimination of All Forms of Discrimination against Women (CEDAW)

The Convention on the Elimination of All Forms of Discrimination against Women (CEDAW) was adopted on 18 December 1979.[49] It is the most comprehensive treaty specifically on the human rights of women, establishing legally binding obligations to end discrimination. Described as the 'International Bill of Rights for Women', the Convention provides for equality between women and men in the enjoyment of civil, political, economic, social and cultural rights. Discrimination against women is to be eliminated through legal, policy and programmatic measures, and through temporary special measures to accelerate women's equality, which are defined as non-discriminatory. States Parties are required to end all forms of discrimination against women and to ensure their equality with men in political and public life with regard to nationality, education, employment, health, and economic and social benefits. The Convention aims at enlarging our understanding of the concept of human rights, as it gives formal recognition to the influence of culture and tradition on restricting women's enjoyment of their fundamental rights through stereotypes, customs and norms which give rise to the multitude of legal, political and economic constraints on the advancement of women. It provides a comprehensive framework for challenging the various forces that have created and sustained discrimination based upon sex.

The Preamble to the Convention on the Elimination of All Forms of Discrimination against Women outlines important ideals, including the need for education and training to combat poverty:

> The States Parties to the present Convention,
>
> Noting that the Charter of the United Nations reaffirms faith in fundamental human rights, in the dignity and worth of the human person and in the equal rights of men and women,
>
> Noting that the Universal Declaration of Human Rights affirms the principle of the inadmissibility of discrimination and proclaims that all human beings are

48 Ibid., at Article 7.

49 United Nations, Convention on the Elimination of All Forms of Discrimination against Women.

born free and equal in dignity and rights and that everyone is entitled to all the rights and freedoms set forth therein, without distinction of any kind, including distinction based on sex,

Noting that the States Parties to the International Covenants on Human Rights have the obligation to ensure the equal rights of men and women to enjoy all economic, social, cultural, civil and political rights,

Considering the international conventions concluded under the auspices of the United Nations and the specialized agencies promoting equality of rights of men and women,

Noting also the resolutions, declarations and recommendations adopted by the United Nations and the specialized agencies promoting equality of rights of men and women,

Concerned, however, that despite these various instruments extensive discrimination against women continues to exist,

Recalling that discrimination against women violates the principles of equality of rights and respect for human dignity, is an obstacle to the participation of women, on equal terms with men, in the political, social, economic and cultural life of their countries, hampers the growth of the prosperity of society and the family and makes more difficult the full development of the potentialities of women in the service of their countries and of humanity,

Concerned that in situations of poverty women have the least access to food, health, education, training and opportunities for employment and other needs,

Convinced that the establishment of the new international economic order based on equity and justice will contribute significantly towards the promotion of equality between men and women,

Emphasizing that the eradication of apartheid, all forms of racism, racial discrimination, colonialism, neo-colonialism, aggression, foreign occupation and domination and interference in the internal affairs of States is essential to the full enjoyment of the rights of men and women,

Affirming that the strengthening of international peace and security, the relaxation of international tension, mutual co-operation among all States irrespective of their social and economic systems, general and complete disarmament, in particular nuclear disarmament under strict and effective international control, the affirmation of the principles of justice, equality and mutual benefit in relations among countries and the realization of the right of peoples under alien and colonial domination and foreign occupation to self-determination and independence, as well as respect for national sovereignty and territorial integrity, will promote social progress and development and as a consequence will contribute to the attainment of full equality between men and women,

Convinced that the full and complete development of a country, the welfare of the world and the cause of peace require the maximum participation of women on equal terms with men in all fields,

Bearing in mind the great contribution of women to the welfare of the family and to the development of society, so far not fully recognized, the social significance of maternity and the role of both parents in the family and in the upbringing of children, and aware that the role of women in procreation should not be a basis for discrimination but that the upbringing of children requires a sharing of responsibility between men and women and society as a whole,

Aware that a change in the traditional role of men as well as the role of women in society and in the family is needed to achieve full equality between men and women,

Determined to implement the principles set forth in the Declaration on the Elimination of Discrimination against Women and, for that purpose, to adopt the measures required for the elimination of such discrimination in all its forms and manifestations,

Have agreed on the following.[50]

Article 1 defines gender discrimination:

1. For the purposes of the present Convention, the term 'discrimination against women' shall mean any distinction, exclusion or restriction made on the basis of sex which has the effect or purpose of impairing or nullifying the recognition, enjoyment or exercise by women, irrespective of their marital status, on a basis of equality of men and women, of human rights and fundamental freedoms in the political, economic, social, cultural, civil or any other field.[51]

Further, Article 4 contains an affirmative action strategy:

4(1) Adoption by States Parties of temporary special measures aimed at accelerating de facto equality between men and women shall not be considered discrimination as defined in the present Convention, but shall in no way entail

50 Ibid., at the Preamble.

51 Ibid., at Article 1.

> as a consequence the maintenance of unequal or separate standards; these measures shall be discontinued when the objectives of equality of opportunity and treatment have been achieved.
> (2) Adoption by States Parties of special measures, including those measures contained in the present Convention, aimed at protecting maternity shall not be considered discriminatory.[52]

Article 5 underscores the need to combat prejudices:

> 5. States Parties shall take all appropriate measures:
> (a) To modify the social and cultural patterns of conduct of men and women, with a view to achieving the elimination of prejudices and customary and all other practices which are based on the idea of the inferiority or the superiority of either of the sexes or on stereotyped roles for men and women;
> (b) To ensure that family education includes a proper understanding of maternity as a social function and the recognition of the common responsibility of men and women in the upbringing and development of their children, it being understood that the interest of the children is the primordial consideration in all cases.[53]

The importance of education as a tool for advancement is outlined in Article 10:

> 10. States Parties shall take all appropriate measures to eliminate discrimination against women in order to ensure to them equal rights with men in the field of education and in particular to ensure, on a basis of equality of men and women:
> (a) The same conditions for career and vocational guidance, for access to studies and for the achievement of diplomas in educational establishments of all categories in rural as well as in urban areas; this equality shall be ensured in pre-school, general, technical, professional and higher technical education, as well as in all types of vocational training;
> (b) Access to the same curricula, the same examinations, teaching staff with qualifications of the same standard and school premises and equipment of the same quality;
> (c) The elimination of any stereotyped concept of the roles of men and women at all levels and in all forms of education by encouraging coeducation and other types of education which will help to achieve this aim and, in particular, by the revision of textbooks and school programmes and the adaptation of teaching methods;
> (d) The same opportunities to benefit from scholarships and other study grants;

52 Ibid., at Article 4.
53 Ibid., at Article 5.

> (e) The same opportunities for access to programmes of continuing education, including adult and functional literacy programmes, particularly those aimed at reducing, at the earliest possible time, any gap in education existing between men and women;
> (f) The reduction of female student drop-out rates and the organization of programmes for girls and women who have left school prematurely;
> (g) The same opportunities to participate actively in sports and physical education;
> (h) Access to specific educational information to help to ensure the health and well-being of families, including information and advice on family planning.[54]

Crucially, Article 11(1) guarantees employment rights for women in terms of access to employment and equal pay:

> 11(1) States Parties shall take all appropriate measures to eliminate discrimination against women in the field of employment in order to ensure, on a basis of equality of men and women, the same rights, in particular:
> (a) The right to work as an inalienable right of all human beings;
> (b) The right to the same employment opportunities, including the application of the same criteria for selection in matters of employment;
> (c) The right to free choice of profession and employment, the right to promotion, job security and all benefits and conditions of service and the right to receive vocational training and retraining, including apprenticeships, advanced vocational training and recurrent training;
> (d) The right to equal remuneration, including benefits, and to equal treatment in respect of work of equal value, as well as equality of treatment in the evaluation of the quality of work;
> (e) The right to social security, particularly in cases of retirement, unemployment, sickness, invalidity and old age and other incapacity to work, as well as the right to paid leave;
> (f) The right to protection of health and to safety in working conditions, including the safeguarding of the function of reproduction.[55]

Article 14 underscores the difficulties rural areas encounter in the fight against class discrimination:

> 14(1) States Parties shall take into account the particular problems faced by rural women and the significant roles which rural women play in the economic survival of their families, including their work in the non-monetized sectors of

54 Ibid., at Article 10.
55 Ibid., at Article 11(1).

> the economy, and shall take all appropriate measures to ensure the application of the provisions of the present Convention to women in rural areas.
> (2) States Parties shall take all appropriate measures to eliminate discrimination against women in rural areas in order to ensure, on a basis of equality of men and women, that they participate in and benefit from rural development and, in particular, shall ensure to such women the right:
> (a) To participate in the elaboration and implementation of development planning at all levels;
> (b) To have access to adequate health care facilities, including information, counselling and services in family planning;
> (c) To benefit directly from social security programmes;
> (d) To obtain all types of training and education, formal and non-formal, including that relating to functional literacy, as well as, inter alia, the benefit of all community and extension services, in order to increase their technical proficiency;
> (e) To organize self-help groups and co-operatives in order to obtain equal access to economic opportunities through employment or self employment;
> (f) To participate in all community activities;
> (g) To have access to agricultural credit and loans, marketing facilities, appropriate technology and equal treatment in land and agrarian reform as well as in land resettlement schemes;
> (h) To enjoy adequate living conditions, particularly in relation to housing, sanitation, electricity and water supply, transport and communications.[56]

The important concept of equality before the law is guaranteed in Article 15:

> 15(1) States Parties shall accord to women equality with men before the law.
> (2) States Parties shall accord to women, in civil matters, a legal capacity identical to that of men and the same opportunities to exercise that capacity. In particular, they shall give women equal rights to conclude contracts and to administer property and shall treat them equally in all stages of procedure in courts and tribunals.
> (3) States Parties agree that all contracts and all other private instruments of any kind with a legal effect which is directed at restricting the legal capacity of women shall be deemed null and void.[57]

Finally, Article 16 ensures special protection to the balance between men and women in everyday life:

56 Ibid., at Article 14.
57 Ibid., at Article 15.

16(1) States Parties shall take all appropriate measures to eliminate discrimination against women in all matters relating to marriage and family relations and in particular shall ensure, on a basis of equality of men and women:

(a) The same right to enter into marriage;

(b) The same right freely to choose a spouse and to enter into marriage only with their free and full consent;

(c) The same rights and responsibilities during marriage and at its dissolution;

(d) The same rights and responsibilities as parents, irrespective of their marital status, in matters relating to their children; in all cases the interests of the children shall be paramount;

(e) The same rights to decide freely and responsibly on the number and spacing of their children and to have access to the information, education and means to enable them to exercise these rights;

(f) The same rights and responsibilities with regard to guardianship, wardship, trusteeship and adoption of children, or similar institutions where these concepts exist in national legislation; in all cases the interests of the children shall be paramount;

(g) The same personal rights as husband and wife, including the right to choose a family name, a profession and an occupation;

(h) The same rights for both spouses in respect of the ownership, acquisition, management, administration, enjoyment and disposition of property, whether free of charge or for a valuable consideration.

(2) The betrothal and the marriage of a child shall have no legal effect, and all necessary action, including legislation, shall be taken to specify a minimum age for marriage and to make the registration of marriages in an official registry compulsory.[58]

Optional Protocol to the Convention on the Elimination of All Forms of Discrimination against Women

The Optional Protocol to the Convention on the Elimination of All Forms of Discrimination against Women (CEDAW) was adopted by the United Nations Commission on the Status of Women on 10 December 1999.[59] Essentially, an optional protocol is an additional enforcement mechanism for the original convention. The motivation behind the development of an Optional Protocol for CEDAW was to bring CEDAW itself on an equal footing with other international human rights instruments, enhancing its enforcement mechanisms. However, the Optional Protocol has provided an opportunity to strengthen the weak

58 Ibid., at Article 16.

59 United Nations, Optional Protocol to the Convention on the Elimination of All Forms of Discrimination against Women.

enforcement ability of CEDAW. The objective of the Optional Protocol is to allow individuals or groups of individuals who have exhausted national remedies to petition the Committee directly about alleged violations of the Convention by their governments. By the Optional Protocol, States Parties undertake to make the Convention and the Protocol widely known and to facilitate access to information about the views and recommendations of the Committee.

United Nations Principles for Older Persons

In the fight against class discrimination, older people are often treated as a separate class. The United Nations Principles for Older Persons, adopted by the UN General Assembly on 16 December 1991 (resolution 46/91) can be divided into five different clusters of relevant issues: independence, participation, care, self-fulfillment and dignity. The Preamble of the Principles for Older Persons states:

> The General Assembly:
>
> Appreciating the contribution that older persons make to their societies,
>
> Recognizing that, in the Charter of the United Nations, the peoples of the United Nations declare ... their determination to reaffirm faith in fundamental human rights, in the dignity and worth of the human person, in the equal rights of men and women and of nations large and small and to promote social progress and better standards of life in larger freedom,
>
> Noting the elaboration of those rights in the Universal Declaration of Human Rights, the International Covenant on Economic, Social and Cultural Rights and the International Covenant on Civil and Political Rights and other declarations to ensure the application of universal standards to particular groups,
>
> In pursuance of the International Plan of Action on Ageing, adopted by the World Assembly on Ageing and endorsed by the General Assembly in its resolution 37/51 of 3 December 1982,
>
> Appreciating the tremendous diversity in the situation of older persons, not only between countries but within countries and between individuals, which requires a variety of policy responses,
>
> Aware that in all countries, individuals are reaching an advanced age in greater numbers and in better health than ever before,
>
> Aware of the scientific research disproving many stereotypes about inevitable and irreversible decline with age,

> Convinced that in a world characterized by an increasing number and proportion of older persons, opportunities must be provided for willing and capable older persons to participate in and contribute to the ongoing activities of society,
>
> Mindful that the strains on family life in both developed and developing countries require support for those providing care to frail older persons,
>
> Bearing in mind the standards already set by the International Plan of Action on Ageing and the conventions, recommendations and resolutions of the International Labour Organization, the World Health Organization and other United Nations entities,
>
> Encourages Governments to incorporate the following principles into their national programmes whenever possible: ... .[60]

There are a number of central themes running through the International Plan of Action on Ageing 2002:

a. The full realization of all human rights and fundamental freedoms of all older persons;
b. The achievement of secure ageing, which involves reaffirming the goal of eradicating poverty in old age and building on the United Nations Principles for Older Persons;
c. The empowerment of older persons to fully and effectively participate in the economic, political and social lives of their societies, including through income-generating and voluntary work;
d. The provision of opportunities for individual development, self-fulfilment and well-being throughout life as well as in late life, through such things as access to lifelong learning and participation in the community while recognizing that older persons are not one homogenous group;
e. The full enjoyment of economic, social and cultural rights, and civil and political rights of people, and the elimination of all forms of violence and discrimination against older persons;
f. The commitment to gender equality among older persons through the elimination of gender-based discrimination;
g. The recognition of the crucial importance of families, intergenerational interdependence, solidarity and reciprocity for social development;
h. The provision of health care, support and social protection for older persons, including preventive and rehabilitative health care;
i. A partnership between all levels of government, civil society, the private sector and older persons themselves in translating the International Plan of Action into practical action;

---

60 United Nations, Principles for Older Persons, at the Preamble.

j. The harnessing of scientific research and expertise, and the realization of the potential of technology to focus on the individual, social and health implications of ageing, in particular in developing countries;
k. The recognition of the situation of ageing of indigenous people, their unique circumstances and the need to seek the means to give them an effective voice in decisions directly affecting them.[61]

Equal Remuneration Convention (ILO No. 100)

Important for workers who suffer class discrimination in the workplace, the General Conference of the International Labor Organization, convened at Geneva, adopted the Equal Remuneration Convention (ILO No. 100) of 9 June 1951. The Preamble of the Equal Remuneration Convention states:

> The General Conference of the International Labour Organisation,
>
> Having been convened at Geneva by the Governing Body of the International Labour Office, and having met in its thirty-fourth session on 6 June 1951, and
>
> Having decided upon the adoption of certain proposals with regard to the principle of equal remuneration for men and women workers for work of equal value, which is the seventh item on the agenda of the session, and
>
> Having determined that these proposals shall take the form of an international Convention, Adopts this twenty-ninth day of June of the year one thousand nine hundred and fifty-one the following Convention, which may be cited as the Equal Remuneration Convention, 1951.[62]

The term "remuneration" is defined in Article 1:

> 1. For the purpose of this Convention:
> (a) The term 'remuneration' includes the ordinary, basic or minimum wage or salary and any additional emoluments whatsoever payable directly or indirectly, whether in cash or in kind, by the employer to the worker and arising out of the worker's employment;

---

61 United Nations, Second World Assembly on Ageism, International Plan of Action on Ageing, 2002.

62 United Nations, Equal Remuneration Convention (ILO No. 100), at the Preamble.

(b) The term 'equal remuneration for men and women workers for work of equal value' refers to rates of remuneration established without discrimination based on sex.[63]

Different methods for equality are envisioned in Article 2:

2(1) Each Member shall, by means appropriate to the methods in operation for determining rates of remuneration, promote and, in so far as is consistent with such methods, ensure the application to all workers of the principle of equal remuneration for … workers for work of equal value.
(2) This principle may be applied by means of:
(a) National laws or regulations;
(b) Legally established or recognized machinery for wage determination;
(c) Collective agreements between employers and workers; or
(d) A combination of these various means.[64]

Further, objective methods of appraisal are ensured in Article 3:

3(1) Where such action will assist in giving effect to the provisions of this Convention, measures shall be taken to promote objective appraisal of jobs on the basis of the work to be performed.
(2) The methods to be followed in this appraisal may be decided upon by the authorities responsible for the determination of rates of remuneration, or, where such rates are determined by collective agreements, by the parties thereto.[65]

Discrimination (Employment and Occupation) Convention (ILO No. 111)

Important for workers who suffer class discrimination in the workplace, the General Conference of the International Labour Organization, convened at Geneva, adopted on 5 July 1958 the Discrimination (Employment and Occupation) Convention (ILO No. 111), which entered into force on 15 June 1960. The Preamble of the Discrimination (Employment and Occupation) Convention states:

Having decided upon the adoption of certain proposals with regard to discrimination in the field of employment and occupation, and

Having determined that these proposals shall take the form of an international Convention, and Considering that the Declaration of Philadelphia affirms that all human beings, irrespective of race, creed or sex, have the right to pursue

63 Ibid., at Article 1.
64 Ibid., at Article 2.
65 Ibid., at Article 3.

> both their material well-being and their spiritual development in conditions of freedom and dignity, of economic security and equal opportunity, and
>
> Considering further that discrimination constitutes a violation of rights enunciated by the Universal Declaration of Human Rights.[66]

The word "discrimination" is defined in Article 1 to include social origin under Article 1(1)(a):

> 1(1) For the purpose of this Convention the term 'discrimination' includes:
> (a) any distinction, exclusion or preference made on the basis of race, colour, sex, religion, political opinion, national extraction or social origin, which has the effect of nullifying or impairing equality of opportunity or treatment in employment or occupation;
> (b) such other distinction, exclusion or preference which has the effect of nullifying or impairing equality of opportunity or treatment in employment or occupation as may be determined by the Member concerned after consultation with representative employers' and workers' organizations, where such exist, and with other appropriate bodies.
> (2) Any distinction, exclusion or preference in respect of a particular job based on the inherent requirements thereof shall not be deemed to be discrimination.
> (3) For the purpose of this Convention the terms 'employment' and 'occupation' include access to vocational training, access to employment and to particular occupations, and terms and conditions of employment.[67]

Member commitment to equality of opportunity and treatment is contained in Article 2:

> 2. Each Member for which this Convention is in force undertakes to declare and pursue a national policy designed to promote, by methods appropriate to national conditions and practice, equality of opportunity and treatment in respect of employment and occupation, with a view to eliminating any discrimination in respect thereof.[68]

Further, Article 3 specifically enunciates Member responsibilities:

> 3. Each Member for which this Convention is in force undertakes, by methods appropriate to national conditions and practice:

---

66 United Nations, Discrimination (Employment and Occupation) Convention (ILO No. 111), at the Preamble.

67 Ibid., at Article 1.

68 Ibid., at Article 2.

> (a) To seek the co-operation of employers' and workers' organizations and other appropriate bodies in promoting the acceptance and observance of this policy;
> (b) To enact such legislation and to promote such educational programs as may be calculated to secure the acceptance and observance of the policy;
> (c) To repeal any statutory provisions and modify any administrative instructions or practices which are inconsistent with the policy;
> (d) To pursue the policy in respect of employment under the direct control of a national authority;
> (e) To ensure observance of the policy in activities of vocational guidance, vocational training and placement services under the direction of a national authority;
> (f) To indicate in its annual reports on the application of the Convention the action taken in pursuance of the policy and the results secured by such action.[69]

Finally, special measures are provided for in Article 5 to include for social origin:

> 5(1) Special measures of protection or assistance provided in other Conventions or Recommendations adopted by the International Labor Conference shall not be deemed to be discrimination.
> (2) Any Member may, after consultation with representative employers' and workers' organizations, where such exist, determine that other special measures designed to meet the particular requirements of persons who, for reasons such as sex, age, disablement, family responsibilities or social or cultural status, are generally recognized to require special protection or assistance, shall not be deemed to be discrimination.[70]

Employment Policy Convention (ILO No. 122)

Important for workers who suffer class discrimination in the workplace, the General Conference of the International Labor Organization, convened in Geneva, adopted on 9 July 1964 the Employment Policy Convention (ILO No. 122), which entered into force on 9 July 1965. The Preamble of the Employment Policy Convention (ILO No. 122) states:

> Considering that the Declaration of Philadelphia recognizes the solemn obligation of the International Labor Organization to further among the nations of the world programs which will achieve full employment and the raising of standards of living, and that the Preamble to the Constitution of the International

69 Ibid., at Article 3.
70 Ibid., at Article 5.

> Labor Organization provides for the prevention of unemployment and the provision of an adequate living wage, and
>
> Considering further that under the terms of the Declaration of Philadelphia it is the responsibility of the International Labor Organization to examine and consider the bearing of economic and financial policies upon employment policy in the light of the fundamental objective that 'all human beings, irrespective of race, creed or sex, have the right to pursue both their material well-being and their spiritual development in conditions of freedom and dignity, of economic security and equal opportunity', and
>
> Considering that the Universal Declaration of Human Rights provides that 'everyone has the right to work, to free choice of employment, to just and favorable conditions of work and to protection against unemployment'.[71]

A commitment to full, productive and freely chosen employment is envisioned in Article 1, including irrespective of social origin in Article 1(2)(c):

> 1(1) With a view to stimulating economic growth and development, raising levels of living, meeting manpower requirements and overcoming unemployment and under-employment, each Member shall declare and pursue, as a major goal, an active policy designed to promote full, productive and freely chosen employment.
> (2) The said policy shall aim at ensuring that:
> (a) There is work for all who are available for and seeking work;
> (b) Such work is as productive as possible;
> (c) There is freedom of choice of employment and the fullest possible opportunity for each worker to qualify for, and to use his skills and endowments in, a job for which he is well suited, irrespective of race, colour, sex, religion, political opinion, national extraction or social origin.
> (3) The said policy shall take due account of the stage and level of economic development and the mutual relationships between employment objectives and other economic and social objectives, and shall be pursued by methods that are appropriate to national conditions and practices.[72]

Respectfully, national conditions are taken into account in the carrying out of the policy:

> 2. Each Member shall, by such methods and to such extent as may be appropriate under national conditions:

71 United Nations, Employment Policy Convention (ILO No. 122), at the Preamble.
72 Ibid., at Article 1.

> (a) Decide on and keep under review, within the framework of a coordinated economic and social policy, the measures to be adopted for attaining the objectives specified in article l;
> (b) Take such steps as may be needed, including when appropriate the establishment of programs, for the application of these measures.[73]

Finally, a consultation process is envisioned in Article 3 for the implementation of the Employment Policy Convention:

> 3. In the application of this Convention, representatives of the persons affected by the measures to be taken, and in particular representatives of employers and workers, shall be consulted concerning employment policies, with a view to taking fully into account their experience and views and securing their full co-operation in formulating and enlisting support for such policies.[74]

Convention against Discrimination in Education

Education is paramount in the fight against class discrimination. The Preamble of the Convention against Discrimination in Education states:

> The General Conference of the United Nations Educational, Scientific and Cultural Organization, meeting in Paris from 14 November to 15 December 1960, at its eleventh session,
>
> *Recalling* that the Universal Declaration of Human Rights asserts the principle of non-discrimination and proclaims that every person has the right to education,
>
> *Considering* that discrimination in education is a violation of rights enunciated in that Declaration,
>
> *Considering* that, under the terms of its Constitution, the United Nations Educational, Scientific and Cultural Organization has the purpose of instituting collaboration among the nations with a view to furthering for all universal respect for human rights and equality of educational opportunity,
>
> *Recognizing* that, consequently, the United Nations Educational, Scientific and Cultural Organization, while respecting the diversity of national educational systems, has the duty not only to proscribe any form of discrimination in education but also to promote equality of opportunity and treatment for all in education,

---

73 Ibid., at Article 2.
74 Ibid., at Article 3.

Having before it proposals concerning the different aspects of discrimination in education, …

Having decided at its tenth session that this question should be made the subject of an international convention as well as of recommendations to Member States,

Adopts this Convention on the fourteenth day of December 1960.[75]

Article 1 defines the terms discirmination to include social origin and economic condition, and also defines education:

1(1) For the purposes of this Convention, the term 'discrimination' includes any distinction, exclusion, limitation or preference which, being based on race, colour, sex, language, religion, political or other opinion, national or social origin, economic condition or birth, has the purpose or effect of nullifying or impairing equality of treatment in education and in particular:

(a) Of depriving any person or group of persons of access to education of any type or at any level;

(b) Of limiting any person or group of persons to education of an inferior standard;

(c) Subject to the provisions of Article 2 of this Convention, of establishing or maintaining separate educational systems or institutions for persons or groups of persons; or

(d) Of inflicting on any person or group of persons conditions which are incompatible with the dignity of man.

(2) For the purposes of this Convention, the term 'education' refers to all types and levels of education, and includes access to education, the standard and quality of education, and the conditions under which it is given.[76]

Certain actions are exempt from being considered as discrimination under Article 2:

2. When permitted in a State, the following situations shall not be deemed to constitute discrimination, within the meaning of Article I of this Convention:

(a) The establishment or maintenance of separate educational systems or institutions for pupils of the two sexes, if these systems or institutions offer equivalent access to education, provide a teaching staff with qualifications of the same standard as well as school premises and equipment of the same

75 United Nations, Convention against Discrimination in Education, at the Preamble.

76 Ibid., at Article 1.

> quality, and afford the opportunity to take the same or equivalent courses of study;
>
> (b) The establishment or maintenance, for religious or linguistic reasons, of separate educational systems or institutions offering an education which is in keeping with the wishes of the pupil's parents or legal guardians, if participation in such systems or attendance at such institutions is optional and if the education provided conforms to such standards as may be laid down or approved by the competent authorities, in particular for education of the same level;
>
> (c) The establishment or maintenance of private educational institutions, if the object of the institutions is not to secure the exclusion of any group but to provide educational facilities in addition to those provided by the public authorities, if the institutions are conducted in accordance with that object, and if the education provided conforms with such standards as may be laid down or approved by the competent authorities, in particular for education of the same level.[77]

Discrimination in education is outlawed under Article 3:

> 3. In order to eliminate and prevent discrimination within the meaning of this Convention, the States Parties thereto undertake:
>
> (a) To abrogate any statutory provisions and any administrative instructions and to discontinue any administrative practices which involve discrimination in education;
>
> (b) To ensure, by legislation where necessary, that there is no discrimination in the admission of pupils to educational institutions;
>
> (c) Not to allow any differences of treatment by the public authorities between nationals, except on the basis of merit or need, in the matter of school fees and the grant of scholarships or other forms of assistance to pupils and necessary permits and facilities for the pursuit of studies in foreign countries;
>
> (d) Not to allow, in any form of assistance granted by the public authorities to educational institutions, any restrictions or preference based solely on the ground that pupils belong to a particular group;
>
> (e) To give foreign nationals resident within their territory the same access to education as that given to their own nationals.[78]

Article 4 guarantees equality of opportunity and treatment in education:

> 4. The States Parties to this Convention undertake furthermore to formulate, develop and apply a national policy which, by methods appropriate to the

77 Ibid., at Article 2.

78 Ibid., at Article 3.

> circumstances and to national usage, will tend to promote equality of opportunity and of treatment in the matter of education and in particular:
>
> (a) To make primary education free and compulsory; make secondary education in its different forms generally available and accessible to all; make higher education equally accessible to all on the basis of individual capacity; assure compliance by all with the obligation to attend school prescribed by law;
>
> (b) To ensure that the standards of education are equivalent in all public educational institutions of the same level, and that the conditions relating to the quality of the education provided are also equivalent;
>
> (c) To encourage and intensify by appropriate methods the education of persons who have not received any primary education or who have not completed the entire primary education course and the continuation of their education on the basis of individual capacity;
>
> (d) To provide training for the teaching profession without discrimination.[79]

Finally, Article 5 underscores the importance of education for the full development of a human being:

> 5(1) The States Parties to this Convention agree that:
>
> (a) Education shall be directed to the full development of the human personality and to the strengthening of respect for human rights and fundamental freedoms; it shall promote understanding, tolerance and friendship among all nations, racial or religious groups, and shall further the activities of the United Nations for the maintenance of peace;
>
> (b) It is essential to respect the liberty of parents and, where applicable, of legal guardians, firstly to choose for their children institutions other than those maintained by the public authorities but conforming to such minimum educational standards as may be laid down or approved by the competent authorities and, secondly, to ensure in a manner consistent with the procedures followed in the State for the application of its legislation, the religious and moral education of the children in conformity with their own convictions; and no person or group of persons should be compelled to receive religious instruction inconsistent with his or their convictions;
>
> (c) It is essential to recognize the right of members of national minorities to carry on their own educational activities, including the maintenance of schools and, depending on the educational policy of each State, the use or the teaching of their own language, provided however:
>
> (i) That this right is not exercised in a manner which prevents the members of these minorities from understanding the culture and language

79 Ibid., at Article 4.

of the community as a whole and from participating in its activities, or which prejudices national sovereignty;

(ii) That the standard of education is not lower than the general standard laid down or approved by the competent authorities; and

(iii) That attendance at such schools is optional.

(2) The States Parties to this Convention undertake to take all necessary measures to ensure the application of the principles enunciated in paragraph 1 of this Article.[80]

Conclusion

Much needs to be done inside and outside the United Nations, in order to specifically outlaw class discrimination. Awareness and information about the situation of those who are suffering discrimination is critical if full participation and equality are to be achieved. The media is a key partner in the process of empowering people, in addressing discrimination, prejudice and ignorance, and in ending stereotypical portrayals. Non-governmental organizations also have a vital role to play in building understanding among society as a whole, with a need to utilize information and communications technologies to empower all people. On the international level, attempts have been made to provide legislatively for equality to end class discrimination. In recycling discrimination, 'the stream always tries to return to its habitual course'.[81] However, international law has made great strides to work toward overcoming class discrimination, in the pursuit of "Class Act".

---

80 Ibid., at Article 5.

81 Canadian Advisory Council on the Status of Women, *Feminist Guide to the Canadian Constitution*, Ottawa, 1992, at p.57.

Chapter 4
Class Act in Australia and New Zealand

Introduction

In the quest for tolerance of class distinctions in *Class Act*, this chapter will examine efforts against class discrimination in Australia and New Zealand. It will examine important legislation impacting class, first in Australia, namely the Human Rights Act, the Human Rights and Equal Opportunity Commission Act, the Discrimination Act and the Anti-Discrimination Act, for minorities the Racial Discrimination Act and the Racial Hatred Act, and for women the Sex Discrimination Act, the Workplace Relations Act and the Fair Work Act; and then in New Zealand, namely the Treaty of Waitangi, the Bill of Rights Act, the Human Rights Act and the Human Rights Amendment Act, for minorities the Race Relations Act, the Employment Contracts Act and the Employment Relations Act.

Australia

Australian laws do impose an obligation on everyone to be vigilant about discrimination and to take action when incidents of prejudice occur, particularly where those incidents might be unlawful. Australia is a party to a number of international conventions and declarations which impose obligations to eliminate discrimination, including class discrimination, when ratified in Australian law, including the Universal Declaration of Human Rights. When Australia becomes a party to an international convention, the terms of the convention create binding obligations in international law. However, international laws do not automatically become a part of Australian law. The Australian government can choose to give effect to its international obligations in various forms, legislative, policy or symbolic. In Australia, they are reflected in a range of government policies and programs, and some are also incorporated in law. Australia has taken practical steps to improve access to justice and protection under the law in the pursuit of equality, and is committed to providing more accessible, low-cost alternative dispute resolution options. Australia has a regime of legislation and institutional mechanisms to protect against discrimination, and is committed to promoting, supporting and protecting human rights.

Commonwealth laws applying in South Australia cover social origin discrimination in work, which could cover a person's social class, family background and local origin, and includes refusing to hire them, hiring them on less favorable terms, denying them access to any benefits that go with the job, dismissing them or subjecting them to other adverse treatment. It is important to note that if the legislation specifies certain categories of discrimination such as race or gender, this is not exhaustive and may extend, but does not limit, the meaning of the provision in which it appears.

Human Rights Act

The Human Rights Act, also known as An Act to Respect, Protect and Promote Human Rights, is the first Bill of Rights in Australia and was effective from 1 January 2009. The Preamble of the Human Rights Act states:

> 1. Human rights are necessary for individuals to live lives of dignity and value.
> 2. Respecting, protecting and promoting the rights of individuals improves the welfare of the whole community.
> 3. Human rights are set out in this Act so that individuals know what their rights are.
> 4. Setting out these human rights also makes it easier for them to be taken into consideration in the development and interpretation of legislation.
> 5. This Act encourages individuals to see themselves, and each other, as the holders of rights, and as responsible for upholding the human rights of others.
> 6. Few rights are absolute. Human rights may be subject only to the reasonable limits in law that can be demonstrably justified in a free and democratic society. One individual's rights may also need to be weighed against another individual's rights.
> 7. Although human rights belong to all individuals, they have special significance for Indigenous people – the first owners of this land, members of its most enduring cultures, and individuals for whom the issue of rights protection has great and continuing importance.[1]

Section 5 defines human rights and Section 6 defines who possesses human rights:

> 5. In this Act:
> *human rights* means the civil and political rights.[2]
>
> 6. Only individuals have human rights.[3]

Important for class discrimination cases, Section 7 notes that the Act is not exhaustive:

1 Human Rights Act, Australia, at the Preamble.
2 Ibid., at Section 5.
3 Ibid., at Section 6.

7. This Act is not exhaustive of the rights an individual may have under domestic or international law.[4]

Equality before the law is recognized in Section 8:

8. Recognition and equality before the law
(1) Everyone has the right to recognition as a person before the law.
(2) Everyone has the right to enjoy his or her human rights without distinction or discrimination of any kind.
(3) Everyone is equal before the law and is entitled to the equal protection of the law without discrimination. In particular, everyone has the right to equal and effective protection against discrimination on any ground.[5]

However, Section 28 is a limiting clause:

28(1) Human rights may be subject only to reasonable limits set by Territory laws that can be demonstrably justified in a free and democratic society.
(2) In deciding whether a limit is reasonable, all relevant factors must be considered, including the following:
(a) the nature of the right affected;
(b) the importance of the purpose of the limitation;
(c) the nature and extent of the limitation;
(d) the relationship between the limitation and its purpose;
(e) any less restrictive means reasonably available to achieve the purpose the limitation seeks to achieve.[6]

Section 31 deals with interpretation of human rights:

31(1) International law, and the judgments of foreign and international courts and tribunals, relevant to a human right may be considered in interpreting the human right.
(2) In deciding whether material mentioned in subsection (1) or any other material should be considered, and the weight to be given to the material, the following matters must be taken into account:
(a) the desirability of being able to rely on the ordinary meaning of this Act, having regard to its purpose and its provisions read in the context of the Act as a whole;
(b) the undesirability of prolonging proceedings without compensating advantage;

4 Ibid., at Section 7.
5 Ibid., at Section 8.
6 Ibid., at Section 28.

(c) the accessibility of the material to the public.[7]

Further, Section 32 covers a declaration of incompatibility with the Act:

> 32(1) This section applies if
> (a) a proceeding is being heard by the Supreme Court; and
> (b) an issue arises in the proceeding about whether a Territory law is consistent with a human right.
> (2) If the Supreme Court is satisfied that the Territory law is not consistent with the human right, the court may declare that the law is not consistent with the human right (the *declaration of incompatibility*).
> (3) The declaration of incompatibility does not affect
> (a) the validity, operation or enforcement of the law; or
> (b) the rights or obligations of anyone.
> (4) The registrar of the Supreme Court must promptly give a copy of the declaration of incompatibility to the Attorney-General.[8]

The Human Rights Commissioner's special role is noted in Section 36:

> 36(1) The human rights commissioner may intervene in a proceeding before a court that involves the application of this Act with the leave of the court.
> (2) The court may give leave subject to conditions.[9]

Finally, it is stressed in Section 40B that Public Authorities are held to a higher standard in terms of respect for the Act:

> 40B Public authorities must act consistently with human rights
> (1) It is unlawful for a public authority
> (a) to act in a way that is incompatible with a human right; or
> (b) in making a decision, to fail to give proper consideration to a relevant human right.
> (2) Subsection (1) does not apply if the act is done or decision made under a law in force in the Territory and
> (a) the law expressly requires the act to be done or decision made in a particular way and that way is inconsistent with a human right; or
> (b) the law cannot be interpreted in a way that is consistent with a human right.[10]

---

7 Ibid., at Section 31.
8 Ibid., at Section 32.
9 Ibid., at Section 36.
10 Ibid., at Section 40B.

Human Rights and Equal Opportunity Commission Act (HREOCA)

Important for equal rights and tolerance of class distinctions, the Human Rights and Equal Opportunity Commission Act 1986 (HREOCA) gives effect to such relevant international conventions and declarations as the International Covenant on Civil and Political Rights, and for employment discrimination the International Labour Organization Convention on Discrimination in Employment and Occupation. The Human Rights and Equal Opportunity Commission (HREOC) inquires into complaints under federal anti-discrimination law and educates the community about obligations under domestic legislation. The HREOCA enables the HREOC to investigate complaints of breaches of conventions by Commonwealth Government agencies and may also investigate complaints of discrimination in employment by any employer.

Discrimination is defined in Section 3, which includes social origin under Section 3(a):

> 3. Discrimination, except in Part IIB, means:
> (a) any distinction, exclusion or preference made on the basis of race, colour, sex, religion, political opinion, national extraction or social origin that has the effect of nullifying or impairing equality of opportunity or treatment in employment or occupation; and
> (b) any other distinction, exclusion or preference that:
> (i) has the effect of nullifying or impairing equality of opportunity or treatment in employment or occupation; and
> (ii) has been declared by the regulations to constitute discrimination for the purposes of this Act;
> but does not include any distinction, exclusion or preference:
> (c) in respect of a particular job based on the inherent requirements of the job.[11]

Further, the duties of the Commission are outlined in Section 10A:

> 10A(1) It is the duty of the Commission to ensure that the functions of the Commission under this or any other Act are performed:
> (a) with regard for:
> (i) the indivisibility and universality of human rights; and
> (ii) the principle that every person is free and equal in dignity and rights; and
> (b) efficiently and with the greatest possible benefit to the people of Australia.

11 Human Rights and Equal Opportunity Commission Act, Australia, at Section 3.

(2) Nothing in this section imposes a duty on the Commission that is enforceable by proceedings in a court.[12]

Finally, the functions of Commission are outlined in Section 11:

11(1) The functions of the Commission are:

(a) such functions as are conferred on the Commission by the *Age Discrimination Act 2004*, the *Racial Discrimination Act 1975*, the *Sex Discrimination Act 1984* or any other enactment;

(aa) to inquire into, and attempt to conciliate, complaints of unlawful discrimination.[13]

Written complaints are contained in Section 46P:

46P(1) A written complaint may be lodged with the Commission, alleging unlawful discrimination.

(2) The complaint may be lodged:

(a) by a person aggrieved by the alleged unlawful discrimination:

(i) on that person's own behalf; or

(ii) on behalf of that person and one or more other persons who are also aggrieved by the alleged unlawful discrimination; or

(b) by 2 or more persons aggrieved by the alleged unlawful discrimination:

(i) on their own behalf; or

(ii) on behalf of themselves and one or more other persons who are also aggrieved by the alleged unlawful discrimination; or

(c) by a person or trade union on behalf of one or more other persons aggrieved by the alleged unlawful discrimination.

(3) A person who is a class member for a representative complaint is not entitled to lodge a separate complaint in respect of the same subject matter.

(4) If it appears to the Commission that:

(a) a person wishes to make a complaint under subsection (1); and

(b) the person requires assistance to formulate the complaint or to reduce it to writing;

the Commission must take reasonable steps to provide appropriate assistance to the person.[14]

12 Ibid., at Section 10A.

13 Ibid., at Section 11.

14 Ibid., at Section 46P.

Discrimination Act and Anti-Discrimination Act

Important in the fight against class discrimination, the Discrimination Act 1991 (Act No. 81 of 1991) provides against discrimination. Section 7 enumerates the grounds:

> 7(1) This Act applies to discrimination on the ground of any of the following attributes:
> (a) sex;
> (b) sexuality;
> (c) transsexuality;
> (d) relationship status;
> (e) status as a parent or carer;
> (f) pregnancy;
> (g) breastfeeding;
> (h) race;
> (i) religious or political conviction;
> (j) disability;
> (k) membership or nonmembership of an association or organisation of employers or employees;
> (l) age;
> (m) profession, trade, occupation or calling;
> (n) association (whether as a relative or otherwise) with a person identified by reference to an attribute referred to in another paragraph of this subsection;
> (o) spent conviction within the meaning of the *Spent Convictions Act 2000*.
> (2) In this Act, a reference to an attribute mentioned in subsection (1) includes
> (a) a characteristic that people with that attribute generally have; and
> (b) a characteristic that people with that attribute are generally presumed to have; and
> (c) such an attribute that a person is presumed to have; and
> (d) such an attribute that the person had in the past but no longer has.[15]

Discrimination is defined under Section 8:

> 8(1) For this Act, a person *discriminates* against another person if
> (a) the person treats or proposes to treat the other person unfavourably because the other person has an attribute referred to in section 7; or
> (b) the person imposes or proposes to impose a condition or requirement that has, or is likely to have, the effect of disadvantaging people because they have an attribute referred to in section 7.

15 Discrimination Act, Australia, at Section 7.

(2) Subsection (1) (b) does not apply to a condition or requirement that is reasonable in the circumstances.
(3) In deciding whether a condition or requirement is reasonable in the circumstances, the matters to be taken into account include
(a) the nature and extent of the resultant disadvantage; and
(b) the feasibility of overcoming or mitigating the disadvantage; and
(c) whether the disadvantage is disproportionate to the result sought by the person who imposes or proposes to impose the condition or requirement.[16]

With regard to employees, Section 10 states:

10(1) It is unlawful for an employer to discriminate against a person
(a) in the arrangements made for the purpose of deciding who should be offered employment; or
(b) in deciding who should be offered employment; or
(c) in the terms or conditions on which employment is offered.
(2) It is unlawful for an employer to discriminate against an employee
(a) in the terms or conditions of employment that the employer affords the employee; or
(b) by denying the employee access, or limiting the employee's access, to opportunities for promotion, transfer or training or to any other benefit associated with employment; or
(c) by dismissing the employee; or
(d) by subjecting the employee to any other detriment.[17]

Finally, the Anti-Discrimination Act 1991 (Act No. 85 of 1991) provides for the protection of an employee under Section 7:

7(1) The Act prohibits discrimination on the basis of the following attributes
a. sex;
b. marital status;
c. pregnancy;
d. parental status;
e. breast feeding;
f. age;
g. race;
h. impairment;
i. religion;
j. political belief or activity;
k. trade union activity;
l. lawful sexual activity;

16 Ibid., at Section 8.
17 Ibid., at Section 10.

m. association with, or relation to, a person identified on the basis of any of the above attributes.[18]

Racial Discrimination Act (RDA) and Racial Hatred Act (RHA)

Important for minorities and class discrimination, the Racial Discrimination Act 1975 (RDA), also known as An Act relating to the Elimination of Racial and other Discrimination, prohibits discrimination on the grounds of race, color, descent and national or ethnic origin.[19] The RDA gives effect to Australia's obligations under the International Convention on the Elimination of All Forms of Racial Discrimination. The RDA aims to ensure that all Australians can enjoy their human rights and freedoms in full equality regardless of their race, color, descent, or national or ethnic origin. The RDA applies to everyone in Australia including businesses, schools, and local, State, Territory and Commonwealth government agencies and departments. It overrides racially discriminatory legislation, making it ineffective. However, Commonwealth legislation which is racially discriminatory is not necessarily overridden by the RDA. Under the RDA, racial discrimination is unlawful whenever it impairs a person's equal enjoyment of his human rights and fundamental freedoms. In addition, the RDA has specific provisions making it unlawful to discriminate in areas such as employment, land, housing and accommodation, provision of goods and services, access to places and facilities for use by the public, advertising and joining a trade union. The RDA also makes indirect racial discrimination unlawful. In some cases, the RDA will permit special measures, which are distinctions based on race where there might be more favorable treatment for one racial group over another. It does so as a form of affirmative action, so that a group which has been traditionally denied human rights and access to rights can receive special treatment to redress the situation and to allow that group to enjoy human rights on an equal footing with the rest of the community. This form of favorable treatment is not unlawful discrimination and the special measure will be removed when equality has been achieved. Government support for special measures is not discriminatory, because the aim is to enhance the access of certain groups to justice, cultural expression and other rights and freedoms. The RDA is administered by the Human Rights and Equal Opportunity Commission (HREOC). HREOC has the responsibility for investigating complaints.

Particularly, Section 9 prohibits racial discrimination:

> 9(1) It is unlawful for a person to do any act involving a distinction, exclusion, restriction or preference based on race, colour, descent or national or ethnic origin which has the purpose or effect of nullifying or impairing the recognition, enjoyment or exercise, on an equal footing, of any human right or fundamental

18 Anti-Discrimination Act, Australia, at Section 7.

19 Racial Discrimination Act, Australia.

> freedom in the political, economic, social, cultural or any other field of public life.
>
> (1A) Where:
>
> (a) a person requires another person to comply with a term, condition or requirement which is not reasonable having regard to the circumstances of the case; and
>
> (b) the other person does not or cannot comply with the term, condition or requirement; and
>
> (c) the requirement to comply has the purpose or effect of nullifying or impairing the recognition, enjoyment or exercise, on an equal footing, by persons of the same race, colour, descent or national or ethnic origin as the other person, of any human right or fundamental freedom in the political, economic, social, cultural or any other field of public life;
>
> the act of requiring such compliance is to be treated, for the purposes of this Part, as an act involving a distinction based on, or an act done by reason of, the other person's race, colour, descent or national or ethnic origin.
>
> (2) A reference in this section to a human right or fundamental freedom in the political, economic, social, cultural or any other field of public life includes any right of a kind referred to in Article 5 of the Convention.
>
> (3) This section does not apply in respect of the employment, or an application for the employment, of a person on a ship or aircraft (not being an Australian ship or aircraft) if that person was engaged, or applied, for that employment outside Australia.[20]

In addition, Section 10 guarantees equality before the law:

> 10(1) If, by reason of, or of a provision of, a law of the Commonwealth or of a State or Territory, persons of a particular race, colour or national or ethnic origin do not enjoy a right that is enjoyed by persons of another race, colour or national or ethnic origin, or enjoy a right to a more limited extent than persons of another race, colour or national or ethnic origin, then, notwithstanding anything in that law, persons of the first-mentioned race, colour or national or ethnic origin shall, by force of this section, enjoy that right to the same extent as persons of that other race, colour or national or ethnic origin.[21]

Also important for minorities, the Racial Hatred Act 1995 (RHA) amended the Racial Discrimination Act (RDA) by adding in new laws specifically dealing with racial vilification. In addition to the RHA extending the coverage of the RDA to allow people to complain about racially offensive or abusive behavior, it also gives effect to some of Australia's obligations under the International Covenant on Civil and Political Rights, and the International Convention on the Elimination of

20 Ibid., at Section 9.

21 Ibid., at Section 10.

All Forms of Racial Discrimination. The RHA aims to strike a balance between two valued rights, namely the right to communicate freely and the right to live free from vilification. It covers public acts, which are done because of the race, color, or national or ethnic origin of a person or group and reasonably likely in all circumstances to offend, insult, humiliate or intimidate that person or group. In bringing a complaint under the RHA, the complainant is responsible for proving that the act was done in public, that it was because of his ethnicity and that it was reasonably likely to offend, insult, humiliate or intimidate a reasonable person of that ethnicity. In claiming an exception, the respondent is responsible for establishing that the act was a genuine exception and that it was done reasonably and in good faith.

Sex Discrimination Act (SDA)

Important for women and class discrimination, the Sex Discrimination Act 1984 (SDA) prohibits discrimination on the grounds of gender, marital status, pregnancy, and potential pregnancy and family responsibilities, and is administered by the Sex Discrimination Commissioner under the auspices of the Human Rights and Equal Opportunity Commission (HREOC).[22] Particularly, Section 5 deals directly with the definition of gender discrimination:

> 5(1) For the purposes of this Act, a person (in this subsection referred to as the discriminator) discriminates against another person (in this subsection referred to as the aggrieved person) on the ground of the sex of the aggrieved person if, by reason of:
>
> (a) the sex of the aggrieved person;
>
> (b) a characteristic that appertains generally to persons of the sex of the aggrieved person; or
>
> (c) a characteristic that is generally imputed to persons of the sex of the aggrieved person; the discriminator treats the aggrieved person less favourably than, in circumstances that are the same or are not materially different, the discriminator treats or would treat a person of the opposite sex.
>
> (2) For the purposes of this Act, a person (the discriminator) discriminates against another person (the aggrieved person) on the ground of the sex of the aggrieved person if the discriminator imposes, or proposes to impose, a condition, requirement or practice that has, or is likely to have, the effect of disadvantaging persons of the same sex as the aggrieved person. [23]

In terms of affirmative action, Section 7D stipulates that a person may take special measures for the purpose of achieving substantive equality between men and

22 Sex Discrimination Act, Australia, at Section 3.

23 Ibid., at Section 5.

women; or people of different marital status; or women who are pregnant and people who are not pregnant.[24]

Further, discrimination in education is prohibited under Section 21:

> 21(1) It is unlawful for an educational authority to discriminate against a person on the ground of the person's sex, marital status, pregnancy or potential pregnancy:
>
> (a) by refusing or failing to accept the person's application for admission as a student; or
>
> (b) in the terms or conditions on which it is prepared to admit the person as a student.
>
> (2) It is unlawful for an educational authority to discriminate against a student on the ground of the student's sex, marital status, pregnancy or potential pregnancy:
>
> (a) by denying the student access, or limiting the student's access, to any benefit provided by the educational authority;
>
> (b) by expelling the student; or
>
> (c) by subjecting the student to any other detriment.
>
> (3) Nothing in this section applies to or in respect of a refusal or failure to accept a person's application for admission as a student at an educational institution where:
>
> (a) the educational institution is conducted solely for students of the opposite sex to the sex of the applicant; or
>
> (b) except in the case of an institution of tertiary education – education or training at the level at which the applicant is seeking education or training is provided by the educational institution only or mainly for students of the opposite sex to the sex of the applicant.
>
> (4) This section binds the Crown in right of a State.[25]

The Act provides an important role for the HREOC in addressing the issue of gender discrimination. Its functions are defined under Section 48, namely to promote an understanding and acceptance of, and compliance with, this Act; to undertake research and educational programs on behalf of the Commonwealth for the purpose of promoting the objects of this Act; to examine enactments for the purpose of ascertaining whether they are inconsistent with or contrary to the objects of this Act, and to report to the Minister the results of any such examination.[26]

---

24 Ibid., at Section 7D.

25 Ibid., at Section 21.

26 Ibid., at Section 48.

Workplace Relations Act

Important for employment rights and class discrimination in the workplace, the Workplace Relations Act 1996 has provisions to safeguard groups of workers. The Act provides for equal remuneration for work of equal value without discrimination. Section 3 enunciates the principal objectives, which specifically mentions social origin under Section 3(m):

> 3. The principal object of this Act is to provide a framework for cooperative workplace relations which promotes the economic prosperity and welfare of the people of Australia by:
>
> (m) respecting and valuing the diversity of the work force by helping to prevent and eliminate discrimination on the basis of race, colour, sex, sexual preference, age, physical or mental disability, marital status, family responsibilities, pregnancy, religion, political opinion, national extraction or social origin.[27]

Employment is not to be terminated on certain grounds, which specifically mentions social origin at Section 659(2):

> 659(2) Except as provided by subsection (3) or (4), an employer must not terminate an employee's employment for any one or more of the following reasons, or for reasons including any one or more of the following reasons:
>
> (f) race, colour, sex, sexual preference, age, physical or mental disability, marital status, family responsibilities, pregnancy, religion, political opinion, national extraction or social origin.[28]

The Commission is to take into account discrimination issues under Section 104, which specifically mentions social origin under Section 104(b):

> 104. In the performance of its functions, the Commission must take into account the following:
>
> (a) the need to apply the principle of equal pay for work of equal value;
>
> (b) the need to prevent and eliminate discrimination because of, or for reasons including, race, colour, sex, sexual preference, age, physical or mental disability, marital status, family responsibilities, pregnancy, religion, political opinion, national extraction or social origin.[29]

Finally, the functions of the Workplace Authority Director are enumerated under Section 150B, which specifically mentions the need to prevent and eliminate social origin, important for class discrimination cases:

27 Workplace Relations Act, Australia, at Section 3.

28 Ibid., at Section 659(2).

29 Ibid., at Section 104.

> 150B(2) In performing his or her functions relating to workplace agreements, the Workplace Authority Director must have particular regard to:
>
> (d) the need to prevent and eliminate discrimination because of, or for reasons including, race, colour, sex, sexual preference, age, physical or mental disability, marital status, family responsibilities, pregnancy, religion, political opinion, national extraction or social origin.[30]

Fair Work Act

Important for employment rights and class discrimination in the workplace, the objects of the Fair Work Act 2009 are outlined under Section 3:

> 3. The object of this Act is to provide a balanced framework for cooperative and productive workplace relations that promotes national economic prosperity and social inclusion for all Australians by:
>
> (a) providing workplace relations laws that are fair to working Australians, are flexible for businesses, promote productivity and economic growth for Australia's future economic prosperity and take into account Australia's international labour obligations; and
>
> (b) ensuring a guaranteed safety net of fair, relevant and enforceable minimum terms and conditions through the National Employment Standards, modern awards and national minimum wage orders; and
>
> (c) ensuring that the guaranteed safety net of fair, relevant and enforceable minimum wages and conditions can no longer be undermined by the making of statutory individual employment agreements of any kind given that such agreements can never be part of a fair workplace relations system; and
>
> (d) assisting employees to balance their work and family responsibilities by providing for flexible working arrangements; and
>
> (e) enabling fairness and representation at work and the prevention of discrimination by*recognising* the right to freedom of association and the right to be represented, protecting against unfair treatment and discrimination,
>
> providing accessible and effective procedures to resolve grievances and disputes and providing effective compliance mechanisms; and
>
> (f) achieving productivity and fairness through an emphasis on enterprise-level collective bargaining underpinned by simple good faith bargaining obligations and clear rules governing industrial action.[31]

The Fair Work Ombudsman can accept complaints about discrimination in employment on the ground of social origin under Section 351(1):

---

30 Ibid., at Section 150B.

31 Fair Work Act, Australia, at Section 3.

> 351(1) An employer must not take adverse action against a person who is an employee, or prospective employee, of the employer because of the person's race, colour, sex, sexual preference, age, physical or mental disability, marital status, family or carer's responsibilities, pregnancy, religion, political opinion, national extraction or social origin.
> (2) However, subsection (1) does not apply to action that is:
> (a) not unlawful under any anti-discrimination law in force in the place where the action is taken; or
> (b) taken because of the inherent requirements of the particular position concerned; or
> (c) if the action is taken against a staff member of an institution conducted in accordance with the doctrines, tenets, beliefs or teachings of a particular religion or creed – taken:
> (i) in good faith; and
> (ii) to avoid injury to the religious susceptibilities of adherents of that religion or creed.
> (3) Each of the following is an *anti-discrimination law*:
> (aa) the *Age Discrimination Act 2004*;
> (ab) the *Disability Discrimination Act 1992*;
> (ac) the *Racial Discrimination Act 1975*;
> (ad) the *Sex Discrimination Act 1984*;
> (a) the *Anti-Discrimination Act 1977* of New South Wales;
> (b) the *Equal Opportunity Act 1995* of Victoria;
> (c) the *Anti-Discrimination Act 1991* of Queensland;
> (d) the *Equal Opportunity Act 1984* of Western Australia;
> (e) the *Equal Opportunity Act 1984* of South Australia;
> (f) the *Anti-Discrimination Act 1998* of Tasmania;
> (g) the *Discrimination Act 1991* of the Australian Capital Territory;
> (h) the *Anti-Discrimination Act* of the Northern Territory.[32]

Finally, Section 772 specifies that employment is not to be terminated under certain grounds, including social origin under Section 772(f):

> 772(1) An employer must not terminate an employee's employment for one or more of the following reasons, or for reasons including one or more of the following reasons:
> (a) temporary absence from work because of illness or injury of a kind prescribed by the regulations;
> (b) trade union membership or participation in trade union activities outside working hours or, with the employer's consent, during working hours;
> (c) non-membership of a trade union;

32 Ibid., at Section 351.

(d) seeking office as, or acting or having acted in the capacity of, a representative of employees;
(e) the filing of a complaint, or the participation in proceedings, against an employer involving alleged violation of laws or regulations or recourse to competent administrative authorities;
(f) race, colour, sex, sexual preference, age, physical or mental disability, marital status, family or carer's responsibilities, pregnancy, religion, political opinion, national extraction or social origin;
(g) absence from work during maternity leave or other parental leave;
(h) temporary absence from work for the purpose of engaging in a voluntary emergency management activity, where the absence is reasonable having regard to all the circumstances.

(2) However, subsection (1) does not prevent a matter referred to in paragraph (1)(f) from being a reason for terminating a person's employment if:
(a) the reason is based on the inherent requirements of the particular position concerned; or
(b) if the person is a member of the staff of an institution that is conducted in accordance with the doctrines, tenets, beliefs or teachings of a particular religion or creed – the employment is terminated:
(i) in good faith; and
(ii) to avoid injury to the religious susceptibilities of adherents of that religion or creed.

(3) To avoid doubt, if:
(a) an employer terminates an employee's employment; and
(b) the reason, or a reason, for the termination is that the position held by the employee no longer exists, or will no longer exist; and
(c) the reason, or a reason, that the position held by the employee no longer exists, or will no longer exist, is the employee's absence, or proposed or probable absence, during maternity leave or other parental leave; the employee's employment is taken, for the purposes of paragraph (1)(g), to have been terminated for the reason, or for reasons including the reason, of absence from work during maternity leave or other parental leave.[33]

Overall, Australia aims to bolster the efforts of all government agencies, the private sector, the community and individuals to achieve equality, through, namely, advancing outcomes in areas where there is discrimination and inequality; improving outcomes for those with special needs, the Indigenous population and those from a non-English speaking background; encouraging increased efforts by State/Territory and Commonwealth agencies to develop inclusive policies, programs and services; encouraging and facilitating the increased involvement of

33 Ibid., at Section 772.

the private sector and community groups in taking responsibility for addressing discrimination and inequality.[34]

In terms of power and decision-making, the critical area of concern is inequality in the sharing of power and decision-making at all levels, with corrective action to take measures to ensure equal access to and full participation in power structures; and increase the capacity of all humans to participate in decision-making and leadership. All peoples have a right and a responsibility to participate in the decision-making processes that shape the nation. Unless human beings are full and active participants in all spheres of public and private life, across a wide range of decision-making positions, the future will not reflect the talents, experience and aspirations of all citizens. Overall, greater diversity should be encouraged among those occupying senior decision-making positions, and opportunities should be expanded to participate in high-level positions, in order to create or strengthen national machineries and other governmental bodies; integrate neutral perspectives in legislation, public policies, programs and projects; and generate and disseminate disaggregated data and information for planning and evaluation. The participation of all humans on equal terms in political, social, economic and cultural life is essential to the progress and the well-being of society in general.

In terms of human rights, the critical area of concern is the lack of respect for and adequate promotion and protection of human rights, with corrective action to fully implement all human rights instruments; ensure equality and non-discrimination under the law and in practice; and achieve legal literacy. Of particular concern is the level of access to and participation in processes relating to Australia's obligations under international instruments on human rights, including reporting and monitoring of obligations. Human rights are an inalienable, integral and indivisible aspect of life, in the legislative protections and the existence of agencies to enable citizens to exercise their rights and responsibilities.[35]

Explicit recognition of a positive duty toward equal rights is balanced by expanding the operation of the unjustifiable hardship defence. Legal adjustments will produce net benefits for the community without imposing undue hardship on the organizations required to make them, and will benefit the whole community. Artificial and real barriers to all people's participation in economic and social life need to be removed, and this will require a different mind set about new infrastructures, which should be friendly for all members of society.

New Zealand

New Zealand is an island nation of 103,000 square miles and a population of 4,180,000. New Zealand has ratified several international covenants, which obligate governments to ensure equality to enjoy all economic, social, cultural, civil and

34 Australia's Beijing Plus Five Action Plan 2001–2005.

35 Ibid.

political rights. Although international agreements do not automatically become part of New Zealand domestic law upon ratification but must be enacted into law by Parliament, jurisprudence has developed in New Zealand that recognizes the value of international agreements as tools for interpreting the legislative provisions which implement them into domestic law.

Treaty of Waitangi

In the late 1830s, there were approximately 125,000 Māori and about 2,000 settlers in New Zealand. More immigrants were arriving all the time though, and Captain William Hobson was sent to act for the British Crown in the negotiation of a treaty between the Crown and Māori. The Colonial Secretary, Lord Normanby, instructed Hobson:

> All dealings with the Aborigines for their Lands must be conducted on the same principles of sincerity, justice, and good faith as must govern your transactions with them for the recognition of Her Majesty's Sovereignty in the Islands. Nor is this all. They must not be permitted to enter into any Contracts in which they might be the ignorant and unintentional authors of injuries to themselves. You will not, for example, purchase from them any Territory the retention of which by them would be essential, or highly conducive, to their own comfort, safety or subsistence. The acquisition of Land by the Crown for the future Settlement of British Subjects must be confined to such Districts as the Natives can alienate without distress or serious inconvenience to themselves. To secure the observance of this rule will be one of the first duties of their official protector.

The Treaty of Waitangi is an important legislative instrument. The Preamble of the English version of the Treaty of Waitangi, which came into effect on 6 February 1840, states:

> HER MAJESTY VICTORIA Queen of the United Kingdom of Great Britain and Ireland regarding with Her Royal favor the Native Chiefs and Tribes of New Zealand and anxious to protect their just Rights and Property and to secure to them the enjoyment of Peace and Good Order has deemed it necessary in consequence of the great number of Her Majesty's Subjects who have already settled in New Zealand and the rapid extension of Emigration both from Europe and Australia which is still in progress to constitute and appoint a functionary properly authorized to treat with the Aborigines of New Zealand for the recognition of Her Majesty's Sovereign authority over the whole or any part of those islands, Her Majesty therefore being desirous to establish a settled form of Civil Government with a view to avert the evil consequences which must result from the absence of the necessary Laws and Institutions alike to the native population and to Her subjects has been graciously pleased to empower and to authorize me William Hobson a Captain in Her Majesty's Royal Navy Consul

> and Lieutenant Governor of such parts of New Zealand as may be or hereafter shall be ceded to her Majesty to invite the confederated and independent Chiefs of New Zealand to concur in the following Articles and Conditions.[36]

In terms of the meaning of the Treaty, the Preamble of the English text states that the British intentions were to protect Māori interests from the encroaching British settlement, provide for British settlement and establish a government to maintain peace and order. The Maori text has a different emphasis, suggesting that the Queen's main promises to Māori were to secure tribal *rangatiratanga* and secure Māori land ownership.

Article 1 states:

> The Chiefs of the Confederation of the United Tribes of New Zealand and the separate and independent Chiefs who have not become members of the Confederation cede to Her Majesty the Queen of England absolutely and without reservation all the rights and powers of Sovereignty which the said Confederation or Individual Chiefs respectively exercise or possess, or may be supposed to exercise or to possess over their respective Territories as the sole Sovereigns thereof.[37]

In terms of the meaning of the Treaty, in the Māori text of Article 1, the Māori gave the British a right of governance, *kawanatanga*, whereas in the English text, the Māori ceded "sovereignty". One of the problems that faced the original translators of the English draft of the Treaty was that "sovereignty" in the British understanding of the word had no direct translation in the context of Māori society. *Rangatira*, the chiefs, held *rangatiratanga*, the autonomy and authority, over their own domains but there was no supreme ruler of the whole country. In the Māori text, the translators used the inadequate term *kawanatanga*, a transliteration of the word "governance", which was then in current use. The Māori understanding of this word came from familiar use in the New Testament of the Bible when referring to the likes of Pontius Pilate, and from their knowledge of the role of the *Kawana*, the Governor of New South Wales, whose jurisdiction then extended to British subjects in New Zealand. As a result, in Article 1, the Māori believe they ceded to the Queen a right of governance in return for the promise of protection, while retaining the authority to manage their own affairs.

Article 2 states:

> Her Majesty the Queen of England confirms and guarantees to the Chiefs and Tribes of New Zealand and to the respective families and individuals thereof the full exclusive and undisturbed possession of their Lands and Estates Forests Fisheries and other properties which they may collectively or individually possess so long

---

36 Treaty of Waitangi, New Zealand, at the Preamble.

37 Ibid., at Article 1.

> as it is their wish and desire to retain the same in their possession; but the Chiefs of the United Tribes and the individual Chiefs yield to Her Majesty the exclusive right of Preemption over such lands as the proprietors thereof may be disposed to alienate at such prices as may be agreed upon between the respective Proprietors and persons appointed by Her Majesty to treat with them in that behalf.[38]

In terms of the meaning of the Treaty, the Māori text of Article 2 uses the word *rangatiratanga* in promising to uphold the authority that tribes had always had over their lands and *taonga*. This choice of wording emphasizes status and authority. In the English text, the Queen guaranteed to the Māori the undisturbed possession of their properties, including their lands, forests, and fisheries, for as long as they wished to retain them, emphasizing property and ownership rights. Article 2 provides for land sales to be effected through the Crown, giving the Crown the right of pre-emption in land sales. The Waitangi Tribunal, after reading the instructions for the Treaty provided by Lord Normanby, concluded that the purpose of this provision was not just to regulate settlement but to ensure that each tribe retained sufficient land for its own purposes and needs.

Article 3 states:

> In consideration thereof Her Majesty the Queen of England extends to the Natives of New Zealand Her royal protection and imparts to them all the Rights and Privileges of British Subjects.
> W HOBSON Lieutenant Governor.
> Now therefore We the Chiefs of the Confederation of the United Tribes of New Zealand being assembled in Congress at Victoria in Waitangi and We the Separate and Independent Chiefs of New Zealand claiming authority over the Tribes and Territories which are specified after our respective names, having been made fully to understand the Provisions of the foregoing Treaty, accept and enter into the same in the full spirit and meaning thereof: in witness of which we have attached our signatures or marks at the places and the dates respectively specified.[39]

In terms of the meaning of the Treaty, in Article 3, the Crown promised to the Māori the benefits of royal protection and full citizenship, emphasizing equality. Further, in the epilogue, the signatories acknowledge that they have entered into the full spirit of the Treaty. It is the principles of the Treaty, rather than the meaning of its strict terms, that is important and the Waitangi Tribunal must have regard for cultural meanings of words, the surrounding circumstances, comments made at the time and the parties' objectives.

38 Ibid., at Article 2.
39 Ibid., at Article 3.

Bill of Rights Act

Important for equal rights and tolerance for class distinctions, according to the Preamble of the Bill of Rights Act 1990, as amended by the Human Rights Act, the Bill of Rights aims to affirm, protect and promote human rights and fundamental freedoms in New Zealand; and to affirm New Zealand's commitment to the International Covenant on Civil and Political Rights.[40] It applies to acts done by the legislative, executive and judicial branches of the Government, or by any person or body in the performance of any public function, power or duty conferred or imposed on that person or body by or pursuant to law.

In addition, freedom from discrimination is guaranteed under Section 19:

> 19(1) Everyone has the right to freedom from discrimination on the grounds of colour, race, ethnic or national origins, sex, marital status, or religious or ethical belief.
> (2) Measures taken in good faith for the purpose of assisting or advancing persons or groups of persons disadvantaged because of colour, race, ethnic or national origins, sex, marital status, or religious or ethical belief do not constitute discrimination.[41]

The right to justice and hence remedies are contained in Section 27:

> 27(1) Every person has the right to the observance of the principles of natural justice by any tribunal or other public authority which has the power to make a determination in respect of that person's right, obligations, or interests protected or recognized by law.
> (2) Every person whose rights, obligations, or interests protected or recognized by law have been affected by a determination of any tribunal or other public authority has the right to apply, in accordance with law, for judicial review of that determination.
> (3) Every person has the right to bring civil proceedings against, and to defend civil proceedings brought by, the Crown, and to have those proceedings heard, according to law, in the same way as civil proceedings between individuals.[42]

Importantly, Section 28 guarantees protection regardless of the Bill of Rights:

> 28. An existing right or freedom shall not be held to be abrogated or restricted by reason only that the right or freedom is not included in this Bill of Rights or is included only in part.[43]

40 Bill of Rights Act, New Zealand, at the Preamble.
41 Ibid., at Section 19.
42 Ibid., at Section 27.
43 Ibid., at Section 28.

Human Rights Act (HRA) and Human Rights Amendment Act

Important for equal rights and tolerance for class distinctions, the Human Rights Act 1993 (HRA), entitled An Act to consolidate and amend the Race Relations Act 19711 and the Human Rights Commission Act 1977 and to provide better protection of human rights in New Zealand in general accordance with the United Nations Covenants or Conventions on Human Rights, protects New Zealanders from unlawful discrimination in a number of areas of life. The Human Rights Commission (HRC) was established by the Human Rights Commission Act 1977 (HRCA), and is empowered under the HRA to protect human rights in accordance with United Nations Covenants and Conventions. The Human Rights Amendment Act 2001 (HRAA) made several significant changes to the HRA, and specifically to the functions and powers of the Commission, and specifically as to the way complaints of unlawful discrimination are received and resolved by the Commission. Some of the key changes to the Commission's functions and powers include: advocating and promoting respect for and appreciation of human rights in New Zealand society, and encouraging the maintenance and development of harmonious relations between individuals and the diverse groups in New Zealand society; advocating and promoting, by education and publicity, respect for, and observance of, human rights; making public statements promoting an understanding of, and compliance with, the New Zealand Bill of Rights Act 1990; developing a national plan of action, in consultation with interested parties, for the promotion and protection of human rights in New Zealand; promoting, by research, education and discussion, a better understanding of the human rights dimensions of the Treaty of Waitangi and their relationship with domestic and international human rights law; bringing civil proceedings for any breach of the Act arising out of any inquiry conducted by the Commission; and applying to a court or tribunal to be appointed as intervener or as counsel, assisting the Court or Tribunal, in facilitating the performance of the Commission's functions relating to advocacy for, or promotion of, human rights.

Further, the functions and powers of the HRC include to encourage, by education and publicity, respect for and observance of human rights; to encourage and coordinate programs and activities in the field of human rights; to make public statements in relation to any matter affecting human rights, including statements promoting an understanding of, and compliance with, the Act; to prepare and publish guidelines for the avoidance of acts or practices that may be inconsistent with the provisions of this Act; to receive representations from members of the public on any matter affecting human rights; to consult and cooperate with other people and bodies concerned with the protection of human rights; to inquire into any matter, including any enactment or law, or any practice, or any procedure, whether governmental or nongovernmental, if it appears to the Commission that human rights are, or may be, infringed thereby; and to report to the Prime Minister from time to time on any matter affecting human rights, including the desirability of legislative, administrative or other action to give better protection to human rights and to ensure better compliance with standards laid down in international instruments on human rights, the desirability of New Zealand becoming bound by any international instrument on human rights, and the implications of any proposed legislation or proposed policy of the Government that the Commission considers may affect human rights.[44] Employment remains the largest area of complaints at about 60 %.

Prohibited grounds are personal characteristics and discrimination because of these characteristics is unlawful. Important for equal rights, Section 21 defines discrimination under prohibited grounds for discrimination:

> Section 21(1) For the purposes of this Act, the prohibited grounds of discrimination are:
>
> (a) sex, which includes pregnancy and childbirth;
> (b) marital status, which means the status of being:
> (i) single; or
> (ii) married; or
> (iii) married but separated; or
> (iv) a party to a marriage now dissolved; or
> (v) widowed; or
> (vi) living in a relationship in the nature of a marriage.
> (c) religious belief;
> (d) ethical belief, which means the lack of a religious belief, whether in respect of a particular religion or religions or all religions;
> (e) colour;
> (f) race;
> (g) ethnic or national origins, which includes nationality or citizenship;
> (h) disability, which means:
> (i) physical disability or impairment;
> (ii) physical illness;
> (iii) psychiatric illness;
> (iv) intellectual or psychological disability or impairment;
> (v) any other loss or abnormality of psychological, physiological, or anatomical structure or function;
> (vi) reliance on a guide dog, wheelchair, or other remedial means;
> (vii) the presence in the body of organisms capable of causing illness;
> (i) age, which means:
> (i) for the purposes of sections 22 to 41 and section 70 of this Act and in relation to any different treatment based on age that occurs in the period beginning with 1 February 1994 and ending with the close of 31 January 1999, any age commencing with the age of 16 years and ending with the date on which persons of the age of the person whose age is in issue qualify for national superannuation under section 3 of the Social

44 Human Rights Act, New Zealand, at Section 5(1).

Welfare (Transitional Provisions) Act 1990 (irrespective of whether or not the particular person qualifies for national superannuation at that age or any other age);

(ii) for the purposes of sections 22 to 41 and section 70 of this Act and in relation to any different treatment based on age that occurs on or after 1 February 1999, any age commencing with the age of 16 years;

(iii) for the purposes of any other provision of Part II of this Act, any age commencing with the age of 16 years;

(j) political opinion, which includes the lack of a particular political opinion or any political opinion;

(k) employment status, which means:

(i) being unemployed; or

(ii) being a recipient of a benefit or compensation under the Social Security Act 1964 or the Accident Rehabilitation and Compensation Insurance Act 1992;

(l) family status, which means:

(i) having the responsibility for parttime care or fulltime care of children or other dependants; or

(ii) having no responsibility for the care of children or other dependants; or

(iii) being married to, or being in a relationship in the nature of a marriage with, a particular person; or

(iv) being a relative of a particular person;

(m) sexual orientation, which means a heterosexual, homosexual, lesbian, or bisexual orientation.

(2) Each of the grounds specified in subsection (1) of this section is a prohibited ground of discrimination, for the purposes of this Act, if:

(a) it pertains to a person or to a relative or associate of a person; and

(b) it either:

(i) currently exists or has in the past existed; or

(ii) is suspected or assumed or believed to exist or to have existed by the person alleged to have discriminated.[45]

Indirect discrimination is defined in Section 65:

65. Where any conduct, practice, requirement, or condition that is not apparently in contravention of any provision of this Part of this Act has the effect of treating a person or group of persons differently on one of the prohibited grounds of discrimination in a situation where such treatment would be unlawful under any provision of this Part of this Act other than this section, that conduct, practice, condition, or requirement shall be unlawful under that provision unless the

45 Ibid., at Section 21.

person whose conduct or practice is in issue, or who imposes the condition or requirement, establishes good reason for it.[46]

Further, as regards discrimination in employment, Section 22(1) states:

22(1) Where an applicant for employment or an employee is qualified for work of any description, it shall be unlawful for an employer, or any person acting or purporting to act on behalf of an employer:

(a) to refuse or omit to employ the applicant on work of that description which is available; or

(b) to offer or afford the applicant or the employee less favourable terms of employment, conditions of work, superannuation or other fringe benefits, and opportunities for training, promotion, and transfer than are made available to applicants or employees of the same or substantially similar capabilities employed in the same or substantially similar circumstances on work of that description; or

(c) to terminate the employment of the employee, or subject the employee to any detriment, in circumstances in which the employment of other employees employed on work of that description would not be terminated, or in which other employees employed on work of that description would not be subjected to such detriment; or

(d) to retire the employee, or to require or cause the employee to retire or resign (applies to all (a), (b), (c) and (d)), by reason of any of the prohibited grounds of discrimination.[47]

Section 35 outlines the general qualification on exceptions:

35. No employer shall be entitled … to accord to any person in respect of any position different treatment based on a prohibited ground of discrimination even though some of the duties of that position would fall within any of those exceptions if, with some adjustment of the activities of the employer (not being an adjustment involving unreasonable disruption of the activities of the employer), some other employee could carry out those particular duties.[48]

Finally, measures to ensure equality are established under Section 73:

73 (1) Anything done or omitted which would otherwise constitute a breach of any of the provisions of this Part of this Act shall not constitute such a breach if:

---

46 Ibid., at Section 65.

47 Ibid., at Section 22(1).

48 Ibid., at Section 35.

> (a) it is done or omitted in good faith for the purpose of assisting or advancing persons or groups of persons, being in each case persons against whom discrimination is unlawful by virtue of this Part of this Act; and
> (b) those persons or groups need or may reasonably be supposed to need assistance or advancement in order to achieve an equal place with other members of the community. [49]

Race Relations Act

Important for minorities and class discrimination, the Race Relations Act 1971 guards against race discrimination in a number of areas, including employment, with Section 5 stating:

> 5(1) It shall be unlawful for any [person who is an] employer, or any person acting or purporting to act on behalf of any [person who is an] employer
> (a) To refuse or omit to employ any person on work of any description which is available and for which that person is qualified; or
> (b) To refuse or omit to offer or afford any person the same terms of employment, conditions of work, fringe benefits, and opportunities for training, promotion, and transfer as are made available for persons of the same or substantially similar qualifications employed in the same or substantially similar circumstances on work of that description; or
> (c) To dismiss any person, or subject any person to any detriment, in circumstances in which other persons employed by that employer on work of that description are not or would not be dismissed or are not or would not be subjected to such detriment by reason of the colour, race, or ethnic or national origins of that person ....
> (3) Nothing in this section shall apply in respect of the employment of any person for any purpose for which persons of a particular ethnic or national origin have or are commonly found to have a particular qualification or aptitude.[50]

In terms of measures to ensure equality, Section 9 provides:

> 9. Anything done or omitted which would otherwise constitute a breach of any of the provisions of sections 4 to 7 of this Act shall not constitute such a breach if
> (a) It is done or omitted in good faith for the purpose of assisting or advancing persons or groups of persons, being in each case persons of a particular colour, race, or ethnic or national origin; and

49 Ibid., at Section 73.
50 Race Relations Act, New Zealand., at Section 5.

> (b) Those groups or persons need or may reasonably be supposed to need assistance or advancement in order to achieve an equal place with other members of the community.[51]

Finally, Section 9A provides for racial harmony:

> 9A(1) It shall be unlawful for any person
>
> (a) To publish or distribute written matter which is threatening, abusive, or insulting, or to broadcast by means of radio or television words which are threatening, abusive, or insulting;
>
> or
>
> (b) To use in any public place … or within the hearing of persons in any such public place, or at any meeting to which the public are invited or have access, words which are threatening, abusive, or insulting,
>
> being matter or words likely to excite hostility or ill-will against, or bring into contempt or ridicule, any group of persons in New Zealand on the ground of the colour, race, or ethnic or national origins of that group of persons.[52]

Employment Contracts Act and Employment Relations Act

Important for employment rights and tolerance for class distinctions in the workplace, the Employment Contracts Act 1991[53] and the Employment Relations Act 2000[54] provide people with the right to take discrimination cases to the Employment Court as a personal grievance. Further, Section 3 of the Employment Relations Act establishes the objectives:

> 3. The object of this Act is
>
> (a) to build productive employment relationships through the promotion of mutual trust and confidence in all aspects of the employment environment and of the employment relationship
>
> (i) by recognising that employment relationships must be built on good faith behaviour; and
>
> (ii) by acknowledging and addressing the inherent inequality of bargaining power in employment relationships; and
>
> (iii) by promoting collective bargaining; and
>
> (iv) by protecting the integrity of individual choice; and
>
> (v) by promoting mediation as the primary problem-solving mechanism; and
>
> (vi) by reducing the need for judicial intervention; and

---

51 Ibid., at Section 9.

52 Ibid., at Section 9A.

53 Employment Contracts Act, New Zealand.

54 Employment Relations Act, New Zealand.

(b) to promote observance in New Zealand of the principles underlying International Labour Organisation Convention 87 on Freedom of Association, and Convention 98 on the Right to Organise and Bargain Collectively.[55]

Finally, the jurisdiction of the Employment Court is established under Section 187 of the Employment Relations Act:

187(1) The Court has exclusive jurisdiction
(a) to hear and determine elections under section 179 for a hearing of a matter previously determined by the Authority, whether under this Act or any other Act conferring jurisdiction on the Authority:
(b) to hear and determine actions for the recovery of penalties under this Act for a breach of any provision of this Act (being a provision that provides for the penalty to be recovered in the Court):
(c) to hear and determine questions of law referred to it by the Authority under section 177:
(d) to hear and determine applications for leave to have matters before the Authority removed into the Court under section 178(3):
(e) to hear and determine matters removed into the Court under section 178:
(f) to hear and determine, under section 6(5), any question whether any person is to be declared to be
(i) an employee within the meaning of this Act; or
(ii) a worker or employee within the meaning of any of the Acts referred to in section 223(1):
(g) to order compliance under section 139:
(h) to hear and determine proceedings founded on tort and resulting from or related to a strike or lockout:
(i) to hear and determine any application for an injunction of a type specified in section 100:
(j) to hear and determine any application for review of the type referred to in section 194:
(k) to issue warrants under section 231:
(l) to exercise its powers in respect of any offence against this Act:
(m) to exercise such other functions and powers as are conferred on it by this or any other Act.
(2) The Court does not have jurisdiction to entertain an application for summary judgment.[56]

In looking at education as a tool for advancement and in the fight against class discrimination, the different socio-economic status of the students and the school

55 Ibid., at Section 3.
56 Ibid., at Section 187.

were found to have an impact on performance.[57] Private secondary school students performed better in school certificate exams than other pupils. In terms of school type, single-sex schools outperformed co-educational schools in school certificate examinations. Students from lower socio-economic backgrounds performed, on average, significantly worse on the combined reading literacy scale. The greater the number of educational resources, such as a dictionary or a quiet place to study, and the greater number of classical possessions, such as classical literature and works of art, that New Zealand students reported in their home, the higher, on average, their score on the combined reading literacy scale. This effect was also seen across the Organization for Economic Co-operation and Development (OECD) countries.

According to the Census of Population and Dwellings, compiled by the OECD, New Zealand students were expected to spend 17.2 years in the formal education system, compared with the OECD country mean of 16.7 years.[58] Interestingly, New Zealand males, at 16.5 years, had the same expected average as the OECD mean. It was the female average, at 17.8 years, that pulled the New Zealand average above that of the OECD, as New Zealand females were more likely to complete tertiary qualifications. There was a rise in the numbers of those achieving tertiary qualifications. The proportion who reported having no qualification was 27.6%, while the proportion that reported having a bachelor or higher degree was 11.8%. As well, the level of educational attainment for males and females was very similar: 28% of males had no qualification, and 12% had a bachelor degree or higher, while the comparable figures for females were 27 % and 11%.

As well, there was an improvement in educational attainment for successive generations of New Zealanders: of all those aged 55 to 64, 9% had a bachelor or higher degree, while 40% had no qualification; of those aged 25 to 34 years, 18% had a bachelor or higher degree and another 18% had no qualification. The most common fields of study for adults' highest post-school qualification were management and commerce, and engineering and related technologies, while the least common field of study was information technology. Among those adults whose highest post-school qualification was a bachelor or higher degree, the most common field of study was society and culture, followed by management and commerce, while the least common field of study was food, hospitality and personal services. The most common post-school qualification field of study for males was engineering and related technologies, while health was the most common amongst females. The least common fields of study for males and females were creative arts and architecture and building respectively.

Finally, a comparison of countries by the OECD, as part of the International Adult Literacy Survey, found that the likelihood of obtaining a tertiary qualification increased for those whose parents also had a tertiary education. There was a positive,

57 OECD (1998), *Human Capital Investment – An International Comparison*, Paris, pp. 15–34.

58 Ibid.

statistically significant, relationship between the years of schooling the parents had, and their 15-year-old children's scores on the combined reading literacy scale. A New Zealander aged between 16 and 65 was 2.1 times as likely to have a tertiary qualification if their parents had completed tertiary education, compared with those whose parents had not completed secondary education. Interestingly, this increased likelihood for those with tertiary educated parents increased from 2 times for 46–55 year-olds, and to 2.8 times for 26–35 year-olds.[59]

Conclusion

Despite strong legislative provisions both in Australia and New Zealand, there is still progress to be made to achieve equal outcomes and opportunities for all. Equality and the rights contained within legislation rely on the overall legal system, as well as cultural attitudes for implementation and enforcement. However, gaps do exist in the coverage of legislation, and in the manner by which it is enforced. Taking concrete action to advance human rights and support opportunity and choice require a concerted effort across the whole of government, in addition to the important ongoing role of specialist human rights monitoring and complaints mechanisms, in the pursuit of "Class Act".

59 Ibid.

Chapter 5
Class Act in Africa and South Africa

Introduction

In the quest for tolerance of class distinctions in *Class Act*, this chapter will examine efforts against class discrimination on the continent of Africa, and in South Africa. It will examine important legislation impacting class, first in Africa, namely the Charter of the Organization of African Unity, the African Charter on Human and Peoples' Rights and the Protocol of the African Charter on Human and Peoples' Rights, and for women, the Protocol on Rights of Women in Africa; and then in South Africa, namely the Interim Constitution Schedule 4 and the Constitution, the Employment Equity Act, and the Promotion of Equality and Prevention of Unfair Discrimination Act.

Africa

Africa is not a single uniform entity. Within Africa, there is much diversity, in terms of class, race, culture, gender relations, disability, age, religion, society, family, geography, economy and natural resources. There is not one formula that can be applied in every case, and as such every community has to make its individual needs heard. In addition, Africa is not static. It is a continent in flux and is rapidly undergoing fundamental changes, namely the growth of urban populations, deterioration of the environment and increasing desertification, growing dependency on world markets, increasing numbers of young people and seniors, and civil strife and conflict. Development policies, plans and programs must be flexible to react and respond to these changes. The knowledge, attitudes and practices of the general African population have some components that are historically accumulated, based on the cultural and institutional heritage of the past. This is especially so among populations where a majority live in traditional ways, a lesser proportion are in transition and a small powerful minority are considered 'modern'. Citizen services during the past several decades seem to have been dominated by the disparate trends and methods of funding from various European countries. Such developments, imported from countries with much stronger economies and longer histories of universal primary and child-centered education, as well as educational research, have seldom been culturally or conceptually appropriate to the countries in which they have taken place. Setting current efforts against a century or more of antiquated foreign development is intended to bring more realistic perspectives.

The current emphases within South Africa on human rights and policy reform go hand in hand with greater empowerment of all people. In terms of international trade, African countries adopted the Dakar/Ngor Declaration in 1992 as the African common position to the International Conference on Population and Development (ICPD). It was recognized that population and development are inextricably linked, and that empowering and meeting people's needs for education and health are necessary for both individual advancement and balanced development. For population and sustainable development in Africa, a key measure must be the promotion of access to equitable distribution of resources. Further, there needs to be a mix of macroeconomic and structural policies and programs for enhancing investment, growth, poverty reduction and social development; infrastructure improvement and institutional support services policies; and policies aimed at strengthening grassroots institutions and local participation. The ICPD+5 Program of Action recommended a set of interdependent quantitative goals and objectives, which included universal access to primary education, with special attention to closing the gap in primary and secondary school education; universal access to primary health care; universal access to a full range of comprehensive reproductive health care services, including family planning; reductions in infant, child and maternal morbidity and mortality; and increased life expectancy impacting seniors.

Overall, in terms of trade and its impact on people in Africa, in 2000, the United States Congress passed the African Growth and Opportunity Act (AGOA), which eliminated American duties on textile imports from eligible sub-Saharan countries.[1] Further, a new round of global trade negotiations, dubbed the Doha Development Round, began in 2002. However, to ensure long-term benefits from better access to American markets, African countries must diversify their economies, investing in infrastructure and in education to attract higher-tech companies. Africa's main goals are to substantially reduce or eliminate all tariffs on agricultural products, including quota duties; substantially reduce or eliminate tariff escalation; simplify complex tariffs by converting all tariffs to an *ad valorem* or fixed percentage of a product's value; substantially reduce or eliminate market-distorting export subsidies and domestic support; and recognize and meet the special needs of the world's least developed countries.

Importantly, the New Partnership for Africa's Development (NEPAD) is a pledge by all of Africa's leaders to eradicate poverty in which many seniors live, and move towards sustainable growth and development. The partnership focuses on African ownership of the development process and seeks to reinvigorate the continent in all areas of human activity. Through cooperation and partnership, African leaders have agreed to promote the role of different groups in social and economic development; promote and protect democracy and human rights by developing standards for accountability, transparency and participatory governance; restore and maintain macroeconomic stability; implement transparent legal and regulatory frameworks; revitalize and extend education, technical training and

1 Economic Commission for Africa, *Economic Report on Africa*, 2002.

health care services; and promote the development of infrastructure, agriculture, agroprocessing and manufacturing to meet the needs of export and domestic markets as well as local employment. NEPAD draws Africa's attention to the seriousness of the continent's economic challenges, the potential for addressing them and the challenge of mobilizing support. The main strategies proposed include pursuing equality in education, business and public service; developing education and human resources at all levels, and in particular increasing the role of information and communication technology in education and training, inducing a 'brain gain' for Africa and eliminating disparities in education; and increasing domestic resource mobilization and accelerating foreign investment, creating a conducive environment for private sector activities, with an emphasis on domestic entrepreneurs.[2]

Charter of the Organization of African Unity

The heads of African States and governments signed the Charter of the Organization of African Unity on 25 May 1963 in Addis Ababa, Ethiopia, and it entered into force on 13 September 1963. The Preamble of the Charter of the Organization of African Unity states:

> Convinced that it is the inalienable right of all people to control their own destiny,
>
> Conscious of the fact that freedom, equality, justice and dignity are essential objectives for the achievement of the legitimate aspirations of the African peoples,
>
> Conscious of our responsibility to harness the natural and human resources of our continent for the total advancement of our peoples in all spheres of human endeavor,
>
> Inspired by a common determination to promote understanding among our peoples and cooperation among our states in response to the aspirations of our peoples for brotherhood and solidarity, in a larger unity transcending ethnic and national differences,
>
> Convinced that, in order to translate this determination into a dynamic force in the cause of human progress, conditions for peace and security must be established and maintained,

2 Ibid.

> Determined to safeguard and consolidate the hard-won independence as well as the sovereignty and territorial integrity of our states, and to fight against neo-colonialism in all its forms,
>
> Dedicated to the general progress of Africa,
>
> Persuaded that the Charter of the United Nations and the Universal Declaration of Human Rights, to the Principles of which we reaffirm our adherence, provide a solid foundation for peaceful and positive cooperation among States,
>
> Desirous that all African States should henceforth unite so that the welfare and well-being of their peoples can be assured,
>
> Resolved to reinforce the links between our states by establishing and strengthening common institutions.[3]

Article I establishes the Organization of African Unity:

> I.1. The High Contracting Parties do by the present Charter establish an Organization to be known as the ORGANIZATION OF AFRICAN UNITY.
> 2. The Organization shall include the Continental African States, Madagascar and other Islands surrounding Africa.[4]

Its purposes are outlined in Article II:

> II.1. The Organization shall have the following purposes:
> (a) To promote the unity and solidarity of the African States;
> (b) To coordinate and intensify their cooperation and efforts to achieve a better life for the peoples of Africa;
> (c) To defend their sovereignty, their territorial integrity and independence;
> (d) To eradicate all forms of colonialism from Africa; and
> (e) To promote international cooperation, having due regard to the Charter of the United Nations and the Universal Declaration of Human Rights.
>
> 2. To these ends, the Member States shall coordinate and harmonize their general policies, especially in the following fields:
> (a) Political and diplomatic cooperation;
> (b) Economic cooperation, including transport and communications;
> (c) Educational and cultural cooperation;
> (d) Health, sanitation and nutritional cooperation;
> (e) Scientific and technical cooperation; and

---

3 Charter of the Organization of African Unity, at the Preamble.
4 Ibid., at Article I.

(f) Cooperation for defense and security.[5]

The various institutions are outlined in Article VII:

> VII. The Organization shall accomplish its purposes through the following principal institutions:
> 1. The Assembly of Heads of State and Government.
> 2. The Council of Ministers.
> 3. The General Secretariat.
> 4. The Commission of Mediation, Conciliation and Arbitration.[6]

The Assembly of Heads of State and Government is contained in Article VIII:

> VIII. The Assembly of Heads of State and Government shall be the supreme organ of the Organization. It shall, subject to the provisions of this Charter, discuss matters of common concern to Africa with a view to coordinating and harmonizing the general policy of the Organization. It may in addition review the structure, functions and acts of all the organs and any specialized agencies which may be created in accordance with the present Charter.[7]

The Council of Ministers is contained in Article XII:

> XII.1. The Council of Ministers shall consist of Foreign Ministers or other Ministers as are designated by the Governments of Member States.
> 2. The Council of Ministers shall meet at least twice a year. When requested by any Member State and approved by two-thirds of all Member States, it shall meet in extraordinary session.[8]

The General Secretariat is contained in Article XVI:

> XVI. There shall be a Secretary-General of the Organization, who shall be appointed by the Assembly of Heads of State and Government. The Secretary-General shall direct the affairs of the Secretariat.[9]

The Commission of Mediation, Conciliation and Arbitration is contained in Article XIX:

5 Ibid., at Article II.
6 Ibid., at Article VII.
7 Ibid., at Article VIII.
8 Ibid., at Article XII.
9 Ibid., at Article XVI.

XIX. Member States pledge to settle all disputes among themselves by peaceful means and, to this end decide to establish a Commission of Mediation, Conciliation and Arbitration, the composition of which and condition of service shall be defined by a separate Protocol to be approved by the Assembly of Heads of State and Government. Said Protocol shall be regarded as forming an integral part of the present Charter.[10]

The Specialized Commission is contained in Article XX:

XX. The Assembly shall establish such Specialized Commissions as it may deem necessary, including the following:
1. Economic and Social Commission.
2. Educational, Scientific, Cultural and Health Commission.
3. Defense Commission.[11]

African Charter on Human and Peoples' Rights

The African Charter on Human and Peoples' Rights was adopted by the Eighteenth Assembly of Heads of State and Government on 27 June 1981 in Nairobi, Kenya, and is one of the most widely accepted regional human rights instruments, having been ratified by more than fifty countries. The Preamble of the African Charter on Human and Peoples' Rights states:

The African States members of the Organization of African Unity, parties to the present Convention entitled African Charter on Human and Peoples' Rights,

Considering the Charter of the Organization of African Unity, which stipulates that 'freedom, equality, justice and dignity are essential objectives for the achievement of the legitimate aspirations of the African peoples';

Reaffirming the pledge they solemnly made in Article 2 of the said Charter to eradicate all forms of colonialism from Africa, to coordinate and intensify their cooperation and efforts to achieve a better life for the peoples of Africa and to promote international cooperation having due regard to the Charter of the United Nations and the Universal Declaration of Human Rights;

Taking into consideration the virtues of their historical tradition and the values of African civilization which should inspire and characterize their reflection on the concept of human and peoples' rights;

---

10 Ibid., at Article XIX.
11 Ibid., at Article XX.

> Recognizing on the one hand, that fundamental human rights stem from the attitudes of human beings, which justifies their international protection, and on the other hand that the reality and respect of peoples' rights should necessarily guarantee human rights;
>
> Considering that the enjoyment of rights and freedoms also implies the performance of duties on the part of everyone;
>
> Convinced that it is henceforth essential to pay particular attention to the right to development and that civil and political rights cannot be dissociated from economic, social and cultural rights in their conception as well as universality and that the satisfaction of economic, social and cultural rights is a guarantee for the enjoyment of civil and political rights;
>
> Conscious of their duty to achieve the total liberation of Africa, the peoples of which are still struggling for their dignity and genuine independence, and undertaking to eliminate colonialism, neo-colonialism, apartheid, zionism and to dismantle aggressive foreign military bases and all forms of discrimination, particularly those based on race, ethnic group, colour, sex, language, religion or political opinions;
>
> Reaffirming their adherence to the principles of human and peoples' rights and freedoms contained in the declarations, conventions and other instruments adopted by the Organization of African Unity, the Movement of Non-Aligned Countries and the United Nations;
>
> Firmly convinced of their duty to promote and protect human and peoples' rights and freedoms and taking into account the importance traditionally attached to these rights and freedoms in Africa.[12]

In terms of rights and duties in general, and human and peoples' rights, specifically, Article 1 states:

> 1. The Member States of the Organization of African Unity, parties to the present Charter shall recognize the rights, duties and freedoms enshrined in the Charter and shall undertake to adopt legislative or other measures to give effect to them.[13]

Article 5 upholds the dignity of the human person:

---

12 African Charter on Human and Peoples' Rights, at the Preamble.

13 Ibid., at Article 1.

> 5. Every individual shall have the right to the respect of the dignity inherent in a human being and to the recognition of his legal status. All forms of exploitation and degradation of man, particularly slavery, slave trade, torture, cruel, inhuman or degrading punishment and treatment shall be prohibited.[14]

The concept of equality is guaranteed in Article 19:

> 19. All peoples shall be equal; they shall enjoy the same respect and shall have the same rights. Nothing shall justify the domination of a people by another.[15]

Further, important for equal rights and class discrimination cases, Article 2 protects against discrimination, specifically mentioning social origin, fortune, birth or any status:

> 2. Every individual shall be entitled to the enjoyment of the rights and freedoms recognized and guaranteed in the present Charter without distinction of any kind such as race, ethnic group, colour, sex, language, religion, political or any other opinion, national and social origin, fortune, birth or any status.[16]

Finally, respect and tolerance without discrimination are espoused in Article 28:

> 28. Every individual shall have the duty to respect and consider his fellow beings without discrimination, and to maintain relations aimed at promoting, safeguarding and reinforcing mutual respect and tolerance.[17]

Article 3 guarantees equal protection of the law, important in class discrimination cases:

> 3. Every individual shall be equal before the law.
> Every individual shall be entitled to equal protection of the law.[18]

Further, important for equal rights and class discrimination in the workplace, employment rights and equal pay for equal work are guaranteed in Article 15:

> 15. Every individual shall have the right to work under equitable and satisfactory conditions, and shall receive equal pay for equal work.[19]

---

14 Ibid., at Article 5.
15 Ibid., at Article 19.
16 Ibid., at Article 2.
17 Ibid., at Article 28.
18 Ibid., at Article 3.
19 Ibid., at Article 15.

Crucially, the right to education, not only for advancement but as a tool against class discrimination, is contained in Article 17:

> 17. Every individual shall have the right to education.
> Every individual may freely take part in the cultural life of his community.
> The promotion and protection of morals and traditional values recognized by the community shall be the duty of the State.[20]

Further, education is used to further the rights and freedoms of the Charter under Article 25:

> 25. States parties to the present Charter shall have the duty to promote and ensure through teaching, education and publication, the respect of the rights and freedoms contained in the present Charter and to see to it that these freedoms and rights as well as corresponding obligations and duties are understood.[21]

Article 20 upholds the right of self-determination of people in their social development:

> 20. All peoples shall have the right to existence. They shall have the unquestionable and inalienable right to self-determination. They shall freely determine their political status and shall pursue their economic and social development according to the policy they have freely chosen.
> Colonized or oppressed peoples shall have the right to free themselves from the bonds of domination by resorting to any means recognized by the international community.
> All peoples shall have the right to the assistance of the State Parties to the present Charter in their liberation struggle against foreign domination, be it political, economic or cultural.[22]

Further, cultural development in the heritage of mankind is recognized in Article 22:

> 22. All peoples shall have the right to their economic, social and cultural development with due regard to their freedom and identity and in the equal enjoyment of the common heritage of mankind.
> States shall have the duty, individually or collectively, to ensure the exercise of the right to development.[23]

---

20 Ibid., at Article 17.
21 Ibid., at Article 25.
22 Ibid., at Article 20.
23 Ibid., at Article 22.

Importantly, duties of individuals towards one another are established in Article 27:

> 27. Every individual shall have duties towards his family and society, the State and other legally recognized communities and the international community.
> The rights and freedoms of each individual shall be exercised with due regard to the rights of others, collective security, morality and common interest.[24]

Further under Article 29, the individual shall contribute to the betterment of society:

> 29. To serve his national community by placing his physical and intellectual abilities at its service;
> To preserve and strengthen positive African cultural values in his relations with other members of the society, in the spirit of tolerance, dialogue and consultation and, in general, to contribute to the promotion of the moral well-being of society.[25]

Article 7 stresses the importance of the courts in safeguarding rights:

> 7.1. Every individual shall have the right to have his cause heard. This comprises: (a) the right to an appeal to competent national organs against acts of violating his fundamental rights as recognized and guaranteed by conventions, laws, regulations and customs in force; (b) the right to be presumed innocent until proved guilty by a competent court or tribunal; (c) the right to defence, including the right to be defended by counsel of his choice; (d) the right to be tried within a reasonable time by an impartial court or tribunal. 2. No one may be condemned for an act or omission which did not constitute a legally punishable offence at the time it was committed. No penalty may be inflicted for an offence for which no provision was made at the time it was committed. Punishment is personal and can be imposed only on the offender.[26]

Further, the paramount role of the Courts is guaranteed in Article 26:

> 26. State Parties to the present Charter shall have the duty to guarantee the independence of the Courts and shall allow the establishment and improvement of appropriate national institutions entrusted with the promotion and protection of the rights and freedoms guaranteed by the present Charter.[27]

---

24 Ibid., at Article 27.
25 Ibid., at Article 29.
26 Ibid., at Article 7.
27 Ibid., at Article 26.

The African Commission on Human and Peoples' Right is established under Article 30:

> 30. An African Commission on Human and Peoples' Rights, hereinafter called 'the Commission', shall be established within the Organization of African Unity to promote human and peoples' rights and ensure their protection in Africa.[28]

The mandate of the Commission is contained in Article 45:

> 45. The functions of the Commission shall be:
> To promote human and peoples' rights and in particular:
> to collect documents, undertake studies and researches on African problems in the field of human and peoples' rights, organize seminars, symposia and conferences, disseminate information, encourage national and local institutions concerned with human and peoples' rights and, should the case arise, give its views or make recommendations to Governments.
> to formulate and lay down principles and rules aimed at solving legal problems relating to human and peoples' rights and fundamental freedoms upon which African Governments may base their legislation.
> cooperate with other African and international institutions concerned with the promotion and protection of human and peoples' rights.
> Ensure the protection of human and peoples' rights under conditions laid down by the present Charter.
> Interpret all the provisions of the present Charter at the request of a State Party, an institution of the OAU or an African Organization recognized by the OAU.
> Perform any other tasks which may be entrusted to it by the Assembly of Heads of State and Government.[29]

The procedure of the Commission is contained in Article 46:

> 46. The Commission may resort to any appropriate method of investigation; it may hear from the Secretary General of the Organization of African Unity or any other person capable of enlightening it.[30]

Communications from States are envisioned in Article 47:

> 47. If a State Party to the present Charter has good reasons to believe that another State Party to this Charter has violated the provisions of the Charter, it may draw, by written communication, the attention of that State to the matter. This Communication shall also be addressed to the Secretary General of the OAU

28 Ibid., at Article 30.
29 Ibid., at Article 45.
30 Ibid., at Article 46.

> and to the Chairman of the Commission. Within three months of the receipt of the Communication, the State to which the Communication is addressed shall give the enquiring State, written explanation or statement elucidating the matter. This should include as much as possible, relevant information relating to the laws and rules of procedure applied and applicable and the redress already given or course of action available.[31]

Article 48 provides for submissions to the Commission:

> 48. If within three months from the date on which the original communication is received by the State to which it is addressed, the issue is not settled to the satisfaction of the two States involved through bilateral negotiation or by any other peaceful procedure, either State shall have the right to submit the matter to the Commission through the Chairman and shall notify the other States involved.[32]

So too under Article 49:

> 49. Notwithstanding the provisions of Article 47, if a State Party to the present Charter considers that another State Party has violated the provisions of the Charter, it may refer the matter directly to the Commission by addressing a communication to the Chairman, to the Secretary General of the Organization of African Unity and the State concerned.[33]

Exhaustion of remedies is recognized under Article 50:

> 50. The Commission can only deal with a matter submitted to it after making sure that all local remedies, if they exist, have been exhausted, unless it is obvious to the Commission that the procedure of achieving these remedies would be unduly prolonged.[34]

A report issued by the Commission is entailed in Article 52:

> 52. After having obtained from the States concerned and from other sources all the information it deems necessary and after having tried all appropriate means to reach an amicable solution based on the respect of human and peoples' rights, the Commission shall prepare, within a reasonable period of time from

---

31 Ibid., at Article 47.
32 Ibid., at Article 48.
33 Ibid., at Article 49.
34 Ibid., at Article 50.

the notification referred to in Article 48, a report to the States concerned and communicated to the Assembly of Heads of State and Government.[35]

In terms of Applicable Principles, Article 60 states:

> 60. The Commission shall draw inspiration from international law on human and peoples' rights, particularly from the provisions of various African instruments on Human and Peoples' Rights, the Charter of the United Nations, the Charter of the Organization of African Unity, the Universal Declaration of Human Rights, other instruments adopted by the United Nations and by African countries in the field of Human and Peoples' Rights, as well as from the provisions of various instruments adopted within the Specialized Agencies of the United Nations of which the Parties to the present Charter are members.[36]

Finally, Article 61 holds:

> 61. The Commission shall also take into consideration, as subsidiary measures to determine the principles of law, other general or special international conventions, laying down rules expressly recognized by Member States of the Organization of African Unity, African practices consistent with international norms on Human and Peoples' Rights, customs generally accepted as law, general principles of law recognized by African States as well as legal precedents and doctrine.[37]

Protocol to the African Charter on Human and Peoples' Rights on the Establishment of an African Court on Human and Peoples' Rights

The Preamble of the Protocol to the African Charter on Human and Peoples' Rights on the Establishment of an African Court on Human and Peoples' Rights 2003 states:

> The Member States of the Organization of African Unity hereinafter referred to as the OAU, States Parties to the African Charter on Human and Peoples' Rights,
>
> Considering that the Charter of the Organization of African Unity recognizes that freedom, equality, justice, peace and dignity are essential objectives for the achievement of the legitimate aspirations of the African Peoples;

35 Ibid., at Article 52.
36 Ibid., at Article 60.
37 Ibid., at Article 61.

> Noting that the African Charter on Human and Peoples' Rights reaffirms adherence to the principles of Human and Peoples' Rights, freedoms and duties contained in the declarations, conventions and other instruments adopted by the Organization of African Unity, and other international organizations;
>
> Recognizing that the two-fold objective of the African Commission on Human and Peoples' Rights is to ensure on the one hand promotion and on the other protection of Human and Peoples' Rights, freedom and duties;
>
> Recognizing further, the efforts of the African Charter on Human and Peoples' Rights in the promotion and protection of Human and Peoples` Rights since its inception in 1987;
>
> Firmly convinced that the attainment of the objectives of the African Charter on Human and Peoples' Rights requires the establishment of an African Court on Human and Peoples' Rights to complement and reinforce the functions of the African Commission on Human and Peoples' Rights.[38]

Important for equal rights and tolerance for class distinctions, an African Court of Human and Peoples' Rights is established under Article 1:

> 1. There shall be established within the Organization of African Unity an African Court of Human and Peoples' Rights hereinafter referred to as 'the Court', the organization, jurisdiction and functioning of which shall be governed by the present Protocol.[39]

The relationship between the Court and the Commission is enunciated under Article 2:

> 2. The Court shall, bearing in mind the provisions of this Protocol, complement the protective mandate of the African Commission on Human and Peoples' Rights hereinafter referred to as 'the Commission', conferred upon it by the African Charter on Human and Peoples' Rights, hereinafter referred to as 'the Charter'.[40]

The Jurisdiction of the Court is established under Article 3:

> 3. The jurisdiction of the Court shall extend to all cases and disputes submitted to it concerning the interpretation and application of the Charter, this Protocol

---

38 Protocol to the African Charter on Human and Peoples' Rights on the Establishment of an African Court on Human and Peoples' Rights, at the Preamble.

39 Ibid., at Article 1.

40 Ibid., at Article 2.

and any other relevant Human Rights instrument ratified by the States concerned. In the event of a dispute as to whether the Court has jurisdiction, the Court shall decide.[41]

The Court may issue advisory opinions as outlined under Article 4:

4. At the request of a Member State of the OAU, the OAU, any of its organs, or any African organization recognized by the OAU, the Court may provide an opinion on any legal matter relating to the Charter or any other relevant human rights instruments, provided that the subject matter of the opinion is not related to a matter being examined by the Commission. The Court shall give reasons for its advisory opinions provided that every judge shall be entitled to deliver a separate or dissenting decision.[42]

Access to the Court is established under Article 5:

5. The following are entitled to submit cases to the Court:
The Commission
The State Party, which had lodged a complaint to the Commission
The State Party against which the complaint has been lodged at the Commission
The State Party whose citizen is a victim of human rights violation
African intergovernmental organizations
When a State Party has an interest in a case, it may submit a request to the Court to be permitted to join.
The Court may entitle relevant non-governmental organizations (NGOs) with observer status before the Commission, and individuals to institute cases directly before it … .[43]

The issue of admissibility of cases is examined in Article 6:

6. The Court, when deciding on the admissibility of a case instituted under Article 5 … of this Protocol, may request the opinion of the Commission which shall give it as soon as possible.
The Court shall rule on the admissibility of cases … .
The Court may consider cases or transfer them to the Commission.[44]

Article 7 establishes the Sources of Law:

---

41 Ibid., at Article 3.
42 Ibid., at Article 4.
43 Ibid., at Article 5.
44 Ibid., at Article 6.

> 7. The Court shall apply the provision of the Charter and any other relevant human rights instruments ratified by the States concerned.[45]

Importantly, the independence of the Court is underlined in Article 17:

> 17. The independence of the judges shall be fully ensured in accordance with international law.
> No judge may hear any case in which the same judge has previously taken part as agent, counsel or advocate for one of the parties or as a member of a national or international court or a commission of enquiry or in any other capacity. Any doubt on this point shall be settled by decision of the Court.[46]

Evidence is stressed under Article 26:

> 26. The Court shall hear submissions by all parties and if deemed necessary, hold an enquiry. The States concerned shall assist by providing relevant facilities for the efficient handling of the case.
> The Court may receive written and oral evidence including expert testimony and shall make its decision on the basis of such evidence.[47]

Findings of the Court are provided for under Article 27:

> 27. If the Court finds that there has been violation of a human or peoples' rights, it shall make appropriate orders to remedy the violation, including the payment of fair compensation or reparation.
> In cases of extreme gravity and urgency, and when necessary to avoid irreparable harm to persons, the Court shall adopt such provisional measures as it deems necessary.[48]

The Judgment of the Court is underlined under Article 28:

> 28. The Court shall render its judgment within ninety (90) days of having completed its deliberations.
> The judgment of the Court decided by majority shall be final and not subject to appeal.
> … the Court may review its decision in the light of new evidence under conditions to be set out in the Rules of Procedure.
> The Court may interpret its own decision.

45 Ibid., at Article 7.
46 Ibid., at Article 17.
47 Ibid., at Article 26.
48 Ibid., at Article 27.

> The judgment of the Court shall be read in open court, due notice having been given to the parties.
> Reasons shall be given for the judgment of the Court.
> If the judgment of the court does not represent, in whole or in part, the unanimous decision of the judges, any judge shall be entitled to deliver a separate or dissenting opinion.[49]

Finally, Article 30 provides for the execution of judgment:

> 30. The States Parties to the present Protocol undertake to comply with the judgment in any case to which they are parties within the time stipulated by the Court and to guarantee its execution.[50]

Protocol on Rights of Women in Africa

Important for women, in the Preamble to the Protocol on Rights of Women in Africa 2003, the State Parties to the Protocol on the Rights of Women in Africa undertake the agreement:

> CONSIDERING that Article 66 of the African Charter on Human and Peoples' Rights provides for special protocols or agreements, if necessary, to supplement the provisions of the African Charter, and that the OAU Assembly of Heads of State and Government meeting in its Thirty-first Ordinary Session in Addis Ababa, Ethiopia, in June 1995, endorsed by resolution AHG/Res.240 (XXXI) the recommendation of the African Commission on Human and Peoples' Rights to elaborate a Protocol on the Rights of Women in Africa;
>
> CONSIDERING that Article 2 of the African Charter on Human and Peoples' Rights enshrines the principle of non-discrimination on the grounds of race, ethnic group, colour, sex, language, religion, political or any other opinion, national and social origin, fortune, birth or other status;
>
> FURTHER CONSIDERING that Article 18 of the African Charter on Human and Peoples' Rights calls on all Member States to eliminate every discrimination against women and to ensure the protection of the rights of women as stipulated in international declarations and conventions;
>
> NOTING that Articles 60 and 61 of the African Charter on Human and Peoples' Rights recognize regional and international human rights instruments and African practices consistent with international norms on human and peoples'

49 Ibid., at Article 28.
50 Ibid., at Article 30.

rights as being important reference points for the application and interpretation of the African Charter;

RECALLING that women's rights have been recognized and guaranteed in all international human rights instruments, notably the Universal Declaration of Human Rights, the International Covenant on Civil and Political Rights, the International Covenant on Economic, Social and Cultural Rights, the Convention on the Elimination of All Forms of Discrimination Against Women and all other international conventions and covenants relating to the rights of women as being inalienable, interdependent and indivisible human rights;

NOTING that women's rights and women's essential role in development have been reaffirmed in the United Nations Plans of Action on the Environment and Development in 1992, on Human Rights in 1993, on Population and Development in 1994 and on Social Development in 1995;

FURTHER NOTING that the Plans of Action adopted in Dakar and in Beijing call on all Member States of the United Nations, which have made a solemn commitment to implement them, to take concrete steps to give greater attention to the human rights of women in order to eliminate all forms of discrimination and of gender-based violence against women;

BEARING IN MIND related Resolutions, Declarations, Recommendations, Decisions and other Conventions aimed at eliminating all forms of discrimination and at promoting equality between men and women;

CONCERNED that despite the ratification of the African Charter on Human and Peoples' Rights and other international human rights instruments by the majority of Member States, and their solemn commitment to eliminate all forms of discrimination and harmful practices against women, women in Africa still continue to be victims of discrimination and harmful practices;

FIRMLY CONVINCED that any practice that hinders or endangers the normal growth and affects the physical, emotional and psychological development of women and girls should be condemned and eliminated, and DETERMINED to ensure that the rights of women are protected in order to enable them to enjoy fully all their human rights.[51]

Under Article 1, "Discrimination against women" is defined as any distinction, exclusion or restriction based on sex, or any differential treatment whose objective or effects compromise or destroy the recognition, enjoyment or the exercise by women, regardless of their marital status, of human rights and fundamental

51 Protocol on the Rights of Women in Africa, at the Preamble.

freedoms in all spheres of life.[52] Important to the right of education and the fight against class discrimination, "Harmful Practices (HPs)" are defined as all behavior, attitudes and practices which negatively affect the fundamental rights of women and girls, such as their right to life, health, dignity, education and physical integrity.[53]

Importantly, Article 2(1) is paramount in the fight for the elimination of discrimination against women who suffer double discrimination:

> 2(1) State Parties shall combat all forms of discrimination against women through appropriate legislative measures. In this regard they shall:
>
> (a) include in their national constitutions and other legislative instruments the principle of equality between men and women and ensure its effective application;
>
> (b) enact and effectively implement appropriate national legislative measures to prohibit all forms of harmful practices which endanger the health and general well-being of women and girls;
>
> (c) integrate a gender perspective in their policy decisions, legislation, development plans, activities and all other spheres of life;
>
> (d) take positive action in those areas where discrimination against women in law and in fact continues to exist;
>
> (e) support the local, national, regional and continental initiatives directed at eradicating all forms of discrimination against women.
>
> (2) States Parties shall commit themselves to modify the social and cultural patterns of conduct of women and men through public education, information, education and communication strategies, with a view to achieving the elimination of harmful cultural and traditional practices and all other practices which are based on the idea of the inferiority or the superiority of either of the sexes, or on stereotyped roles for women and men.[54]

Access to justice and equal protection before the law are guaranteed under Article 8:

> 8. Women and men are equal before the law and shall have the right to equal protection and benefit of the law. States Parties shall take all appropriate measures to ensure:
>
> (a) effective access by women to judicial and legal services, including legal aid;
>
> (b) support to local, national, regional and continental initiatives directed at providing women access to legal services, including legal aid;

---

52 Ibid., at Article 1.

53 Ibid., at Article 1.

54 Ibid., at Article 2.

> (c) the establishment of adequate educational and other appropriate structures with particular attention to women and to sensitise everyone to the rights of women;
> (d) that law enforcement organs at all levels are equipped to effectively interpret and enforce gender equality rights;
> (e) that women are represented equally in the judiciary and law enforcement organs;
> (f) reform of existing discriminatory laws and practices in order to promote and protect the rights of women.[55]

Important in the fight against class discrimination, the right to education and training is guaranteed under Article 12:

> 12(1) States Parties shall take all appropriate measures to:
> (a) eliminate all forms of discrimination against women and guarantee equal opportunity and access in the sphere of education and training;
> (b) eliminate all stereotypes in textbooks, syllabuses and the media, that perpetuate such discrimination;
> (c) protect women, especially the girl-child from all forms of abuse, including sexual harassment in schools and other educational institutions and provide for sanctions against the perpetrators of such practices;
> (d) provide access to counselling and rehabilitation services to women who suffer abuses and sexual harassment;
> (e) integrate gender sensitisation and human rights education at all levels of education curricula including teacher training.
> 2. States Parties shall take specific positive action to:
> (a) promote literacy among women;
> (b) promote education and training for women at all levels and in all disciplines, particularly in the fields of science and technology;
> (c) promote the enrolment and retention of girls in schools and other training institutions and the organisation of programmes for women who leave school prematurely.[56]

Finally, in looking at the important concern of economic and social welfare rights, Article 13 is critical for equal rights in employment:

> 13. State Parties shall guarantee women equal opportunities to work. In this respect, they shall:
> i. promote equality in access to employment;
> ii. promote the right to equal remuneration for jobs of equal value for men and women;

55 Ibid., at Article 8.
56 Ibid., at Article 12.

iii. ensure transparency in employment and dismissal relating to women in order to address issues of sexual harassment in the workplace;
iv. allow women freedom to choose their occupation, and protect them from exploitation by their employers;
v. create conditions to promote and support the occupations and economic activities dominated by women, in particular, within the informal sector;
vi. encourage the establishment of a system of protection and social insurance for women working in the informal sector;
vii. introduce a minimum age of work and prohibit children below that age from working, and prohibit the exploitation of children, especially the girl-child;
viii. take the necessary measures to recognise the economic value of the work of women in the home;
ix. guarantee adequate pre and post-natal maternity leave;
x. ensure equality in taxation for men and women;
xi. recognise the right of salaried women to the same allowances and entitlements as those granted to salaried men for their spouses and children;
xii. recognise motherhood and the upbringing of children as a social function for which the State, the private sector and both parents must take responsibility.[57]

South Africa

In the fight against class discrimination, Apartheid has had a devastating impact on South Africa, including on its education system. Despite high rates of enrollment, educational attainment remains a challenge in South Africa, with many young people progressing slowly through school.[58] Being from a poor household or belonging to a traditionally disadvantaged population group strongly reduces educational advancement and achievement, with the negative effects on education of being poor larger for females than males. Among 14–15 year-olds, 40% of girls in the poorest quintile of households have not advanced beyond primary school, versus only 3% among the richest one-fifth of respondents; among 20–22 year-olds, only 16% in the poorest wealth quintile have achieved primary school or less, while over one-half of the richest quintile had their 'matric', a secondary school completion certificate, plus some post-secondary education. Educational attainment of males also shows very strong wealth patterns as well. Among 14–15 year-olds, just over one-half of boys in the poorest two wealth quintiles

57 Ibid., at Article 13.

58 Population Council, *Horizons* research summary, "Poverty, Educational Attainment, and Livelihoods: How Well Do Young People Fare in KwaZulu Natal, South Africa?", Washington, D.C., 2004.

have not advanced past primary school versus 10% among the richest one-fifth of respondents; among 20–22 year-olds, 18% in the poorest quintile have achieved only primary education or less, while over a third of the richest one-fifth have their 'matric' plus some post-secondary education. While most young people have attained at least primary education by age 20, there are large differences by population group: Africans fare worse than Asians, who in turn have lower educational attainment than whites. Only one-third of Africans in the 20–22 years old age group completed secondary school compared with 80% of Asians and 90% of whites.[59]

Interim Constitution and Schedule 4

Important for tolerance for class distinctions, the Preamble of the Interim Constitution of the Republic of South Africa, 1993 (Act No. 200) states:

> In humble submission to Almighty God,
>
> We, the people of South Africa declare that
>
> WHEREAS there is a need to create a new order in which all South Africans will be entitled to a common South African citizenship in a sovereign and democratic constitutional state in which there is equality between men and women and people of all races so that all citizens shall be able to enjoy and exercise their fundamental rights and freedoms;
>
> AND WHEREAS in order to secure the achievement of this goal, elected representatives of all the people of South Africa should be mandated to adopt a new Constitution in accordance with a solemn pact recorded as Constitutional Principles;
>
> AND WHEREAS it is necessary for such purposes that provision should be made for the promotion of national unity and the restructuring and continued governance of South Africa while an elected Constitutional Assembly draws up a final Constitution;
>
> NOW THEREFORE the following provisions are adopted as the Constitution of the Republic of South Africa.[60]

The Constitutional Principles for the Republic of South Africa are contained in Schedule 4 of the Interim Constitution, and important for equal rights and class discrimination cases, Principle I guarantees equality:

59 Ibid.

60 Interim Constitution of South Africa, at the Preamble.

> I. The Constitution of South Africa shall provide for the establishment of one sovereign state, a common South African citizenship and a democratic system of government committed to achieving equality between men and women and people of all races.[61]

In addition, Principle II also guarantees fundamental rights, freedoms and civil liberties:

> II. Everyone shall enjoy all universally accepted fundamental rights, freedoms and civil liberties, which shall be provided for and protected by entrenched and justiciable provisions in the Constitution … .[62]

Important for equal rights and class discrimination cases, the prohibition against discrimination and the promotion of equality are contained within Principle III, which includes "all other forms of discrimination":

> III. The Constitution shall prohibit racial, gender and all other forms of discrimination and shall promote racial and gender equality and national unity.[63]

Further, the fundamental guarantee of equality of all before the law is contained in Principle V, which includes all disadvantaged by discrimination:

> V. The legal system shall ensure the equality of all before the law and an equitable legal process. Equality before the law includes laws, programmes or activities that have as their object the amelioration of the conditions of the disadvantaged, including those disadvantaged on the grounds of race, colour or gender.[64]

The Supremacy clause is contained in Principle IV, which states that the Constitution shall be the supreme law of the land; it shall be binding on all organs of state at all levels of government.[65] In addition, the separation of powers for objectivity and accountability is contained in Principle VI, which establishes that there shall be a separation of powers between the legislature, executive and judiciary, with appropriate checks and balances to ensure accountability, responsiveness and openness.[66] Finally, the important role of the judiciary is outlined in Principle VII:

---

61 Ibid., at Schedule 4, Principle I.
62 Ibid., at Principle II.
63 Ibid., at Principle III.
64 Ibid., at Principle V.
65 Ibid., at Principle IV.
66 Ibid., at Principle VI.

> VII. The judiciary shall be appropriately qualified, independent and impartial and shall have the power and jurisdiction to safeguard and enforce the Constitution and all fundamental rights.[67]

Under Fundamental Rights contained in Chapter 3, Section 8 deals with equality:

> 8(1) Every person shall have the right to equality before the law and to equal protection of the law.
> (2) No person shall be unfairly discriminated against, directly or indirectly, and, without derogating from the generality of this provision, on one or more of the following grounds in particular: race, gender, sex, ethnic or social origin, colour, sexual orientation, age, disability, religion, conscience, belief, culture or language.
> (3)(a) This section shall not preclude measures designed to achieve the adequate protection and advancement of persons or groups or categories of persons disadvantaged by unfair discrimination, in order to enable their full and equal enjoyment of all rights and freedoms.
> (b) Every person or community dispossessed of rights in land before the commencement of this Constitution under any law which would have been inconsistent with subsection (2) had that subsection been in operation at the time of the dispossession, shall be entitled to claim restitution of such rights subject to and in accordance with sections 121, 122 and 123.
> (4) *Prima facie* proof of discrimination on any of the grounds specified in subsection (2) shall be presumed to be sufficient proof of unfair discrimination as contemplated in that subsection, until the contrary is established.[68]

Constitution of South Africa

The Constitution of the Republic of South Africa was first adopted by the Constitutional Assembly on 8 May 1996 (Act 108 of 1996), and was signed into law on 10 December 1996. As an integration of ideas from ordinary citizens, civil society and political parties represented in and outside of the Constitutional Assembly, the Constitution of South Africa represents the collective wisdom of the South African people and has been arrived at by general agreement. The objective in this process was to ensure that the final Constitution be legitimate, credible and accepted by all South Africans.

The Preamble of the Constitution of the Republic of South Africa reads:

> We, the people of South Africa,
> Recognize the injustices of our past;
> Honour those who suffered for justice and freedom in our land;

67 Ibid., at Principle VII.
68 Ibid., at Section 8.

> Respect those who have worked to build and develop our country; and
> Believe that South Africa belongs to all who live in it, united in our diversity.
> We therefore, through our freely elected representatives, adopt this Constitution as the supreme law of the Republic so as to
> Heal the divisions of the past and establish a society based on democratic values, social justice and fundamental human rights;
> Lay the foundations for a democratic and open society in which government is based on the will of the people and every citizen is equally protected by law;
> Improve the quality of life of all citizens and free the potential of each person; and
> Build a united and democratic South Africa able to take its rightful place as a sovereign state in the family of nations.
> May God protect our people.
> Nkosi Sikelel' iAfrika. Morena boloka setjhaba sa heso.
> God seën Suid-Afrika. God bless South Africa.
> Mudzimu fhatutshedza Afurika. Hosi katekisa Afrika.[69]

The Founding Provisions of the Republic of South Africa are found in Chapter 1, with Section 1 of the Constitution, stressing equality and the advancement of human rights:

> 1. The Republic of South Africa is one, sovereign, democratic state founded on the following values:
> (a) Human dignity, the achievement of equality and the advancement of human rights and freedoms.
> (b) Non-racialism and non-sexism.
> (c) Supremacy of the constitution and the rule of law.
> (d) Universal adult suffrage, a national common voters roll, regular elections and a multi-party system of democratic government, to ensure accountability, responsiveness and openness.[70]

The Supremacy Clause is found in Section 2:

> 2. This Constitution is the supreme law of the Republic; law or conduct inconsistent with it is invalid, and the obligations imposed by it must be fulfilled.[71]

Important for equal rights, the right to equality is espoused in Section 3:

> 3(2) All citizens are

69 Constitution of South Africa, at the Preamble.
70 Ibid., at Section 1.
71 Ibid., at Section 2.

(a) equally entitled to the rights, privileges and benefits of citizenship; and
(b) equally subject to the duties and responsibilities of citizenship.[72]

The Bill of Rights for South Africa is contained in Chapter 2. Section 7 states:

> 7(1) This Bill of Rights is a cornerstone of democracy in South Africa. It enshrines the rights of all people in our country and affirms the democratic values of human dignity, equality and freedom.
> (2) The state must respect, protect, promote and fulfil the rights in the Bill of Rights.
> (3) The rights in the Bill of Rights are subject to the limitations contained … in the Bill.[73]

Further, the limitation of rights is strictly contained in Section 36:

> 36(1) The rights in the Bill of Rights may be limited only in terms of law of general application to the extent that the limitation is reasonable and justifiable in an open and democratic society based on human dignity, equality and freedom, taking into account all relevant factors, including
> (a) the nature of the right;
> (b) the importance of the purpose of the limitation;
> (c) the nature and extent of the limitation;
> (d) the relation between the limitation and its purpose; and
> (e) less restrictive means to achieve the purpose.
> (2) Except as provided in subsection (1) or in any other provision of the Constitution, no law may limit any right entrenched in the Bill of Rights.[74]

Application and jurisdiction of the Bill of Rights are outlined in Section 8:

> 8(1) The Bill of Rights applies to all law, and binds the legislature, the executive, the judiciary and all organs of state.
> (2) A provision of the Bill of Rights binds a natural or a juristic person if, and to the extent that, it is applicable, taking into account the nature of the right and the nature of any duty imposed by the right.
> (3) When applying a provision of the Bill of Rights to a natural or juristic person in terms of subsection (2), a court:
> (a) in order to give effect to a right in the Bill, must apply, or if necessary develop, the common law to the extent that legislation does not give effect to that right; and

72 Ibid., at Section 3.
73 Ibid., at Section 7.
74 Ibid., at Section 36(1).

> (b) may develop rules of the common law to limit the right, provided that the limitation is in accordance with Section 36(1).
> (4) A juristic person is entitled to the rights in the Bill of Rights to the extent required by the nature of the rights and the nature of that juristic person.[75]

In terms of equality for all regardless of class, Section 9 goes on to outline and guarantee the important concept of equal protection, including against horizontal and vertical class discrimination under Section 9(3), which specifies social origin:

> 9(1) Everyone is equal before the law and has the right to equal protection and benefit of the law.
> (2) Equality includes the full and equal enjoyment of all rights and freedoms. To promote the achievement of equality, legislative and other measures designed to protect or advance persons, or categories of persons, disadvantaged by unfair discrimination may be taken.
> (3) The state may not unfairly discriminate directly or indirectly against anyone on one or more grounds, including race, gender, sex, pregnancy, marital status, ethnic or social origin, colour, sexual orientation, age, disability, religion, conscience, belief, culture, language and birth.
> (4) No person may unfairly discriminate directly or indirectly against anyone on one or more grounds in terms of subsection (3). National legislation must be enacted to prevent or prohibit unfair discrimination.
> (5) Discrimination on one or more of the grounds listed in subsection (3) is unfair unless it is established that the discrimination is fair.[76]

On human dignity, Section 10 states that everyone has inherent dignity and the right to have their dignity respected and protected.[77]

Further, Section 16 provides for freedom of expression, which does not extend to hatred:

> 16(1) Everyone has the right to freedom of expression … .
> (2) The right in subsection (1) does not extend to
> (a) propaganda for war;
> (b) incitement of imminent violence; or
> (c) advocacy of hatred that is based on race, ethnicity, gender or religion, and that constitutes incitement to cause harm.[78]

---

75 Ibid., at Section 8.
76 Ibid., at Section 9.
77 Ibid., at Section 10.
78 Ibid., at Section 16.

In the interpretation of the Bill of Rights, Section 39 stresses the importance of human dignity and equality:

> 39(1) When interpreting the Bill of Rights, a court, tribunal or forum:
> (a) must promote the values that underlie an open and democratic society based on human dignity, equality and freedom;
> (b) must consider international law; and
> (c) may consider foreign law.
> (2) When interpreting any legislation, and when developing the common law or customary law, every court, tribunal or forum must promote the spirit, purport and objects of the Bill of Rights.
> (3) The Bill of Rights does not deny the existence of any other rights or freedoms that are recognized or conferred by common law, customary law or legislation, to the extent that they are consistent with the Bill.[79]

In safeguarding the right to employment under the principle of freedom of trade, occupation and profession, important for equal rights, Section 22 states that every citizen has the right to choose their trade, occupation or profession freely, and the practice of a trade, occupation or profession may be regulated by law.[80] In terms of labor relations, Section 23 establishes that everyone has the right to fair labor practices, and every worker has the right to form and join a trade union; to participate in the activities and programs of a trade union; and to strike.[81]

Important in the fight against class discrimination, education is guaranteed as a tool for advancement under Section 29:

> 29(1) Everyone has the right
> (a) to a basic education, including adult basic education; and
> (b) to further education, which the state, through reasonable measures, must make progressively available and accessible.
> (2) Everyone has the right to receive education in the official language or languages of their choice in public educational institutions where that education is reasonably practicable. In order to ensure the effective access to, and implementation of, this right, the state must consider all reasonable educational alternatives, including single medium institutions, taking into account
> (a) equity;
> (b) practicability; and
> (c) the need to redress the results of past racially discriminatory laws and practices.
> (3) Everyone has the right to establish and maintain, at their own expense, independent educational institutions that

79 Ibid., at Section 39.
80 Ibid., at Section 22.
81 Ibid., at Section 23.

(a) do not discriminate on the basis of race;
(b) are registered with the state; and
(c) maintain standards that are not inferior to standards at comparable public educational institutions.

(4) Subsection (3) does not preclude state subsidies for independent educational institutions.[82]

In guaranteeing the right to administrative action, Section 33 states that everyone has the right to administrative action that is lawful, reasonable and procedurally fair.[83] Importantly, the right to access to the courts is outlined in Section 34, which holds that everyone has the right to have any dispute that can be resolved by the application of law decided in a fair public hearing before a court or, where appropriate, another independent and impartial tribunal or forum.[84] In order to guarantee rights enumerated under the Constitution, Section 38 ensures the enforcement of such rights, by holding that anyone listed has the right to approach a competent court, alleging that a right in the Bill of Rights has been infringed or threatened, and the court may grant appropriate relief, including a declaration of rights. The persons who may approach a court are anyone acting in their own interest; anyone acting on behalf of another person who cannot act in their own name; anyone acting as a member of, or in the interest of, a group or class of persons; anyone acting in the public interest; and an association acting in the interest of its members.[85]

The importance of the Constitutional Court is outlined in Section 167:

167(3) The Constitutional Court
(a) is the highest court in all constitutional matters;
(b) may decide only constitutional matters, and issues connected with decisions on constitutional matters; and
(c) makes the final decision whether a matter is a constitutional matter or whether an issue is connected with a decision on a constitutional matter.[86]

Further, the powers of the courts in constitutional matters are outlined in Section 172(1):

172(1) When deciding a constitutional matter within its power, a court
(a) must declare that any law or conduct that is inconsistent with the Constitution is invalid to the extent of its inconsistency; and
(b) may make any order that is just and equitable, including

82 Ibid., at Section 29.
83 Ibid., at Section 33.
84 Ibid., at Section 34.
85 Ibid., at Section 38.
86 Ibid., at Section 167.

> (i) an order limiting the retrospective effect of the declaration of invalidity; and
> (ii) an order suspending the declaration of invalidity for any period and on any conditions, to allow the competent authority to correct the defect.[87]

Under the establishment and governing principles, Section 181 lists several important institutions mandated to strengthen constitutional democracy, namely the Public Protector; the Human Rights Commission; the Commission for the Promotion and Protection of the Rights of Cultural, Religious and Linguistic Communities; the Auditor-General; and the Electoral Commission.[88] The functions of the Human Rights Commission are listed under Section 184, which states that it must promote respect for human rights and a culture of human rights; promote the protection, development and attainment of human rights; and monitor and assess the observance of human rights in the Republic. Finally, the Human Rights Commission has the powers, as regulated by national legislation, necessary to perform its functions, including the power to investigate and to report on the observance of human rights; to take steps to secure appropriate redress where human rights have been violated; and to carry out research; and to educate.[89]

Employment Equity Act

Important for tolerance for class distinctions, the Preamble of the Employment Equity Act 1998, an Act to provide for employment equity and to provide for matters incidental thereto, states:

> Recognizing
>
> that as a result of apartheid and other discriminatory laws and practices, there are disparities in employment, occupation and income within the national labor market; and that those disparities create such pronounced disadvantages for certain categories of people that they cannot be redressed simply by repealing discriminatory laws,
>
> Therefore, in order to
>
> promote the constitutional right of equality and the exercise of true democracy; eliminate unfair discrimination in employment; ensure the implementation of employment equity to redress the effects of discrimination; achieve a diverse workforce broadly representative of our people; promote economic development

87 Ibid., at Section 172.
88 Ibid., at Section 181.
89 Ibid., at Section 184.

and efficiency in the workforce; and give effect to the obligations of the Republic as a member of the International Labour Organisation.[90]

Section 3 deals with interpretation of the Act:

> 3. This Act must be interpreted
> (a) in compliance with the Constitution;
> (b) so as to give effect to its purpose;
> (c) taking into account any relevant code of good practice issued in terms of this Act or any other employment law; and
> (d) in compliance with the international law obligations of the Republic, in particular those contained in the International Labour Organisation Convention (No. 111) concerning Discrimination in Respect of Employment and Occupation.[91]

Important for equal rights and class discrimination cases, the purpose of the Act is defined in Section 2:

> 2. The purpose of this Act is to achieve equity in the workplace by
> (a) promoting equal opportunity and fair treatment in employment through the elimination of unfair discrimination; and
> (b) implementing affirmative action measures to redress the disadvantages in employment experienced by designated groups, in order to ensure their equitable representation in all occupational categories and levels in the workforce.[92]

Crucially, the elimination and the prohibition of unfair discrimination for people regardless of social origin are called for in Sections 5 and 6(1) respectively:

> 5. Every employer must take steps to promote equal opportunity in the workplace by eliminating unfair discrimination in any employment policy or practice.[93]
>
> 6(1) No person may unfairly discriminate, directly or indirectly, against an employee, in any employment policy or practice, on one or more grounds, including race, gender, sex, pregnancy, marital status, family responsibility, ethnic or social origin, colour, sexual orientation, age, disability, religion, HIV status, conscience, belief, political opinion, culture, language and birth.[94]

---

90 Employment Equity Act, South Africa, at the Preamble.
91 Ibid., at Section 3.
92 Ibid., at Section 2.
93 Ibid., at Section 5.
94 Ibid., at Section 6(1).

Article 6(2) allows for affirmative action programs and bona fide occupational qualifications:

> 6(2) It is not unfair discrimination to:
> (a) take affirmative action measures consistent with the purpose of this Act; or
> (b) distinguish, exclude or prefer any person on the basis of an inherent requirement of a job.[95]

Further, Section 15 goes on to outline affirmative action measures which are permitted:

> 15(1) Affirmative action measures are measures designed to ensure that suitably qualified people from designated groups have equal employment opportunities and are equitably represented in all occupational categories and levels in the workforce of a designated employer.
> (2) Affirmative action measures implemented by a designated employer must include:
> (a) measures to identify and eliminate employment barriers, including unfair discrimination, which adversely affect people from designated groups;
> (b) measures designed to further diversity in the workplace based on equal dignity and respect of all people;
> (c) making reasonable accommodation for people from designated groups in order to ensure that they enjoy equal opportunities and are equitably represented in the workforce of a designated employer;
> (d) subject to subsection (3), measures to:
> (i) ensure the equitable representation of suitably qualified people from designated groups in all occupational categories and levels in the workforce; and
> (ii) retain and develop people from designated groups and to implement appropriate training measures, including measures in terms of an Act of Parliament providing for skills development.
> (3) The measures referred to in subsection (2)(d) include preferential treatment and numerical goals, but exclude quotas.[96]

According to the burden of proof outlined in Section 11, whenever unfair discrimination is alleged in terms of this Act, the employer against whom the allegation is made must establish that it is fair.[97]

Further, to combat class discrimination in the workplace, Section 20 outlines the requirement of an employment equity plan:

95 Ibid., at Section 6(2).
96 Ibid., at Section 15.
97 Ibid., at Section 11.

> 20(1) A designated employer must prepare and implement an employment equity plan which will achieve reasonable progress towards employment equity in that employer's workforce.
> (2) An employment equity plan prepared in terms of subsection (1) must state:
> (a) the objectives to be achieved for each year of the plan;
> (b) the affirmative action measures to be implemented as required by subsection 15(2);
> (c) where underrepresentation of people from designated groups has been identified by the analysis, the numerical goals to achieve the equitable representation of suitably qualified people from designated groups within each occupational category and level in the workforce, the timetable within which this is to be achieved, and the strategies intended to achieve those goals;
> (d) the timetable for each year of the plan for the achievement of goals and objectives other than numerical goals;
> (e) the duration of the plan, which may not be shorter than one year or longer than five years;
> (f) the procedures that will be used to monitor and evaluate the implementation of the plan and whether reasonable progress is being made towards implementing employment equity;
> (g) the internal procedures to resolve any dispute about the interpretation or implementation of the plan;
> (h) the persons in the workforce, including senior managers, responsible for monitoring and implementing the plan; and
> (i) any other prescribed matter.[98]

The functions of the Commission for Employment Equity are enumerated in Section 30:

> 30(1) The Commission advises the Minister on:
> (a) codes of good practice issued by the Minister;
> (b) regulations made by the Minister; and
> (c) policy and any other matter concerning this Act.
> (2) In addition to the functions in subsection (1) the Commission may:
> (a) make awards recognizing achievements of employers in furthering the purpose of this Act;
> (b) research and report to the Minister on any matter relating to the application of this Act, including appropriate and well-researched norms and benchmarks for the setting of numerical goals in various sectors; and
> (c) perform any other prescribed function.[99]

98 Ibid., at Section 20.
99 Ibid., at Section 30.

Under Section 35, a labor inspector has the authority to enter, question and inspect as provided,[100] and under Section 36, he must request and obtain a written undertaking from a designated employer to comply within a specified period, if the inspector has reasonable grounds to believe that the employer has failed to consult with employees; conduct an analysis; prepare and implement an employment equity plan; submit and publish its annual report; prepare a successive employment equity plan; assign responsibility to a senior manager; inform its employees; or keep records.[101] Under Section 37, a labor inspector may issue a compliance order to a designated employer if that employer has failed to act,[102] and finally, under Section 40, a designated employer may appeal to the Labor Court against a compliance order of the Director-General within 21 days after receiving that order.[103]

In terms of a Code of Good Practice, the process of developing a plan has three sequential phases: planning, development, and implementation and monitoring, according to the Employment Equity Act. The planning phase of the process should include assignment of responsibility and accountability to senior managers; a communication, awareness and training program; consultation with relevant stakeholders; an analysis of existing employment policies, procedures and practices; an analysis of the existing workforce profile; an analysis of relevant demographic information; and the development of meaningful benchmark comparisons. The development phase should include objectives set; corrective measures formulated; time frames established; the plan drawn up; resources identified and allocated for the implementation of the plan; and the plan communicated. The implementation and monitoring phase should include implementation; monitoring and evaluating progress; reviewing the plan; and reporting on progress.

In order to identify any barriers that may be responsible for the underrepresentation or under-utilization of employees from designated groups, including senior workers, a review of all employment policies, practices and procedures specifically, as well as the working environment in general, should be undertaken of employment policy or practices, such as recruitment, selection, pre-employment testing and induction that could be biased, inappropriate or unaffirming; practices related to succession and experience planning, and related promotions and transfers to establish whether designated groups are excluded or adversely impacted; utilization and job assignments to establish whether designated groups are able meaningfully to participate and contribute; current training and development methodologies and strategies; remuneration structures and practices such as equal remuneration for work of equal value; employee benefits related to retirement, risk and medical aid to establish whether designated groups have equal access; disciplinary practices which may have a disproportionately adverse effect on designated groups that may not be justified; the number and nature of dismissals,

100 Ibid., at Section 35.
101 Ibid., at Section 36.
102 Ibid., at Section 37.
103 Ibid., at Section 40.

voluntary terminations and retrenchments of employees from designated groups that may indicate internal or external equity-related factors contributing to such terminations; and corporate culture which may be characterized by exclusionary social and other practices. All practices should be assessed in terms of cross-group fairness, and the review should take into account more subtle or indirect forms of discrimination and stereotyping, which could result in certain groups of people not being employed in particular jobs, or which could preclude people from being promoted.

Finally, affirmative action measures should be developed in terms of appointing members from designated groups for transparent and unbiased recruitment strategies; increasing the pool of available candidates; training, promoting and retaining people from designated groups; ensuring that members of designated groups are appointed in such positions that they are able meaningfully to participate in corporate decision-making processes; and transforming the corporate culture of the past in a way that affirms diversity in the workplace and harnesses the potential of all employees, regardless of class.

Promotion of Equality and Prevention of Unfair Discrimination Act

Important for tolerance for class distinctions, the Preamble of the Promotion of Equality and Prevention of Unfair Discrimination Act 2000 states:

> The consolidation of democracy in our country requires the eradication of social and economic inequalities, especially those that are systematic in nature, which were generated in our history by colonialism, apartheid and patriarchy, and which brought pain and suffering to the great majority of our people … ;
> The Constitution provides for the enactment of national legislation to prevent or prohibit unfair discrimination and to promote the achievement of equality;
> This implies the advancement, special legal and other measures, of historically disadvantaged individuals, communities and social groups who were dispossessed of their land and resources, deprived of their human dignity and who continue to endure the consequences;
> This Act endeavours to facilitate the transition to a democratic society, united in its diversity, marked by human relations that are caring and compassionate, and guided by the principles of equality, fairness, equity, social progress, justice human dignity and freedom.[104]

'Prohibited grounds' are defined under Section 1, which includes social origin:

104 Promotion of Equality and Prevention of Unfair Discrimination Act, South Africa, at the Preamble.

> (xxii)(a) race, gender, sex, pregnancy, marital status, ethnic or social origin, colour, sexual orientation, age, disability, religion, conscience, belief, culture, language and birth; or
> (b) any other ground where discrimination based on that other ground:
> (i) causes or perpetuates systemic disadvantage:
> (ii) undermines human dignity; or
> (iii) adversely affects the equal enjoyment of a person's rights and freedoms in a serious manner that is comparable to discrimination on a ground in paragraph (a).[105]

The objects of the Act are enumerated in Section 2, including the eradication of discrimination:

> 2. The objects of this Act are:
> (a) to enact legislation required by section 9 of the Constitution;
> (b) to give effect to the letter and spirit of the Constitution, in particular:
> (i) the equal enjoyment of all rights and freedoms by every person;
> (ii) the promotion of equality;
> (iii) the values of non-racialism and non-sexism contained in section 1 of the Constitution;
> (iv) the prevention of unfair discrimination and protection of human dignity as contemplated in sections 9 and 10 of the Constitution;
> (v) the prohibition of advocacy of hatred, based on race, ethnicity, gender or religion, that constitutes incitement to cause harm as contemplated in section 16(2)*(c)* of the Constitution and section 12 of this Act;
> (c) to provide for measures to facilitate the eradication of unfair discrimination, hate speech and harassment, particularly on the grounds of race, gender and disability;
> (d) to provide for procedures for the determination of circumstances under which discrimination is unfair;
> (e) to provide for measures to educate the public and raise public awareness on the importance of promoting equality and overcoming unfair discrimination, hate speech and harassment;
> (f) to provide remedies for victims of unfair discrimination, hate speech and harassment and persons whose right to equality has been infringed;
> (g) to set out measures to advance persons disadvantaged by unfair discrimination;
> (h) to facilitate further compliance with international law obligations including treaty obligations in terms of, amongst others, the Convention on the Elimination of All Forms of Racial Discrimination and the Convention on the Elimination of All Forms of Discrimination against Women.[106]

105 Ibid., at Chapter 1, Section 1.
106 Ibid., at Section 2.

Further, the guiding principles are contained in Section 4:

> 4(1) In the adjudication of any proceedings which are instituted in terms of or under this Act, the following principles should apply:
> (a) The expeditious and informal processing of cases, which facilitate participation by the parties to the proceedings;
> (b) access to justice to all persons in relevant judicial and other dispute resolution forums;
> (c) the use of rules of procedure … and criteria to facilitate participation;
> (d) the use of corrective or restorative measures in conjunction with measures of a deterrent nature;
> (e) the development of special skills and capacity for persons applying this Act in order to ensure effective implementation and administration thereof.
> (2) In the application of this Act the following should be recognised and taken into account:
> (a) The existence of systemic discrimination and inequalities, particularly in respect of race, gender and disability in all spheres of life as a result of past and present unfair discrimination, brought about by colonialism, the apartheid system and patriarchy; and
> (b) the need to take measures at all levels to eliminate such discrimination and inequalities.[107]

In terms of the prevention and general prohibition of unfair discrimination, Section 6 states:

> 6. Neither the State nor any person may unfairly discriminate against any person.[108]

In looking at the burden of proof in class discrimination cases, Section 13 stipulates:

> 13(1) If the complainant makes out a prima facie case of discrimination:
> (a) the respondent must prove, in the facts before the court, that the discrimination did not take place as alleged; or
> (b) the respondent must prove that the conduct is not based on one or more of the prohibited grounds.
> (2) If the discrimination did take place:
> (a) on a ground in paragraph (a) of the definition of 'prohibited grounds' … then it is unfair, unless the respondent proves that the discrimination is fair;
> (b) on a ground in paragraph (b) of the definition of 'prohibited grounds', then it is unfair

107 Ibid., at Section 4.
108 Ibid., at Section 6.

(i) if one or more of the conditions set out in paragraph (b) of the definition of 'prohibited grounds' is established; and
(ii) unless the respondent proves that the discrimination is fair.[109]

Further, Section 14 establishes the determination of fairness or unfairness:

> 14(1) It is not unfair discrimination to take measures designed to protect or advance persons or categories of persons disadvantaged by unfair discrimination or the members of such groups or categories of persons.
> (2) In determining whether the respondent has proved that the discrimination is fair, the following must be taken into account:
> (a) The context;
> (b) the factors referred to in subsection (3);
> (c) whether the discrimination reasonably and justifiably differentiates between persons according to objectively determinable criteria, intrinsic to the activity concerned.
> (3) The factors referred to in subsection (2)(b) include the following:
> (a) Whether the discrimination impairs or is likely to impair human dignity;
> (b) the impact or likely impact of the discrimination on the complainant;
> (c) the position of the complainant in society and whether he or she suffers from patterns of disadvantage or belongs to a group that suffers from patterns of disadvantage;
> (d) the nature and extent of the discrimination;
> (e) whether the discrimination is systematic in nature;
> (f) whether the discrimination has a legitimate purpose;
> (g) whether and to what extent the discrimination achieves its purpose;
> (h) whether there are less restrictive and less disadvantageous means to achieve the purpose;
> (i) whether and to what extent the respondent has taken such steps as being reasonable in the circumstances to:
> (i) address the disadvantage which arises from or is related to one or more of the prohibited grounds; or
> (ii) accommodate diversity.[110]

Importantly, under Section 25, the State has a duty to promote equality and, as such, the State must, where necessary with the assistance of the relevant constitutional institutions, develop awareness of fundamental rights in order to promote a climate of understanding, mutual respect and equality; take measures to develop and implement programs in order to promote equality; and where necessary or appropriate develop action plans to address any unfair discrimination, hate speech

109 Ibid., at Section 13.
110 Ibid., at Section 14.

or harassment. It must also enact further legislation that seeks to promote equality and to establish a legislative framework in line with the objectives of the Act; develop codes of practice as contemplated in the Act in order to promote equality; develop guidelines, including codes in respect of reasonable accommodation; provide assistance, advice and training on issues of equality; develop appropriate internal mechanisms to deal with complaints of unfair discrimination, hate speech or harassment; and conduct information campaigns to popularize the Act.[111]

Finally, Section 28 provides for special measures to promote equality and end discrimination:

> 28(1) If it is proved in the prosecution of any offence that unfair discrimination on the grounds of race, gender or disability played a part in the commission of the offence, this must be regarded as an aggravating circumstance for purposes of sentence.
> (2) The South African Human Rights Commission must, in its report referred to in
> section 15 of the Human Rights Commission Act, 1994 (Act No. 54 of 1994), include an assessment on the extent to which unfair discrimination on the grounds of race, gender and disability persists in the Republic, the effects thereof and recommendations on how best to address the problems.
> (3)(a) The State, institutions performing public functions and all persons have a duty and responsibility, in particular to:
> (i) eliminate discrimination on the grounds of race, gender and disability;
> (ii) promote equality in respect of race, gender and disability.
> (b) In carrying out the duties and responsibilities referred to in paragraph *(a)*, the State, institutions performing public functions and, where appropriate and relevant, juristic and non-juristic entities, must:
> (i) audit laws, policies and practices with a view to eliminating all discriminatory aspects thereof;
> (ii) enact appropriate laws, develop progressive policies and initiate codes of practice in order to eliminate discrimination on the grounds of race, gender and disability;
> (iii) adopt viable action plans for the promotion and achievement of equality in respect of race, gender and disability; and
> (iv) give priority to the elimination of unfair discrimination and the promotion of equality in respect of race, gender and disability.[112]

The Constitution represents a radical rupture with the past based on intolerance and exclusion, and the movement forward to the acceptance of the need to develop a society based on equality, tolerance and respect by all for all. The test of tolerance

111 Ibid., at Section 25.
112 Ibid., at Section 28.

for the Court is not how one finds space for people with whom, and practices with which, one feels comfortable, but how one accommodates the expression of what is discomforting:

> The law may not automatically and of itself eliminate stereotyping and prejudice. Yet it serves as a great teacher, establishes public norms that become assimilated into daily life and protects vulnerable people from unjust marginalisation and abuse. It needs to be remembered that not only the courts are responsible for vindicating the rights enshrined in the Bill of Rights. The legislature is in the frontline in this respect. One of its principal functions is to ensure that the values of the Constitution as set out in the Preamble and section 1 permeate every area of the law.[113]

The way to combat class discrimination is neither to deny its existence or its systemic roots, nor to trivialise its impact, and those who deny it must be challenged because it is such denial that potentially entrenches inherited inequalities. We need to strengthen and in some cases revolutionize the democratic institutions and their capacity to deal with the barriers that perpetuate social exclusion and discrimination on the grounds of class. In order to change entrenched discriminatory perceptions and prejudices, educational programs that popularise a rights-based approach to addressing discrimination should be developed for civil society as a whole. It is necessary to address discrimination and inequality in its many institutional and social forms. This includes changing the skewed distribution of resources through the equitable distribution of State funds, a program of economic empowerment, including senior economic empowerment, affirmative action, land reform and social development. It requires the transformation, in terms of composition, culture and focus, of institutions such as the judiciary, public service, private sector and academia. Essential to this are programs to promote tolerance in all institutions of social development. It is clear that much needs to be done to ensure that all people, including those from different classes and social origins, rightfully enjoy their constitutional rights.

Conclusion

African States should share experiences on best practices in order to complement each other so as to ensure effective class mainstreaming in legislation and court cases; continue to ensure that equal rights issues are integrated in all development programs and plans; develop common indicators for monitoring equal rights issues

113 *Minister of Home Affairs and Another v Fourie and Another (Doctors For Life Internationaland Others, Amicus Curiae); Lesbian and Gay Equality Project and Others v. Minister of Home Affairs and Others*, (CCT 60/04), (CCT 10/05); 2006 (1) SA 524 (CC); 2006 (3) BCLR 355 (CC) (1 December 2005).

at local, regional, national and international levels; and encourage and support the initiation and coordination of periodical conference/seminars on equal rights and development. Indeed, a renewal of commitment to class equality is overdue in Africa, where there is a great disparity in the level of human rights protection available to its inhabitants. Almost all African countries have constitutions or civil codes that prohibit discrimination. However, the level of protection varies from nation to nation, and entrenched attitudes and practices, as well as limited resources, limit the practical effect, in the pursuit of "Class Act".

at local/regional, national and transnational levels and encompassing [illegible] the [illegible]

Chapter 6
Class Act in Canada, Mexico and the United States

Introduction

In the quest for tolerance of class distinctions in *Class Act*, this chapter will examine efforts against class discrimination in North America. It will examine important legislation impacting class, in Canada, namely the Canadian Constitution, the Canadian Bill of Rights, the Canadian Human Rights Act and the Canada Employment Equity Act; then minimally in Mexico, namely the *Constitución Política de los Estados Unidos Mexicanos*, *Ley Federal de Trabajo* and the *Ley del Seguro Social*; and finally in the United States, namely the Declaration of Independence, the Federalist Papers, the American Constitution, the Equal Pay Act and the Civil Rights Act. Although neighbors, Canada and the United States have had separate histories and thus have undergone very different paths, with some rights having more of an impact in one country than the other.

Canada

The British model of government, which has influenced greatly the Canadian structure, sees the legislature making the laws and the judiciary applying them, with parliamentary supremacy not founded on democratic ideals, but rather a narrow power struggle.[1] Canada is a relatively young nation, founded officially by Confederation in 1867. While present Canada endorses multiculturalism, it is a country founded on the tale of "two solitudes", English and French or Anglophone and Francophone, which lies at the heart of many a legal debate. While Canada is an officially bilingual country composed of ten provinces and three territories, it is important to note that the province of Quebec now remains by contrast officially unilingually Francophone.

Canadian Constitution

The Canadian Constitution is made up of the Constitution Act of 1867 (formerly the British North America Act) and its various amendments, and the Constitution

1 Mandel, Michael, *The Charter of Rights and the Legalization of Politics in Canada*, Toronto, 1989, p. 4.

Act of 1982, which includes the Canadian Charter of Rights and Freedoms, encompassing Articles 1 to 34. It was proclaimed into force and entrenched on 17 April 1982.

The Constitution Act of 1867 sets out the division of powers between the Federal Government and the Provincial Governments. The exclusive powers of the Parliament of Canada are found in Section 91:

> 91. It shall be lawful for the Queen, by and with the Advice and Consent of the Senate and House of Commons, to make laws for the Peace, Order, and good Government of Canada, in relation to all Matters not coming within the Classes of Subjects by this Act assigned exclusively to the Legislatures of the Provinces; and for greater Certainty, but not so as to restrict the Generality of the foregoing Terms of this Section, it is hereby declared that (notwithstanding anything in this Act) the exclusive Legislative Authority of the Parliament of Canada extends to all Matters coming within the Classes of Subjects next hereinafter enumerated; that is to say,
>
> 1A. The Public Debt and Property.
> 2. The Regulation of Trade and Commerce.
> 2A. Unemployment insurance.
> 3. The raising of Money by any Mode or System of Taxation.
> 4. The borrowing of Money on the Public Credit.
> 5. Postal Service.
> 6. The Census and Statistics.
> 7. Militia, Military and Naval Service, and Defence.
> 8. The fixing of and providing for the Salaries and Allowances of Civil and other Officers of the Government of Canada.
> 9. Beacons, Buoys, Lighthouses, and Sable Island.
> 10. Navigation and Shipping.
> 11. Quarantine and the Establishment and Maintenance of Marine Hospitals.
> 12. Sea Coast and Inland Fisheries.
> 13. Ferries between a Province and any British or Foreign Country or between Two Provinces.
> 14. Currency and Coinage.
> 15. Banking, Incorporation of Banks, and the Issue of Paper Money.
> 16. Savings Banks.
> 17. Weights and Measures.
> 18. Bills of Exchange and Promissory Notes.
> 19. Interest.
> 20. Legal Tender.
> 21. Bankruptcy and Insolvency.
> 22. Patents of Invention and Discovery.
> 23. Copyrights.
> 24. Indians, and Lands reserved for the Indians.
> 25. Naturalization and Aliens.

26. Marriage and Divorce.
27. The Criminal Law, except the Constitution of Courts of Criminal Jurisdiction, but including the Procedure in Criminal Matters.
28. The Establishment, Maintenance, and Management of Penitentiaries.
29. Such Classes of Subjects as are expressly excepted in the Enumeration of the Classes of Subjects by this Act assigned exclusively to the Legislatures of the Provinces.

And any Matter coming within any of the Classes of Subjects enumerated in this section shall not be deemed to come within the Class of Matters of a local or private Nature comprised in the Enumeration of the Classes of Subjects by this Act assigned exclusively to the Legislatures of the Provinces.[2]

The exclusive powers of provincial legislatures are found in Section 92:

92 In each Province the Legislature may exclusively make Laws in relation to Matters coming within the Classes of Subject next hereinafter enumerated; that is to say,

1. Repealed.
2. Direct Taxation within the Province in order to the raising of a Revenue for Provincial Purposes.
3. The borrowing of Money on the sole Credit of the Province.
4. The Establishment and Tenure of Provincial Offices and the Appointment and Payment of Provincial Officers.
5. The Management and Sale of the Public Lands belonging to the Province and of the Timber and Wood thereon.
6. The Establishment, Maintenance, and Management of Public and Reformatory Prisons in and for the Province.
7. The Establishment, Maintenance, and Management of Hospitals, Asylums, Charities, and Eleemosynary Institutions in and for the Province, other than Marine Hospitals.
8. Municipal Institutions in the Province.
9. Shop, Saloon, Tavern, Auctioneer, and other Licences in order to the raising of a Revenue for Provincial, Local, or Municipal Purposes.
10. Local Works and Undertakings other than such as are of the following Classes:
    (a) Lines of Steam or other Ships, Railways, Canals, and other Works and Undertakings connecting the Province with any other or others of the Provinces, or extending beyond the Limits of the Province;
    (b) Lines of Steam Ships between the Province and any British or Foreign Country;
    (c) Such Works as, although wholly situate within the Province, are before or after the Execution declared by the Parliament of Canada to be for the

2 Constitution Act of 1867, Canada, at Section 91.

general Advantage of Canada or for the Advantage of Two or more of the Provinces.

11. The Incorporation of Companies with Provincial Objects.
12. The Solemnization of Marriage in the Province.
13. Property and Civil Rights in the Province.
14. The Administration of Justice in the Province, including the Constitution, Maintenance, and Organization of Provincial Courts, both of Civil and of Criminal Jurisdiction, and including Procedure in Civil Matters in those Courts.
15. The Imposition of Punishment by Fine, Penalty, or Imprisonment for enforcing any Law of the Province made in relation to any Matter coming within any of the Classes of Subjects enumerated in this Section.
16. Generally all Matters of a merely local or private Nature in the Province.[3]

In terms of education as a tool to combat class discrimination, the division of power on education is found in Section 93:

> 93. In and for each Province the Legislature may exclusively make Laws in relation to Education, subject and according to the following Provisions:
> 1. Nothing in any such Law shall prejudicially affect any Right or Privilege with respect to Denominational Schools which any Class of Persons have by Law in the Province at the Union:
> 2. All the Powers, Privileges and Duties at the Union by Law conferred and imposed in Upper Canada on the Separate Schools and School Trustees of the Queen's Roman Catholic Subjects shall be and the same are hereby extended to the Dissentient Schools of the Queen's Protestant and Roman Catholic Subjects in Quebec:
> 3. Where in any Province a System of Separate or Dissentient Schools exists by Law at the Union or is thereafter established by the Legislature of the Province, an Appeal shall lie to the Governor General in Council from any Act or Decision of any Provincial Authority affecting any Right or Privilege of the Protestant or Roman Catholic Minority of the Queen's Subjects in relation to Education:
> 4. In case any such Provincial Law as from Time to Time seems to the Governor General in Council requisite for the Execution of the Provisions of this Section is not made, or in case any Decision of the Governor General in Council on any Appeal under this Section is not duly executed by the proper Provincial Authority in that Behalf, then and in every such Case, and as far as the Circumstances of each Case require, the Parliament of Canada may make remedial Laws for the due Execution of the Provisions of this Section and of any Decision of the Governor General in Council under this Section.[4]

---

3 Ibid., at Section 92.
4 Ibid., at Section 93.

Further, the purpose of the Constitution Act of 1982 and the Charter of Rights and Freedoms is to protect and safeguard the rights and freedoms enumerated, and to contain governmental action within reasonable limits. The supremacy of the Constitution is contained in Section 52(1):

> 52 (1) The Constitution of Canada is the supreme law of Canada and any law that is inconsistent with the provisions of the Constitution is, to the extent of the inconsistency, of no force or effect.[5]

Section 32 provides for its application to the Parliament and government of Canada, as well as to the legislature and government of each province.[6]

Civil Rights—Important for protection against discrimination, which should include class, Section 15 of the Charter, which came into effect on 17 April 1985 after a three-year implemented delay, guarantees equality of rights, and also deals with affirmative action programs to help reverse the discrimination process:

> 15(1) Every individual is equal before and under the law and has the right to the equal protection and equal benefit of the law without discrimination and, in particular, without discrimination based on race, national or ethnic origin, colour, religion, sex, age or mental or physical disability.
> (2) Subsection (1) does not preclude any law, program or activity that has as its object the amelioration of conditions of disadvantaged individuals or groups including those that are disadvantaged because of race, national or ethnic origin, colour, religion, sex, age or mental or physical disability.[7]

Further, the Charter implements equality through Section 28, which cannot be overridden by legislation or act of Parliament:

> 28. Notwithstanding anything in this Charter, the rights and freedoms referred to in it are guaranteed equally to male and female persons.[8]

Fundamental Freedoms—Important for discrimination cases, fundamental freedoms are protected under Section 2 of the Charter:

> 2. Everyone has the following fundamental freedoms:
> (a) freedom of conscience and religion;
> (b) freedom of thought, belief, opinion and expression, including freedom of the press and other means of communication;

5 Constitution Act of 1982, Canada, at Section 52(1).
6 Ibid., at Section 32.
7 Ibid., at Section 15.
8 Ibid., at Section 28.

(c) freedom of peaceful assembly; and
(d) freedom of association.[9]

Multiculturalism and Aboriginal Rights Multiculturalism is established under Section 27:

> 27. This Charter shall be interpreted in a manner consistent with the preservation and enhancement of the multicultural heritage of Canadians.[10]

Further, the protection of the Aboriginal Peoples of Canada is included in Section 35:

> 35(1) The existing aboriginal and treaty rights of the aboriginal peoples of Canada are hereby recognized and affirmed.
> (2) In this Act, 'aboriginal peoples of Canada' includes the Indian, Inuit and Métis peoples of Canada.[11]

Official Languages The Official Languages of Canada are recognized in Section 16:

> 16.1(1) The English linguistic community and the French linguistic community in New Brunswick have equality of status and equal rights and privileges, including the right to distinct educational institutions and such distinct cultural institutions as are necessary for the preservation and promotion of those communities.
> (2) The role of the legislature and government of New Brunswick to preserve and promote the status, rights and privileges referred to in subsection (1) is affirmed.[12]

Minority Language Educational Rights Section 23 covers education and the language of instruction:

> 23(1) Citizens of Canada
> *(a)* whose first language learned and still understood is that of the English or French linguistic minority population of the province in which they reside, or
> *(b)* who have received their primary school instruction in Canada in English or French and reside in a province where the language in which they received that instruction is the language of the English or French linguistic minority

9 Ibid., at Section 2.
10 Ibid., at Section 27.
11 Ibid., at Section 35.
12 Ibid., at Section 16.

population of the province, have the right to have their children receive primary and secondary school instruction in that language in that province.
(2) Citizens of Canada of whom any child has received or is receiving primary or secondary school instruction in English or French in Canada, have the right to have all their children receive primary and secondary school instruction in the same language.
(3) The right of citizens of Canada under subsections (1) and (2) to have their children receive primary and secondary school instruction in the language of the English or French linguistic minority population of a province
(a) applies wherever in the province the number of children of citizens who have such a right is sufficient to warrant the provision to them out of public funds of minority language instruction; and
(b) includes, where the number of those children so warrants, the right to have them receive that instruction in minority language educational facilities provided out of public funds.[13]

Mobility Rights—Mobility rights, including the right to move and gain livelihood, are contained in Section 6:

6(1) Every citizen of Canada has the right to enter, remain in and leave Canada.
(2) Every citizen of Canada and every person who has the status of a permanent resident of Canada has the right
(a) to move to and take up residence in any province; and
(b) to pursue the gaining of a livelihood in any province.
(3) The rights specified in subsection (2) are subject to
(a) any laws or practices of general application in force in a province other than those that discriminate among persons primarily on the basis of province of present or previous residence; and
(b) any laws providing for reasonable residency requirements as a qualification for the receipt of publicly provided social services.
(4) Subsections (2) and (3) do not preclude any law, program or activity that has as its object the amelioration in a province of conditions of individuals in that province who are socially or economically disadvantaged if the rate of employment in that province is below the rate of employment in Canada.[14]

Enforcement of Guaranteed Rights and Freedoms—The enforcement of rights and freedoms is contained under Section 24:

13 Ibid., at Section 23.
14 Ibid., at Section 6.

> 24(1) Anyone whose rights or freedoms, as guaranteed by this Charter, have been infringed or denied may apply to a court of competent jurisdiction to obtain such remedy as the court considers appropriate and just in the circumstances.
> (2) Where, in proceedings under subsection (1), a court concludes that evidence was obtained in a manner that infringed or denied any rights or freedoms guaranteed by this Charter, the evidence shall be excluded if it is established that, having regard to all the circumstances, the admission of it in the proceedings would bring the administration of justice into disrepute.[15]

Provisions in Denial of Rights—The infamous "notwithstanding" clause is Section 33, allowing the Canadian provinces to opt out of the Constitution for successive and infinite five-year periods:

> 33. Parliament or the legislature of a province may expressly declare in an Act of Parliament or of the legislature ... that the Act or a provision thereof shall operate notwithstanding a provision included in ... Section ... 15 of this Charter.[16]

The Canadian Constitution extends power to judges to review legislative action on the basis of congruence with protected values in the Charter, and treats the judicial branch of government as a partner with the legislative and executive branches, in determining the rights of citizens. However, Section 33, the overriding clause, will ensure that legislatures rather than judges have the final say on important matters of public policy, so that laws offensive to certain provisions of the Charter may be upheld.

Importantly, Section 1 of the Charter is also an overriding clause:

> 1. The Canadian Charter of Rights and Freedoms set out is subject only to such reasonable limits prescribed by law as can be demonstrably justified in a free and democratic society.[17]

Thus, fundamental freedoms, as well as legal and equality rights, can be subjected to this notwithstanding clause. Remarkably, the right against **class** discrimination is not absolute, since the Canadian Charter of Rights and Freedoms may be used to strengthen inequalities, by weighing in on the side of power, and undermine popular movements.

In terms of the burden of proof, Section 1 of the Charter has two functions: first, it guarantees the rights and freedoms set out in the provisions which follow it; and second, it states explicitly the exclusive justificatory criteria, outside of Section 33 of the Charter, against which limitations on those rights and freedoms

15 Ibid., at Section 24.
16 Ibid., at Section 33.
17 Ibid., at Section 1.

may be measured. The onus of proving that a limitation on any Charter right is reasonable and demonstrably justified in a free and democratic society rests upon the party seeking to uphold the limitation. Limits on constitutionally guaranteed rights are clearly exceptions to the general guarantee. The presumption is that Charter rights are guaranteed unless the party invoking Section 1 can bring itself within the exceptional criteria justifying their being limited. The standard of proof under Section 1 is a preponderance of probabilities. Proof beyond a reasonable doubt would be unduly onerous on the party seeking to limit the right, because concepts such as "reasonableness", "justifiability" and "free and democratic society" are not amenable to such a standard. Nevertheless, the preponderance of probability test must be applied rigorously.

The Supreme Court of Canada uses the purposive approach to interpret the Charter, whereby the underlying purpose of the legislative provision and the nature of the interest are identified. A two-step procedure is utilized to see whether the limit of the Charter contained in Section 1 can uphold an infringement of a right. Two questions are asked: (1) has the right been violated?; and (2) can the violation be justified under Section 1? The burden of proof is such that the onus of establishing a prima facie infringement of the Charter is on the person alleging it, while the onus of justifying a reasonable limit on the protected right is on the party invoking Section 1. Two criteria must be satisfied in order to come within Section 1 of the Charter: (1) the objective of the limiting measure must be sufficiently important, and the concerns must be pressing and substantial to justify overriding a constitutionally protected right; and (2) the means must be reasonable and demonstrably justified according to a proportionality test, which balances the interests of society against those of individuals. There are three components to the test: (1) the measure must be carefully designed to achieve the stated objective, and must not be arbitrary, unfair or irrational; (2) the measure should impair the right as little as possible; and (3) proportionality must exist between the effect of the limiting measure and its objectives (*Regina v. Oakes*, [1986] 1 SCR 103).[18]

Canadian Bill of Rights

In addition to the Canadian Constitution, there is the Canadian Bill of Rights, enacted on 10 August 1960.

Fundamental Freedoms—Human rights and fundamental freedoms are guaranteed in Section 1, which mentions equality before the law and the protection of the law and should include class:

> 1. It is hereby recognized and declared that in Canada there have existed and shall continue to exist without discrimination by reason of race, national origin,

18 *Regina v. Oakes*, [1986] 1 SCR 103.

colour, religion or sex, the following human rights and fundamental freedoms, namely,
(a) the right of the individual to life, liberty, security of the person and enjoyment of property and the right not to be deprived thereof except by due process of law;
(b) the right of the individual to equality before the law and the protection of the law;
(c) freedom of religion;
(d) freedom of speech;
(e) freedom of assembly and of association; and
(f) freedom of the press.[19]

Canadian Human Rights Act (CHRA)

The Canadian Human Rights Act (CHRA) was implemented and came into force on 1 March 1978, and prohibits discrimination in all federal and federally regulated organizations. The provinces and territories have similar laws forbidding discrimination in their areas of jurisdiction. Complaints are handled by the Canadian Human Rights Commission and a number of provincial commissions.

The CHRA has been very influential for those seeking relief from human rights abuses and discrimination through a channel other than the traditional court system, namely the Canadian Human Rights Tribunal (CHRT). It implements a complaint process through a commission, which assumes that systemic discrimination does not exist but for a few cases. This differs from a proactive approach, which places an obligation on the employer to determine if systemic wage discrimination exists and to remedy it within a time frame. The Canadian Human Rights Commission (CHRC) administers the CHRA, in trying to ensure the principles of equal opportunity and non-discrimination within the federal jurisdiction that is the federal public service and federally regulated employers. The CHRA features a "duty of accommodation" which requires employers to address the needs of people who are protected under the CHRA, and creates a smaller permanent human rights tribunal, which will improve the ability to hear and make decisions about cases effectively and efficiently.

Importantly, the purpose of the CHRA is outlined in Section 2, which specifically mentions:

> 2. The purpose of this Act is to extend the laws in Canada to give effect, within the purview of matters coming within the legislative authority of Parliament, to the principle that all individuals should have an opportunity equal with other individuals to make for themselves the lives that they are able and wish to have and to have their needs accommodated, consistent with their duties and obligations as members of society, without being hindered in or prevented from

19 Bill of Rights, Canada, at Section 1.

> doing so by discriminatory practices based on race, national or ethnic origin, colour, religion, age, sex, sexual orientation, marital status, family status, disability or conviction for an offence for which a pardon has been granted.[20]

Further, important for class discrimination cases, Section 3(1) states:

> 3(1) For all purposes of this Act, race, national or ethnic origin, colour, religion, age, sex, marital status, family status, disability and conviction for which a pardon has been granted are prohibited grounds of discrimination.[21]

Sections 7 and 10 go on to enumerate what is considered to be discriminatory in the workplace:

> 7. It is a discriminatory practice, directly or indirectly:
>
> (a) to refuse to employ or continue to employ any individual, or
>
> (b) in the course of employment, to differentiate adversely in relation to an employee, on a prohibited ground of discrimination.[22]
>
> 10. It is a discriminatory practice for an employer, employee organization or organization of employers:
>
> (a) to establish or pursue a policy or practice, or
>
> (b) to enter into an agreement affecting recruitment, referral, hiring, promotion, training, apprenticeship, transfer or any other matter relating to employment or prospective employment, that deprives or tends to deprive an individual or class of individuals of any employment opportunities on a prohibited ground of discrimination.[23]

Further, under Section 11, it is discriminatory directly or indirectly to refuse to employ or, in the course of employment, to differentiate adversely against an employee in recruitment, referral, hiring, promotion, training or transfer policies:

> 11(2) In assessing the value of work performed by employees employed in the same establishment, the criterion to be applied is the composite of the skill, effort and responsibility required in the performance of the work and the conditions under which the work is performed.[24]

However, Section 15(1) allows for a bona fide occupational exception:

> 15(1) It is not a discriminatory practice if

---

20 Canadian Human Rights Act, Canada, at Section 2.
21 Ibid., at Section 3(1).
22 Ibid., at Section 7.
23 Ibid., at Section 10.
24 Ibid., at Section 11.

> *(a)* any refusal, exclusion, expulsion, suspension, limitation, specification or preference in relation to any employment is established by an employer to be based on a *bona fide* occupational requirement.[25]

Further, special programs are allowed under Section 16 for those classes of individuals who have suffered discrimination:

> 16. It is not a discriminatory practice for a person to adopt or carry out a special program, plan or arrangement designed to prevent disadvantages that are likely to be suffered by, or to eliminate or reduce disadvantages that are suffered by, any group of individuals when those disadvantages would be or are based on or related to the race, national or ethnic origin, colour, religion, age, sex, marital status, family status or disability of members of that group, by improving opportunities respecting goods, services, facilities, accommodation or employment in relation to that group.[26]

The CHRA looks at comparable worth, applying the same wages where respective work is shown to be equal in value through a combination of skill, effort, responsibility and working conditions, and thereby makes comparisons between dissimilar jobs. It is a discriminatory practice to establish different wages, so that if people do work of equal value in the same establishment then they must be paid equally. Discriminatory practices for wage inequities include segregated employment, exclusion of those categorically from the existing evaluation system, under-valuation of certain positions, fewer promotion opportunities, senior rules disadvantaging some groups, and discriminatory transfers, promotion and layoffs.[27] Discrimination includes practices or attitudes, whether by design or impact, which have the effect of limiting the individual's right to the opportunities generally available, because of attributes such as class rather than actual characteristics. There are, however, some reasonable factors to permit a pay difference, such as periodic pay increases for length of service or working in remote locations. The CHRC only has jurisdiction over the federal public service and federally regulated employers in the quest for equal pay for work of equal value, and one drawback to the federal law is that it is limited to comparisons within the same establishment.

In terms of the onus of proof with respect to a complaint under the Act, the evidentiary burden in discrimination cases involving the refusal of employment appears clear and constant through all Canadian jurisdictions: a complainant must first establish a prima facie case of discrimination, and once that is done the burden shifts to the respondent to provide a reasonable explanation for the otherwise discriminatory behavior. Thereafter, assuming the employer has provided an explanation, the complainant has the eventual burden of showing that

---

25 Ibid., at Section 15(1).

26 Ibid., at Section 16.

27 Labor Canada, *Equal Pay for Work of Equal Value*, Ottawa, 1986, p. 21.

the explanation provided was merely "pretext" and that the true motivation behind the employer's actions was in fact discriminatory (*Basi v. Canadian National Railway* (1984), 9 CHRR 4. D/5029, 5037 (CHRTribunal)).[28]

Thus, in an employment complaint, the Commission usually establishes a prima facie case by proving that: (1) the complainant was qualified for the particular employment; (2) the complainant was not hired; and (3) someone no better qualified but lacking the distinguishing feature which is the gravamen of the human rights complaint subsequently obtained the position. If these elements are proved, there is an evidentiary onus on the respondent to provide an explanation of events equally consistent with the conclusion that discrimination on the basis prohibited by the Code is not the correct explanation of what occurred (*Shakes v._Rex Pak Ltd.* (1982), 3 CHRR D/1001, 1002).[29] Should the respondent provide evidence of a non-discriminatory reason for refusing to employ the complainant, then the complainant and the Commission can still establish that the reason advanced for non-employment is in fact a pretext, and that discrimination on an unlawful ground was one of the operative reasons for the respondent's actions (*Blake v. Ministry of Correctional Services and Mimico Correctional Institute* (1984), 5 CHRR D/2417 (Ontario)).[30] The ultimate onus of proof to establish the complaint on a balance of probabilities lies with the complainant and the Commission. Discrimination can be established by direct evidence or by circumstantial evidence, which is evidence that is consistent with the fact that is sought to be proven and inconsistent with any other rational conclusion, since it is not necessary to find that the respondent intended to discriminate against the complainant, it is sufficient to establish the complaint if it is found, on the balance of probabilities, that the respondent in fact discriminated against the complainant on one of the grounds alleged in their complaint (*Ontario Human Rights Commission v. Simpsons-Sears Ltd.*, [1985] SCR 536, 547).[31]

There are three essential steps in developing a special program: to identify as problems, areas within the organization in which the labor force is unrepresentative; to determine how the problems relate to organization policies, practices and procedures, both formal and informal; and to formulate solutions that aim to remove existing barriers and to provide for equitable representation. The criteria that indicate the need for a special program are: observable absence of members of certain groups in particular job categories or in the organization as a whole; existence of particularly high unemployment rates among certain groups; internal complaints and grievances from employees; external complaints by individuals

28 *Basi v. Canadian National Railway* (1984), 9 CHRR 4. D/5029, 5037 (CHR Tribunal).

29 *Shakes v. Rex Pak Ltd.* (1982), 3 CHRR D/1001, 1002.

30 *Blake v. Ministry of Correctional Services and Mimico Correctional Institute* (1984), 5 CHRR D/2417 (Ontario).

31 *Ontario Human Rights Commission v. Simpsons-Sears Ltd.*, [1985] SCR 536, 547.

or groups; inability of the organization to recruit or retain employees in terms of high turnover; and complaints filed with the CHRC alleging discriminatory practices. The primary objective of a special program is to increase the overall representation of the organization's labor force in some specific way. In setting objectives specific to the organization, the following factors must be considered: objectives should be quantitative, namely targets or goals; objectives should aim to correct underutilization or overconcentration where they occur in an organization; objectives must be specific as to target group and should also specify job category and geographical area; and objectives must be attainable within specific and reasonable timeframes. A special program is intended to be a temporary measure that should not outlive the identified problem of disadvantage, although the achievement of objectives will result in permanent organizational changes; objectives should realistically reflect the ability of the organization to respond to change; objectives must take into consideration the continuing rights of individuals, especially employees, not belonging to designated target groups; and objectives should be framed with care to be sensitive to the feelings and expectations of staff, including members of the target groups.

As used in human rights laws, "discrimination" means making a distinction between certain individuals or groups based on a prohibited ground of discrimination. The Canadian Human Rights Act and provincial human rights codes forbid discrimination in employment, with exceptions in some cases regarding mandatory retirement and bona fide occupational requirements. Roughly 17.9% of all anti-discrimination clauses found in major Canadian collective agreements specifically refer to the federal or provincial human rights code.[32] According to the Canadian Human Rights Commission, "discrimination" means treating people differently, negatively or adversely because of prohibited grounds of discrimination. The province of Quebec, by amending the Quebec Charter of Rights and Freedoms, which is both a charter of rights and a human rights act, prohibits discrimination based on class and social condition in Section 10 entitled Right to Equal Recognition and Exercise of Rights and Freedoms:

> 10. Every person has a right to full and equal recognition and exercise of his human rights and freedoms, without distinction, exclusion or preference based on race, colour, sex, pregnancy, sexual orientation, civil status, age except as provided by law, religion, political convictions, language, ethnic or national origin, social condition, a handicap or the use of any means to palliate a handicap. Discrimination exists where such a distinction, exclusion or preference has the effect of nullifying or impairing such right.[33]

---

32 Human Resources and Social Development Canada, Anti-Discrimination Clauses and Practices, 2006.

33 Quebec Charter of Rights and Freedoms, Quebec, at Section 10.

Canada Employment Equity Act

Important for workers, the purpose of the Canada Employment Equity Act, assented to 15 December 1995, as outlined in Section 2, is to achieve equality in the workplace so that no person shall be denied employment opportunities or benefits for reasons unrelated to ability and, in the fulfilment of that goal, to correct the conditions of disadvantage in employment experienced by members of certain groups, and by giving effect to the principle that employment equity means more than treating persons in the same way but also requires special measures and the accommodation of differences.[34] It covers the federal government, including the public service and crown corporations, as well as federally-regulated private sector employers with 100 or more employees, and addresses four designated groups: persons with disabilities, women, Aboriginal peoples and visible minorities. The Canadian Human Rights Commission (CHRC) is responsible for enforcing the obligations of employers to implement employment equity.

Section 5 establishes a duty on employers:

> 5. Every employer shall implement employment equity by
>
> *(a)* identifying and eliminating employment barriers against persons in designated groups that result from the employer's employment systems, policies and practices that are not authorized by law; and
>
> *(b)* instituting such positive policies and practices and making such reasonable accommodations as will ensure that persons in designated groups achieve a degree of representation in each occupational group in the employer's workforce that reflects their representation in
>
> (i) the Canadian workforce, or
>
> (ii) those segments of the Canadian workforce that are identifiable by qualification, eligibility or geography and from which the employer may reasonably be expected to draw employees.[35]

However, Section 6 exempts employers from certain obligations:

> 6. The obligation to implement employment equity does not require an employer
>
> *(a)* to take a particular measure to implement employment equity where the taking of that measure would cause undue hardship to the employer;
>
> *(b)* to hire or promote unqualified persons;
>
> *(c)* with respect to the public sector, to hire or promote persons without basing the hiring or promotion on selection according to merit in cases where the *Public Service Employment Act* requires that hiring or promotion be based on selection according to merit; or

34 Canada Employment Equity Act, Canada, at Section 2.

35 Ibid., at Section 5.

> *(d)* to create new positions in its workforce.[36]

Section 10 provides for the implementation of an employment equity plan:

> 10(1) The employer shall prepare an employment equity plan that
> *(a)* specifies the positive policies and practices that are to be instituted by the employer in the short term for the hiring, training, promotion and retention of persons in designated groups and for the making of reasonable accommodations for those persons, to correct the underrepresentation of those persons identified by the analysis …;
> *(b)* specifies the measures to be taken by the employer in the short term for the elimination of any employment barriers identified by the review …;
> *(c)* establishes a timetable for the implementation of the matters referred to in paragraphs (*a*) and (*b*);
> *(d)* where underrepresentation has been identified by the analysis, establishes short term numerical goals for the hiring and promotion of persons in designated groups in order to increase their representation in each occupational group in the workforce in which underrepresentation has been identified and sets out measures to be taken in each year to meet those goals;
> *(e)* sets out the employer's longer term goals for increasing the representation of persons in designated groups in the employer's workforce and the employer's strategy for achieving those goals; and
> *(f)* provides for any other matter that may be prescribed.[37]

Finally, under Section 29, a Tribunal may, in the same manner and to the same extent as a superior court of record, summon and enforce the attendance of witnesses and compel them to give oral and written evidence on oath and to produce such documents and things as the Tribunal considers necessary for a full review; administer oaths; and receive and accept such evidence and other information, whether on oath or by affidavit or otherwise, as the Tribunal sees fit, whether or not that evidence or information would be admissible in a court of law.[38]

Citizenship offers a sense of belonging in one's country and gives each individual the right to participate in society and in its economic and political systems. It confers the protection of the State within Canada and abroad, while requiring individuals to obey this country's laws. In terms of a more complete set of rights, popular conceptions of citizenship incorporate an increasingly complete set of rights. From "civil rights" such as freedom of speech, thought and faith, citizenship came to include "political rights" as expressed by the right to hold office or to vote. Most recently, twentieth century citizenship is understood to comprise not only these but also "social and economic rights". These are the level

36 Ibid., at Section 6.
37 Ibid., at Section 10.
38 Ibid., at Article 29.

of well-being and security that are required to exist in a society. They represent a commitment that there will be no internal "borders" and that all those who call a particular country home can participate fully in the life of the community. Section 15 of the Charter has become a touchstone for people's rights. However, as we have seen, the Charter has its limits.[39] In terms of the legislative review process, the Government needs to establish an ongoing strategy and process to review laws, regulations, policies, practices and rules to remove barriers to full participation and ensure the equality of all people. Canada's labor market is evolving. New types of jobs are appearing in the workplace as others disappear. Governments are trying to respond to these changes and are working to ensure that all Canadians can participate in the new economy.

The legal workplace duty to accommodate requires the elimination of employment standards, rules, practices or other requirements that discriminate on prohibited grounds.[40] Two Supreme Court of Canada cases, *Meiorin: British Columbia (Public Service Employee Relations Commission) (BCPSERC) v. The British Columbia Government and Service Employees Union (BCGSEU)* [1999], 35 C.H.R.R. D/257 (S.C.C.)[41] (gender discrimination at the workplace) and *Grismer: Terry Grismer (Estate)* v. *The British Columbia Superintendent of Motor Vehicles et al.*, [1999] 3 S.C.R. 868[42] (service discrimination to a person with a disability), established that accommodation is to be the norm, in line with affirmative action and employment equity work. The Supreme Court decision in *Meiorin: British Columbia (Public Service Employee Relations Commission) (BCPSERC) v. The British Columbia Government and Service Employees Union (BCGSEU)* [1999], 35 C.H.R.R. D/257 (S.C.C.) requires employers to design workplace standards that do not discriminate, and developed the three-step *Merion* Test to determine if the employer has established a standard that is a bona fide occupational requirement; the employer must: 1. Demonstrate the standard was adopted for a purpose rationally connected to the performance of the job; 2. Honestly believe the standard is necessary to fulfill the legitimate, work-related purpose; and 3. Show the standard is reasonably necessary to the accomplishment of the legitimate, work-related purpose, so that it is impossible to accommodate workers without undue hardship to the employer.[43] To deal with step 3, the following questions are

39 Federal Task Force on Disability Issues, *Equal Citizenship for Canadians with Disabilities: The Will to Act*, 1996.

40 Hatfield, Robert, "Duty to Accommodate", *Just Labour*, vol. 5 (Winter 2005), p. 23.

41 *Meiorin: British Columbia (Public Service Employee Relations Commission) (BCPSERC) v. The British Columbia Government and Service Employees Union (BCGSEU)* [1999], 35 C.H.R.R. D/257 (S.C.C.).

42 *Grismer: Terry Grismer (Estate) v. The British Columbia Superintendent of Motor Vehicles et al.*, [1999] 3 S.C.R. 868.

43 *Meiorin: British Columbia (Public Service Employee Relations Commission) (BCPSERC) v. The British Columbia Government and Service Employees Union (BCGSEU)* [1999], 35 C.H.R.R. D/257 (S.C.C.).

asked: Have alternatives been considered?; If so, why were these alternatives not adopted?; Must all workers meet a single standard, or could different standards be adopted?; Does the standard treat some more harshly than others?; If so, was the standard designed to minimize this differential treatment?; What steps were taken to find accommodations?; Is there evidence of undue hardship if accommodation were to be provided?; Have all parties who are required to accommodate played their roles? The Court did say accommodation would be the norm "in so far as is reasonably possible", and accommodation is not required if it causes undue hardship.[44] To be considered undue hardship, financial costs must be so great as to alter the essential nature of the enterprise or affect its viability, and may include: financial cost, health and safety, impact on the collective agreement, interference with other workers' rights, employee morale, the size of the operation and the adaptability of the workforce and facilities.[45]

In terms of inclusion, the principle of inclusiveness implied in Canadian citizenship gives the Government a base for its approach to today's requirements. The federal government should promote the equality commitments contained in the international and national instruments that underpin full citizenship. It should also support programs and policies that help all Canadians participate effectively in the economic and social mainstream.

It is essential for the principles and values in the Charter be applied in a more effective way to new laws, regulations, policies, programs and procedures as they are developed; and existing laws, regulations, policies, programs and procedures that put Canadians from minority groups at a disadvantage, before these are challenged in the courts. While the federal government aims for and expects that its laws will not discriminate in their intent or effect, the reality is that, while many laws do not actively discriminate against Canadians from minority groups, their effects are discriminatory. In terms of an inclusive labor market, a vision of inclusion is one in which programs and services are designed in consultation with people from various groups, in which employers hire individuals on the basis of their skills and abilities, and accommodating different ways to get work done happens as a matter of course in the workplace. Inclusiveness should be a matter of "business as usual". The Government should put in place operational, administrative and evaluative mechanisms to ensure that the labor market needs of people from all walks of life regardless of **class** are served by programs and services for which it retains or shares responsibility. It should provide appropriate supports to local managers to help them include people from minority groups among their clients and ensure that local managers are aware that they will be measured or evaluated on their ability to serve all people. A secure income is

44 Ibid.

45 *Central Alberta Dairy Pool v. Alberta (Human Rights Commission)* [1990] 2 S.C.R. 489.

fundamental to the ability to enjoy the rights of citizenship, since without a secure income, an individual cannot satisfy the most basic living needs.[46]

Canada entered the twenty-first century with a population better educated than ever.[47] The hallmark of the 1990s was the tremendous growth in the number of Canadians with a college or university education, a trend that began at the end of the Second World War. Three developments set the stage for advances in education: 1 – a labour market preference for skilled workers to compete in a global and technologically advanced economy; 2 – immigration rules designed to attract highly skilled immigrants; and 3 – the recession of the early1990s that was especially difficult for Canadian youth.

According to the 2001 census, 28% of all individuals aged 25–34 had university qualifications, 21% held a college diploma, and another 12% had trade credentials. In all, 61% of individuals in this age group had qualifications beyond high school. Further, education levels rose for both men and women. In the case of men aged 25 and over, 21% were university graduates. The growth among women aged 25 and over was even greater with 18% having college credentials. In 2001, 1.1 million people in the working-age population aged 25–64 had doctorates, master's degrees and other qualifications above the bachelor level, such as degrees in law, medicine, dentistry and veterinary science. The largest increases occurred at the master's level, up 60% to more than 580,000 in 2001. About 109,000 Canadians had earned doctorates in 2001, up 48%, representing 7% of the working age population, up from 5% a decade earlier. The census also revealed that 61% of immigrants of working age who arrived in the 1990s held trade, college or university credentials.

The census has tracked trends in the education of Canadians aged 15 and over for many decades. In 1951, just 2% had education beyond high school. In 2001, for the first time, more than half did. In 1951, only 2% of all Canadians aged 15 and over had university qualifications. Over the next five decades, the proportion of university graduates climbed steadily. In 1971, it was 5%; in 1991, it had more than doubled to 11%; and by 2001, it was 15%. Meanwhile, during the 1960s and 1970s, a strong college system developed throughout Canada, including the CEGEP system in Quebec. By 2001, the proportion of the population with non-university post-secondary credentials had more than doubled to 36%. This, added to the 15% with university qualifications, meant that more than one-half, 51%, of all Canadians aged 15 and over had post-secondary qualifications in 2001. The total number of Canadians aged 25 and over with a university education reached about 4 million in 2001. Another 3.2 million held a college certificate, while 2.4 million were qualified in a trade.

Women have made great inroads. In 1991, almost three million women aged 25–64, or 41% of the total, had a trade, college or university education. By 2001, this had jumped to almost 4.4 million, or 53%, and 23% had graduated from a

46 Ibid.

47 Census Canada.

university. As a result of this growth, women in 2001 accounted for 51% of all working-age university graduates and 59% of all college graduates. In 2001, exactly one-half of all university graduates aged 25 and over were women.

The number of adults not completing high school has dropped dramatically over the years, with under 5.8 million or 15% of adults aged 25 and over in 2001 who had less than a high school diploma. There is now a highly educated working-age population (aged 25–64), and the trend to higher education in the past decade has had a profound impact on the educational profile of this age group. The 2001 Census marked the first time that a majority of the working-age population had post-secondary credentials.

There was a dramatic increase in education levels in all provinces and territories, with education levels among the working-age population improving dramatically in every province and territory during the past 10 years, according to the census (see Table 6.1). In terms of university, college and trade school, in Nova Scotia, Ontario and the Northwest Territories, 55% of the population had qualifications in one of the three levels beyond high school compared to 53% in the nation overall. In British Columbia and Alberta, it was 56% and in the Yukon, it was 62%.[48]

Canada is now a world leader in education. In terms of university and college graduates combined, no other OECD (Organization for Economic Cooperation and Development) country had a higher proportion than Canada. In 2000, 41% of Canada's population aged 25–64 had either a college or university education, compared with 37% in the United States, 36% in Ireland and 34% in Japan.[49] With high attendance rates of Canadians, there is promise for an even more highly-skilled population in the future.

Mexico

Constitución Política de los Estados Unidos Mexicanos

The equality of all persons before the law is guaranteed by the *Constitución Política de los Estados Unidos Mexicanos*, the Political Constitution of the United Mexican States. The supremacy of the Constitution with its rights is covered under Article 1:

> 1. Every person in the United Mexican States shall enjoy the guarantees granted by this Constitution, which cannot be restricted or suspended except in such cases and under such conditions as are herein provided.[50]

---

48 Ibid.
49 Ibid.
50 Constitución Política de los Estados Unidos Mexicanos, Mexico, at Article 1.

Table 6.1 Level of Educational Attainment, Canada (2001)

	Level of Educational Attainment					
Name	**No high school certificate**	**High school**	**Trades certificate**	**College**	**University**	**Total**
Canada	**3,698,235**	**3,898,405**	**2,097,140**	**2,917,895**	**3,676,630**	**16,288,310**
Newfoundland and Labrador	100,470	45,430	61,535	39,450	39,970	286,855
Prince Edward Island	20,460	14,325	11,045	12,945	11,920	70,700
Nova Scotia	131,090	90,010	86,220	88,295	100,045	495,650
New Brunswick	116,545	96,630	55,050	66,670	64,805	399,695
Quebec	979,960	1,018,715	505,650	637,890	866,455	4,008,675
Ontario	1,274,225	1,509,585	677,755	1,194,425	1,528,665	6,184,650
Manitoba	162,600	128,575	74,855	93,215	112,395	571,640
Saskatchewan	134,580	103,880	76,050	74,400	87,010	475,915
Alberta	349,940	363,210	245,885	299,825	343,500	1,602,355
British Columbia	416,245	518,150	295,180	401,755	512,715	2,144,050
Yukon Territory	2,795	3,615	3,045	3,510	3,960	16,925
Northwest Territories	4,970	3,990	3,380	3,600	3,845	19,785
Nunavut	4,355	2,300	1,500	1,915	1,355	11,410

Source: Statistics Canada, 2001

Importantly, education is guaranteed under Article 3:

> 3. The education imparted by the Federal State shall be designed to develop harmoniously all the faculties of the human being and shall foster in him at the same time a love of country and a consciousness of international solidarity, in independence and justice.
>
> (1) Freedom of religious beliefs being guaranteed by Article 24, the standard which shall guide such education shall be maintained entirely apart from any religious doctrine and, based on the results of scientific progress, shall strive against ignorance and its effects, servitudes, fanaticism, and prejudices. Moreover:
>
> > (a) It shall be democratic, considering democracy not only as a legal structure and a political regimen, but as a system of life founded on a constant economic, social, and cultural betterment of the people;
> >
> > (b) It shall be national insofar as, without hostility or exclusiveness,– it shall achieve the understanding of our problems, the utilization of our resources, the defense of our political independence, the assurance of our economic independence, and the continuity and growth of our culture; and
> >
> > (c) It shall contribute to better human relationships, not only with the elements which it contributes toward strengthening and at the same time inculcating, together with respect for the dignity of the person and the integrity of the family, the conviction of the general interest of society, but also by the care which it devotes to the ideals of brotherhood and equality of rights of all men, avoiding privileges of race, creed, class, sex, or persons.
>
> (2) Private persons may engage in education of all kinds and grades. But as regards elementary, secondary, and normal education (and that of any kind or grade designed for laborers and farm workers) they must previously obtain, in every case, the express authorization of the public power. Such authorization may be refused or revoked by decisions against which there can be no judicial proceedings or recourse.
>
> (3) Private institutions devoted to education of the kinds and grades specified in the preceding section must be without exception in conformity with the provisions of sections I and II of the first paragraph of this article and must also be in harmony with official plans and programs.
>
> (4) Religious corporations, ministers of religion, stock companies which exclusively or predominantly engage in educational activities, and associations or companies devoted to propagation of any religious creed shall not in any way participate in institutions giving elementary, secondary and normal education and education for laborers or field workers.
>
> (5) The State may in its discretion withdraw at any time the recognition of official validity of studies conducted in private institutions.
>
> (6) Elementary education shall be compulsory.
>
> (7) All education given by the State shall be free.

> (8) The Congress of the Union, with a view to unifying and coordinating education throughout the Republic, shall issue the necessary laws for dividing the social function of education among the Federation, the States and the Municipalities, for fixing the appropriate financial allocations for this public service and for establishing the penalties applicable to officials who do not comply with or enforce the pertinent provisions, as well as the penalties applicable to all those who infringe such provisions.[51]

Article 4 protects employment rights:

> 4. No person can be prevented from engaging in the profession, industrial or commercial pursuit, or occupation of his choice, provided it is lawful. The exercise of this liberty shall only be forbidden by judicial order when the rights of third parties are infringed, or by administrative order, issued in the manner provided by law, when the rights of society are violated. No one may be deprived of the fruits of his labor except by judicial decision. The law in each state shall determine the professions which may be practiced only with a degree, and set forth the requirements for obtaining it and the authorities empowered to issue it.[52]

Finally, in terms of equality in employment, Article 123(7) establishes that equal work performed in the same post with the same hours worked and conditions of efficiency shall also be remunerated with the same salary.[53]

Ley Federal de Trabajo

The entitlement to equal opportunities is set down in Article 3 and Article 164 of the *Ley Federal de Trabajo* (LFT), the Federal Labor Law.[54] Article 1 provides that no discrimination may be established between workers.[55] Article 86 establishes that equal work performed in the same post with the same hours worked and conditions of efficiency shall also be remunerated with the same salary.[56] Although there is no unemployment insurance per se, Articles 50 and 52 of the LFT establish an obligation on the part of employers to pay compensation to unfairly dismissed workers, and they would also have the option to be reinstated to the same job.[57] If the worker is discharged without justification and his employment is for a specified period, the worker is entitled to receive a severance payment equal to the wages received for half of the time of work with the same employer. For those workers

51 Ibid., at Article 3.
52 Ibid., at Article 4.
53 Ibid., at Article 123(7).
54 *Ley Federal de Trabajo*, Mexico, at Articles 3 and 164.
55 Ibid., at Article 1.
56 Ibid., at Article 86.
57 Ibid., at Articles 50 and 52.

with more than one year of service, the severance payment is equal to six months' wages for the first year of service plus 20 days' wages for each additional year of service. For workers with labor contracts of unspecified duration, the severance payment is equal to three months' wages, and they would also have the right to receive wages for the period between the day of dismissal and the day the severance compensation is paid. If a worker asks to be reinstated and the employer refuses, he has the right to receive 20 days' wages for each year of service in addition to the above.

Ley del Seguro Social

In terms of retirement income and health benefits, the social security system covers a broad range of social insurance, including retirement and dismissal due to old age, work risks, illness and maternity, disability and life, and nursery facilities for children, as well as other social benefits. The system is financed by premiums paid by employers and employees, and by contributions from the federal government. Premiums paid by the employer are equal to 8.5% of insurable earnings plus 13.9%of the minimum wage in the Distrito Federal for illness insurance plus a variable portion for work risks insurance. Employees' premiums are equal to two per cent of their insurable earnings. In the case of workers receiving the minimum wage, according to Article 36, employers are obliged to pay the entire premium.[58] Contributions to the retirement insurance scheme are administered by means of individual accounts handled by private companies known as *Administradores de Fondos para el Retiro de los Trabajadores* (AFORES), Worker Retirement Fund Administrators.

In terms of employment, while Mexico boasts very high employment rates for men with 82.5% of males aged between 15 and 64 were in employment in 2004, the third highest figure among OECD countries, in contrast, there are low employment rates for women at 41.3%, the second lowest figure among OECD countries). However, the share of women in the labour market has increased, growing from 34.2% in 1991 to 41.3% in 2004. Further, there are three times more male employers at 5.4% than female employers, while there are twice as many women than men in unpaid employment, a ration of 13.2% to 7%. Further, the significant pay gap is more pronounced amongst professionals at -5.6 pesos/hour, supervisors and managers at -5.2 pesos, and public servants and privator sector managers at -4.4 pesos. In terms of education, females represented 50% of enrolments in undergraduate programs in 2003. Although there are programs where men predominate such as engineering or women predominate such as nursing, education and liberal studies, there are other areas where the ratio has been inverted, such as health sciences with women at 60% and social sciences and business administration at 55%. However, the gender gap in postgraduate programs persists with the percentage of females at 39.2% in 2003, ranked 22nd

58 *Ley del Seguro Social*, Mexico, at Article 36.

for the 28 OECD countries for which data are available. In the fight for equality, all women received the right to vote in 1953, although some provinces allowed women the right to vote in provincial elections as early as 1922. In 2006, the Parliament of Mexico adopted the General Act on Equality between Women and Men, which aimed at establishing a mandatory link between the federal and the state level in the formulation of policies and legal provisions.

United States of America

According to the latest statistics of 2007, college graduate in the United States account for 29.5% of men and 28% of women, with whites accounting for 29.9% of men and 28.3% of women, blacks accounting for 18% of men and 19% women, asians and pacific islanders accounting for 55.2% of men and 49.3% of women, and hispanics accounting for 11.8% of men and 13.7% women.[59] Education is a tool to overcome class discrimination.

The American model sees judicial activism and the judicial power as fundamentally legislative in character, with royal power displaced and overthrown, but class power remaining, with the upper class combining the popular republican form of government.

Declaration of Independence

The concepts of equality and good government, found in the American judicial system, were equally important principles to the Founding Fathers of the United States. The Declaration of Independence, the bedrock of the United States' jurisprudence system, was enshrined on 4 July 1776. It fundamentally states:

> We hold these truths to be self-evident, that all men are created equal; that they are endowed by their Creator with certain unalienable rights; that among these are life, liberty and the pursuit of happiness. That, to secure these rights, governments are instituted among men, deriving their just powers from the consent of the governed; that whenever any form of government becomes destructive of these ends, it is the right of the people to alter or to abolish it, and to institute a new government, laying its foundation on such principles, and organize its powers in such form, as to them shall seem most likely to effect their safety and happiness.[60]

---

59 U.S. Census Bureau, U.S. Census of Population.

60 Declaration of Independence, United States.

Federalist Papers

Influential thinkers, such as Jefferson, Madison and Jay, believed in a national government and a Bill of Rights, which they outlined in the Federalist Papers 1787–88. Government is seen as essential to the security of liberty, with every citizen ceding some rights for the protection thereof. The diversities in the faculties of men are recognized as where property rights originate. The objective of government is to secure the public good and private rights against the danger of factions, with the most common source of faction being the unequal distribution of property. The purpose of the Union is the common defense of the members, so that the means are proportionate to the ends. Government must act before the public and must be derived from the body of society. The Constitution is founded on the assent and ratification of the people, and every man who values liberty must cherish the attachment to the Union and preserve it.

Among the three branches of government, the Judicial branch is considered the least dangerous to the political rights of the Constitution. The Executive branch dispenses the honors and holds the sword, the Legislative branch controls the purse and prescribes the rules to regulate duties and rights, and the Judiciary has no influence over the sword or the purse, needing the aid of the Executive for the efficacy of judgments. Oppression can proceed from the Courts, but liberty will not be endangered if the branches are separate. The Constitution is the fundamental law of the land. "We, the people of the United States, to secure the blessings of liberty to ourselves and our prosperity, do ordain and establish this Constitution for the United States of America." As a recognition of popular rights, the judgments of many unite into one, with the voluntary consent of a whole people.[61] The Federalist Papers give us an important insight into the making of the Constitution, showing us early on the concept of equality of man and the formation of one government out of many people. The importance of the Judiciary must not be overlooked, as it is a major contributor of policy through its judgments, often itself influencing the sword, the Executive, and the purse, the Legislative. American constitutionalism is the product of the revolutionary movement in political thought of Hobbes, the parent of the modern American political process.[62] The chief purpose of political institutions is the management of social conflict. According to Hobbes, the only source of public authority is the private need of independently situated political actors, with a prior right to act based on self-defined standards of conscience and interest. If used wisely, the Constitution can serve to remedy injustices, including **class** discrimination.

---

61 Federalist Papers, United States.

62 Coleman, Frank, *Hobbes and America*, Toronto, 1977, p. 3.

United States Constitution

Fundamental Freedoms—The First Amendment to the Constitution, enacted in 1791, guarantees the freedoms of religion and expression:

> Amendment I
> Congress shall make no law respecting an establishment of religion, or prohibiting the free exercise thereof; or abridging the freedom of speech, or of the press; or the right of the people peaceably to assemble, and to petition the government for a redress of grievances.[63]

Civil Rights—The Fifth and Fourteenth Amendments of the Constitution, ratified in 15 December 1791 and 9 July 1868 respectively, are of paramount importance in the fight for human rights, including class. With the due process clause of the Fifth Amendment including an equal protection component, the Fifth and Fourteenth Amendments provide due process of law and equal protection to citizens from federal and state actions respectively. Thus, they prohibit government from invidious discrimination:

> Amendment V
> No person shall … be deprived of life, liberty, or property, without due process of law … .[64]

> Amendment XIV
> 1. No state shall make or enforce any law which shall abridge the privileges or immunities of citizens of the United States; nor shall any state deprive any person of life, liberty, or property, without due process of law; nor deny to any person within its jurisdiction the equal protection of the laws.[65]

The 39th Article of the Magna Carta of 1215 is a foundation for the Fifth and Fourteenth Amendments of the American Constitution regarding due process and the rights of life, liberty and property. The Magna Carta states:

> No free man shall be taken or imprisoned or dispossessed, or outlawed or banished, or in any way destroyed, nor will we go upon him nor send upon him, except by the legal judgement of his peers or by the law of the land.[66]

---

63 United States Constitution, at Amendment I.
64 Ibid., at Amendment V.
65 Ibid., at Amendment XIV.
66 Magna Carta, Great Britain.

Further, the Thirteenth Amendment, ratified 6 December 1865, was the initial step in ending a great injustice in the United States, which had lasted for centuries, namely slavery:

> Amendment XIII
> 1. Neither slavery nor involuntary servitude, except as a punishment for crime whereof the party shall have been duly convicted, shall exist within the United States, or any place subject to their jurisdiction.[67]

In addition, the Nineteenth Amendment, ratified 18 August 1920, was an initial step in granting equality for women:

> Amendment XIX
> The right of citizens of the United States to vote shall not be denied or abridged by the United States or by any State on account of sex.
> Congress shall have power to enforce this article by appropriate legislation.[68]

The American Founding Fathers designed the United States Constitution to be a set of broad guidelines established by free and intelligent men for the government of free and intelligent people for successive generations. It has survived for over two hundred years due to the common sense of the American people, the prudence of their representatives and the calculated wisdom of its judicial interpreters, the Supreme Court of the United States.[69] Chief Justice Marshall said of the Constitution: "It was intended to endure for ages to come and consequentially to be adapted to the various crises of human affairs" (*McCullough v. Maryland*, 4 Wheaton 415 (1819)).[70] It was a common opinion that each branch of government in matters pertaining to itself be the final judge of its own powers. However, it was the function of the judiciary, and especially the Supreme Court, to construe in the last resort the meaning of the Constitution, with its opinion final and binding. Justice Hughes stated: "We are under a Constitution but the Constitution is what the judges say it is." The United States Constitution, through Article 6(2), known as the Supremacy Clause, is the supreme law of the land:

> 6(2) This Constitution, and the Laws of the United States which shall be made in Pursuance thereof; and all Treaties made, or which shall be made, under the Authority of the United States, shall be the supreme Law of the Land; and the

---

67 United States Constitution, at Amendment XIII.

68 Ibid., at Amendment XIX.

69 North, Arthur, *The Supreme Court, Judicial Process and Judicial Politics*, New York, 1964, p. 2.

70 *McCullough v. Maryland*, 4 Wheaton 415 (1819).

> Judges in every State shall be bound thereby, any Thing in the Constitution or Laws of any State to the Contrary notwithstanding.[71]

The seminal case of *Marbury v. Madison*, 1 Cranch 137 (1803), brought forth the important principles that (1) the Constitution is the supreme law of the land; (2) the powers granted to various branches of government are limited; and (3) the sole and essential function of the Court is to determine which law should prevail in conflict of laws.[72]

In a dynamic society, the creativity of judges is important for the development of the law and the adaptability of the Constitution to the needs of modern society, according to the Realist Theory. Courts are the best means for recognizing social change, in order to focus social attitudes on unachieved goals and assist in their attainment through a decision-making process of judgments and thus policy-making, according to the Free Legal Decision Sociological Jurisprudence Theory.[73] History has a record of the past and provides the Court with a reservoir of social wisdom and political insight. It points out the evils against which the great constitutional clauses were designed as remedies. The adjudicative process depends on a delicate symbiotic relationship, whereby the Court must know us better than we know ourselves, acting as a voice of the spirit to remind us of our better selves.[74] It provides a stimulus and quickens moral education. However, the roots of the Supreme Court's decisions must be already in the nation. The aspirations voiced by the Court must be those the community is willing not only to avow but in the end to live by. For the power of the great constitutional decisions rests upon the accuracy of the Court's perceptions of this kind of common will and upon its ability ultimately to command a consensus. The rule of law, the capacity to command free assent, is the substitute for power.[75] Law is the fabric of a free society, organized with a minimum of force and a maximum of reason, in an ideal sense of right and justice. Thus, a neutral government, with its various branches, serves only as a participant in the inhumanities of its citizens.

In terms of the burden of proof in discrimination cases, the United States Supreme Court examines the cause of action to see whether a Plaintiff is a member of a class or group, which as a matter of law can invoke the power of the court, and thus, the equal protection clause and the due process clause of the Constitutional Amendments confer a constitutional right to be free from discrimination (*Davis*

71 United States Constitution, United States, at Article 6(2).

72 *Marbury v. Madison*, 1 Cranch 137 (1803).

73 North, Arthur, *The Supreme Court, Judicial Process and Judicial Politics*, New York, 1964, p. 8.

74 Cox Archibald, *The Role of the Supreme Court in American Government*, New York, 1976, p. 117.

75 Cox, Archibald, *Civil Rights, The Constitution and the Court*, Cambridge, MA, 1967, p. 21.

v. Passman, 442 US 228 (1979)).[76] Importantly, over the years, in examining court challenges, the United States Supreme Court has developed three different levels of review and accompanying burden of proof, depending upon the type of action brought in a legal proceeding. The Court will first examine the legislative purpose of the governmental action alleged to be contrary to the constitutional amendments, and the plaintiff's burden to prove his case will then come into play. The three levels of review are: (1) the minimum rationality level applied to see the rational basis for the means to the ends so that a law will survive as long as it does not serve an important government objective or is not substantially related to the achievement of the objective; (2) the heightened scrutiny level where the defendant government must show that the restriction has a substantial relationship to an important government interest, applied in quasi-suspect classifications, such as gender discrimination cases; and (3) most importantly, the strict scrutiny level where the defendant government must show a compelling interest for the restriction, a hard burden to meet, applied in suspect classifications affecting fundamental rights, such as racial discrimination cases. Thus, the concept of the burden of proof is an important element in court cases. In the fight for equal rights without regard to class distinction, some would say one's class should be considered suspect and thus be subject to the highest level of review of strict scrutiny.

In addition, although the American Constitution is the paramount tool for redressing wrongs, the judicial system in the United States has seen the use of two acts, the Equal Pay Act and the Civil Rights Act as alternatives to the Constitution, with the latter having been the most successful in guarding against discrimination.

Equal Pay Act

The Equal Pay Act's declaration of purpose is:

> The Congress hereby finds that the existence … of wage differentials based on sex
>
> (1) depresses wages and living standards for employees necessary for their health and efficiency;
>
> (2) prevents the maximum utilization of the available labor resources;
>
> (3) tends to cause labor disputes, thereby burdening, affecting, and obstructing commerce;
>
> (4) burdens commerce and the free flow of goods in commerce; and
>
> (5) constitutes an unfair method of competition.[77]

Important for women, the Equal Pay Act 1963 establishes that it is unlawful for an employer to pay unequal wages for equal work based on a discriminatory

76 *Davis v. Passman*, 442 US 228 (1979).

77 Equal Pay Act, United States.

distinction. An exception is made where there is a system of (1) seniority; (2) merit; (3) earnings based on quantity or quality of production; or (4) something other than gender. Section 16 of the Equal Pay Act states:

> 206(d)(1) No employer having employees ... shall discriminate, within any establishment ... between employees on the basis of sex by paying wages to employees in such establishment at a rate less than the rate at which he pays wages to employees of the opposite sex in such establishment for equal work on jobs the performance of which requires equal skill, effort and responsibility, and which are performed under similar working conditions except where such payment is made pursuant to 1) a seniority system, 2) a merit system, 3) a system which measures earnings by quantity or quality of product or 4) a differential based on any other factor other than sex.[78]

The Equal Pay Act only includes jobs that are very much alike or closely related, considered virtually or substantially identical (*Brennan v. City Stores*, 479 F.2d. 235 (1973)).[79] Jobs though not identical can be considered equal for Equal Pay Act standards, if there is only an insubstantial difference in skill, effort and responsibility (*Murphy v. Miller Brewer Co.*, 307 F.Supp. 829 (1969)).[80] For the Equal Pay Act, there is discrimination when there is a different wage rate for equal work, that is work which requires equal skill, effort and responsibility under similar working conditions (*Corning Glass v. Brennan*, 417 US 188 (1974)).[81] Equal protection is violated only by intentional discrimination, and a different impact standing alone is not enough. Further, there is no legal duty to undo the effects of previous discrimination (*American Nurses' Association v. State of Illinois*, 783 F.2d. 716 (1986)).[82] In terms of the burden of proof, the Plaintiff has the burden of establishing that equal pay for equal work was not received, and then the Defendant, in rebutting a prima facie case, must show the different wages were based on seniority, merit, a quantitative or qualitative system, or reasons other than sex (*Spaulding v. University of Washington*, 740 F.2d. 686 (1984)).[83] The court, however, is concerned with the actual job performance and content, not job description, titles or classifications, and the scrutiny is done on a case-by-case basis so that if skill is irrelevant to job requirements, it is not considered. Therefore, a non-job-related pretext can act as a shield for invidious discrimination.

---

78 Ibid., at Section 206(d)(1).

79 *Brennan v. City Stores*, 479 F.2d. 235 (1973).

80 *Murphy v. Miller Brewer Co.*, 307 F.Supp. 829 (1969).

81 *Corning Glass Works v. Brennan*, 417 US 188 (1974).

82 *American Nurses' Association v. State of Illinois*, 783 F.2d. 716 (1986).

83 *Spaulding v. University of Washington*, 740 F.2d. 686 (1984).

Civil Rights Act

Important for discrimination cases, including class discrimination, Title VII, the Civil Rights Act 1964, incorporating some of the provisions of the earlier Equal Pay Act with the Bennett Act Amendment, was implemented to safeguard important civil liberties, and serves to strengthen legislation, thereby helping the courts rule against discrimination.

Importantly, Section 703(a) guards against discrimination in employment:

> 703(a) It shall be an unlawful employment practice for an employer, (1) to fail or refuse to hire or to discharge any individual, or otherwise to discriminate against any individual with respect to his compensation, terms, conditions, or privilege of employment, because of such individual's race, color, religion, sex, or national origin, or (2) to limit, segregate, or classify his employees or applicants for employment in any way which would deprive or tend to deprive any individual of employment opportunities or otherwise adversely affect his status as an employee, because of such individual's race, color, religion, sex, or national origin.[84]

Further, employment agencies and labor organizations are covered under Section 703(b) and 703(c) respectively:

> 703(b) It shall be an unlawful employment practice for an employment agency to fail or refuse to refer for employment, or otherwise to discriminate against, any individual because of his race, color, religion, sex, or national origin, or to classify or refer for employment any individual on the basis of his race, color, religion, sex, or national origin.[85]

> 703(c) It shall be an unlawful employment practice for a labor organization
>
> (1) to exclude or to expel from its membership, or otherwise to discriminate against, any individual because of his race, color, religion, sex, or national origin;
>
> (2) to limit, segregate, or classify its membership or applicants for membership, or to classify or fail or refuse to refer for employment any individual, in any way which would deprive or tend to deprive any individual of employment opportunities, or would limit such employment opportunities or otherwise adversely affect his status as an employee or as an applicant for employment, because of such individual's race, color, religion, sex, or national origin.[86]

---

84 Ibid., Section 703(a).
85 Ibid., at Section 703(b).
86 Ibid., at Section 703(c).

Finally, training programs are covered under Section 703(d):

> 703(d) It shall be an unlawful employment practice for any employer, labor organization, or joint labor-management committee controlling apprenticeship or other training or retraining, including on-the-job training programs to discriminate against any individual because of his race, color, religion, sex, or national origin in admission to, or employment in, any program established to provide apprenticeship or other training.[87]

A bona fide occupational qualification exception is outlined in Section 703(e):

> 703(e) Notwithstanding any other provision of this subchapter, (1) it shall not be an unlawful employment practice for an employer to hire and employ employees, for an employment agency to classify, or refer for employment any individual, for a labor organization to classify its membership or to classify or refer for employment any individual, or for an employer, labor organization, or joint labor-management committee controlling apprenticeship or other training or retraining programs to admit or employ any individual in any such program, on the basis of his religion, sex, or national origin in those certain instances where religion, sex, or national origin is a bona fide occupational qualification reasonably necessary to the normal operation of that particular business or enterprise, and (2) it shall not be an unlawful employment practice for a school, college, university, or other educational institution or institution of learning to hire and employ employees of a particular religion if such school, college, university, or other educational institution or institution of learning is, in whole or in substantial part, owned, supported, controlled, or managed by a particular religion or by a particular religious corporation, association, or society, or if the curriculum of such school, college, university, or other educational institution or institution of learning is directed toward the propagation of a particular religion.[88]

Section 703(h) covers unequal pay:

> 703(h) Notwithstanding any other provision of this title, it shall be a lawful employment practice for an employer to apply different standards of compensation, or different terms, conditions, or privileges of employment pursuant to a bona fide seniority or merit system, or a system which measures earnings by quantity or quality of production or to employees who work different locations, provided that such are not the result of an intention to discriminate because of race, color, religion, sex, or national origin. It shall not be an unlawful employment practice under this title for any employer to differentiate upon the basis of sex

87 Ibid., at Section 703(d).
88 Ibid., at Section 703(e).

> in determining the amount of wages or compensation paid to employees of such employer if such differentiation is authorized by the provisions of Section 6(d) of the Fair Standards Act.[89]

Section 703(j) guards against preferential treatment:

> 703(j) Nothing contained in this subchapter shall be interpreted to require any employer, employment agency, labor organization, or joint labor management committee subject to this subchapter to grant preferential treatment to any individual or to any group because of the race, color, religion, sex, or national origin of such individual or group on account of an imbalance which may exist with respect to the total number or percentage of persons of any race, color, religion, sex, or national origin employed by any employer, referred or classified for employment by any employment agency or labor organization, admitted to membership or classified by any labor organization, or admitted to, or employed in, any apprenticeship or other training program, in comparison with the total number or percentage of persons of such race, color, religion, sex, or national origin in any community, State, section, or other area, or in the available work force in any community, State, section, or other area.[90]

In addition, discriminatory advertising is outlawed under Section 704(b):

> 704(b) It shall be an unlawful employment practice for an employer, labor organization, or employment agency to print or publish or cause to be printed or published any notice or advertisement relating to employment by such an employer or membership in or any classification or referral for employment by such a labor organization, or relating to any classification or referral for employment by such an employment agency, indicating any preference, limitation, specification, or discrimination, based on race, color, religion, sex, or national origin, except that such a notice or advertisement may indicate a preference, limitation, specification, or discrimination based on religion, sex, or national origin when religion, sex, or national origin is a bona fide occupational qualification for employment.[91]

The establishment of a discriminatory employment practice based on disparate impact is noted in Section 703(k):

> 703(k)(1)(A) An unlawful employment practice based on disparate impact is established under this title only if

89 Ibid., at Section 703(h).
90 Ibid., at Section 703(j).
91 Ibid., at Section 704(b).

> (i) a complaining party demonstrates that a respondent uses a particular employment practice that causes a disparate impact on the basis of race, color, religion, sex, or national origin and the respondent fails to demonstrate that the challenged practice is job related for the position in question and consistent with business necessity.[92]

Further, the duty of a complainant party in a discrimination case is outlined in Section 703(m):

> 703(m) Except as otherwise provided in this title, an unlawful employment practice is established when the complaining party demonstrates that race, color, religion, sex, or national origin was a motivating factor for any employment practice, even though other factors also motivated the practice.[93]

Section 706(g) provides for adjudicative relief:

> 706(g) If the court finds that the respondent has intentionally engaged in or is intentionally engaging in an unlawful employment practice charged in the complaint, the court may enjoin the respondent from engaging in such unlawful employment practice, and order such affirmative action as may be appropriate, which may include, but is not limited to, reinstatement or hiring of employees, with or without back pay … or any other equitable relief as the court deems appropriate … . No order of the court shall require the admission or reinstatement of an individual as a member of a union, or the hiring, reinstatement, or promotion of an individual as an employee, or the payment to him of any back pay, if such individual was refused admission, suspended, or expelled, or was refused employment or advancement or was suspended or discharged for any reason other than discrimination on account of race, color, religion, sex, or national origin or in violation of section 704(a).[94]

Finally, opposition to a discriminatory practice is protected under Section 704(a):

> 704(a) It shall be an unlawful employment practice for an employer to discriminate against any of his employees or applicants for employment, for an employment agency, or joint labor management committee controlling apprenticeship or other training or retraining, including on the job training programs, to discriminate against any individual, or for a labor organization to discriminate against any member thereof or applicant for membership, because he has opposed any practice made an unlawful employment practice by this

92 Ibid., at Section 703(k).
93 Ibid., at Section 703(m).
94 Ibid., at Section 706(g).

> subchapter, or because he has made a charge, testified, assisted, or participated in any manner in an investigation, proceeding, or hearing under this subchapter.[95]

In general, the Civil Rights Act eliminates artificial, arbitrary and unnecessary barriers to employment in the form of invidious discrimination, unless there is a demonstrably reasonable measure of job performance (*Griggs v. Duke Power Co.*, 401 US 424 (1971)).[96] Title VII prohibits discrimination allowing for compensation, thus recognizing equal pay as a legal right (*American Federation of State, County and Municipal Employees v. Washington*, 770 F.2d. 1401 (1985)).[97] In terms of the burden of proof, the Plaintiff has the burden to show he belongs to a group, has applied for a job, was qualified for the job that the employer tried to fill but was rejected, and the employer continued to seek applicants (*McDonnell Douglas Corp. v. Green*, 411 U.S. 792 (1973)),[98] and then the Defendant, in rebutting a prima facie case, is required to show the absence of a discriminatory motive for his actions. However, this was later revised by the court, so that the Defendant is not required to show the absence, but must merely articulate a legitimate non-discriminatory reason for the employee's rejection (*Board of Trustees of Keene State College v. Sweeney*, 439 US 24 (1978)).[99]

The Civil Rights Act is often used to fight discrimination in compensation, with a differentiation made between disparate treatment and disparate impact. Disparate treatment is concerned with direct or circumstantial discriminatory motives, which lack well-defined criteria (*Spaulding v. University of Washington*, 740 F.2d. 686 (1984)),[100] and involves intent or motive as an essential element of liability concerning the effects of a chosen policy, with awareness alone of adverse consequences on a group being insufficient (*American Federation of State, County and Municipal Employees v. Washington*, 770 F.2d. 1401 (1985)).[101] In a disparate treatment approach, the Plaintiff is required to show by a preponderance of the evidence the overt motive, and then the Defendant, in rebutting a prima facie case, must prove that it was non-discriminatory either by the four exceptions, by necessity or by a bona fide occupational qualification. On the other hand, disparate impact is more than an inference of discriminatory impact of outwardly neutral employment practices and adversity (*Spaulding v. University of Washington*, 740 F.2d. 686 (1984)),[102] and does not need a profession of intent by the employer

95 Ibid., at Section 704(a).

96 *Griggs v. Duke Power Co.*, 401 US 424 (1971).

97 *American Federation of State, County and Municipal Employees v. Washington*, 770 F.2d. 1401 (1985).

98 *McDonnell Douglas Corp. v. Green*, 411 US 792 (1973).

99 *Board of Trustees of Keene State College v. Sweeney*, 439 US 24 (1978).

100 *Spaulding v. University of Washington*, 740 F.2d. 686 (1984).

101 *American Federation of State, County and Municipal Employees v. Washington*, 770 F.2d. 1401 (1985).

102 *Spaulding v. University of Washington*, 740 F.2d. 686 (1984).

to discriminate, only a clearly delineated employment practice (*American Federation of State, County and Municipal Employees v. Washington*, 770 F.2d. 1401 (1985)).[103] In a disparate impact approach, the Plaintiff need only show the disproportionate impact, and then the Defendant, in rebutting a prima facie case, must show that it was non-discriminatory.

Legislation has indeed made an impact on discrimination. However, while legislation has had a marked effect on some forms of direct discrimination, such as in advertising vacancies or in the process of selection for promotion, there is no clear evidence so far of a total shift in the attitude of employers and society to workers from different classes, since this is likely to be a long-term process. Evidence shows that legislation can only help to change attitudes if it operates in conjunction with other policies to promote equal rights and educate employers and workers about their obligations and rights; experience has shown that changing hearts and minds on discrimination is far from easy, and that it is only through doing so that equal respect and treatment of all people will become possible.[104]

Conclusion

The keys to the future for equal rights and tolerance of class distinctions in North America are the implementation and development of the law, the deepening in understanding of specific legal issues relating to human rights in the courts, and the raising of the level of awareness of legal rights and obligations, in the pursuit of "Class Act". Martin Luther King Jr. in his struggle for civil rights stated:

> I have a dream that one day every valley shall be exalted, every hill and mountain shall be made plain, and the crooked places shall be made straight and the glory of the Lord will be revealed and all flesh shall see it together. This is our hope … And when we allow freedom to ring, when we let it ring from every village and hamlet, from every state and city, we will be able to join hands and to sing in the words of the old Negro spiritual, 'Free at last, free at last; thank God Almighty, we are free at last'.[105]

---

103 *American Federation of State, County and Municipal Employees v. Washington*, 770 F.2d. 1401 (1985).

104 Hornstein, Zmira, *Outlawing Age Discrimination: Foreign Lessons, UK Choices*, Bristol, 2001.

105 King Jr., Martin Luther, March on Washington, 28 August 1963.

Chapter 7
Class Act in the North American Free Trade Agreement

Introduction

In the quest for tolerance of class distinctions in employment and trade in *Class Act*, this chapter will examine efforts against class discrimination in the area of the North American Free Trade Agreement (NAFTA), which at the time was the largest economic and legal undertaking ever attempted, having an important impact on the labor force generally and on particular classes of workers specifically. It will look at NAFTA from its inception, examining first its benefits and then its drawbacks. It will also look at the North American Agreement on Labor Cooperation (NAALC) and the Free Trade Area of the Americas (FTAA), as well as legislation of the Americas, namely the American Declaration of the Rights and Duties of Man, the American Convention on Human Rights, the Statute of the Inter-American Court on Human Rights and the Inter-American Democratic Charter.

Toward the North American Free Trade Agreement (NAFTA)

An economic association for "free trade" was first brought about in North America in 1854. Prior to this, however, there were several developments in the relationship between the United States and British North America, what was to become Canada. The War of 1812 brought an end to the fear of American annexation of Canada, with a new view of commercial and economic rivalry between the two countries. The Canadian national sentiment favored trade with the United States through transportation via the railways and the waterways. With the industrial movement in the 1850s came the Grand Trunk Railway system, with an investment of $100 million in transportation and communication.[1] The construction of canals and railways were a move toward the avoidance of continental integration with the United States. However, the United States, with these developments, was not seen as the enemy but a concurrent competitor, with Canada furnishing natural resources. It was more economical for the United States to pass exports by Montreal through the St. Lawrence Seaway in order to lower transportation costs, and to assist them, the British, who controlled Canada at the time, would exempt the American traders from duties, treating them like Canadians. Among the market terminals of

1 Hamelin, Jean, *Histoire du Québec*, Edisem, 1976, p. 371.

North America, Mississippi, the Hudson, New Orleans, New York and Montreal, the latter two were rivals, with New York prevailing. North American seaboard centers participated actively in the prosperity brought about by commercialism.

The Elgin-Marcy Reciprocity Treaty of 1854 was the first major trade pact between the United States and Canada. Reciprocity was an attempt to create, in North America, a single market area covering several distinct political jurisdictions, where specified types of products were freely exchanged for a partial and limited economic union between British North America and the United States.[2] It was thought to be the only feasible alternative to annexation. However, the American Civil War influenced the economic development of British North America, with new markets in the United States opening for Canadian exports. At the end of the war, the removal of restraints on the expansion of American settlement west of the Mississippi jeopardized the security of the Canadian west and hastened Confederation.[3] However, the waterways were a uniting force. The businessmen from Upper Canada, what was to become the Canadian Province of Ontario, were the first to seize the idea of reciprocity. Nevertheless, immediate economic and political union with the United States would have sacrificed for Canada valued institutions, national identity and loyalty to Britain. In the United States, the South with its plantations wanted low tariffs to lower prices of imported goods and to reduce the costs of production for exports of raw materials. On the other hand, the North, with its small farms and factories, was protectionist with little enthusiasm for reciprocity. It was seen as simply a concession for the inclusion of fisheries, the immediate and urgent objective.

Thus, the Treaty was abrogated by the United States on 17 March 1866, due to several antagonizing factors for the United States, namely British support for the Confederacy during the Civil War, new Canadian tariffs, the disastrous effects on timber- and grain-growing regions of the United States, the resentment by farming and lumber interests to Canadian competition, the jealousy by shipping and forwarding interests in Buffalo and Philadelphia of the St. Lawrence Route and of the Grand Trunk Railway system with the Victoria Bridge completion in Montreal in 1860 furthering competition, and the manufacturing interests blaming Canadian tariffs for the decline of certain exports.[4] While Canada's policy in economic relations was to favor east–west relations, the natural tendencies were the opposite, north–south. Shortly after the death of the Reciprocity Treaty until the advent of the 1911 "free trade" election in Canada, free trade with the United States had been the central issue in Canadian politics. Canadian Prime Minister

---

2 Easterbrook, W.T. and Aitken, Hugh, *Canadian Economic History*, Toronto, 1976, p. 362.

3 Ibid., at p. 361.

4 Fry, Earl, "Trends in Canada-U.S. Free Trade Discussions", in A. R. Riggs and Tom Welk, *Canadian-American Free Trade: Historical, Political and Economic Dimensions*, Montreal, 1987, p. 28.

Laurier was the first continentalist Prime Minister to appreciate that Canada shares North America with the United States, which shapes the national destiny.

With the 1911 Free Trade Agreement, Canada built up its own manufacturing protection tariff. At the time, there was the sentiment in Canada of "no truck or trade with the Yankees".[5] However, with the exception of Britain, Canada was the chief trading partner of the United States, and in 1910 alone, Canada bought $242 million and sold $97 million to the United States.[6] American President Taft negotiated for full-scale reciprocity for better trade relations between the United States and Canada, since common interests called for special arrangements, and Canadians and Americans were reminded that there were 3,000 miles of joint border between the two countries. The 1911 free trade agreement was similar to the 1854 pact, but was not a treaty, and thus did not require the two-thirds approval of the US Senate. Most American tariffs on manufacturing goods were reduced, while most Canadian manufacturing tariffs remained. It was passed by Congress and signed by US President Taft. However, Canadian Prime Minister Borden, who defeated Prime Minister Laurier in 1911, opposed the trade legislation and did not put the reciprocity agreement to a vote, with the United States rescinding its vote eight years later.

Other agreements were entered into over the years, one of which was the General Agreement on Tariffs and Trade (GATT) 1947, whose purpose was to promote global trade between members through a reduction in tariffs. Canada wished for trade on a liberalized basis, the first Article of GATT, and same treatment. GATT provided for an impressive reduction of tariffs, with some even impeding economic efficiency, production, competition and growth. It permitted the United States and Canada to enter into free trade, with an agreement to remove customs duties and other restrictions on substantially all bilateral trade.[7] Over the last years of GATT and the advent of the World Trade Organization (WTO), Canadian exports multiplied ten times, the national wealth more than tripled and the number of jobs doubled.[8] On the other hand, unemployment has also risen over this period, which raises important questions about the benefits of free trade. Wartime demands required greater cooperation on a continental basis, with Canada and Mexico being prime sources of raw materials for American factories. Private negotiations on free trade once again took place in 1947 between American

5 d'Aquino, Thomas, "Truck and Trade with the Yankees, The Case for a Canada-U.S. Comprehensive Trade Agreement", in A.R. Riggs and Tom Velk, *Canadian-American Free Trade: Historical, Political and Economic Dimensions*, Montreal, 1987, p. 74.

6 Velk, Tom, and Riggs, A.R., "The Ongoing Debate Over Free Trade", in A.R. Riggs and Tom Velk, *Canadian-American Free Trade: (The Sequel) Historical, Political and Economic Dimensions*, Montreal, 1988, p. 93.

7 General Agreement on Tariffs and Trade, at Article 24.

8 Laun, Louis, "U.S.-Canada Free Trade Negotiations: Historical Opportunities", in A.R. Riggs and Tom Velk, *Canadian-American Free Trade: Historical, Political and Economic Dimensions*, Montreal, 1987, p. 205.

President Truman and Canadian Prime Minister King, in an era of the Marshall Plan, and of US economic assistance to Western Europe and Japan post World War II. King approved the agreement in October 1947, but it was later vetoed in May 1948, because he feared the Canadian public would label it continentalist and anti-British.[9]

Overall, by examining the years leading to the advent of the Free Trade Agreement of the 1980s, we can observe a number of characteristics of the trade relationship between the two countries that are notable: (1) Canada has been the initiator in free trade on almost all the occasions; (2) the United States has been largely indifferent except for President Taft in 1911; (3) in the two most important negotiations of the twentieth century, 1911 and 1947, Canada had second thoughts and put an end to the agreement; (4) the United States has been a formidable obstacle to closer economic ties between the two nations; (5) the 1911 and 1947 deals provided for more US concessions; (6) statements made by the United States were cannon fodder for groups in Canada which were opposed to annexation; (7) Canadian opponents say that economic costs to free trade outweigh economic benefits, and react on an emotional, loyal, national, love of country level, branding those in favor as stooges of American financial interests; (8) while there is more emphasis today on business, commercial and economic issues, Canada has cultural, regional economic development, social welfare and sovereignty concerns; and (9) when times are tough, Canada wants improved access to United States markets while the United States turns inward toward protectionism.[10]

There is a regional aspect to the overall economic evolution of the North American continent. Canada's industrial development has been North American, with its development based on its natural resources, and its expansion characterized by large-scale monopolistic industries. Over time, Canada's dealings with Britain and the United States changed. Canada once had an autonomous relationship with Britain, producing an un-American sentiment. Britain use to be the major investor in Canada. However, over the years, the United States has replaced it. Canada went from dependence on Britain to dependence on the United States, thus producing a foreign-controlled economy. In addition, the nature of foreign investment had changed, since the British invested indirectly through obligations and finance, while the Americans invested directly, usually as proprietors funding production. Tariffs and natural resources attracted US enterprises, and Canada benefited from their capital, technological advancement and mass production. The United States invested $168 billion in 1900 and $881 billion in 1914. The Canadian policy, interestingly, was to increase tariffs and oblige US companies wishing to do business to build factories in Canada. Therefore, the United States penetrated the Canadian economy by installing branch plants for American-made products. By 1932, the United States

9 Fry, Earl, "Trends in Canada-U.S. Free Trade Discussions", in AR. Riggs and Tom Welk, *Canadian-American Free Trade: Historical, Political and Economic Dimensions*, Montreal, 1987, p. 9.

10 Ibid., at p. 34.

had dominated the industrial sector, accounting for 82 % of car production, 68 % of electricity, one-third of pulp and paper, and was solidly ahead in petroleum, pharmaceuticals, rubber, machinery and non-metallic minerals. Of the US enterprises in Canada, 36% of them were established in the period between 1920 and 1929. Today, Canada sends more than three-quarters of all its exports to the United States, accounting for 25% of its annual gross national product.[11]

The policy process resulted in the overwhelming trade dependence of Canada on the United States over the years. American policies are destined to affect the policies of Canada and North America as a whole. Canada is carried into the whirlpool of common points of view, to the advantage of the United States, and its own point of view is easily overwhelmed. Approaches should be adopted by which cultural traits of civilization might persist, with the least possible depreciation of the national sensibility of Canadians upon the US. Canada's trade pattern from the outset was based on the importing of manufactured goods in return for the exporting of staples to more advanced industrialized economies as the engine of growth of the Canadian economy.[12] The commercial rather than industrial bias of the Canadian capitalist **class**, along with dependent branch plant industrialization, flowed from the unequal alliance with American foreign ownership and capital. Canada was within the tight embrace of the American empire, and occupied whatever room was left open by US capital, becoming the exemplary client State. Today, the United States takes up 70% of Canada's total exports, and Canada takes in over 20% of United States exports, which has a direct investment of roughly $20 billion.[13] It is not a zero sum gain with one benefiting at the expense of the other. Canada's prosperity depends on trade with other countries, with one-third of its jobs and one-quarter of its wealth tied to international trade.[14] From the outset, Canada was torn between republicanism and conservatism, trying to forge a national identity. Canada has wished to be more independent in its foreign policy, while at the same time it has had to guard against the departure of Canadian firms going south in search of cheaper labor and less regulation.

Free trade continentalism, according to its advocates, involves: (1) tariff liberalization; (2) a high volume of trade with the United States; (3) meager diversification; (4) some protectionism by the United States; (5) restructuring of the Canadian economy for a more competitive industrial society; and (6) transborder transregionalism between Provinces and States. Continentalism is a process of microregional (subcontinental) integration, which is transnational (multinational

11 Ibid., at p. 27.

12 Watkins, Mel, "The Political Economy of Growth", in Wallace Clement and Glen Williams, *The New Canadian Political Economy*, Kingston, 1989, p. 17.

13 Laun, Louis, "U.S.-Canada Free Trade Negotiations: Historical Opportunities", in A.R. Riggs and Tom Velk, *Canadian-American Free Trade: Historical, Political and Economic Dimensions*, , Montreal, 1987, p.205.

14 Government of Canada, *The North American Free Trade Agreement At A Glance*, Ottawa, 1993, p. 1.

corporations, unions, economic elites) and transgovernmental (direct contacts between two central bureaucracies and relations between Provinces and States), with closer Canada United States transactional ties (diplomatic, administrative, commercial, cultural) and structural interpenetration (economic).[15] Thus, Canada and the United States are somewhat similar as societies with transnational and transgovernmental relationships, attitudes and values, strong social factors and a deep-rooted structural economic interpenetration, in a widespread integration pattern. Canada is strategically situated, with its border and large cities close to US development centers.

While the free trade zone has eliminated trade barriers as to goods, the movement of capital in production has caused negative integration generating disturbances and distortions in the economy. This occurs especially if there is asymmetry within society, causing imbalances, both regionally and between partners in interactions. The freeing of circulation of goods creates initial imbalances and economic distortions. Before World War II, Canada's prosperity depended on resource industries, which required a high cost in order to protect the manufacturing sector serving the home market. However, in the 1980s, the prosperity of resource-based industries was seriously hurt by international development in the areas of new sources of supply and man-made substitutes for natural materials.[16] Export- and service-related products depended on hard pressed resource-based industries, and this created uncertainties in business and job dislocations.[17] Textile and clothing industries are vulnerable in trade liberalization. The clothing industry would be hardpressed in lowering prices, except for high volume segments that are successful when moving into particular niches for export. Canada has specialized and expanded its primary and manufacturing sectors, which the proponents of free trade argue has afforded a net benefit through access to the vital US market that is less restrictive and more secure. However, free trade advocates argue that it is important to secure continued access to the United States market and to work against protectionism, for benefits to producers in sales and to consumers in prices.[18]

Overall, greater specialization in North America brings greater international competition, encouraging more rapid diffusion of new technology, new management

---

15 Soldatos, P., "Canada's Foreign Policy in Search of a Fourth Option: Continuity and Change in Orientation Towards the U.S.", in A.R. Riggs and Tom Velk, *Canadian-American Free Trade: (The Sequel) Historical, Political and Economic Dimensions*, Montreal, 1988, p. 41.

16 Lipsey, Richard, "Canada's Trade Options", in A.R. Riggs and TomVelk, *Canadian-American Free Trade: Historical, Political and Economic Dimensions*, Montreal, 1987, p. 59.

17 Brecher, Irving, "The Free Trade Initiative, On Course or Off", in A.R. Riggs and Tom Velk, *Canadian-American Free Trade: Historical, Political and Economic Dimensions*, Montreal, 1987, p. 67.

18 Neufeld, E.P, "Financial and Economic Dimensions of Free Trade", in A.R. Riggs and Tom Velk, *Canadian-American Free Trade: Historical, Political and Economic Dimensions*, Montreal, 1987, p. 152.

and organizational production. The tertiary service industries are more sharply differentiated among countries by the varied regulatory environments. In the goods-producing industries, tariffs or quotas have been the main barrier. The service industry has subtle impediments, with discrimination being a barrier because of immigration labor laws, which are most evident today with illegal immigration at an all time high. National treatment calls for no regulatory distinction between foreign and domestic firms, which is good if there are similar industries for reciprocity and market access.[19] These laws restrict one country's firms transferring staff to the other country. Trade in services encompasses a large number of areas, having different characteristics of trade and efforts for international rule-making.

Considering these factors, sectoral trade discussions in 1983 later gave way to a comprehensive free trade approach in 1985. US President Reagan and Canadian Prime Minister Mulroney launched an initiative for a bilateral trade agreement, with its goal to remove all or most remaining barriers to cross-border trade in goods and services, and to create an enlarged body of agreed rules to govern trade, which produced the 1989 Canada United States Free Trade Agreement (FTA). President Reagan called the document, signed on 2 January 1988, the most important bilateral trade negotiation ever undertaken by the United States. It was horizontal not sectoral for market access, and called for mutual restraint on unilateral commercial policies. It was believed that there would be a direct link between productivity and jobs,[20] affording a longer cycle of production, investment and specialization. This Free Trade Agreement was the biggest trade agreement ever reached between two countries, in excess of $200 billion in trade of goods and services.[21] Canada exports more per citizen than any counterpart in any other industrial power. Some 30% of its national income is generated by exports with more than three million jobs depending on these exports. The United States absorbs 80% of Canada's exports, in a southward flow,[22] having an economy ten times bigger than Canada's, and affording the latter greater access to opportunities. The relationship encourages lower-cost production in factories, and more specialized and efficient industries, thereby strengthening the capacity to compete in the global market. The goal is to generate growth and production, in order to increase the standard of living for challenging and rewarding careers. The United States, thereby, consolidates access to the biggest export market.

19 Ibid., at p. 155.

20 Layton, Robert, "Why Canada Needs Free Trade", in A.R. Riggs and Tom Velk, *Canadian-American Free Trade: Historical, Political and Economic Dimensions*, Montreal, 1987, p. 200.

21 Velk, Tom, and Riggs, A.R., "The Ongoing Debate Over Free Trade", in A.R. Riggs and Tom Velk, *Canadian-American Free Trade: (The Sequel) Historical, Political and Economic Dimensions*, Montreal, 1988, p. 3.

22 d'Aquino, Thomas, "Truck and Trade with the Yankees, The Case for a Canada-U.S. Comprehensive Trade Agreement", in A.R. Riggs and Tom Velk, *Canadian-American Free Trade: Historical, Political and Economic Dimensions*, Montreal, 1987, p. 74.

North American Free Trade Agreement (NAFTA)

In 1991, Canada, the United States and Mexico began negotiations for the North American Free Trade Agreement (NAFTA). The free trade agenda shifted from a sectoral approach to a comprehensive accord among the three countries, because of a difficulty in matching sectors and in accommodating regional concerns. The 1989 Canada United States Free Trade Agreement laid the foundation for NAFTA, which secured Canada's economic relationship with the United States.

Prior to NAFTA coming into effect on 1 January 1994, trade between the United States and Canada had never been larger and was growing faster than the rest of the economy. In addition, the flow of trade and investment among the United States, Canada and Mexico was $500 billion per year. Mexico has a rapidly growing market of over 85 million people, which historically was hard to penetrate because of strict Mexican barriers to trade. Before NAFTA, Mexico was restrictive on foreign investment. However, with NAFTA, Mexican tariffs are phased out over time. Mexico's border is aligned with the United States and its coastline faces Europe and Asia. It has a key global strategic advantage with its unique geographic position, and is considered the gateway to Latin America, being ranked twelfth in area among the world's nations.[23] Regulations give legal security to market transactions, protect consumers and the environment, and safeguard intellectual property rights. Free trade promotes competition and provides adequate incentives for private decision-making in a free market. However, the regulatory environment must ensure the rules of the game are clear and uniformly applied, subject to monitoring.

NAFTA was the biggest trade agreement ever signed at the time, covering 360 million consumers and far-reaching to remove all tariffs and liberalize non-tariff barriers to trade. It regulates trade in services, liberalizes investment, promotes specialization and implements a mechanism for a binding resolution to disputes, which is unprecedented in free trade. The objectives of NAFTA are the removal of tariff and non-tariff barriers for goods and services, the neutralization of government policies, practices and procedures, and a consistency with the GATT agreement to cover all trade.[24] The long-term goals of free trade are the improvement of real income wages and production, an increase in the number of jobs, a reduction of protectionism, a decrease in competitive pressures from

23 Mexican Investment Board, *Mexico Your Partner for Growth, Regulatory Reform and Competition Policy, Setting the Incentives for an Efficient Economy*, Mexico City, 1994, p. 1.

24 Laun, Louis, "U.S.-Canada Free Trade Negotiations: Historical Opportunities", in A.R. Riggs and Tom Velk, *Canadian-American Free Trade: Historical, Political and Economic Dimensions*, Montreal, 1987, p. 208.

developing and newly industrialized countries, and the mitigation of pressures due to global imbalances.[25]

The United States had several objectives of its own, namely the elimination of tariffs, the reduction of non-tariff barriers, the development of rules governing trade in services, trucking and insurance, the improvement of protection to intellectual property, greater discipline over subsidies, and an open and secure environment for foreign investment. Canada had several goals of its own, as well, namely the improved access to the United States and Mexico for goods and services, the strengthening of the initial Canada United States Free Trade Agreement, and the guarantee of its position as a prime location for investors to serve all the North American Continent. Canada hoped that NAFTA would supply it with a sharper edge for international competitiveness, by widening trade horizons and providing a bigger stage on which to demonstrate and prove its economic expertize and leadership.

NAFTA provided that tariffs would be removed within ten years in the traditional sectors, accounting for half of the trade, and removed either immediately, in five years or exceptionally in twenty years for the remainder, moving toward a harmonized system of tariff nomenclature. It has quantitative restrictions, which build on GATT, and has a sectoral perspective as to agriculture, foods, automotives and energy. There are new elements to the agreement, which include the restriction of investment, the freedom in the future to regulate in conformity with the basic principles of non-discrimination, and the principles of national treatment, right of establishment and right of commercial presence. NAFTA sets out strict rules of origin to qualify for preferential duties, requiring that products originate in North America. For those not meeting this, larger quotas for preferential access to the American market have been included, with these new levels helping textile and apparel manufacturers expand their exports of products to the lucrative American market. Canadian and Mexican tariffs on apparel were eliminated within ten years, and tariffs on textiles within eight years. Mexico has concentrated on less expensive lower-quality items, while Canada has moved toward higher-value textiles and quality designer fashions. Further, the financial industry was first included in the Canadian United States Free Trade Agreement, and it was believed that freer market access for financial services would help trade flow more easily. The United States agreed to national treatment, market access and most favored nation status being applied to financial services, fully subjecting the sector to dispute settlement.

The NAFTA Secretariat, comprising the Canadian, American and Mexican Sections, is an organization established by the Free Trade Commission, pursuant to the North American Free Trade Agreement. It is responsible for the administration of the dispute settlement provisions of the Agreement, and its mandate includes the provision of assistance to the Commission, and support for various non-dispute-

25 Harris, Richard, "Some Observations on the Canada-U.S. Free Trade Deal", in A.R. Riggs and Tom Velk, *Canadian-American Free Trade: (The Sequel) Historical, Political and Economic Dimensions*, Montreal 1988, p. 52.

related committees and working groups. Each national Section maintains a court-like registry relating to panel, committee and tribunal proceedings. A similar administrative body, the Binational Secretariat, existed under the Canada United States Free Trade Agreement (FTA). The Parties have established permanent national Section offices, which are "mirror-images" of one another, and are located in Ottawa, Washington and Mexico City respectively.

Importantly, the principal dispute settlement mechanisms of NAFTA are found in Chapters 11, 14, 19 and 20 of the Agreement. NAFTA establishes a mechanism for the settlement of disputes that assures both equal treatment among Parties in accordance with the principle of international reciprocity and due process before an impartial tribunal. Alternatively, the investor may choose the remedies available in the host country's domestic courts. An important feature of the arbitral provisions is the enforceability in domestic courts of final awards by arbitration tribunals. NAFTA provides for a trade commission in charge of political management, which includes a dispute settlement mechanism in the form of a panel, with an important role of the Commission to consider matters relating to the Agreement which are under dispute. When general disputes concerning NAFTA are not resolved through consultation within a specified period of time, the matter may be referred at the request of either Party to a non-binding panel. Various third-Party provisions are necessarily included, as a third Party that considers it has a substantial interest in a disputed matter is entitled to join consultations or a proceeding as a complaining Party on written notice, but if it does not join as a complainant, upon written notice, it is entitled to attend hearings, make written and oral submissions and receive written submissions of the disputing Parties. There is also a provision for an advisory committee to be established to provide recommendations to the Commission on the use of arbitration and other procedures for the resolution of international private commercial disputes, and if nothing results from the notification of a consultation action, then a panel review ensues with recommendations that are binding if both sides agree. The dispute settlement is also binding when one side believes that a surge of imports is damaging to it, thereby receiving compensation while the other side is snapped back to a most-favored nation tariff. This procedure was in effect for the first ten years of the agreement, providing steps for negotiation, legislation specificity and panel review. The settlement mechanism calls for compulsory consultation on changes of law and an evaluation procedure by a panel, with the right to retaliate or withdraw if the panel so favors. NAFTA also provides, for the first time, a system of settling private investment disputes in that those between an investor from a NAFTA country and another NAFTA government can be settled at the investor's option by binding international arbitration, with all investors treated equally. The dispute settlement provisions call for the rapid and fair settlement of disputes, including the use of impartial panels, and there are three basic steps to the process: first, consultation among the three countries for a satisfactory settlement; second, if the first round fails, the NAFTA trade commission, comprised of cabinet-level representatives, will examine the case for interpretation of trade rules; and third, if the second round fails, in order to promote an impartial decision, the issue will be reviewed by a specially selected panel, which is composed of five members chosen from a trilaterally agreed roster, with two panellists from the complaining party selected by the defending party, two from the defending party nominated by the complainant and the panel's chair allowed to be a representative from the third NAFTA country or another neutral country chosen by mutual agreement or drawn by lot.

The elimination of tariffs is important for a reduction of protectionism and a climate of open investment. Cross-border trade in services was first included in the Canada United States Free Trade Agreement, and NAFTA has extended these codes of binding rules and principles with procedures to encourage the recognition of licenses and certificates through mutually acceptable professional standards and criteria, such as education, experience and professional development. It opens up temporary entry across the border for over 60 professions. Further, there is a provision as to access for temporary personnel in the service and manufacturing sectors, as well as business recognition of professional and sales services in the spirit of freedom of movement. This latter aspect, however, has not yet been extended to blue-collar workers. As such, Canada's service industry is the fastest growing sector of the economy, accounting for the employment of roughly ten million Canadians and two-thirds of the workforce, as well as providing 90% of all new jobs in Canada in the last several years. Canada's export of services around the world totals an average of $24 billion per year, with business and professional services accounting for 20% of these exports. NAFTA obliges one country's service providers to treat the other country's no less favorably than their own for domestic and cross-border sales, distribution and the right of establishment of facilities, providing for mutually acceptable professional licensing standards. However, this equal employment provision in the Member States must go further to protect against any form of discrimination, including **class**.

While the Canada United States Free Trade Agreement established the first comprehensive set of principles governing trade in services, NAFTA broadens these protections and extends them to Mexico. Virtually all services are covered by NAFTA, with key sectors being: accounting, architecture, land transport, publishing, consulting, commercial education, environmental services, enhanced telecommunications, advertising, broadcasting, construction, tourism, engineering, health care, management and legal services. Each country has also excluded certain sensitive sectors from coverage, such that Mexico will not liberalize services of public notaries, which are specifically reserved to Mexicans by the Mexican Constitution, and Canada has retained its cultural exclusion, which affects the entertainment and publishing industries. NAFTA does not remove or weaken licensing and certification requirements but, consistent with the principle of non-discrimination, licensing of professionals, such as lawyers, doctors and accountants, are based on objective criteria aimed at ensuring competence, not nationality, so that NAFTA does not permit American, Mexican or Canadian professionals to practice in the other Member countries, unless they have undergone the same licensing and certification procedures as a National professional.

The Preamble of the North American Free Trade Agreement states:

> The Government of Canada, the Government of the United Mexican States and the Government of the United States of America, resolved to:
>
> STRENGTHEN the special bonds of friendship and cooperation among their nations;
>
> CONTRIBUTE to the harmonious development and expansion of world trade and provide a catalyst to broader international cooperation;
>
> CREATE an expanded and secure market for the goods and services produced in their territories;
>
> REDUCE distortions to trade;
>
> ESTABLISH clear and mutually advantageous rules governing their trade;
>
> ENSURE a predictable commercial framework for business planning and investment;
>
> BUILD on their respective rights and obligations under the *General Agreement on Tariffs and Trade* and other multilateral and bilateral instruments of cooperation;
>
> ENHANCE the competitiveness of their firms in global markets;
>
> FOSTER creativity and innovation, and promote trade in goods and services that are the subject of intellectual property rights;
>
> CREATE new employment opportunities and improve working conditions and living standards in their respective territories;
>
> UNDERTAKE each of the preceding in a manner consistent with environmental protection and conservation;
>
> PRESERVE their flexibility to safeguard the public welfare;
>
> PROMOTE sustainable development;
>
> STRENGTHEN the development and enforcement of environmental laws and regulations; and

PROTECT, enhance and enforce basic workers' rights.[26]

Under the agreement, in terms of service providers, Article 1201 applies to measures adopted or maintained by a Party relating to cross-border trade in services by service providers of another Party, including measures respecting the production, distribution, marketing, sale and delivery of a service; the purchase or use of, or payment for, a service; the access to and use of distribution and transportation systems in connection with the provision of a service; the presence in its territory of a service provider of another Party; and the provision of a bond or other form of financial security as a condition for the provision of a service.[27]

Articles 1202 and 1203 provide that each Party shall accord to service providers of another Party treatment no less favorable than that it accords, in like circumstances, to service providers of any other Party or of a non-Party.[28] Further, Article 1208 maintains that each Party shall set out in its Schedule to Annex VI its commitments to liberalize quantitative restrictions, licensing requirements, performance requirements or other non-discriminatory measures.[29]

Professional services are defined in Article 1213 as services, the provision of which requires specialized post-secondary education, or equivalent training or experience, and for which the right to practice is granted or restricted by a Party, but does not include services provided by trades-persons or vessel and aircraft crew members.[30]

Important to all workers, especially those who are educated, Article 1210 provides for licensing and certification requirements:

> 1210.1. With a view to ensuring that any measure adopted or maintained by a Party relating to the licensing or certification of nationals of another Party does not constitute an unnecessary barrier to trade, each Party shall endeavor to ensure that any such measure:
>
> (a) is based on objective and transparent criteria, such as competence and the ability to provide a service;
>
> (b) is not more burdensome than necessary to ensure the quality of a service; and
>
> (c) does not constitute a disguised restriction on the cross-border provision of a service.
>
> 2. … a Party shall not be required to extend to a service provider of another Party the benefits of recognition of education, experience, licenses or certifications obtained in another country, whether such recognition was accorded unilaterally or by arrangement or agreement with that other country. The Party according

26 North American Free Trade Agreement, at the Preamble.
27 Ibid., at Article 1201.
28 Ibid., at Article 1202, 1203.
29 Ibid., at Article 1208.
30 Ibid., at Article 1213.

> such recognition shall afford any interested Party an adequate opportunity to demonstrate that education, experience, licenses or certifications obtained in that other Party's territory should also be recognized or to negotiate and enter into an agreement or arrangement of comparable effect.
> 3. … a Party shall eliminate any citizenship or permanent residency requirement for the licensing and certification of professional service providers in its territory… .[31]

Further, licensing and certification standards for professionals are provided for in Annex 1210.5.A.2:

> Annex 1210.5.A.2. The Parties shall encourage the relevant bodies in their respective territories to develop mutually acceptable standards and criteria for licensing and certification of professional service providers and to provide recommendations on mutual recognition to the Commission.[32]

Additionally, important in the fight against class discrimination, Annex 1210.5.A.3. provides for standards and education criteria to be developed:

> Annex 1210.5.A.3. The standards and criteria referred to in paragraph 2 may be developed with regard to the following matters:
> (a) education: accreditation of schools or academic programs;
> (b) examinations: qualifying examinations for licensing, including alternative methods of assessment such as oral examinations and interviews;
> (c) experience: length and nature of experience required for licensing;
> (d) conduct and ethics: standards of professional conduct and the nature of disciplinary action for non-conformity with those standards;
> (e) professional development and re-certification: continuing education and ongoing requirements to maintain professional certification;
> (f) scope of practice: extent of, or limitations on, permissible activities;
> (g) local knowledge: requirements for knowledge of such matters as local laws, regulations, language, geography or climate; and
> (h) consumer protection: alternatives to residency requirements, including bonding, professional liability insurance and client restitution funds, to provide for the protection of consumers.[33]

Finally, Annex 1210.5.B.1. provides that each Party shall, in implementing its obligations and commitments regarding foreign legal consultants as set out in its relevant Schedules and subject to any reservations therein, ensure that a national

31 Ibid., at Article 1210.
32 Ibid., at Annex 1210.5.A.2.
33 Ibid., at Annex 1210.5.A.3.

of another Party is permitted to practice or advise on the law of any country in which that national is authorized to practice as a lawyer.[34]

Article 1213 defines professional services as:

> services, the provision of which requires specialized post-secondary education, or equivalent training or experience, and for which the right to practice is granted or restricted by a Party, but does not include services provided by trades-persons or vessel and aircraft crew members.[35]

In terms of the temporary entry for people to conduct business, Chapter 16 and specifically Article 1601 specify:

> 1601. This Chapter reflects the preferential trading relationship between the Parties, the desirability of facilitating temporary entry on a reciprocal basis and of establishing transparent criteria and procedures for temporary entry, and the need to ensure border security and to protect the domestic labor force and permanent employment in their respective territories.[36]

Article 1602 outlines the general obligations:

> 1602.1. Each Party shall apply its measures relating to the provisions of this Chapter in accordance with Article 1601 and, in particular, shall apply expeditiously those measures so as to avoid unduly impairing or delaying trade in goods or services or conduct of investment activities under this Agreement.
> 2. The Parties shall endeavor to develop and adopt common criteria, definitions and interpretations for the implementation of this Chapter.[37]

Additional requirements are noted in Annex 1603, in order to gain entry for different classes of individuals in employment situations. Section A provides for business visitors:

> Annex 1603.A.1. Each Party shall grant temporary entry to a business person seeking to engage in a business activity set out in Appendix 1603.A.1, without requiring that person to obtain an employment authorization, provided that the business person otherwise complies with existing immigration measures applicable to temporary entry, on presentation of:
> (a) proof of citizenship of a Party;
> (b) documentation demonstrating that the business person will be so engaged and describing the purpose of entry; and

34 Ibid., at Annex 1210.5.B.1.
35 Ibid., at Article 1213.
36 Ibid., at Article 1601.
37 Ibid., at Article 1602.

(c) evidence demonstrating that the proposed business activity is international in scope and that the business person is not seeking to enter the local labor market.

2. Each Party shall provide that a business person may satisfy the requirements of paragraph 1(c) by demonstrating that:

(a) the primary source of remuneration for the proposed business activity is outside the territory of the Party granting temporary entry; and

(b) the business person's principal place of business and the actual place of accrual of profits, at least predominantly, remain outside such territory.

A Party shall normally accept an oral declaration as to the principal place of business and the actual place of accrual of profits. Where the Party requires further proof, it shall normally consider a letter from the employer attesting to these matters as sufficient proof.

3. Each Party shall grant temporary entry to a business person seeking to engage in a business activity other than those set out in Appendix 1603.A.1, without requiring that person to obtain an employment authorization, on a basis no less favorable than that provided under the existing provisions of the measures set out in Appendix 1603.A.3, provided that the business person otherwise complies with existing immigration measures applicable to temporary entry.

4. No Party may:

(a) as a condition for temporary entry under paragraph 1 or 3, require prior approval procedures, petitions, labor certification tests or other procedures of similar effect; or

(b) impose or maintain any numerical restriction relating to temporary entry under paragraph 1 or 3.

5. Notwithstanding paragraph 4, a Party may require a business person seeking temporary entry under this Section to obtain a visa or its equivalent prior to entry. Before imposing a visa requirement, the Party shall consult with a Party whose business persons would be affected with a view to avoiding the imposition of the requirement. With respect to an existing visa requirement, a Party shall consult, on request, with a Party whose business persons are subject to the requirement with a view to its removal.[38]

Section B provides for traders and investors:

Annex 1603.B.1. Each Party shall grant temporary entry and provide confirming documentation to a business person seeking to:

(a) carry on substantial trade in goods or services principally between the territory of the Party of which the business person is a citizen and the territory of the Party into which entry is sought, or

(b) establish, develop, administer or provide advice or key technical services to the operation of an investment to which the business person

38 Ibid., at Annex 1603.A.

or the business person's enterprise has committed, or is in the process of committing, a substantial amount of capital, in a capacity that is supervisory, executive or involves essential skills, provided that the business person otherwise complies with existing immigration measures applicable to temporary entry.

2. No Party may:

(a) as a condition for temporary entry under paragraph 1, require labor certification tests or other procedures of similar effect; or

(b) impose or maintain any numerical restriction relating to temporary entry under paragraph 1.

3. Notwithstanding paragraph 2, a Party may require a business person seeking temporary entry under this Section to obtain a visa or its equivalent prior to entry.[39]

Section C provides for intra-company transferees:

Annex 1603.C.1. Each Party shall grant temporary entry and provide confirming documentation to a business person employed by an enterprise who seeks to render services to that enterprise or a subsidiary or affiliate thereof, in a capacity that is managerial, executive or involves specialized knowledge, provided that the business person otherwise complies with existing immigration measures applicable to temporary entry. A Party may require the business person to have been employed continuously by the enterprise for one year within the three-year period immediately preceding the date of the application for admission.

2. No Party may:

(a) as a condition for temporary entry under paragraph 1, require labor certification tests or other procedures of similar effect; or

(b) impose or maintain any numerical restriction relating to temporary entry under paragraph 1.

3. Notwithstanding paragraph 2, a Party may require a business person seeking temporary entry under this Section to obtain a visa or its equivalent prior to entry. Before imposing a visa requirement, the Party shall consult with a Party whose business persons would be affected with a view to avoiding the imposition of the requirement. With respect to an existing visa requirement, a Party shall consult, on request, with a Party whose business persons are subject to the requirement with a view to its removal.[40]

Section D provides for professionals:

Annex 1603.D.1. Each Party shall grant temporary entry and provide confirming documentation to a business person seeking to engage in a business activity at a

---

39 Ibid., at Annex 1603.B.

40 Ibid., at Annex 1603.C.

professional level in a profession set out in Appendix 1603.D.1, if the business person otherwise complies with existing immigration measures applicable to temporary entry, on presentation of:

(a) proof of citizenship of a Party; and

(b) documentation demonstrating that the business person will be so engaged and describing the purpose of entry.

2. No Party may:

(a) as a condition for temporary entry under paragraph 1, require prior approval procedures, petitions, labor certification tests or other procedures of similar effect; or

(b) impose or maintain any numerical restriction relating to temporary entry under paragraph 1.

3. Notwithstanding paragraph 2, a Party may require a business person seeking temporary entry under this Section to obtain a visa or its equivalent prior to entry. Before imposing a visa requirement, the Party shall consult with a Party whose business persons would be affected with a view to avoiding the imposition of the requirement. With respect to an existing visa requirement, a Party shall consult, on request, with a Party whose business persons are subject to the requirement with a view to its removal.

4. Notwithstanding paragraphs 1 and 2, a Party may establish an annual numerical limit, which shall be set out in Appendix 1603.D.4, regarding temporary entry of business persons of another Party seeking to engage in business activities at a professional level in a profession set out in Appendix 1603.D.1, if the Parties concerned have not agreed otherwise prior to the date of entry into force of this Agreement for those Parties. In establishing such a limit, the Party shall consult with the other Party concerned.

5. A Party establishing a numerical limit pursuant to paragraph 4, unless the Parties concerned agree otherwise:

(a) shall, for each year after the first year after the date of entry into force of this Agreement, consider increasing the numerical limit set out in Appendix 1603.D.4 by an amount to be established in consultation with the other Party concerned, taking into account the demand for temporary entry under this Section;

(b) shall not apply its procedures established pursuant to paragraph 1 to the temporary entry of a business person subject to the numerical limit, but may require the business person to comply with its other procedures applicable to the temporary entry of professionals; and

(c) may, in consultation with the other Party concerned, grant temporary entry under paragraph 1 to a business person who practices in a profession where accreditation, licensing, and certification requirements are mutually recognized by those Parties.

6. Nothing in paragraph 4 or 5 shall be construed to limit the ability of a business person to seek temporary entry under a Party's applicable immigration measures

relating to the entry of professionals other than those adopted or maintained pursuant to paragraph 1.[41]

Finally, Appendix 1603.D.1 outlines the different professions provided for under NAFTA, along with the minimum educational requirements and alternative credentials, with education an important tool for advancement to end class discrimination:

Appendix 1603D.1.

Accountant – Baccalaureate or Licenciatura Degree; or C.P.A., C.A., C.G.A. or C.M.A.

Architect – Baccalaureate or Licenciatura Degree; or state/provincial license(2)

Computer Systems Analyst – Baccalaureate or Licenciatura Degree; or Post-Secondary Diploma(3) or Post-Secondary Certificate(4), and three years experience

Disaster Relief Insurance Claims Adjuster (claims adjuster employed by an insurance company located in the territory of a Party, or an independent claims adjuster) – Baccalaureate or Licenciatura Degree, and successful completion of training in the appropriate areas of insurance adjustment pertaining to disaster relief claims; or three years experience in claims adjustment and successful completion of training in the appropriate areas of insurance adjustment pertaining to disaster relief claims

Economist – Baccalaureate or Licenciatura Degree

Engineer – Baccalaureate or Licenciatura Degree; or state/provincial license

Forester – Baccalaureate or Licenciatura Degree; or state/provincial license

Graphic Designer – Baccalaureate or Licenciatura Degree; or Post-Secondary Diploma or Post-Secondary Certificate, and three years experience

Hotel Manager – Baccalaureate or Licenciatura Degree in hotel/restaurant management; or Post-Secondary Diploma or Post-Secondary Certificate in hotel/restaurant management, and three years experience in hotel/restaurant management

41 Ibid., at Annex 1603.D.

Industrial Designer – Baccalaureate or Licenciatura Degree; or Post-Secondary Diploma or Post-Secondary Certificate, and three years experience

Interior Designer – Baccalaureate or Licenciatura Degree; or Post-Secondary Diploma or Post-Secondary Certificate, and three years experience

Land Surveyor – Baccalaureate or Licenciatura Degree; or state/provincial/federal license

Landscape Architect – Baccalaureate or Licenciatura Degree

Lawyer (including Notary in the Province of Quebec) – LL.B., J.D., LL.L., B.C.L. or Licenciatura Degree (five years); or membership in a state/provincial bar

Librarian – M.L.S. or B.L.S. (for which another Baccalaureate or Licenciatura Degree was a prerequisite)

Management Consultant – Baccalaureate or Licenciatura Degree; or equivalent professional experience as established by statement or professional credential attesting to five years experience as a management consultant, or five years experience in a field of specialty related to the consulting agreement

Mathematician (including Statistician) – Baccalaureate or Licenciatura Degree

Range Manager/ Range Conservationalist – Baccalaureate or Licenciatura Degree

Research Assistant (working in a post-secondary educational institution) – Baccalaureate or Licenciatura Degree

Scientific Technician/Technologist(5) – Possession of

a. theoretical knowledge of any of the following disciplines: agricultural sciences, astronomy, biology, chemistry, engineering, forestry, geology, geophysics, meteorology or physics; and
b. the ability to solve practical problems in any of those disciplines, or the ability to apply principles of any of those disciplines to basic or applied research

Social Worker – Baccalaureate or Licenciatura Degree

Sylviculturist (including Forestry Specialist) – Baccalaureate or Licenciatura Degree

Technical Publications Writer – Baccalaureate or Licenciatura Degree; or Post-Secondary Diploma or Post-Secondary Certificate, and three years experience

Urban Planner (including Geographer) – Baccalaureate or Licenciatura Degree

Vocational Counsellor – Baccalaureate or Licenciatura Degree

Medical/Allied Professional

Dentist – D.D.S., D.M.D., Doctor en Odontologia or Doctor en Cirugia Dental; or state/provincial license

Dietitian – Baccalaureate or Licenciatura Degree; or state/provincial license

Medical Laboratory Technologist (Canada)/Medical Technologist (Mexico)(6) – Baccalaureate or Licenciatura Degree; or Post-Secondary Diploma or Post-Secondary *Certificate, and three years experience*

Nutritionist – Baccalaureate or Licenciatura Degree

Occupational Therapist – Baccalaureate or Licenciatura Degree; or state/provincial license

Pharmacist – Baccalaureate or Licenciatura Degree; or state/provincial license

Physician (teaching or research only) – M.D. or Doctor en Medicina; or state/provincial license

Physiotherapist/Physical Therapist – Baccalaureate or Licenciatura Degree; or state/provincial license

Psychologist – State/provincial license; or Licenciatura Degree

Recreational Therapist – Baccalaureate or Licenciatura Degree

Registered Nurse – State/provincial license; or Licenciatura Degree

Veterinarian – D.V.M., D.M.V. or Doctor en Veterinaria; or state/provincial license

Scientist

Agriculturist (including Agronomist) – Baccalaureate or Licenciatura Degree

Animal Breeder – Baccalaureate or Licenciatura Degree

Animal Scientist – Baccalaureate or Licenciatura Degree

Apiculturist – Baccalaureate or Licenciatura Degree

Astronomer – Baccalaureate or Licenciatura Degree

Biochemist – Baccalaureate or Licenciatura Degree

Biologist – Baccalaureate or Licenciatura Degree

Chemist – Baccalaureate or Licenciatura Degree

Dairy Scientist – Baccalaureate or Licenciatura Degree

Entomologist – Baccalaureate or Licenciatura Degree

Epidemiologist – Baccalaureate or Licenciatura Degree

Geneticist – Baccalaureate or Licenciatura Degree
Geologist – Baccalaureate or Licenciatura Degree
Geochemist – Baccalaureate or Licenciatura Degree
Geophysicist (including Oceanographer in Mexico and the United States) – Baccalaureate or Licenciatura Degree
Horticulturist – Baccalaureate or Licenciatura Degree
Meteorologist – Baccalaureate or Licenciatura Degree
Pharmacologist – Baccalaureate or Licenciatura Degree
Physicist (including Oceanographer in Canada) – Baccalaureate or Licenciatura Degree
Plant Breeder – Baccalaureate or Licenciatura Degree
Poultry Scientist – Baccalaureate or Licenciatura Degree
Soil Scientist – Baccalaureate or Licenciatura Degree
Zoologist – Baccalaureate or Licenciatura Degree

Teacher
College – Baccalaureate or Licenciatura Degree
Seminary – Baccalaureate or Licenciatura Degree
University – Baccalaureate or Licenciatura Degree[42]

There are a number of institutions that are part of NAFTA. Article 2001 provides for the Free Trade Commission:

> 2001.1. The Parties hereby establish the Free Trade Commission, comprising cabinet-level representatives of the Parties or their designees.
> 2. The Commission shall:
> (a) supervise the implementation of this Agreement;
> (b) oversee its further elaboration;
> (c) resolve disputes that may arise regarding its interpretation or application;
> (d) supervise the work of all committees and working groups established under this Agreement, referred to in Annex 2001.2; and
> (e) consider any other matter that may affect the operation of this Agreement.
> 3. The Commission may:
> (a) establish, and delegate responsibilities to, ad hoc or standing committees, working groups or expert groups;
> (b) seek the advice of nongovernmental persons or groups; and
> (c) take such other action in the exercise of its functions as the Parties may agree.[43]

42 Ibid., at Appendix 1603.D.1.
43 Ibid., at Article 2001.

Further, Article 2002 provides for the Secretariat:

> 2002.1. The Commission shall establish and oversee a Secretariat comprising national Sections.
> 2. Each Party shall:
> (a) establish a permanent office of its Section;
> (b) be responsible for
> (i) the operation and costs of its Section, and
> (ii) the remuneration and payment of expenses of panelists and members of committees and scientific review boards established under this Agreement, as set out in Annex 2002.2;
> (c) designate an individual to serve as Secretary for its Section, who shall be responsible for its administration and management; and
> (d) notify the Commission of the location of its Section's office.
> 3. The Secretariat shall:
> (a) provide assistance to the Commission;
> (b) provide administrative assistance to
> (i) panels and committees established under Chapter Nineteen (Review and Dispute Settlement in Antidumping and Countervailing Duty Matters), in accordance with the procedures established pursuant to Article 1908, and
> (ii) panels established under this Chapter, in accordance with procedures established pursuant to Article 2012; and
> (c) as the Commission may direct
> (i) support the work of other committees and groups established under this Agreement, and
> (ii) otherwise facilitate the operation of this Agreement.[44]

Importantly, in terms of a dispute settlement, cooperation is stressed under Article 2003:

> 2003. The Parties shall at all times endeavor to agree on the interpretation and application of this Agreement, and shall make every attempt through cooperation and consultations to arrive at a mutually satisfactory resolution of any matter that might affect its operation.[45]

Recourse to dispute settlement procedures is enunciated under Articles 1606 and 2004:

> 1606.1. A Party may not initiate proceedings under Article 2007 (Commission – Good Offices, Conciliation and Mediation) regarding a refusal to grant

44 Ibid., at Article 2002.
45 Ibid., at Article 2003.

temporary entry under this Chapter or a particular case arising under Article 1602(1) unless:

(a) the matter involves a pattern of practice; and

(b) the business person has exhausted the available administrative remedies regarding the particular matter.

2. The remedies referred to in paragraph (1) (b) shall be deemed to be exhausted if a final determination in the matter has not been issued by the competent authority within one year of the institution of an administrative proceeding, and the failure to issue a determination is not attributable to delay caused by the business person.[46]

2004. Except for the matters covered in Chapter Nineteen (Review and Dispute Settlement in Antidumping and Countervailing Duty Matters) and as otherwise provided in this Agreement, the dispute settlement provisions of this Chapter shall apply with respect to the avoidance or settlement of all disputes between the Parties regarding the interpretation or application of this Agreement or wherever a Party considers that an actual or proposed measure of another Party is or would be inconsistent with the obligations of this Agreement or cause nullification or impairment in the sense of Annex 2004.[47]

Further, in terms of panel proceedings, a request for an arbitral panel is contained in Article 2008:

2008.1. If the Commission has convened pursuant to Article 2007(4), and the matter has not been resolved within:

(a) 30 days thereafter,

(b) 30 days after the Commission has convened in respect of the matter most recently referred to it, where proceedings have been consolidated pursuant to Article 2007(6), or

(c) such other period as the consulting Parties may agree,

any consulting Party may request in writing the establishment of an arbitral panel. The requesting Party shall deliver the request to the other Parties and to its Section of the Secretariat.

2. On delivery of the request, the Commission shall establish an arbitral panel.

3. A third Party that considers it has a substantial interest in the matter shall be entitled to join as a complaining Party on delivery of written notice of its intention to participate to the disputing Parties and its Section of the Secretariat. The notice shall be delivered at the earliest possible time, and in any event no later than seven days after the date of delivery of a request by a Party for the establishment of a panel.

46 Ibid., at Article 1606.

47 Ibid., at Article 2004.

> 4. If a third Party does not join as a complaining Party in accordance with paragraph 3, it normally shall refrain thereafter from initiating or continuing:
> (a) a dispute settlement procedure under this Agreement, or
> (b) a dispute settlement proceeding in the GATT on grounds that are substantially equivalent to those available to that Party under this Agreement,
> regarding the same matter in the absence of a significant change in economic or commercial circumstances.
> 5. Unless otherwise agreed by the disputing Parties, the panel shall be established and perform its functions in a manner consistent with the provisions of this Chapter.[48]

The rules of procedure are outlined in Article 2012:

> 2012.1. The Commission shall establish by January 1, 1994, Model Rules of Procedure, in accordance with the following principles:
> (a) the procedures shall assure a right to at least one hearing before the panel as well as the opportunity to provide initial and rebuttal written submissions; and
> (b) the panel's hearings, deliberations and initial report, and all written submissions to and communications with the panel shall be confidential.
> 2. Unless the disputing Parties otherwise agree, the panel shall conduct its proceedings in accordance with the Model Rules of Procedure.
> 3. Unless the disputing Parties otherwise agree within 20 days from the date of the delivery of the request for the establishment of the panel, the terms of reference shall be:
> 'To examine, in the light of the relevant provisions of the Agreement, the matter referred to the Commission (as set out in the request for a Commission meeting) and to make findings, determinations and recommendations as provided in Article 2016(2)'.[49]

Third party participation is permitted under Article 2013:

> 2013. A Party that is not a disputing Party, on delivery of a written notice to the disputing Parties and to its Section of the Secretariat, shall be entitled to attend all hearings, to make written and oral submissions to the panel and to receive written submissions of the disputing Parties.

The panel's final report is contained in Article 2017:

48 Ibid., at Article 2008.
49 Ibid., at Article 2012.

> 2017.1. The panel shall present to the disputing Parties a final report, including any separate opinions on matters not unanimously agreed, within 30 days of presentation of the initial report, unless the disputing Parties otherwise agree.[50]

Implementation of the final report is stressed under Article 2018:

> 2018.1. On receipt of the final report of a panel, the disputing Parties shall agree on the resolution of the dispute, which normally shall conform with the determinations and recommendations of the panel, and shall notify their Sections of the Secretariat of any agreed resolution of any dispute.[51]

Importantly, non-implementation and the suspension of benefits are provided for under Article 2019:

> 2019.1. If in its final report a panel has determined that a measure is inconsistent with the obligations of this Agreement or causes nullification or impairment in the sense of Annex 2004 and the Party complained against has not reached agreement with any complaining Party on a mutually satisfactory resolution pursuant to Article 2018(1) within 30 days of receiving the final report, such complaining Party may suspend the application to the Party complained against of benefits of equivalent effect until such time as they have reached agreement on a resolution of the dispute.
>
> 2. In considering what benefits to suspend pursuant to paragraph 1:
>
> (a) a complaining Party should first seek to suspend benefits in the same sector or sectors as that affected by the measure or other matter that the panel has found to be inconsistent with the obligations of this Agreement or to have caused nullification or impairment in the sense of Annex 2004; and
>
> (b) a complaining Party that considers it is not practicable or effective to suspend benefits in the same sector or sectors may suspend benefits in other sectors.[52]

In terms of domestic proceedings and a private commercial dispute settlement, Article 2020 provides for referrals of matters from judicial or administrative proceedings:

> 2020.1. If an issue of interpretation or application of this Agreement arises in any domestic judicial or administrative proceeding of a Party that any Party considers would merit its intervention, or if a court or administrative body solicits the views of a Party, that Party shall notify the other Parties and its Section of the

50 Ibid., at Article 2017.
51 Ibid., at Article 2018.
52 Ibid., at Article 2019.

> Secretariat. The Commission shall endeavor to agree on an appropriate response as expeditiously as possible.
> 2. The Party in whose territory the court or administrative body is located shall submit any agreed interpretation of the Commission to the court or administrative body in accordance with the rules of that forum.
> 3. If the Commission is unable to agree, any Party may submit its own views to the court or administrative body in accordance with the rules of that forum.[53]

Further, private rights are guaranteed under Article 2021:

> 2021. No Party may provide for a right of action under its domestic law against any other Party on the ground that a measure of another Party is inconsistent with this Agreement.[54]

Finally, Article 2022 provides for alternative dispute resolution:

> 2022.1. Each Party shall, to the maximum extent possible, encourage and facilitate the use of arbitration and other means of alternative dispute resolution for the settlement of international commercial disputes between private parties in the free trade area.
> 2. To this end, each Party shall provide appropriate procedures to ensure observance of agreements to arbitrate and for the recognition and enforcement of arbitral awards in such disputes.[55]

North American Agreement on Labor Cooperation (NAALC)

The North American Agreement on Labor Cooperation (NAALC) 1993, a side agreement to NAFTA, promotes the enforcement of national labor laws and transparency in their administration, important for equal rights of workers. Through NAALC, the NAFTA partners seek to improve working conditions and living standards in all three countries, and commit themselves to promoting principles that protect, enhance and enforce basic workers' rights. To accomplish these goals, the NAALC creates mechanisms for cooperative activities and intergovernmental consultations, as well as for independent evaluations and dispute settlement related to the enforcement of labor laws. Public submissions made under the NAALC have led to public hearings, ministerial consultations and action plans to address concerns raised. In addition, the NAFTA partners have established cooperative programs and technical exchanges on a number of issues such as industrial relations, health and safety, child labor, gender equity and migrant worker issues.

---

53 Ibid., at Article 2020.
54 Ibid., at Article 2021.
55 Ibid., at Article 2022.

The agreement reflects the shared recognition of the United States, Mexico and Canada that their mutual prosperity depends on the promotion of fair and open competition based on innovation and rising levels of productivity and quality with due regard for the importance of labor laws and principles. The Agreement increases cooperation and promotes greater understanding among the Parties in a broad range of labor areas; establishes the obligation of each Party to ensure the enforcement of its domestic labor laws; provides mechanisms to permit problem-solving consultations; enables the Parties to initiate evaluations of patterns of practice by independent committees of experts; and allows for dispute settlement procedures.

The general obligation of each Party is to ensure the effective enforcement of its own labor law. Specific obligations refer to publication of labor laws and related regulations and procedures, and to promotion of awareness of and compliance with them. Other obligations include government enforcement actions for promoting compliance and effective enforcement of its labor law, covering such matters as: appointing and training of inspectors, monitoring compliance and examining suspected violations; carrying out inspections, mandatory reporting and record keeping; encouraging worker–management committees; providing mediation, conciliation, or arbitration services; and initiating in a timely manner enforcement actions seeking appropriate remedies. Each Party is committed to ensuring access by persons with a legally recognized interest to administrative, judicial and related tribunals, including recourse to procedures by which labor rights can be enforced in a binding fashion. The Agreement also provides that such tribunals and proceedings before them would be fair and comply with due process.

A trinational Labor Commission is created to facilitate the achievement of the objectives of the Agreement and to deal with labor issues in a cooperative and consultative manner that duly respects the three nations' sovereignty. The Labor Commission consists of a Ministerial Council, an International Coordinating Secretariat (ICS) and three National Administrative Offices (NAOs). The Ministerial Council consists of the labor Ministers from the three signatory countries, who supervise the implementation of the Agreement, including directing the work of the ICS, and promote cooperative activities. An ICS, under the direction of the Ministerial Council, carries out the day-to-day work of the Commission, and is responsible for assisting the Council in its work, for gathering and periodically publishing information on labor matters in Canada, the United States and Mexico, for planning and coordinating cooperative activities, and for supporting any working groups or evaluation committees established by the Ministerial Council. The NAOs, established by each Party, serve as a point of contact for and facilitate the provision of information to other Parties on domestic law and practice, receive public communications, conduct preliminary reviews and promote the exchange of information relevant to the Agreement.

As to resolution of disputes, if the Council cannot resolve a dispute involving a Party's alleged persistent pattern of failure to effectively enforce labor laws with respect to health and safety, child labor and minimum wage, relating to a situation involving mutually recognized labor laws and the production of goods or services traded between the Parties, any Party may request an arbitral panel, which will be established on a two-thirds vote of the council, and panelists will normally be chosen from a previously agreed roster of experts, including experts on labor matters. With the approval of the disputing Parties, a panel may seek information and technical advice from any person or body that it deems appropriate, and the report of the panel will be made publicly available five days after it is transmitted to the Parties. If a panel makes a finding that a Party has engaged in a persistent pattern of failure to effectively enforce its labor laws, the Parties may, within 60 days, agree on a mutually satisfactory action plan to remedy the non-enforcement. If there is no agreed action plan, then between 60 and 120 days after the final panel report, the panel may be reconvened to evaluate an action plan proposed by the Party complained against or to set out an action plan in its stead. Further, the panel would also make a determination on the imposition of monetary enforcement assessments on the alleged offending Party. The panel may be reconvened at any time to determine if an action plan is being fully implemented, and if not, the panel is to impose a monetary enforcement assessment on the alleged offending Party. In the event that a Party complained against fails to pay a monetary enforcement assessment or continues in its failure to enforce its labor law and minimum wage, the Party is liable for ongoing enforcement actions. In the case of Canada, the Commission, on the request of a complaining Party, collects the monetary enforcement assessment and enforces an action plan in summary proceedings before a Canadian court of competent jurisdiction. In the case of Mexico and the United States, the complaining Party or Parties may suspend NAFTA benefits based on the amount of the assessment.

The Preamble to the North American Agreement on Labor Cooperation (NAALC) states that the Government of the United States of America, the Government of Canada and the Government of the United Mexican States undertake the agreement:

> RECALLING their resolve in the North American Free Trade Agreement (NAFTA) to:
> create an expanded and secure market for the goods and services produced in their territories,
> enhance the competitiveness of their firms in global markets,
> create new employment opportunities and improve working conditions and living standards in their respective territories, and
> protect, enhance and enforce basic workers' rights;
>
> AFFIRMING their continuing respect for each Party's constitution and law;
>
> DESIRING to build on their respective international commitments and to strengthen their cooperation on labor matters;

> RECOGNIZING that their mutual prosperity depends on the promotion of competition based on innovation and rising levels of productivity and quality;
>
> SEEKING to complement the economic opportunities created by the NAFTA with the human resource development, labor-management cooperation and continuous learning that characterize high-productivity economies;
>
> ACKNOWLEDGING that protecting basic workers' rights will encourage firms to adopt high-productivity competitive strategies;
> RESOLVED to promote, in accordance with their respective laws, high-skill, high-productivity economic development in North America by:
> investing in continuous human resource development, including for entry into the workforce and during periods of unemployment;
> promoting employment security and career opportunities for all workers through referral and other employment services;
> strengthening labor-management cooperation to promote greater dialogue between worker organizations and employers and to foster creativity and productivity in the workplace;
> promoting higher living standards as productivity increases;
> encouraging consultation and dialogue between labor, business and government both in each country and in North America;
> fostering investment with due regard for the importance of labor laws and principles;
> encouraging employers and employees in each country to comply with labor laws and to work together in maintaining a progressive, fair, safe and healthy working environment;
>
> BUILDING on existing institutions and mechanisms in Canada, Mexico and the United States to achieve the preceding economic and social goals; and
>
> CONVINCED of the benefits to be gained from further cooperation between them on labor matters.[56]

The objectives of the agreement are outlined in Article 1:

> 1(a) improve working conditions and living standards in each Party's territory;
> (b) promote, to the maximum extent possible, the labor principles set out in Annex 1;
> (c) encourage cooperation to promote innovation and rising levels of productivity and quality;

56 North American Agreement on Labor Cooperation (NAALC), at the Preamble.

> (d) encourage publication and exchange of information, data development and coordination, and joint studies to enhance mutually beneficial understanding of the laws and institutions governing labor in each Party's territory;
> (e) pursue cooperative labor-related activities on the basis of mutual benefit;
> (f) promote compliance with, and effective enforcement by each Party of, its labor law; and
> (g) foster transparency in the administration of labor law.[57]

As such, the Preamble to NAALC reaffirms relevant provisions of the Preamble to NAFTA and adds further shared goals related to labor matters while not specifically mentioning **class** rights. Importantly, each Party is committed, in accordance with its domestic laws, to promote equal pay and to eliminate employment discrimination, important for equal rights in employment. Further, each is committed to the following labor principles: the freedom of association, the right to bargain collectively, the right to strike, prohibition of forced labor, restrictions on labor by children and young people, minimum employment standards, prevention of occupational accidents and diseases, compensation in cases of work accidents or occupational diseases, and protection of migrant workers. The Agreement sets forth the following general objectives: improving working conditions and living standards, promoting compliance with and effective enforcement of labor laws, promoting the Agreement's principles through cooperation and coordination, and promoting the publication and exchange of information to enhance the mutual understanding of the Parties' laws, institutions and legal systems.

Specifically, in terms of Obligations of the Parties and the Levels of Protection, Article 2 holds:

> 2. Affirming full respect for each Party's constitution, and recognizing the right of each Party to establish its own domestic labor standards, and to adopt or modify accordingly its labor laws and regulations, each Party shall ensure that its labor laws and regulations provide for high labor standards, consistent with high quality and productivity workplaces, and shall continue to strive to improve those standards in that light.[58]

Importantly, government enforcement action is established under Article 3, which states that each Party shall promote compliance with and effectively enforce its labor law through appropriate government action, such as:

> 3(a) appointing and training inspectors;
> (b) monitoring compliance and investigating suspected violations, including through on-site inspections;
> (c) seeking assurances of voluntary compliance;

57 Ibid., at Article 1.
58 Ibid., at Article 2.

(d) requiring record keeping and reporting;
(e) encouraging the establishment of worker-management committees to address labor regulation of the workplace;
(f) providing or encouraging mediation, conciliation and arbitration services; or
(g) initiating, in a timely manner, proceedings to seek appropriate sanctions or remedies for violations of its labor law.[59]

Critical for discrimination cases, the agreement safeguards private action in Article 4:

4.1. Each Party shall ensure that persons with a legally recognized interest under its law in a particular matter have appropriate access to administrative, quasijudicial, judicial or labor tribunals for the enforcement of the Party's labor law.
2. Each Party's law shall ensure that such persons may have recourse to, as appropriate, procedures by which rights arising under:
(a) its labor law, including in respect of occupational safety and health, employment standards, industrial relations and migrant workers, and
(b) collective agreements,
can be enforced.[60]

Further, under procedural guarantees, Article 5 establishes:

5.1. Each Party shall ensure that its administrative, quasijudicial, judicial and labor tribunal proceedings for the enforcement of its labor law are fair, equitable and transparent and, to this end, each Party shall provide that:
(a) such proceedings comply with due process of law;
(b) any hearings in such proceedings are open to the public, except where the administration of justice otherwise requires;
(c) the parties to such proceedings are entitled to support or defend their respective positions and to present information or evidence; and
(d) such proceedings are not unneccessarily complicated and do not entail unreasonable charges or time limits or unwarranted delays.
2. Each Party shall provide that final decisions on the merits of the case in such proceedings are:
(a) in writing and preferably state the reasons on which the decisions are based;
(b) made available without undue delay to the parties to the proceedings and, consistent with its law, to the public; and
(c) based on information or evidence in respect of which the parties were offered the opportunity to be heard.

59 Ibid., at Article 3.
60 Ibid., at Article 4.

3. Each Party shall provide, as appropriate, that parties to such proceedings have the right, in accordance with its law, to seek review and, where warranted, correction of final decisions issued in such proceedings.
4. Each Party shall ensure that tribunals that conduct or review such proceedings are impartial and independent and do not have any substantial interest in the outcome of the matter.
5. Each Party shall provide that the parties to administrative, quasijudicial, judicial or labor tribunal proceedings may seek remedies to ensure the enforcement of their labor rights. Such remedies may include, as appropriate, orders, compliance agreements, fines, penalties, imprisonment, injunctions or emergency workplace closures.
6. Each Party may, as appropriate, adopt or maintain labor defense offices to represent or advise workers or their organizations.
7. Nothing in this Article shall be construed to require a Party to establish, or to prevent a Party from establishing, a judicial system for the enforcement of its labor law distinct from its system for the enforcement of laws in general.
8. For greater certainty, decisions by each Party's administrative, quasijudicial, judicial or labor tribunals, or pending decisions, as well as related proceedings shall not be subject to revision or reopened under the provisions of this Agreement[61]

In terms of cooperation for tolerance for class distinctions in the workplace, Article 11 underlines the importance of labor practices and cooperative activities for equality:

11.1. The Council shall promote cooperative activities between the Parties, as appropriate, regarding:

a. occupational safety and health;
b. child labor;
c. migrant workers of the Parties;
d. human resource development;
e. labor statistics;
f. work benefits;
g. social programs for workers and their families;
h. programs, methodologies and experiences regarding productivity improvement;
i. labor-management relations and collective bargaining procedures;
j. employment standards and their implementation;
k. compensation for work-related injury or illness;
l. legislation relating to the formation and operation of unions, collective bargaining and the resolution of labor disputes, and its implementation;
m. the equality of women and men in the workplace;

61 Ibid., at Article 5.

n. forms of cooperation among workers, management and government;
o. the provision of technical assistance, at the request of a Party, for the development of its labor standards; and
p. such other matters as the Parties may agree.

2. In carrying out the activities referred to in paragraph 1, the Parties may, commensurate with the availability of resources in each Party, cooperate through:
a. seminars, training sessions, working groups and conferences;
b. joint research projects, including sectoral studies;
c. technical assistance; and
d. such other means as the Parties may agree.

3. The Parties shall carry out the cooperative activities referred to in paragraph 1 with due regard for the economic, social, cultural and legislative differences between them.[62]

Importantly, Article 49 defines labor law, which should include class in Article 49.1(g) under "other grounds":

49.1. For purposes of this Agreement:
'labor law' means laws and regulations, or provisions thereof, that are directly related to:
(a) freedom of association and protection of the right to organize;
(b) the right to bargain collectively;
(c) the right to strike;
(d) prohibition of forced labor;
(e) labor protections for children and young persons;
(f) minimum employment standards, such as minimum wages and overtime pay, covering wage earners, including those not covered by collective agreements;
(g) elimination of employment discrimination on the basis of grounds such as race, religion, age, sex, or other grounds as determined by each Party's domestic laws;
(h) equal pay for men and women;
(i) prevention of occupational injuries and illnesses;
(j) compensation in cases of occupational injuries and illnesses;
(k) protection of migrant workers.[63]

Further, in Article 7 of Annex 1, labor principles are outlined, which stress the elimination of employment discrimination, and should include class discrimination under "other grounds":

62 Ibid., at Article 11.
63 Ibid., at Article 49.

> Annex 1. The following are guiding principles that the Parties are committed to promote, subject to each Party's domestic law, but do not establish common minimum standards for their domestic law. They indicate broad areas of concern where the Parties have developed, each in its own way, laws, regulations, procedures and practices that protect the rights and interests of their respective workforces.
>
> 7. Elimination of employment discrimination on such grounds as race, religion, age, sex or other grounds, subject to certain reasonable exceptions, such as, where applicable, *bona fide* occupational requirements or qualifications and established practices or rules governing retirement ages, and special measures of protection or assistance for particular groups designed to take into account the effects of discrimination.[64]

In terms of the benefits and concerns of NAFTA, the advocates argue, provides several benefits: (1) improved access to the North American market of 360 million consumers, as to manufactured goods, and business and professional services; (2) opportunities to export more products and services to Mexico, which needs capital goods, services and investment; (3) new export and investment opportunities for companies in different markets; (4) a more equitable trading relationship through the elimination of almost all Mexican tariffs and imports, with Mexico being the largest trading partner in Latin America; (5) strengthened and precise North American rules of origin to determine which goods qualify for duty free treatment in North America; 6. opportunities to bid on large government procurement contracts, with equal access to the bidding process in some sectors; (7) improved methods to settle trade disputes among Canada, Mexico and the United States; (8) protection of key domestic interests, including culture, education, water, health and social services, such as childcare, the environment and aboriginal people; (9) increased market opportunities in Latin America; and (10) enhancement of the area as a foreign investment destination through secure access to the North American market for foreign investors, with key selling points of strong transportation and telecommunication infrastructures, abundant energy resources, a highly educated and skilled workforce, comprehensive social and health services, and a stable political and economic environment.[65] Further, the benefits of free trade, according to its advocates, are: (1) increased specialization; (2) rationalization, eliminating some production and expanding in others while introducing new production techniques, entailing (a) a reduction in the number of manufacturing plants, (b) an increase in production runs, (c) an increase in trade among the Parties, and (d) a reduction in production costs;[66] (3) longer production runs in larger specialized

64 Ibid., at Annex 1, Article 7.

65 Government of Canada, *The North American Free Trade Agreement At A Glance*, Ottawa, p. 3.

66 Wigle, Randall, "The Received Wisdom of the Canada-U.S. Free Trade Qualifications", in A.R. Riggs and Tom Velk, *Canadian-American Free Trade: Historical,*

plants; and (4) easier transfer of technology. The costs of free trade are (1) transition; and (2) harmonization requirements.[67] Therefore, those in favor of the North American Free Trade Agreement argue that free trade improves efficiency and competition, stimulates production and economic growth, and opens new opportunities, supplementing and broadening the General Agreement on Tariffs and Trade (GATT) out of which grew the World Trade Organization (WTO).[68]

Overall, NAFTA eliminates the majority of current tariffs and import licenses on all manufactured goods, provides greater access for service industries, permits more mobility for professional and business workers, and allows easier entry into the North American market. By lowering trade barriers, the agreement has expanded trade in all three countries. This, some argue, has led to increased employment, more choices for consumers at competitive prices and rising prosperity. From 1993, the year preceding the start of NAFTA implementation, to 2001, trade among the NAFTA nations climbed 109%, from US$297 billion to US$622 billion, and each day the NAFTA parties conduct nearly US$1.7 billion in trilateral trade. Because of NAFTA, North America is one of the most competitive, prosperous and economically integrated regions in the world. Looking at the Canadian situation, Canada's merchandise exports to its NAFTA partners climbed 95%, from US$117 billion to US$229 billion, while such exports to the rest of the world in the period increased only 5%. Looking at the Mexican situation, Mexico exported US$139 billion to its NAFTA partners, an increase of 225%, while such exports to the rest of the world increased 93%, with growth in Mexican exports accounting for more than half of the increase in Mexico's real gross domestic product. In looking at the American situation, United States merchandise exports to NAFTA partners nearly doubled from US$142 billion to US$265 billion, which was significantly higher than the 44% growth in exports to the rest of the world. [69]

An increasingly integrated North American market has stimulated capital flows, promoted the spread of technology, and contributed to increasing productivity and higher wages. Between 1994 and 2000, foreign direct investment (FDI) inflows in the NAFTA countries reached US$1.3 trillion, or about 28% of the world total, spurring economic development and growth throughout North America. The dynamic performance of exports and investment in North America has boosted economic activity and production in the region, and some argue, has contributed to the creation of more and better paying jobs in all three countries. Looking at the Canadian situation, the hourly wage rate in export-supported jobs is 35%

Political and Economic Dimensions, Montreal, 1987, p. 92.

67 Raynauld, André, "Looking Outward Again", in A.R. Riggs and Tom Velk, *Canadian American Free Trade: Historical, Political and Economic Dimensions*, Montreal, 1987, p. 86.

68 Stone, Frank, "Removing Barriers to Canada", in A. R. Riggs and Tom Velk, *Canadian-American Free Trade: Historical, Political and Economic Dimensions*, The Institute for Research in Public Policy, Montreal, 1987, p.183.

69 Government of Canada, *NAFTA at Eight*, Ottawa, 2002.

higher than in the non-export sector. Looking at the Mexican situation, Mexico's annual average capital inflow reached US$11.7 billion, three times the annual received in the seven years prior to the Agreement, and the export sector is the country's leading job creation engine, accounting for more than half of Mexican manufacturing jobs gained, with these jobs paying nearly 40% more than those in the rest of the manufacturing sector. Looking at the American situation, the United States received large flows of foreign capital, approximately US$110.2 billion per year, and employment supported by merchandise exports to NAFTA countries grew to an estimated 2.9 million jobs, with these paying between 13 and 18% more than the average American national wage.

NAFTA, according to its critics who paint a more realistic picture, is not free, since Canada has paid a high price to gain greater access to the American and Mexican markets. Canadian consumers have seen prices rise along with the advent of the Goods and Services Tax, and thousands of jobs have been lost, with unemployment hovering around the 9% level.[70] The structural adjustment costs, such as a rise in unemployment, tend to be underestimated by free trade advocates. Further, the agreement is also not about trade, and is more about the creation of a new continental model of development for the regulation of capitalism.[71] It serves more as a corporate bill of rights entrenching deregulation and market orientation in an international treaty, while at the same time eroding the national economic, as well as social and political institutions. Neo-conservatives in Canada and the Unites States wanted a deregulated continental model of development to increase capital mobility in order to restore profitability. Unfortunately, corporate managers have worked in a continent-wide drive to bring down wages and welfare state spending, by playing communities off against one another, doing away with crucial social programs. The hidden goal is to harmonize and integrate Canadian standards and institutions with the United States, and as a result, Canada's economy, political system and labor practices have been significantly altered due to closer ties with the United States economy. Canada has been forced to acquiesce to the continental model of development by continental market forces and American geopolitical pressures. Free trade is designed to restructure society to suit corporate needs, causing a threat to communities by capital-enhanced geographic mobility, which is not universally beneficial.

Many have benefited, but in the eyes of the critics, many more have been hurt by class distinctions. Sovereignty has been compromised, and the three most important industries for Canada, wood exports, agriculture and automobile manufacturing, have been hurt. Noting class discrimination, "the burden of Free Trade driven restructuring was shared unequally on a national, regional, class and gender basis".[72] The critics argue that the new capital labor accord relies on

---

70 Merrett, Christopher, *Free Trade, Neither Free Nor About Trade*, New York, 1996, p. 270.

71 Ibid., at p. 95.

72 Ibid., at p. 271.

domination instead of negotiation. Canadian workers are suffering from a "whiplash process", being forced concessions on wage benefits and work rules, and failure to acquiesce has resulted in relocation out of Canada. Mergers, temporary and part-time workers, and cheap labor increase competitiveness at a cost, free-trade-generated jobs not materializing as promised by the advocates. The Continental Model has led to polarization and segmentation of the Canadian labor force, and the discourse of universality has ended, so that there is more social inequality across Canada. The Welfare State is viewed as an impediment to profit in the eyes of business, which has chipped away at it, giving way to a "policy of stealth"; and with deregulation, budget cuts and privatization, importance is given to corporate profit at the expense of social equality.

"Continental free trade has helped to create a neo-conservative utopia where issues such as social justice and regional equality have become relics" of a bygone era.[73] While opponents of free trade are said to suffer from "emporiophobia", a fear of free trade, the effects of free trade are something to fear, since hemispheric free trade is now a possibility. It was argued that there would be a "sucking sound" of jobs going south of the border, ultimately to Mexico.[74] However, no tripartite treaty will disturb the overwhelming dominance that accrues to the United States, because of its geographic position, between Canada and Mexico. A borderland is a region jointly shared by two nations that houses people with common social characteristics in spite of the political boundaries between them, and thus the United States has a strong influence on the other two countries bordering it. The outflow of investment and the haemorrhaging of profits and service payments out of Canada is intrinsically intertwined with NAFTA.[75] According to the critics, the human and economic debris will be with us for as long as we can see into the future. The single most important impact of NAFTA is the decline in the overall standard of living of Canadians, which has coincided with the agreements. We must be careful to reform democracy and political institutions so citizens and not just corporate business benefit from change. There is presently more foreign ownership and control in Canada, with fewer and poorer jobs. More imports of goods and services should be sourced in Canada, but there is a failure to develop new competitive products while at the same time having less diversification of exports.

Northrop Frye pointed out long ago about Canada, "Why go to the trouble of annexing a country that is so easy to exploit without taking any responsibility for it?"[76] Economic penetration has proven simpler than military force. NAFTA, according to its critics, is a neo-conservative Americanization of Canada.[77] The pre-agreement years saw trade on a multilateral level, without abandoning

73 Ibid., at p. 279.

74 McPhail, Brenda, *NAFTA Now*, Lanham, 1985, p. 44.

75 Hurtig, Mel, *The Betrayal of Canada*, Toronto, 1991, p. 303.

76 Ibid., at p. 89.

77 Watkins, Mel, "The Political Economy of Growth", in Wallace Clement and Glen Williams, *The New Canadian Political Economy*, Kingston, 1989, p. 3.

national control of the foreign market. However, the agreement itself is seen as a straitjacket, because it is difficult to introduce new measures to strengthen or expand national control of firms and industries. It can be argued that it is a dangerous and indefensible gamble for Canada to commit to a binding dispute settlement mechanism with a trading partner, the United States, which has such a disproportionate power. NAFTA has set up a trading bloc designed to fit Canada and Mexico into the American model of development, keeping Europe and Japan out. Mexico is an attractive site for low-wage production of standardized industrial goods, and with this comes Canadian and American job losses, with production shifts to Mexico and a downward pressure on wages. Workers have been displaced from industries and are vulnerable to competition from low-wage countries, with the loss especially to low-income jobs. While the job crisis existed before free trade and was not confined to Canada, NAFTA does nothing for basic labor.

There is a conflict between the profitability of individual corporations and the pressures of global capabilities against human needs for high employment levels, decent pay, healthy working conditions and job security. To serve the corporate profit, what has occurred is a decrease in full-time employment and an increase in part-time and temporary employment at the expense of benefits, as well as an increase in unemployment and in welfare levels. As such, this has been "the longest and deepest unemployment crisis since the Great Depression", with inappropriate monetary policy playing a major role.[78]

There is a gap in the free trade effect between the top corporate executive and the average shop floor worker. Free trade encourages self-reinforcing cycles of destructive competition, exerting great pressure on the continent. It has eliminated jobs, depressed incomes and standards. The effects of investment diversion and export harassment far outweigh the positive effects of tariff reductions. There is a one-sided advantage for a corporate elite that is globally competitive, increasing profits, surviving and growing unfettered by government controls, and securing the highest rate of return for the interests of financial capital. Decent jobs and decent living standards have become unimportant. However, the employment needs of society must be paramount, and therefore, corporate interests must yield to broader public interests. NAFTA is tilted in the wrong direction. Multilateral trading arrangements with the European Community and Japan would be alternatives to NAFTA and its shortfalls. Canada's social programs are a contrast to those of the United States. Americanization is balkanizing Canada. Regional equality is promised, but individuals, families, communities and regions are being abandoned. Canada was founded on the national principle of building strong communities and regions to serve the needs of residents, not to deplete these areas in order to supply land and factories for economic interests. With lay-offs and closures, there is a bitter legacy of unemployment, poverty and inequality, with society becoming distinctly harsher. Those who are able to thrive are doing very well, but the societal gap is growing so that there is a chasm between rich and poor,

78 Campbell, Bruce, *Free Trade, Destroyer of Jobs*, Ottawa, 1993, p. 2.

young and old, black and white, men and women, non-disabled and disabled, with a disappearing middle **class**. There is a severe strain on the societal fabric, with a sacrificing of the needs of many for the demands of few.

Among those who were opposed to NAFTA, well-known Canadian Mitchell Sharp stated it best:

> From the very beginnings of our country, we have sought to preserve a separate identity, to live in harmony with our next door neighbour but as an independent country. By entering into this … preferential agreement, we would be deciding no longer to resist the continental pull. On the contrary, we would be accelerating the process of the Americanisation of Canada.[79]

Many believe that free trade challenges the fundamentals of Canada's nationhood, with its powers limited by interdependence and domination from foreign multinationals. The benefits of free trade do not fall equally. Free trade serves to undermine full employment,[80] but the first essential ingredient for free trade should be a commitment to full employment. Sufficient independence for blueprint choices and for flexible alternatives for long-term planning is needed, looking away from integration.

By operating under the deceptive banner of "free" trade, multinational corporations are working hard to expand their control over the international economy, and to dismantle vital health, safety and environmental protections, which in recent decades have been won by citizens' movements across the globe. According to consumer advocate Ralph Nader, this serves to devalue jobs, depress wage levels, make workplaces less safe, destroy family farms and undermine consumer protections.[81] Because of NAFTA, large global companies have capitalized on poverty in the Third World, by lowering safety and wages in employment. As such, workers, consumers and communities will continue to lose, while short-term profits soar and big business wins, in a threat to move South. Thus the centralization of commercial power is unsound, as the allocation of power to lower levels of government bodies tends to increase citizen power. There is a need for community-oriented production in smaller-scale operations, along with more flexibility and adaptability to local needs for sustainable production methods and democratic controls. There is a race "to the bottom", pitting State against State, for the lowest wage levels, lowest environmental policies and lowest consumer safety standards.[82]

---

79 Axworthy, Lloyd, "Free Trade, The Costs for Canada", in A.R. Riggs and Tom Velk, *Canadian-American Free Trade: (The Sequel) Historical, Political and Economic Dimensions*, The Institute for Research on Public Policy, Montreal, 1988, p. 38.

80 Ibid., at p. 39.

81 Nader, Ralph, *The Case Against Free Trade*, San Francisco, 1993, p. 1.

82 Ibid., at p. 6.

NAFTA has forced Canada to harmonize its social and economic policies to conform to the United States at the expense of its citizens. Free trade calls for privatization and deregulation, but policy intervention is needed to reduce unemployment and raise wage rates. There has been a shift away from service-type jobs, with pressure to decrease wages and provide fewer benefits for the sake of the almighty American dollar. There has been major job loss by sourcing services outside Canada but also outside the United States.[83] It is important to negotiate over the right of establishment and the right to national treatment. Manufacturing is vulnerable to trade liberalization, which will lead to an increase in unemployment and adverse working conditions, and the United States has an advantage over Canada, because of cheap material, capital intensiveness and technological advancement. As well, in the food industry, Canada is again at a disadvantage due to its size and climate. So too in the electrical field where the United States is again favored, because of a rationalization of production for specializations. Overall, there is a "going South" policy, since Canadian firms want to locate elsewhere, while still having access to the Canadian market, but at the same time, by phasing out import restrictions, the domestic sector is not protected.

American legislation for North American realignment, it is argued, will curtail equal rights legislation, since equal pay is too costly for the industry. Free trade erodes the domestic service economy.[84] Of the three major categories of sectors, the primary (agriculture and resource extracting), the secondary (construction and manufacturing) and the tertiary (service), the service sector accounts for two-thirds of the national income and 70% of jobs in Canada. Foreign service industry activity is limited by non-tariff barriers, through control over investment, ownership and trade levels. The United States, however, believes that government intervention as a matter of security and sovereignty is an unfair practice. Since, the United States accounts for roughly 80% of Canada's trade, the Canadian market is vulnerable, because of the large percentage of US-owned businesses, which causes an indirect pressure to conform to United States policy. Interestingly, the United States has easier access to Canada than Canada to the United States, and the American trade remedy legislation imposes pressure upon Canada to harmonize, which impacts social services, availability of and types of employment, job loss, wages and working conditions. Because of all of these factors, it is found that trade-led growth is not always an adequate economic policy. Free trade is a means, not an end.

83 Griffin Cohen, Marjorie, *Free Trade and the Future of Women's Work, Manufacturing and Service Industries*, Toronto, 1987, p. 16.

84 Ibid., at p. 49.

American Declaration of the Rights and Duties of Man

Important for equal rights, including tolerance for class distinctions, the Preamble of the American Declaration of the Rights and Duties of Man 1948 states:

> All men are born free and equal, in dignity and in rights, and, being endowed by nature with reason and conscience, they should conduct themselves as brothers one to another.
>
> The fulfilment of duty by each individual is a prerequisite to the rights of all. Rights and duties are interrelated in every social and political activity of man. While rights exalt individual liberty, duties express the dignity of that liberty. Duties of a juridical nature presuppose others of a moral nature which support them in principle and constitute their basis.
>
> In as much as spiritual development is the supreme end of human existence and the highest expression thereof, it is the duty of man to serve that end with all his strength and resources.
>
> Since culture is the highest social and historical expression of that spiritual development, it is the duty of man to preserve, practice and foster culture by every means within his power.
>
> And, since moral conduct constitutes the noblest flowering of culture, it is the duty of every man always to hold it in high respect.
>
> WHEREAS:
>
> The American peoples have acknowledged the dignity of the individual, and their national constitutions recognize that juridical and political institutions, which regulate life in human society, have as their principal aim the protection of the essential rights of man and the creation of circumstances that will permit him to achieve spiritual and material progress and attain happiness;
>
> The American States have on repeated occasions recognized that the essential rights of man are not derived from the fact that he is a national of a certain state, but are based upon attributes of his human personality;
>
> The international protection of the rights of man should be the principal guide of an evolving American law;

> The affirmation of essential human rights by the American States together with the guarantees given by the internal regimes of the states establish the initial system of protection considered by the American States as being suited to the present social and juridical conditions, not without a recognition on their part that they should increasingly strengthen that system in the international field as conditions become more favourable.[85]

In terms of equal rights and equality, Article II guarantees the right to equality before the law, which should include class under "any other factor":

> II. All persons are equal before the law and have the rights and duties established in this Declaration, without distinction as to race, sex, language, creed or any other factor.[86]

Further, important for advancement and for a higher standard of living, the right to education is guaranteed under Article XII:

> XII. Every person has the right to an education, which should be based on the principles of liberty, morality and human solidarity.
> Likewise every person has the right to an education that will prepare him to attain a decent life, to raise his standard of living, and to be a useful member of society. The right to an education includes the right to equality of opportunity in every case, in accordance with natural talents, merit and the desire to utilize the resources that the state or the community is in a position to provide. Every person has the right to receive, free, at least a primary education.[87]

In addition, important in the fight against class discrimination in employment, the right to work and to fair remuneration are contained in Article XIV:

> XIV. Every person has the right to work, under proper conditions, and to follow his vocation freely, in so far as existing conditions of employment permit. Every person who works has the right to receive such remuneration as will, in proportion to his capacity and skill, assure him a standard of living suitable for himself and for his family.[88]

The scope of the rights of man is outlined in Article XXVIII:

---

85 American Declaration of the Rights and Duties of Man, at the Preamble.
86 Ibid., at Article II.
87 Ibid., at Article XII.
88 Ibid., at Article XIV.

> XXVIII. The rights of man are limited by the rights of others, by the security of all, and by the just demands of the general welfare and the advancement of democracy.[89]

In terms of duties, the duty to obey the law is contained in Article XXXIII:

> XXXIII. It is the duty of every person to obey the law and other legitimate commands of the authorities of his country and those of the country in which he may be.[90]

Finally, the duty to work is contained in Article XXXVII:

> XXXVII. It is the duty of every person to work, as far as his capacity and possibilities permit, in order to obtain the means of livelihood or to benefit his community.[91]

American Convention on Human Rights

The Preamble of the American Convention on Human Rights 1978, which entered into force on 18 July 1978, states:

> The American states signatory to the present Convention,
>
> *Reaffirming* their intention to consolidate in this hemisphere, within the framework of democratic institutions, a system of personal liberty and social justice based on respect for the essential rights of man;
>
> *Recognizing* that the essential rights of man are not derived from one's being a national of a certain state, but are based upon attributes of the human personality, and that they therefore justify international protection in the form of a convention reinforcing or complementing the protection provided by the domestic law of the American states;
>
> *Considering* that these principles have been set forth in the Charter of the Organization of American States, in the American Declaration of the Rights and Duties of Man, and in the Universal Declaration of Human Rights, and that they have been reaffirmed and refined in other international instruments, worldwide as well as regional in scope;

89 Ibid., at Article XXVIII.
90 Ibid., at Article XXXIII.
91 Ibid., at Article XXXVII.

> *Reiterating* that, in accordance with the Universal Declaration of Human Rights, the ideal of free men enjoying freedom from fear and want can be achieved only if conditions are created whereby everyone may enjoy his economic, social, and cultural rights, as well as his civil and political rights.[92]

Important for equal rights, Article 1 stresses the obligation to respect rights, which specifically mentions social origin and also should include class under "any other social condition":

> 1.1. The States Parties to this Convention undertake to respect the rights and freedoms recognized herein and to ensure to all persons subject to their jurisdiction the free and full exercise of those rights and freedoms, without any discrimination for reasons of race, color, sex, language, religion, political or other opinion, national or social origin, economic status, birth, or any other social condition.
> 2. For the purposes of this Convention, 'person' means every human being.[93]

Further, freedom of thought and expression are safeguarded as pertaining to hatred incited because of such things as class in Article 13.5:

> 13.5. Any propaganda for war and any advocacy of national, racial, or religious hatred that constitute incitements to lawless violence or to any other similar action against any person or group of persons on any grounds including those of race, color, religion, language, or national origin shall be considered as offenses punishable by law.[94]

Important for class discrimination cases, the right to equal protection is guaranteed under Article 24:

> 24. All persons are equal before the law. Consequently, they are entitled, without discrimination, to equal protection of the law.[95]

Further, freedom of movement and residence, critical for employment opportunities, is guaranteed under Article 22:

> 22.1. Every person lawfully in the territory of a State Party has the right to move about in it, and to reside in it subject to the provisions of the law.
> 2. Every person has the right to leave any country freely, including his own.

---

92 American Convention on Human Rights, at the Preamble.
93 Ibid., at Article 1.
94 Ibid., at Article 13.5.
95 Ibid., at Article 24.

> 3. The exercise of the foregoing rights may be restricted only pursuant to a law to the extent necessary in a democratic society to prevent crime or to protect national security, public safety, public order, public morals, public health, or the rights or freedoms of others.
> 4. The exercise of the rights recognized in paragraph 1 may also be restricted by law in designated zones for reasons of public interest.
> 5. No one can be expelled from the territory of the state of which he is a national or be deprived of the right to enter it.
> 6. An alien lawfully in the territory of a State Party to this Convention may be expelled from it only pursuant to a decision reached in accordance with law.
> 7. Every person has the right to seek and be granted asylum in a foreign territory, in accordance with the legislation of the state and international conventions, in the event he is being pursued for political offenses or related common crimes.
> 8. In no case may an alien be deported or returned to a country, regardless of whether or not it is his country of origin, if in that country his right to life or personal freedom is in danger of being violated because of his race, nationality, religion, social status, or political opinions.
> 9. The collective expulsion of aliens is prohibited.[96]

In terms of civil and political rights, the right to Juridical Personality is contained in Article 3:

> 3. Every person has the right to recognition as a person before the law.[97]

Further, domestic legal effects are outlined in Article 2:

> 2. Where the exercise of any of the rights or freedoms referred to in Article 1 is not already ensured by legislative or other provisions, the States Parties undertake to adopt, in accordance with their constitutional processes and the provisions of this Convention, such legislative or other measures as may be necessary to give effect to those rights or freedoms.[98]

Crucially, the right to judicial protection is guaranteed under Article 25:

> 25.1. Everyone has the right to simple and prompt recourse, or any other effective recourse, to a competent court or tribunal for protection against acts that violate his fundamental rights recognized by the constitution or laws of the state concerned or by this Convention, even though such violation may have been committed by persons acting in the course of their official duties.
> 2. The States Parties undertake:

96 Ibid., at Article 22.
97 Ibid., at Article 3.
98 Ibid., at Article 2.

a. to ensure that any person claiming such remedy shall have his rights determined by the competent authority provided for by the legal system of the state;
b. to develop the possibilities of judicial remedy; and
c. to ensure that the competent authorities shall enforce such remedies when granted.[99]

In addition, Article 28 contains a federal clause:

28.1. Where a State Party is constituted as a federal state, the national government of such State Party shall implement all the provisions of the Convention over whose subject matter it exercises legislative and judicial jurisdiction.[100]

As well, in terms of economic and social rights, Article 26 provides for progressive development:

26. The States Parties undertake to adopt measures, both internally and through international cooperation, especially those of an economic and technical nature, with a view to achieving progressively, by legislation or other appropriate means, the full realization of the rights implicit in the economic, social, educational, scientific, and cultural standards set forth in the Charter of the Organization of American States … .[101]

There are a number of competent organs involved as outlined in Article 33:

33. The following organs shall have competence with respect to matters relating to the fulfilment of the commitments made by the States Parties to this Convention:
a. the Inter-American Commission on Human Rights, referred to as 'The Commission'; and
b. the Inter-American Court of Human Rights, referred to as 'The Court'.[102]

In terms of the Inter-American Commission on Human Rights, Article 35 outlines the organization:

35. The Commission shall represent all the member countries of the Organization of American States.[103]

99 Ibid., at Article 25.
100 Ibid., at Article 28.
101 Ibid., at Article 26.
102 Ibid., at Article 33.
103 Ibid., at Article 35.

The functions of the Inter-American Commission on Human Rights are outlined in Article 41:

> 41. The main function of the Commission shall be to promote respect for and defense of human rights. In the exercise of its mandate, it shall have the following functions and powers:
>
> a. to develop an awareness of human rights among the peoples of America;
>
> b. to make recommendations to the governments of the member states, when it considers such action advisable, for the adoption of progressive measures in favor of human rights within the framework of their domestic law and constitutional provisions as well as appropriate measures to further the observance of those rights;
>
> c. to prepare such studies or reports as it considers advisable in the performance of its duties;
>
> d. to request the governments of the member states to supply it with information on the measures adopted by them in matters of human rights;
>
> e. to respond, through the General Secretariat of the Organization of American States, to inquiries made by the member states on matters related to human rights and, within the limits of its possibilities, to provide those states with the advisory services they request;
>
> f. to take action on petitions and other communications pursuant to its authority under the provisions of Articles 44 through 51 of this Convention; and
>
> g. to submit an annual report to the General Assembly of the Organization of American States.[104]

The competency to lodge petitions is outlined in Article 44:

> 44. Any person or group of persons, or any nongovernmental entity legally recognized in one or more member states of the Organization, may lodge petitions with the Commission containing denunciations or complaints of violation of this Convention by a State Party.[105]

Admissibility of petitions is outlined in Article 46:

> 46.1. Admission by the Commission of a petition or communication … shall be subject to the following requirements:
>
> a. that the remedies under domestic law have been pursued and exhausted in accordance with generally recognized principles of international law;

104 Ibid., at Article 41.
105 Ibid., at Article 44.

b. that the petition or communication is lodged within a period of six months from the date on which the party alleging violation of his rights was notified of the final judgment;
c. that the subject of the petition or communication is not pending in another international proceeding for settlement.

2 The provisions of paragraphs 1.a and 1.b of this article shall not be applicable when:

a. the domestic legislation of the state concerned does not afford due process of law for the protection of the right or rights that have allegedly been violated;
b. the party alleging violation of his rights has been denied access to the remedies under domestic law or has been prevented from exhausting them; or
c. there has been unwarranted delay in rendering a final judgment under the aforementioned remedies.[106]

The procedure is outlined in Article 48:

48.1. When the Commission receives a petition or communication alleging violation of any of the rights protected by this Convention, it shall proceed as follows:

a. If it considers the petition or communication admissible, it shall request information from the government of the state indicated as being responsible for the alleged violations and shall furnish that government a transcript of the pertinent portions of the petition or communication. This information shall be submitted within a reasonable period to be determined by the Commission in accordance with the circumstances of each case.
b. After the information has been received, or after the period established has elapsed and the information has not been received, the Commission shall ascertain whether the grounds for the petition or communication still exist. If they do not, the Commission shall order the record to be closed.
c. The Commission may also declare the petition or communication inadmissible or out of order on the basis of information or evidence subsequently received.
d. If the record has not been closed, the Commission shall, with the knowledge of the parties, examine the matter set forth in the petition or communication in order to verify the facts. If necessary and advisable, the Commission shall carry out an investigation, for the effective conduct of which it shall request, and the states concerned shall furnish to it, all necessary facilities.
e. The Commission may request the states concerned to furnish any pertinent information and, if so requested, shall hear oral statements or receive written statements from the parties concerned.

106 Ibid., at Article 46.

f. The Commission shall place itself at the disposal of the parties concerned with a view to reaching a friendly settlement of the matter on the basis of respect for the human rights recognized in this Convention.

2. However, in serious and urgent cases, only the presentation of a petition or communication that fulfils all the formal requirements of admissibility shall be necessary in order for the Commission to conduct an investigation with the prior consent of the state in whose territory a violation has allegedly been committed.[107]

In terms of the Inter-American Court of Human Rights, the right of submission is outlined in Article 61:

61.1. Only the States Parties and the Commission shall have the right to submit a case to the Court.[108]

The safeguarding of rights and the provision of measures are contained in Article 63:

63. 1. If the Court finds that there has been a violation of a right or freedom protected by this Convention, the Court shall rule that the injured party be ensured the enjoyment of his right or freedom that was violated. It shall also rule, if appropriate, that the consequences of the measure or situation that constituted the breach of such right or freedom be remedied and that fair compensation be paid to the injured party.

2. In cases of extreme gravity and urgency, and when necessary to avoid irreparable damage to persons, the Court shall adopt such provisional measures as it deems pertinent in matters it has under consideration. With respect to a case not yet submitted to the Court, it may act at the request of the Commission.[109]

In terms of procedure, Article 66 calls for reasons for judgments:

66.1. Reasons shall be given for the judgment of the Court.[110]

Further, finality of judgment is contained in Article 67:

67. The judgment of the Court shall be final and not subject to appeal. In case of disagreement as to the meaning or scope of the judgment, the Court shall interpret it at the request of any of the parties, provided the request is made within ninety days from the date of notification of the judgment.[111]

---

107 Ibid., at Article 48.
108 Ibid., at Article 61.
109 Ibid., at Article 63.
110 Ibid., at Article 66.
111 Ibid., at Article 67.

Finally, compliance with the judgment is underlined in Article 68:

> 68.1. The States Parties to the Convention undertake to comply with the judgment of the Court in any case to which they are parties.
> 2. That part of a judgment that stipulates compensatory damages may be executed in the country concerned in accordance with domestic procedure governing the execution of judgments against the state.[112]

Statute of the Inter-American Court on Human Rights

More specifically and carrying on from the American Convention on Human Rights, Article 1 of the Statute of the Inter-American Court on Human Rights 1980, which entered into force on 1 January 1980, outlines the nature of the legal organization:

> 1. The Inter-American Court of Human Rights is an autonomous judicial institution whose purpose is the application and interpretation of the American Convention on Human Rights. The Court exercises its functions in accordance with the provisions of the aforementioned Convention and the present Statute.[113]

The jurisdiction of the Court is contained in Article 2:

> 2. The Court shall exercise adjudicatory and advisory jurisdiction … .[114]

The seat of the Court is contained in Article 3:

> 3.1. The seat of the Court shall be San Jose, Costa Rica; however, the Court may convene in any member state of the Organization of American States (OAS) when a majority of the Court considers it desirable, and with the prior consent of the State concerned.[115]

Further, the composition of the Court is contained in Article 4:

> 4.1. The Court shall consist of seven judges, nationals of the member states of the OAS, elected in an individual capacity from among jurists of the highest moral authority and of recognized competence in the field of human rights, who possess the qualifications required for the exercise of the highest judicial

112 Ibid., at Article 68.
113 Statute of the Inter-American Court on Human Rights, at Article 1.
114 Ibid., at Article 2.
115 Ibid., at Article 3.

> functions under the law of the State of which they are nationals or of the State that proposes them as candidates.
> 2. No two judges may be nationals of the same State.[116]

The structure of the Court includes the Presidency as outlined in Article 12 and the Secretariat as outlined in Article 14:

> 12.1. The Court shall elect from among its members a President and Vice-President who shall serve for a period of two years; they may be reelected.
> 2. The President shall direct the work of the Court, represent it, regulate the disposition of matters brought before the Court, and preside over its sessions.[117]

> 14.1. The Secretariat of the Court shall function under the immediate authority of the Secretary, in accordance with the administrative standards of the OAS General Secretariat, in all matters that are not incompatible with the independence of the Court.
> 2. The Secretary shall be appointed by the Court. He shall be a full-time employee serving in a position of trust to the Court, shall have his office at the seat of the Court and shall attend any meetings that the Court holds away from its seat.
> 3. There shall be an Assistant Secretary who shall assist the Secretary in his duties and shall replace him in his temporary absence.
> 4. The Staff of the Secretariat shall be appointed by the Secretary General of the OAS, in consultation with the Secretary of the Court.[118]

In terms of the workings of the Court, Article 24 outlines the hearings, deliberations and decisions:

> 24.1. The hearings shall be public, unless the Court, in exceptional circumstances, decides otherwise.
> 2. The Court shall deliberate in private. Its deliberations shall remain secret, unless the Court decides otherwise.
> 3. The decisions, judgments and opinions of the Court shall be delivered in public session, and the parties shall be given written notification thereof. In addition, the decisions, judgments and opinions shall be published, along with judges' individual votes and opinions and with such other data or background information that the Court may deem appropriate.[119]

---

116 Ibid., at Article 4.
117 Ibid., at Article 12.
118 Ibid., at Article 14.
119 Ibid., at Article 24.

Article 27 stresses the importance of relations with the host country, governments and organizations:

> 27.1. The relations of the Court with the host country shall be governed through a headquarters agreement. The seat of the Court shall be international in nature.
> 2. The relations of the Court with governments, with the OAS and its organs, agencies and entities and with other international governmental organizations involved in promoting and defending human rights shall be governed through special agreements.[120]

Finally, Article 28 stresses the importance of the relations with the Inter-American Commission on Human Rights:

> 28. The Inter-American Commission on Human Rights shall appear as a party before the Court in all cases within the adjudicatory jurisdiction of the Court, pursuant to Article 2(1) of the present Statute.[121]

Inter-American Democratic Charter

The Preamble of the Inter-American Democratic Charter 2001, which came into force on 11 September 2001, espouses the ideals of liberty, equality and social justice, including the eradication of poverty, and the importance of education for human resource development:

> THE GENERAL ASSEMBLY,
>
> CONSIDERING that the Charter of the Organization of American States recognizes that representative democracy is indispensable for the stability, peace, and development of the region, and that one of the purposes of the OAS is to promote and consolidate representative democracy, with due respect for the principle of nonintervention;
>
> RECOGNIZING the contributions of the OAS and other regional and sub-regional mechanisms to the promotion and consolidation of democracy in the Americas;
>
> RECALLING that the Heads of State and Government of the Americas, gathered at the Third Summit of the Americas, held from April 20 to 22, 2001 in Quebec City, adopted a democracy clause which establishes that any unconstitutional

120 Ibid., at Article 27.
121 Ibid., at Article 28.

alteration or interruption of the democratic order in a state of the Hemisphere constitutes an insurmountable obstacle to the participation of that state's government in the Summits of the Americas process;

BEARING IN MIND that existing democratic provisions in regional and subregional mechanisms express the same objectives as the democracy clause adopted by the Heads of State and Government in Quebec City;

REAFFIRMING that the participatory nature of democracy in our countries in different aspects of public life contributes to the consolidation of democratic values and to freedom and solidarity in the Hemisphere;

CONSIDERING that solidarity among and cooperation between American states require the political organization of those states based on the effective exercise of representative democracy, and that economic growth and social development based on justice and equity, and democracy are interdependent and mutually reinforcing;

REAFFIRMING that the fight against poverty, and especially the elimination of extreme poverty, is essential to the promotion and consolidation of democracy and constitutes a common and shared responsibility of the American states;

BEARING IN MIND that the American Declaration on the Rights and Duties of Man and the American Convention on Human Rights contain the values and principles of liberty, equality, and social justice that are intrinsic to democracy;

REAFFIRMING that the promotion and protection of human rights is a basic prerequisite for the existence of a democratic society, and recognizing the importance of the continuous development and strengthening of the inter-American human rights system for the consolidation of democracy;

CONSIDERING that education is an effective way to promote citizens' awareness concerning their own countries and thereby achieve meaningful participation in the decision-making process, and reaffirming the importance of human resource development for a sound democratic system;

RECOGNIZING that a safe environment is essential to the integral development of the human being, which contributes to democracy and political stability;

BEARING IN MIND that the Protocol of San Salvador on Economic, Social, and Cultural Rights emphasizes the great importance of the reaffirmation, development, improvement, and protection of those rights in order to consolidate the system of representative democratic government;

RECOGNIZING that the right of workers to associate themselves freely for the defense and promotion of their interests is fundamental to the fulfillment of democratic ideals;

TAKING INTO ACCOUNT that, in the Santiago Commitment to Democracy and the Renewal of the Inter-American System, the ministers of foreign affairs expressed their determination to adopt a series of effective, timely, and expeditious procedures to ensure the promotion and defense of representative democracy, with due respect for the principle of nonintervention; and that resolution AG/RES. 1080 (XXI-O/91) therefore established a mechanism for collective action in the case of a sudden or irregular interruption of the democratic political institutional process or of the legitimate exercise of power by the democratically-elected government in any of the Organization's member states, thereby fulfilling a long-standing aspiration of the Hemisphere to be able to respond rapidly and collectively in defense of democracy;

RECALLING that, in the Declaration of Nassau [AG/DEC. 1 (XXII-O/92)], it was agreed to develop mechanisms to provide assistance, when requested by a member state, to promote, preserve, and strengthen representative democracy, in order to complement and give effect to the provisions of resolution AG/RES. 1080 (XXI-O/91);

BEARING IN MIND that, in the Declaration of Managua for the Promotion of Democracy and Development [AG/DEC. 4 (XXIII-O/93)], the member states expressed their firm belief that democracy, peace, and development are inseparable and indivisible parts of a renewed and integral vision of solidarity in the Americas; and that the ability of the Organization to help preserve and strengthen democratic structures in the region will depend on the implementation of a strategy based on the interdependence and complementarity of those values;

CONSIDERING that, in the Declaration of Managua for the Promotion of Democracy and Development, the member states expressed their conviction that the Organization's mission is not limited to the defense of democracy wherever its fundamental values and principles have collapsed, but also calls for ongoing and creative work to consolidate democracy as well as a continuing effort to prevent and anticipate the very causes of the problems that affect the democratic system of government;

BEARING IN MIND that the Ministers of Foreign Affairs of the Americas, at the thirty-first regular session of the General Assembly, held in San Jose, Costa Rica, in keeping with express instructions from the Heads of State and Government gathered at the Third Summit of the Americas, in Quebec City, accepted the base document of the Inter-American Democratic Charter and entrusted the Permanent Council of the Organization with strengthening and expanding the document, in accordance with the OAS Charter, for final adoption at a special session of the General Assembly in Lima, Peru;

RECOGNIZING that all the rights and obligations of member states under the OAS Charter represent the foundation on which democratic principles in the Hemisphere are built; and

BEARING IN MIND the progressive development of international law and the advisability of clarifying the provisions set forth in the OAS Charter and related basic instruments on the preservation and defense of democratic institutions, according to established practice,

RESOLVES:

To adopt the following.[122]

Democracy and the rule of law are paramount in Article 1:

1. The peoples of the Americas have a right to democracy and their governments have an obligation to promote and defend it.
Democracy is essential for the social, political, and economic development of the peoples of the Americas.[123]

The anti-discrimination provision is contained in Article 9, which should include class under all forms of discrimination:

9. The elimination of all forms of discrimination, especially gender, ethnic and race discrimination, as well as diverse forms of intolerance, the promotion and protection of human rights of indigenous peoples and migrants, and respect for ethnic, cultural and religious diversity in the Americas contribute to strengthening democracy and citizen participation.[124]

Article 16 recognizes the value of education in the fight against class discrimination:

16. Education is key to strengthening democratic institutions, promoting the development of human potential, and alleviating poverty and fostering greater understanding among our peoples. To achieve these ends, it is essential that a

122 Inter-American Democratic Charter, at the Preamble.
123 Ibid., at Article 1.
124 Ibid., at Article 9.

quality education be available to all, including girls and women, rural inhabitants, and minorities.[125]

Further, social development is covered under Article 11

> 11. Democracy and social and economic development are interdependent and are mutually reinforcing.[126]

Importantly, Article 12 deals with the issues of poverty and illiteracy:

> 12. Poverty, illiteracy, and low levels of human development are factors that adversely affect the consolidation of democracy. The OAS member states are committed to adopting and implementing all those actions required to generate productive employment, reduce poverty, and eradicate extreme poverty, taking into account the different economic realities and conditions of the countries of the Hemisphere. This shared commitment regarding the problems associated with development and poverty also underscores the importance of maintaining macroeconomic equilibria and the obligation to strengthen social cohesion and democracy.[127]

Workers' rights and labor standards are emphasized in Article 10:

> The promotion and strengthening of democracy requires the full and effective exercise of workers' rights and the application of core labor standards, as recognized in the International Labour Organization (ILO) Declaration on Fundamental Principles and Rights at Work … adopted in 1998, as well as other related fundamental ILO conventions. Democracy is strengthened by improving standards in the workplace and enhancing the quality of life for workers in the Hemisphere.[128]

The importance of claims and redress for grievances is outlined in Article 8:

> 8. Any person or group of persons who consider that their human rights have been violated may present claims or petitions to the inter-American system for the promotion and protection of human rights in accordance with its established procedures.

---

125 Ibid., at Article 16.
126 Ibid., at Article 11.
127 Ibid., at Article 12.
128 Ibid., at Article 10.

> Member states reaffirm their intention to strengthen the inter-American system for the protection of human rights for the consolidation of democracy in the Hemisphere.[129]

Further, in terms of democracy and the inter-American system, Article 4 espouses the importance of transparency:

> 4. Transparency in government activities, probity, responsible public administration on the part of governments, respect for social rights, and freedom of expression and of the press are essential components of the exercise of democracy.
> The constitutional subordination of all state institutions to the legally constituted civilian authority and respect for the rule of law on the part of all institutions and sectors of society are equally essential to democracy.[130]

Finally, in terms of human rights, Article 7 stresses the importance of democracy:

> 7. Democracy is indispensable for the effective exercise of fundamental freedoms and human rights in their universality, indivisibility and interdependence, embodied in the respective constitutions of states and in inter-American and international human rights instruments.[131]

Conclusion

By recognizing that we share a hemisphere, NAFTA sets an important precedent for north-south continental trade, and looks toward the future by allowing for participation by other countries, if they meet the membership criteria set by the three founding nations. Latin American countries have expressed an interest in becoming signatory members of the Free Trade Agreement. In addition, the Canadian Province of Quebec has already given thought to joining as a separate member in the event it becomes a separate nation, but wishes to maintain the current division of legislative powers, respect fully its unique social policy, language and culture, maintain a leeway to modernize and develop its economy, provide for transitional periods for businesses in less competitive sectors, adopt a dispute settlement mechanism, maintain its special status for agriculture and fisheries, and protect its right to decide on the Agreement in light of its interests. The Parties to the North American Free Trade Agreement (NAFTA) are cooperating to advance trade liberalization not only within North America with the NAFTA Superhighway, but also in the negotiations for the Free Trade Area of the Americas

129 Ibid., at Article 8.
130 Ibid., at Article 4.
131 Ibid., at Article 7.

(FTAA). Recognizing their shared interests, the NAFTA partners have worked together to advance trade liberalization. In 2001, Canada hosted the Summit of the Americas, a gathering of the 34 democratically elected Heads of State of the Western Hemisphere. The FTAA would eliminate trade and investment barriers on virtually all goods and services traded by member countries, reduce prices for consumers and create new markets for producers throughout the hemisphere.

However, more needs to be done to legislate for equal rights and tolerance for all workers. President John F. Kennedy stated with regard to the relationship between Canada and the United States: "Geography has made us neighbors, history has made us friends, the economy has made us partners and necessity has made us allies."[132] In this spirit, important in the fight against class discrimination, we need to work together to bring about full equality in the Americas, in the pursuit of "Class Act".

132 Kennedy, President John F., Address to the Canadian Parliament, 17 May 1961.

Chapter 8

Class Act in the United Kingdom and Ireland

Introduction

In the quest for tolerance of class distinctions in *Class Act*, this chapter will examine efforts against class discrimination in the United Kingdom and Ireland. It will examine important legislation impacting class, first in the United Kingdom, which encompasses England, Scotland, Wales and Northern Ireland, namely the Human Rights Act, the Equality Act 2006 and 2010, for minorities the Race Relations Act and the Race Relations Act (Amendment) Regulations and for women the Sexual Discrimination Act, and the Equal Pay Act, the Equal Opportunities Commission (EOC) and the Code of Practice on Equal Pay; and then in the Republic of Ireland, namely the Constitution, the Employment Equality Act and the Equal Status Act. At the outset, if a court determines that it is impossible to interpret an Act of Parliament in a way which is compatible with European convention rights, a formal declaration of incompatibility may be made, and it is then for the Government and Parliament to decide whether or not to amend it. There is a need for intervention in the application of human rights law to those of different classes.

United Kingdom

Human Rights Act (HRA)

The Human Rights Act (HRA) 1998, entitled An Act to give further effect to rights and freedoms guaranteed under the European Convention on Human Rights, came into force mostly on 2 October 2000. Regarding the interpretation of legislation, Section 3 states:

> 3(1) So far as it is possible to do so, primary legislation and subordinate legislation must be read and given effect in a way which is compatible with the Convention rights.
>
> (2) This section
>
> (a) appliestoprimarylegislationandsubordinatelegislationwheneverenacted;
>
> (b) does not affect the validity, continuing operation or enforcement of any incompatible primary legislation; and

(c) does not affect the validity, continuing operation or enforcement of any incompatible subordinate legislation if (disregarding any possibility of revocation) primary legislation prevents removal of the incompatibility.[1]

Further, the concept of declaration of incompatibility is covered under Section 4:

4(1) Subsection (2) applies in any proceedings in which a court determines whether a provision of primary legislation is compatible with a Convention right.
(2) If the court is satisfied that the provision is incompatible with a Convention right, it may make a declaration of that incompatibility.
(3) Subsection (4) applies in any proceedings in which a court determines whether a provision of subordinate legislation, made in the exercise of a power conferred by primary legislation, is compatible with a Convention right.
(4) If the court is satisfied
(a) that the provision is incompatible with a Convention right, and
(b) that (disregarding any possibility of revocation) the primary legislation concerned prevents removal of the incompatibility,
it may make a declaration of that incompatibility.[2]

Finally, in terms of Acts of Public Authorities, Section 6 states:

6(1) It is unlawful for a public authority to act in a way which is incompatible with a Convention right.
(2) Subsection (1) does not apply to an act if
(a) as the result of one or more provisions of primary legislation, the authority could not have acted differently; or
(b) in the case of one or more provisions of, or made under, primary legislation which cannot be read or given effect in a way which is compatible with the Convention rights, the authority was acting so as to give effect to or enforce those provisions.
(3) In this section 'public authority' includes
(a) a court or tribunal, and
(b) any person certain of whose functions are functions of a public nature,
but does not include either House of Parliament or a person exercising functions in connection with proceedings in Parliament.
(5) In relation to a particular act, a person is not a public authority by virtue only of subsection (3)(b) if the nature of the act is private.
(6) 'An act' includes a failure to act but does not include a failure to
(a) introduce in, or lay before, Parliament a proposal for legislation; or

1 Human Rights Act, UK, at Section 3.
2 Ibid., at Section 4.

(b) make any primary legislation or remedial order.[3]

Equality Act 2006 and 2010

In the fight against class discrimination, Section 3 of the Equality Act 2006 outlines the general duty of the Commission:

> 3. The Commission shall exercise its functions under this Part with a view to encouraging and supporting the development of a society in which
> (a) people's ability to achieve their potential is not limited by prejudice or discrimination,
> (b) there is respect for and protection of each individual's human rights,
> (c) there is respect for the dignity and worth of each individual,
> (d) each individual has an equal opportunity to participate in society, and
> (e) there is mutual respect between groups based on understanding and valuing of diversity and on shared respect for equality and human rights.[4]

Equality and diversity are to be promoted under Section 8:

> 8(1) The Commission shall, by exercising the powers conferred by this Part
> (a) promote understanding of the importance of equality and diversity,
> (b) encourage good practice in relation to equality and diversity,
> (c) promote equality of opportunity,
> (d) promote awareness and understanding of rights under the equality enactments,
> (e) enforce the equality enactments,
> (f) work towards the elimination of unlawful discrimination, and
> (g) work towards the elimination of unlawful harassment.[5]

Human rights are to be promoted under Section 9:

> 9(1) The Commission shall, by exercising the powers conferred by this Part
> (a) promote understanding of the importance of human rights,
> (b) encourage good practice in relation to human rights,
> (c) promote awareness, understanding and protection of human rights, and
> (d) encourage public authorities to comply with section 6 of the Human Rights Act (compliance with Convention rights).[6]

Important for class discrimination cases, Section 10 states:

3 Ibid., at Section 6.
4 Equality Act 2006, UK, at Section 3.
5 Ibid., at Section 8.
6 Ibid., at Section 9.

> 10(1) The Commission shall, by exercising the powers conferred by this Part
> (a) promote understanding of the importance of good relations
> (i) between members of different groups, and
> (ii) between members of groups and others,
> (b) encourage good practice in relation to relations
> (i) between members of different groups, and
> (ii) between members of groups and others,
> (c) work towards the elimination of prejudice against, hatred of and hostility towards members of groups, and
> (d) work towards enabling members of groups to participate in society.
> (2) In this Part 'group' means a group or class of persons who share a common attribute in respect of any of the following matters
> (a) age,
> (b) disability,
> (c) gender,
> (d) proposed, commenced or completed reassignment of gender (within the meaning given by section 82(1) of the Sex Discrimination Act 1975 (c. 65)),
> (e) race,
> (f) religion or belief, and
> (g) sexual orientation.
> (3) For the purposes of this Part a reference to a group (as defined in subsection (2) includes a reference to a smaller group or smaller class, within a group, of persons who share a common attribute (in addition to the attribute by reference to which the group is defined) in respect of any of the matters specified in subsection (2)(a) to (g).[7]

Further, Section 49 prohibits discrimination in educational institutions, so important as a tool for advancement:

> 49(1) It is unlawful for the responsible body of an educational establishment listed
> in the Table to discriminate against a person
> (a) in the terms on which it offers to admit him as a pupil,
> (b) by refusing to accept an application to admit him as a pupil, or
> (c) where he is a pupil of the establishment
> (i) in the way in which it affords him access to any benefit, facility or service,
> (ii) by refusing him access to a benefit, facility or service,
> (iii) by excluding him from the establishment, or
> (iv) by subjecting him to any other detriment.[8]

7 Ibid., at Section 10.
8 Ibid., at Section 49.

Finally, in terms of monitoring of the law, Section 11 states:

> 11(1) The Commission shall monitor the effectiveness of the equality and human rights enactments.
> (2) The Commission may
> (a) advise central government about the effectiveness of any of the equality and human rights enactments;
> (b) recommend to central government the amendment, repeal, consolidation (with or without amendments) or replication (with or without amendments) of any of the equality and human rights enactments;
> (c) advise central or devolved government about the effect of an enactment (including an enactment in or under an Act of the Scottish Parliament);
> (d) advise central or devolved government about the likely effect of a proposed change of law.[9]

Turning to the Equality Act 2010, in terms of socio-economic inequalities, Section 1 deals with the public sector duty regarding socio-economic inequalities:

> 1(1) An authority to which this section applies must, when making decisions of a strategic nature about how to exercise its functions, have due regard to the desirability of exercising them in a way that is designed to reduce the inequalities of outcome which result from socio-economic disadvantage.
> (2) In deciding how to fulfil a duty to which it is subject under subsection (1), an authority must take into account any guidance issued by a Minister of the Crown.[10]

Section 4 outlines the protected characteristics:

> 4. The following characteristics are protected characteristics
> age;
> disability;
> gender reassignment;
> marriage and civil partnership;
> pregnancy and maternity;
> race;
> religion or belief;
> sex;
> sexual orientation.[11]

Section 13 defines direct discrimination:

9 Ibid., at Section 11.
10 Equality Act 2010, UK, at Section 1.
11 Ibid., at Section 4.

13(1) A person (A) discriminates against another (B) if, because of a protected characteristic, A treats B less favourably than A treats or would treat others.
(2) If the protected characteristic is age, A does not discriminate against B if A can
show A's treatment of B to be a proportionate means of achieving a legitimate aim.
(3) If the protected characteristic is disability, and B is not a disabled person, A does not discriminate against B only because A treats or would treat disabled persons more favourably than A treats B.
(4) If the protected characteristic is marriage and civil partnership, this section applies to a contravention of Part 5 (work) only if the treatment is because it is B who is married or a civil partner.
(5) If the protected characteristic is race, less favourable treatment includes segregating B from others.
(6) If the protected characteristic is sex
(a) less favourable treatment of a woman includes less favourable treatment of her because she is breast-feeding;
(b) in a case where B is a man, no account is to be taken of special treatment afforded to a woman in connection with pregnancy or childbirth.[12]

Further, Section 14 defines combined discrimination and its dual characteristics:

14(1) A person (A) discriminates against another (B) if, because of a combination of two relevant protected characteristics, A treats B less favourably than A treats or would treat a person who does not share either of those characteristics.
(2) The relevant protected characteristics are
(a) age;
(b) disability;
(c) gender reassignment;
(d) race
(e) religion or belief;
(f) sex;
(g) sexual orientation.
(3) For the purposes of establishing a contravention of this Act by virtue of subsection (1) B need not show that A's treatment of B is direct discrimination because of each of the characteristics in the combination (taken separately).
(4) But B cannot establish a contravention of this Act by virtue of subsection (1) if, in reliance on another provision of this Act or any other enactment, A shows that A's treatment of B is not direct discrimination because of either or both of the characteristics in the combination.

12 Ibid., at Section 13.

(5) Subsection (1) does not apply to a combination of characteristics that includes disability in circumstances where, if a claim of direct discrimination because of disability were to be brought, it would come within section 116 (special educational needs).[13]

Finally, Section 19 defines indirect discrimination:

19(1) A person (A) discriminates against another (B) if A applies to B a provision, criterion or practice which is discriminatory in relation to a relevant protected characteristic of B's.
(2) For the purposes of subsection (1), a provision, criterion or practice is discriminatory in relation to a relevant protected characteristic of B's if
(a) A applies, or would apply, it to persons with whom B does not share the characteristic,
(b) it puts, or would put, persons with whom B shares the characteristic at a particular disadvantage when compared with persons with whom B does not share it,
(c) it puts, or would put, B at that disadvantage, and
(d) A cannot show it to be a proportionate means of achieving a legitimate aim.
(3) The relevant protected characteristics are
age;
disability;
gender reassignment;
marriage and civil partnership;
race;
religion or belief;
sex;
sexual orientation.[14]

Section 26 outlaws with harassment:

26(1) A person (A) harasses another (B) if
(a) A engages in unwanted conduct related to a relevant protected characteristic, and
(b) the conduct has the purpose or effect of
(i) violating B's dignity, or
(ii) creating an intimidating, hostile, degrading, humiliating or offensive environment for B.
(2) A also harasses B if
(a) A engages in unwanted conduct of a sexual nature, and

13 Ibid., at Section 14.
14 Ibid., at Section 19.

(b) the conduct has the purpose or effect referred to in subsection (1)(b).

(3) A also harasses B if

(a) A or another person engages in unwanted conduct of a sexual nature or that is related to gender reassignment or sex,

(b) the conduct has the purpose or effect referred to in subsection (1)(b), and

(c) because of B's rejection of or submission to the conduct, A treats B less favourably than A would treat B if B had not rejected or submitted to the conduct.

(4) In deciding whether conduct has the effect referred to in subsection (1)(b), each of the following must be taken into account

(a) the perception of B;

(b) the other circumstances of the case;

(c) whether it is reasonable for the conduct to have that effect.

(5) The relevant protected characteristics are

age;
disability;
gender reassignment;
race;
religion or belief;
sex;
sexual orientation.[15]

Further, Section 27 outlaws victimization:

27(1) A person (A) victimises another person (B) if A subjects B to a detriment because

(a) B does a protected act, or

(b) A believes that B has done, or may do, a protected act.

(2) Each of the following is a protected act

(a) bringing proceedings under this Act;

(b) giving evidence or information in connection with proceedings under this Act;

(c) doing any other thing for the purposes of or in connection with this Act;

(d) making an allegation (whether or not express) that A or another person has contravened this Act.

(3) Giving false evidence or information, or making a false allegation, is not a protected act if the evidence or information is given, or the allegation is made, in bad faith.

(4) This section applies only where the person subjected to a detriment is an individual.

---

15 Ibid., at Section 26.

(5) The reference to contravening this Act includes a reference to committing a breach of an equality clause or rule.[16]

Finally, Section 39 deals with discrimination involving employees and applicants:

39(1) An employer (A) must not discriminate against a person (B)

(a) in the arrangements A makes for deciding to whom to offer employment;

(b) as to the terms on which A offers B employment;

(c) by not offering B employment.

(2) An employer (A) must not discriminate against an employee of A's (B)

(a) as to B's terms of employment;

(b) in the way A affords B access, or by not affording B access, to opportunities for promotion, transfer or training or for receiving any other benefit, facility or service;

(c) by dismissing B;

(d) by subjecting B to any other detriment.

(3) An employer (A) must not victimise a person (B)

(a) in the arrangements A makes for deciding to whom to offer employment;

(b) as to the terms on which A offers B employment;

(c) by not offering B employment.

(4) An employer (A) must not victimise an employee of A's (B)

(a) as to B's terms of employment;

(b) in the way A affords B access, or by not affording B access, to opportunities for promotion, transfer or training or for any other benefit, facility or service;

(c) by dismissing B;

(d) by subjecting B to any other detriment.

(5) A duty to make reasonable adjustments applies to an employer.

(6) Subsection (1)(b), so far as relating to sex or pregnancy and maternity, does not apply to a term that relates to pay

(a) unless, were B to accept the offer, an equality clause or rule would have effect in relation to the term, or

(b) if paragraph (a) does not apply, except in so far as making an offer on terms including that term amounts to a contravention of subsection (1)(b) by virtue of section 13, 14 or 18.

(7) In subsections (2)(c) and (4)(c), the reference to dismissing B includes a reference to the termination of B's employment

(a) by the expiry of a period (including a period expiring by reference to an event or circumstance);

16 Ibid., at Section 27.

(b) by an act of B's (including giving notice) in circumstances such that B is entitled, because of A's conduct, to terminate the employment without notice.

(8) Subsection (7)(a) does not apply if, immediately after the termination, the employment is renewed on the same terms.[17]

Race Relations Act (RRA) and Race Relations Act (Amendment) Regulations

Important for minorities, the Race Relations Act 1976 (RRA) defines direct and indirect discrimination, and victimization. The Act outlaws racial discrimination in employment, training, education, housing, public appointments, and the provision of goods, facilities and services. The Commission for Racial Equality (CRE) has the power to enforce the duties specified in the Act, as it will issue a compliance notice and if necessary seek a court order to enforce the notice. It places a general duty on a range of public authorities to promote race equality, with the duty's aim to make the promotion of race equality central to the work of the listed public authorities, which includes public functions carried out by private sector organizations and has only limited exemption. The public duty requires public bodies to implement race equality in all aspects of employment matters, such as recruitment and selection, training, promotion, discipline and dismissal. In relation to policy development and service delivery, the duty will encourage policy-makers to be more aware of possible problems; contribute to more informed decision-making; make sure that policies are properly targeted; improve the authority's ability to deliver suitable and accessible services that meet varied needs; encourage greater openness about policy making; increase confidence in public services, especially among ethnic minority communities; help to develop good practice; and help to avoid claims of unlawful racial discrimination. Four principles should govern public authorities' efforts to meet their duty to promote race equality: promoting race equality is obligatory for all public authorities listed; public authorities must meet the duty to promote race equality in all relevant functions; the weight given to race equality should be proportionate to its relevance; and the elements of the duty are complementary, which means they are all necessary to meet the whole duty. The general duty has three parts: eliminating unlawful racial discrimination; promoting equality of opportunity; and promoting good relations between people of different racial groups.[18]

Under the Race Relations Act 1976 and the Race Relations Act (Amendment) Regulations 2006, racial discrimination is defined under Section 1:

---

17 Ibid., at Section 39.

18 Commission for Racial Equality, *Code of Practice on the Duty to Promote Race Equality*, 2002.

1(1) A person discriminates against another in any circumstances relevant for the purposes of any provision of this Act if

(a) on racial grounds he treats that other less favourably than he treats or would treat other persons; or

(b) he applies to that other a requirement or condition which he applies or would apply equally to persons not of the same racial group as that other but

(i) which is such that the proportion of persons of the same racial group as that other who can comply with it is considerably smaller than the proportion of persons not of that racial group who can comply with it; and

(ii) which he cannot show to be justifiable irrespective of the colour, race, nationality or ethnic or national origins of the person to whom it is applied; and

(iii) which is to the detriment of that other because he cannot comply with it.

(1A) A person also discriminates against another if, in any circumstances relevant for the purposes of any provision referred to in subsection (1B), he applies to that other a provision, criterion or practice which he applies or would apply equally to persons not of the same race or ethnic or national origins as that other, but

(a) which puts or would put persons of the same race or ethnic or national origins as that other at a particular disadvantage when compared with other persons, (b) which puts that other at that disadvantage, and

(c) which he cannot show to be a proportionate means of achieving a legitimate aim.[19]

Further, Section 2 covers discrimination by way of victimization:

2(1) A person ('the discriminator') discriminates against another person ('the person victimised) in any circumstances relevant for the purposes of any provision of this Act if he treats the person victimised less favourably than in those circumstances he treats or would treat other persons, and does so by reason that the person victimised has

(a) brought proceedings against the discriminator or any other person under this Act; or

(b) given evidence or information in connection with proceedings brought by any person against the discriminator or any other person under this Act; or

(c) otherwise done anything under or by reference to this Act in relation to the discriminator or any other person; or

---

19 Race Relations Act 1976 and the Race Relations Act (Amendment) Regulations 2006, UK, at Section 1.

> (d) alleged that the discriminator or any other person has committed an act which (whether or not the allegation so states) would amount to a contravention of this Act, or by reason that the discriminator knows that the person victimised intends to do any of those things, or suspects that the person victimised has done, or intends to do, any of them.
>
> (2) Subsection (1) does not apply to treatment of a person by reason of any allegation made by him if the allegation was false and not made in good faith.[20]

As well, harassment is covered:

> 3A(1) A person subjects another to harassment in any circumstances relevant for the purposes of any provision referred to in section 1(1B) where, on grounds of race or ethnic or national origins, he engages in unwanted conduct which has the purpose or effect of
>
> (a) violating that other person's dignity, or
>
> (b) creating an intimidating, hostile, degrading, humiliating or offensive environment for him.
>
> (2) Conduct shall be regarded as having the effect specified in paragraph (a) or (b) of subsection (1) only if, having regard to all the circumstances, including in particular the perception of that other person, it should reasonably be considered *as having that effect.*[21]

Section 4 outlaws discrimination by employers:

> 4(1) It is unlawful for a person, in relation to employment by him at an establishment in Great Britain, to discriminate against another
>
> (a) in the arrangements he makes for the purpose of determining who should be offered that employment; or
>
> (b) in the terms on which he offers him that employment; or
>
> (c) by refusing or deliberately omitting to offer him that employment.
>
> (2) It is unlawful for a person, in the case of a person employed by him at an establishment in Great Britain, to discriminate against that employee
>
> (a) in the terms of employment which he affords him; or
>
> (b) in the way he affords him access to opportunities for promotion, transfer or training, or to any other benefits, facilities or services, or by refusing or deliberately omitting to afford him access to them; or
>
> (c) by dismissing him, or subjecting him to any other detriment.
>
> (2A) It is unlawful for an employer, in relation to employment by him at an establishment in Great Britain, to subject to harassment a person whom he employs or who has applied to him for employment.

---

20 Ibid., at Section 2.

21 Ibid., at Section 3A.

(3) Except in relation to discrimination falling within section 2 or discrimination on grounds of race or ethnic or national origins], subsections (1) and (2) do not apply to employment for the purposes of a private household.
(4) Subsection (2) does not apply to benefits, facilities or services of any description if the employer is concerned with the provision (for payment or not) of benefits, facilities or services of that description to the public, or to a section of the public comprising the employee in question, unless

(a) that provision differs in a material respect from the provision of the benefits, facilities or services by the employer to his employees; or

(b) the provision of the benefits, facilities or services to the employee in question is regulated by his contract of employment; or

(c) the benefits, facilities or services relate to training.

(4A) In subsection (2)(c) reference to the dismissal of a person from employment includes, where the discrimination is on grounds of race or ethnic or national origins, reference

(a) to the termination of that person's employment by the expiration of any period (including a period expiring by reference to an event or circumstance), not being a termination immediately after which the employment is renewed on the same terms; and

(b) to the termination of that person's employment by any act of his (including the giving of notice) in circumstances such that he is entitled to terminate it without notice by reason of the conduct of the employer.[22]

Finally, in terms of a General Statutory duty, Section 71(1) states:

71(1) Every body or other person specified in Schedule 1A or a description falling within that Schedule shall, in carrying out its functions, have due regard to the need

(a) to eliminate unlawful racial discrimination; and

(b) to promote equality of opportunity and good relations between persons of different racial groups.[23]

Sex Discrimination Act (SDA)

Important for women, the Sex Discrimination Act 1975 (SDA) defines direct and indirect discrimination. Further, under the SDA, it is first up to the applicant to establish facts, which constitute a "prima facie" case of discrimination, as the burden of proof is initially on the employee to show on the balance of probabilities that her male comparator is doing the same or broadly similar work, or that her work has been rated as equivalent to his, or that her work is of equal value, and that his contract contains a more favorable term. The burden of proof then shifts from

22 Ibid., at Section 4.

23 Ibid., at Section 71(1).

the applicant to the employer to show that there is a nondiscriminatory reason for their actions: that is, the difference between the contracts is genuinely due to a material factor which is not the difference of gender. The material factor defense is the reason put forward by the employer to explain why the comparator, although doing equal work, is paid more than the applicant; to succeed in a defense, this factor must be significant and relevant; that is, it must be an important cause of the difference and apply to the jobs in question. The difference in pay must be genuinely due to the material factor which must not be tainted by gender discrimination. If the reason given for paying the comparator more is that he has certain skills which the applicant does not have, then the employer would have to demonstrate that these skills are necessary for the job, and genuinely applied during the performance of the job, and are not simply rewarded because past pay agreements recognized and rewarded skills which are no longer applicable; to succeed in a defense, the employer needs to show that the material factor accounts for the whole of the difference in pay.

Direct and indirect discrimination are defined in Section 1:

> 1(1) In any circumstances relevant for the purposes of any provision of this Act … a person discriminates against a woman if:
>
> (a) on the ground of her sex he treats her less favourably than he treats or would treat a man, or
>
> (b) he applies to her a requirement or condition which he applies or would apply equally to a man but:
>
> (i) which is such that the proportion of women who can comply with it is considerably smaller than the proportion of men who can comply with it, and
>
> (ii) which he cannot show to be justifiable irrespective of the sex of the person to whom it is applied, and
>
> 1(1)(b)(iii) which is to her detriment because she cannot comply with it.[24]

In looking at discrimination in the employment stage, Section 6(2) states:

> 6(2) It is unlawful for a person, in the case of a woman employed by him at an establishment in Great Britain, to discriminate against her:
>
> (a) in the way he affords her access to opportunities for promotion, transfer or training, or to any other benefits, facilities or services, or by refusing or deliberately omitting to afford her access to them, or
>
> (b) by dismissing her, or subjecting her to any other detriment.[25]

There is an exception to the rule where sex is a genuine occupational qualification, which is contained in Section 7:

---

24 Sex Discrimination Act, UK, at Section 1.

25 Ibid., at Section 6(2).

> 7(1) In relation to sex discrimination:
> (a) section 6(1)(a) or (c) does not apply to any employment where being a man is a genuine occupational qualification for the job.
> 7(2) Being a man is a genuine occupational qualification for a job only where:
> (a) the essential nature of the job calls for a man for reasons of physiology (excluding physical strength or stamina) or, in dramatic performances or other entertainment, for reasons of authenticity, so that the essential nature of the job would be materially different if carried out by a woman; or
> (b) the job needs to be held by a man to preserve decency or privacy … or
> (c) the nature or location of the establishment makes it impracticable for the holder of the job to live elsewhere than in premises provided by the employer …
> (d) the nature of the establishment, or of the part of it within which the work is done, requires it to be held by a man … or
> (e) the job needs to be held by a man because of restrictions imposed by the laws regulating the employment of women, or
> (f) the holder of the job provides individuals with personal services promoting their welfare or education, or similar personal services, and those services can most effectively be provided by a man, or
> (g) the job needs to be held by a man because it is likely to involve the performance of duties outside the United Kingdom in a country whose laws or customs are such that the duties could not, or could not effectively, be performed by a woman, or
> (h) the job is one of two to be held by a married couple.[26]

Equal Pay Act (EPA), Equal Opportunities Commission (EOC) and the Code of Practice on Equal Pay

Important for equal rights in employment and in particular women, the Equal Pay Act 1970 (EPA) covers all contractual terms and not simply those relating to pay, with claims taken initially to an Industrial Tribunal. Genuine occupational qualification is recognized in Section 1(3):

> 1(3) An equality clause shall not operate in relation to a variation between the woman's contract and the man's contract if the employer proves that the variation is genuinely due to a material factor which is not the difference of sex and that factor … must be a material difference between the woman's case and the man's … .[27]

Section 2(1) guarantees the important right of tribunal recourse for redress:

26 Ibid., at Section 7.
27 Equal Pay Act, UK, at Section 1(3).

> 2(1) Any claim in respect of the contravention of a term modified or included by virtue of an equality clause, including a claim for arrears of remuneration or damages in respect of the contravention, may be presented by way of a complaint to an employment tribunal.[28]

In terms of class discrimination cases, the Code of Practice on Equal Pay is the main source of advice on implementing equal pay in the workplace and was issued by the Equal Opportunities Commission (EOC) in 1997. Employers must include an equality clause in individual contracts of employment. The EOC issued a Code of Practice for the purposes of the elimination of discrimination in employment; for guidance to employers, trade unions and employment agencies on measures that can be taken to achieve equality, and on what steps it is reasonably practicable for employers to take to ensure that their employees do not in the course of their employment act contrary to the law; and for the promotion of equality of opportunity in employment. The primary responsibility at law rests with each employer to ensure that there is no unlawful discrimination. The Code recommends the establishment and use of consistent criteria for selection, training, promotion, redundancy and dismissal that are made known to all employees, as part of good employment practices in eliminating disability discrimination. It is recommended that each individual should be assessed according to his personal capability to carry out a given job.

The EOC recommends that a pay systems review should involve the following stages. Stage 1: undertake a thorough analysis of the pay system to produce a breakdown of all employees, which covers job title, grade, whether part-time or full-time, with basic pay, performance ratings and all other elements of remuneration; stage 2: examine each element of the pay system against the data obtained in stage 1; stage 3: identify any elements of the pay system that the review indicates may be the source of any discrimination; stage 4: change any rules or practices, including those in collective agreements, which stages 1 to 3 have identified as likely to give rise to discrimination in pay, in consultation with employees, trade unions or staff representatives where appropriate. Stages 1 to 3 may reveal that practices and procedures in relation to recruitment, selection and access to training have contributed to discrimination in pay, and these should be addressed; stage 5: analyze the likely effects of any proposed changes in practice to the pay system before implementation, in order to identify and rectify any discrimination that could be caused; stage 6: give equal pay to current employees. Where the review shows that some employees are not receiving equal pay for equal work and the reasons cannot be shown to be free of bias, then a plan must be developed for dealing with this; stage 7: set up a system of regular monitoring to allow checks to be made to pay practices; and stage 8: draw up and publish an equal pay policy

28 Ibid., at Section 2(1).

with provision for assessing the new pay system or modification to a system in terms of discrimination.[29]

Ireland

In looking at discrimination in the Republic of Ireland, protection is afforded under the Constitution. Further, the two main pieces of legislation guarding against discrimination are the Employment Equality Act and the Equal Status Act.

Constitution of Ireland

The Constitution of Ireland (Bunreacht Na hEireann) was enacted by the People on 1 July 1937 and came into operation as from 29 December 1937. The Preamble of the Constitution of Ireland states:

> In the Name of the Most Holy Trinity, from Whom is all authority and to Whom, as our final end, all actions both of men and States must be referred,
>
> We, the people of Éire,
>
> Humbly acknowledging all our obligations to our Divine Lord, Jesus Christ, Who sustained our fathers through centuries of trial,
>
> Gratefully remembering their heroic and unremitting struggle to regain the rightful independence of our Nation,
>
> And seeking to promote the common good, with due observance of Prudence, Justice and Charity, so that the dignity and freedom of the individual may be assured, true social order attained, the unity of our country restored, and concord established with other nations,
>
> Do hereby adopt, enact, and give to ourselves this Constitution.[30]

Fundamental freedoms are guaranteed as personal rights under Article 40, and class discrimination is specifically mentioned under Article 40.6(2), one of few laws anywhere that mentions specifically class:

> 40.1. All citizens shall, as human persons, be held equal before the law.
> This shall not be held to mean that the State shall not in its enactments have due regard to differences of capacity, physical and moral, and of social function.

29 Equal Opportunities Commission, *Code of Practice on Equal Pay*.
30 Constitution of Ireland, Ireland, at the Preamble.

2(1) Titles of nobility shall not be conferred by the State.
(2) No title of nobility or of honour may be accepted by any citizen except with the prior approval of the Government.
3(1) The State guarantees in its laws to respect, and, as far as practicable, by its laws to defend and vindicate the personal rights of the citizen.
(2) The State shall, in particular, by its laws protect as best it may from unjust attack and, in the case of injustice done, vindicate the life, person, good name, and property rights of every citizen.
(3) The State acknowledges the right to life of the unborn and, with due regard to the equal right to life of the mother, guarantees in its laws to respect, and, as far as practicable, by its laws to defend and vindicate that right.
This subsection shall not limit freedom to travel between the State and another state.
This subsection shall not limit freedom to obtain or make available, in the State, subject to such conditions as may be laid down by law, information relating to services lawfully available in another state.
4(1) No citizen shall be deprived of his personal liberty save in accordance with law.
(2) Upon complaint being made by or on behalf of any person to the High Court or any judge thereof alleging that such person is being unlawfully detained, the High Court and any and every judge thereof to whom such complaint is made shall forthwith enquire into the said complaint and may order the person in whose custody such person is detained to produce the body of such person before the High Court on a named day and to certify in writing the grounds of his detention, and the High Court shall, upon the body of such person being produced before that Court and after giving the person in whose custody he is detained an opportunity of justifying the detention, order the release of such person from such detention unless satisfied that he is being detained in accordance with the law.
(3) Where the body of a person alleged to be unlawfully detained is produced before the High Court in pursuance of an order in that behalf made under this section and that Court is satisfied that such person is being detained in accordance with a law but that such law is invalid having regard to the provisions of this Constitution, the High Court shall refer the question of the validity of such law to the Supreme Court by way of case stated and may, at the time of such reference or at any time thereafter, allow the said person to be at liberty on such bail and subject to such conditions as the High Court shall fix until the Supreme Court has determined the question so referred to it.
(4) The High Court before which the body of a person alleged to be unlawfully detained is to be produced in pursuance of an order in that behalf made under this section shall, if the President of the High Court or, if he is not available, the senior judge of that Court who is available so directs in respect of any particular case, consist of three judges and shall, in every other case, consist of one judge only.

(5) Nothing in this section, however, shall be invoked to prohibit, control, or interfere with any act of the Defence Forces during the existence of a state of war or armed rebellion.
(6) Provision may be made by law for the refusal of bail by a court to a person charged with a serious offence where it is reasonably considered necessary to prevent the commission of a serious offence by that person.
5. The dwelling of every citizen is inviolable and shall not be forcibly entered save in accordance with law.
6. (1) The State guarantees liberty for the exercise of the following rights, subject to public order and morality:

i. The right of the citizens to express freely their convictions and opinions. The education of public opinion being, however, a matter of such grave import to the common good, the State shall endeavour to ensure that organs of public opinion, such as the radio, the press, the cinema, while preserving their rightful liberty of expression, including criticism of Government policy, shall not be used to undermine public order or morality or the authority of the State.
The publication or utterance of blasphemous, seditious, or indecent matter is an offence which shall be punishable in accordance with law.
ii. The right of the citizens to assemble peaceably and without arms. Provision may be made by law to prevent or control meetings which are determined in accordance with law to be calculated to cause a breach of the peace or to be a danger or nuisance to the general public and to prevent or control meetings in the vicinity of either House of the Oireachtas.
iii. The right of the citizens to form associations and unions. Laws, however, may be enacted for the regulation and control in the public interest of the exercise of the foregoing right.

(2) Laws regulating the manner in which the right of forming associations and unions and the right of free assembly may be exercised shall contain no political, religious or class discrimination.[31]

Finally, Article 42 covers education as a tool for advancement:

42.1. The State acknowledges that the primary and natural educator of the child is the Family and guarantees to respect the inalienable right and duty of parents to provide, according to their means, for the religious and moral, intellectual, physical and social education of their children.
2. Parents shall be free to provide this education in their homes or in private schools or in schools recognised or established by the State.
3(1) The State shall not oblige parents in violation of their conscience and lawful preference to send their children to schools established by the State, or to any particular type of school designated by the State.

31 Ibid., at Article 40.

> (2) The State shall, however, as guardian of the common good, require in view of actual conditions that the children receive a certain minimum education, moral, intellectual and social.
> 4. The State shall provide for free primary education and shall endeavour to supplement and give reasonable aid to private and corporate educational initiative, and, when the public good requires it, provide other educational facilities or institutions with due regard, however, for the rights of parents, especially in the matter of religious and moral formation.
> 5 In exceptional cases, where the parents for physical or moral reasons fail in their duty towards their children, the State as guardian of the common good, by appropriate means shall endeavour to supply the place of the parents, but always with due regard for the natural and imprescriptible rights of the child.[32]

Employment Equality Act

In Ireland, the Employment Equality Act (1998) prohibits discrimination in employment and in other spheres of life on a number of grounds, which should include class. The conception of equality in the EEA is based on individual merit, and moves towards the "equality as rationality" end of the spectrum, addressing discrimination based on prejudice or stereotypes. The Act creates some positive duties to promote equality, despite the limits to positive action in favor of individuals. In addition, it established an Equality Authority with powers to develop codes of practice that have enhanced legal standing, and to promote equality through Equality Reviews and Action Plans. Positive measures are permitted under the Employment Equality Act, where the measures are "intended to reduce or eliminate the effects of discrimination", and various provisions prevent challenges to measures targeted to disadvantaged groups, including seniors.

Important for equal rights and for class discrimination cases, discrimination is outlined in Section 6:

> 6(1) For the purposes of this Act, discrimination shall be taken to occur where, on any of the grounds in *subsection (2)* (in this Act referred to as 'the discriminatory grounds'), one person is treated less favourably than another is, has been or would be treated.
> (2) As between any 2 persons, the discriminatory grounds (and the descriptions of those grounds for the purposes of this Act) are:
> (*a*) that one is a woman and the other is a man (in this Act referred to as 'the gender ground'),
> (*b*) that they are of different marital status (in this Act referred to as 'the marital status ground'),
> (*c*) that one has family status and the other does not (in this Act referred to as 'the family status ground'),

32 Ibid., at Article 42.

(*d*) that they are of different sexual orientation (in this Act referred to as 'the sexual orientation ground'),
(*e*) that one has a different religious belief from the other, or that one has a religious belief and the other has not (in this Act referred to as 'the religion ground'),
(*f*) that they are of different ages, but subject to *subsection (3)* (in this Act referred to as 'the age ground'),
(*g*) that one is a person with a disability and the other either is not or is a person with a different disability (in this Act referred to as 'the disability ground'),
(*h*) that they are of different race, colour, nationality or ethnic or national origins (in this Act referred to as 'the ground of race'),
(*i*) that one is a member of the traveller community and the other is not (in this Act referred to as 'the traveller community ground').[33]

Further, in terms of comparators, Section 28 states:

28(1) For the purpose of this Part, 'C' and 'D' represent 2 persons who differ as follows:
(*a*) in relation to the marital status ground, C and D have different marital status;
(*b*) in relation to the family status ground, C has family status and D does not, or *vice versa*;
(*c*) in relation to the sexual orientation ground, C and D are of different sexual orientations;
(*d*) in relation to the religion ground, C and D have different religious beliefs or C has a religious belief and D does not, or *vice versa*;
(*e*) in relation to the age ground, C and D are of different ages;
(*f*) in relation to the disability ground, C is a person with a disability and D is not, or *vice versa*, or C and D are persons with different disabilities;
(*g*) in relation to the ground of race, C and D differ as to race, colour, nationality or ethnic or national origins or any combination of those factors;
(*h*) in relation to the traveller community ground, C is a member of the traveller community and D is not, or *vice versa*.
(2) In the following provisions of this Part, any reference to C and D which does not apply to a specific discriminatory ground shall be treated as a reference to C and D in the context of each of the discriminatory grounds (other than the gender ground) considered separately.
(3) Any reference in this Act to persons having the same relevant characteristic as C (or as D) shall be construed by reference to the discriminatory ground in

33 Ibid., at Section 6.

relation to which the reference applies or, as the case may be, in relation to each of the discriminatory grounds (other than the gender ground) separately, so that

(*a*) in relation to the marital status ground, the relevant characteristic is having the same marital status as C (or, as the case may be, as D), and

(*b*) in relation to the family status ground, the relevant characteristic is having the same, or the same lack of, family status as C (or, as the case may be, as D),

and so on for each of the other discriminatory grounds.[34]

Further, discrimination by employers is outlined under Section 8:

8(1) In relation to:

(*a*) access to employment,
(*b*) conditions of employment,
(*c*) training or experience for or in relation to employment,
(*d*) promotion or re-grading, or
(*e*) classification of posts,

an employer shall not discriminate against an employee or prospective employee and a provider of agency work shall not discriminate against an agency worker.

(5) Without prejudice to the generality of *subsection (1)*, an employer shall be taken to discriminate against an employee or prospective employee in relation to access to employment if the employer discriminates against the employee or prospective employee:

(*a*) in any arrangements the employer makes for the purpose of deciding to whom employment should be offered, or

(*b*) by specifying, in respect of one person or class of persons, entry requirements for employment which are not specified in respect of other persons or classes of persons, where the circumstances in which both such persons or classes would be employed are not materially different.

(6) Without prejudice to the generality of *subsection (1)*, an employer shall be taken to discriminate against an employee or prospective employee in relation to conditions of employment if, on any of the discriminatory grounds, the employer does not offer or afford to that employee or prospective employee or to a class of persons of whom he or she is one:

(*a*) the same terms of employment (other than remuneration and pension rights),

(*b*) the same working conditions, and

(*c*) the same treatment in relation to overtime, shift work, short time, transfers, lay-offs, redundancies, dismissals and disciplinary measures,

as the employer offers or affords to another person or class of persons, where the circumstances in which both such persons or classes are or would be employed are not materially different.

---

34 Ibid., at Section 28.

(7) Without prejudice to the generality of *subsection (1)*, an employer shall be taken to discriminate against an employee in relation to training or experience for, or in relation to, employment if, on any of the discriminatory grounds, the employer refuses to offer or afford to that employee the same opportunities or facilities for employment counseling, training (whether on or off the job) and work experience as the employer offers or affords to other employees, where the circumstances in which that employee and those other employees are employed are not materially different.

(8) Without prejudice to the generality of *subsection (1)*, an employer shall be taken to discriminate against an employee in relation to promotion if, on any of the discriminatory grounds:

(*a*) the employer refuses or deliberately omits to offer or afford the employee access to opportunities for promotion in circumstances in which another eligible and qualified person is offered or afforded such access, or

(*b*) the employer does not in those circumstances offer or afford the employee access in the same way to those opportunities.[35]

As well, discrimination as to bodies is covered under Section 13:

13. A body which

(*a*) is an organisation of workers or of employers,

(*b*) is a professional or trade organisation, or

(*c*) controls entry to, or the carrying on of, a profession, vocation or occupation,

shall not discriminate against a person in relation to membership of that body or any benefits, other than pension rights, provided by it or in relation to entry to, or the carrying on of, that profession, vocation or occupation.[36]

In addition, indirect discrimination is covered in Section 31:

31(1) Where a provision (whether in the nature of a requirement, practice or otherwise) relating to employment:

(*a*) applies to all the employees or prospective employees of a particular employer who include C and D or, as the case may be, to a particular class of those employees or prospective employees which includes C and D,

(*b*) operates to the disadvantage of C, as compared with D, in relation to any of the matters specified in *paragraphs (a)* to *(e)* of *section 8(1)*,

(*c*) in practice can be complied with by a substantially smaller proportion of the employees or prospective employees having the same relevant characteristic as C when compared with the employees or prospective employees having the same relevant characteristic as D, and

---

35 Ibid., at Section 8.

36 Ibid., at Section 13.

> (*d*) cannot be justified as being reasonable in all the circumstances of the case,
>
> then … for the purposes of this Act the employer shall be regarded as discriminating against C, contrary to *section 8,* on whichever of the discriminatory grounds gives rise to the relevant characteristics referred to in *paragraph (c).*[37]

The Employment Equality Act makes the principle of "equal pay for like work" a term of every employment contract. Proving "like work" means showing that the work of the person claiming equal pay, the claimant, is the same, similar or equal in value to the work of the appropriate comparator, the person with whom the claimant is comparing himself. The comparator must, among other things, be employed by the same or an associated employer, at the same time or during the previous or following three years. Section 7(1) establishes like work:

> 7(1) Subject to *subsection (2)*, for the purposes of this Act, in relation to the work which one person is employed to do, another person shall be regarded as employed to do like work if:
>
> (*a*) both perform the same work under the same or similar conditions, or each is interchangeable with the other in relation to the work,
>
> (*b*) the work performed by one is of a similar nature to that performed by the other and any differences between the work performed or the conditions under which it is performed by each either are of small importance in relation to the work as a whole or occur with such irregularity as not to be significant to the work as a whole, or
>
> (*c*) the work performed by one is equal in value to the work performed by the other, having regard to such matters as skill, physical or mental requirements, responsibility and working conditions.
>
> (3) In any case where:
>
> (*a*) the remuneration received by one person ('the primary worker') is less than the remuneration received by another ('the comparator'), and
>
> (*b*) the work performed by the primary worker is greater in value than the work performed by the comparator, having regard to the matters mentioned in *subsection (1)(c)*,
>
> then, for the purposes of *subsection (1)(c)*, the work performed by the primary worker shall be regarded as equal in value to the work performed by the comparator.[38]

In addition, entitlement to equal remuneration is covered under Section 29:

37 Ibid., at Section 31.

38 Ibid., at Section 7.

29(1) It shall be a term of the contract under which C is employed that, subject to this Act, C shall at any time be entitled to the same rate of remuneration for the work which C is employed to do as D who, at that or any other relevant time, is employed to do like work by the same or an associated employer.
(3) For the purposes of this Part, where D's employer is an associated employer of C's employer, C and D shall not be regarded as employed to do like work unless they both have the same or reasonably comparable terms and conditions of employment.
(4) Where a term of a contract of employment or a criterion applied to employees (including C and D):

(*a*) applies to all employees of a particular employer or to a particular class of such employees (including C and D),
(*b*) is such that the remuneration of those who fulfil the term or criterion is different from that of those who do not,
(*c*) is such that the proportion of employees who can fulfil the term or criterion is substantially smaller in the case of the employees having the same relevant characteristic as C when compared with the employees having the same relevant characteristic as D, and
(*d*) cannot be justified as being reasonable in all the circumstances of the case,

then, for the purposes of *subsection (1)*, C and D shall each be treated as fulfilling or, as the case may be, as not fulfilling the term or criterion, whichever results in the higher remuneration.
(5) Subject to *subsection (4)*, nothing in this Part shall prevent an employer from paying, on grounds other than the discriminatory grounds, different rates of remuneration to different employees.[39]

Important for equal rights, an equality clause is outlined under Section 30:

30(1) If and so far as the terms of a contract of employment do not include (expressly or by reference to a collective agreement or otherwise) a non-discriminatory equality clause, they shall be taken to include one.
(2) A non-discriminatory equality clause is a provision relating to the terms of a contract of employment, other than a term relating to remuneration or pension rights, which has the effect that if:

(*a*) C is employed in circumstances where the work done by C is not materially different from that done by D in the same employment, and
(*b*) at any time C's contract of employment would (but for the non-discriminatory equality clause):

(i) contain a term which is or becomes less favourable to C than a term of a similar kind in D's contract of employment, or

39 Ibid., at Section 29.

(ii) not include a term corresponding to a term in D's contract of employment which benefits D,

then the terms of C's contract of employment shall be treated as modified so that the term in question is not less favourable to C or, as the case may be, so that they include a similar term benefiting C.

(3) A non-discriminatory equality clause shall not operate in relation to a difference between C's contract of employment and D's contract of employment if the employer proves that the difference is genuinely based on grounds which are not among those specified in *paragraphs (a)* to *(h)* of *section 28(1)*.[40]

Harassment in the workplace is also covered under Section 32:

> 32(1) If, at a place where C is employed (in this section referred to as 'the workplace'), or otherwise in the course of C's employment, another individual ('E') harasses C by reference to the relevant characteristic of C and:
>
> (*a*) C and E are both employed at that place or by the same employer,
>
> (*b*) E is C's employer, or
>
> (*c*) E is a client, customer or other business contact of C's employer and the circumstances of the harassment are such that C's employer ought reasonably to have taken steps to prevent it,
>
> then, for the purposes of this Act, the harassment constitutes discrimination by C's employer, in relation to C's conditions of employment, on whichever discriminatory ground is relevant to persons having the same relevant characteristic as C.
>
> (6) If, as a result of any act or conduct of E another person ('F') who is C's employer would, apart from this subsection, be regarded … as discriminating against C, it shall be a defence for F to prove that F took such steps as are reasonably practicable:
>
> (*a*) … to prevent C being treated differently in the workplace or otherwise in the course of C's employment and, if and so far as any such treatment has occurred, to reverse the effects of it, and
>
> (*b*) … to prevent E from harassing C (or any class of persons of whom C is one).[41]

Importantly, positive action for workers is permitted as contained in Section 33, and in particular Section 33(1)(*a*):

> 33(1) Nothing in this Part or *Part II* shall prevent the taking of such measures … in order to facilitate the integration into employment, either generally or in particular areas or a particular workplace …

40 Ibid., at Section 30.

41 Ibid., at Section 32.

> (3) Nothing in this Part or *Part II* shall render unlawful the provision, by or on behalf of the State, of training or work experience for a disadvantaged group of persons if the Minister certifies that, in the absence of the provision in question, it is unlikely that that disadvantaged group would receive similar training or work experience.[42]

The Equality Authority has important legal powers, not to decide on disputes but to work generally for the elimination of discrimination and the promotion of equal opportunities. It can develop Codes of Practice, carry out equality reviews in particular employment, draw up Equality Action Plans and serve Substantive Notices. The Authority has broad powers to ensure the development of a proactive equality-conscious approach to equal opportunities in the workplace. The functions of the Equality Authority are outlined under Section 39:

> 39 The Authority shall have, in addition to the functions assigned to it by any other provision of this Act or of any other Act, the following general functions:
> (*a*) to work towards the elimination of discrimination in relation to employment;
> (*b*) to promote equality of opportunity in relation to the matters to which this Act applies.[43]

The composition of the Equality Authority shall be diverse, with members taken from various groups including those with knowledge or experience in the gay community, as outlined in Section 44(1)(c)(i):

> 44(1) Of the ordinary members of the Authority
> (*a*) two, one male and one female, shall be persons appointed on the nomination by such organisations representative of employees as the Minister considers appropriate,
> (*b*) two, one male and one female, shall be persons appointed on the nomination by such organisations representative of employers as the Minister considers appropriate, and
> (*c*) the remaining number shall be such persons as appear to the Minister to be persons who have knowledge of, or experience in
> (i) consumer, social affairs or equality issues, including issues related to the experience and circumstances of groups who are disadvantaged by reference to gender, marital status, family status, **class**, religion, age, disability, race, colour, nationality, ethnic or national origin or membership of the traveller community,
> (ii) issues related to the provision of goods or services, or

42 Ibid., at Section 33.
43 Ibid., at Section 39.

(iii) such other subject-matter (including law, finance, management or administration) as appears to the Minister to be relevant to the issues to which the
functions of the Authority relate.[44]

The forum for seeking redress is covered under Section 77:

77(1) A person who claims:
(*a*) to have been discriminated against by another in contravention of this Act,
(*b*) not to be receiving remuneration in accordance with an equal remuneration term,
(*c*) not to be receiving a benefit under an equality clause, or
(*d*) to have been penalised in circumstances amounting to victimisation,
may, subject to *subsections (2)* to *(8)*, seek redress by referring the case to the Director.
(2) If a person claims to have been dismissed:
(*a*) in circumstances amounting to discrimination by another in contravention of this Act, or
(*b*) in circumstances amounting to victimisation,
then, subject to *subsection (3)*, a claim for redress for the dismissal may be brought to the Labour Court and shall not be brought to the Director.
(3) If the grounds for such a claim as is referred to in *subsection (1)* or *(2)* arise:
(*a*) under *Part III*, or
(*b*) in any other circumstances (including circumstances amounting to victimisation) to which the Equal Pay Directive or the Equal Treatment Directive is relevant,
then … the person making the claim may seek redress by referring the case to the Circuit Court, instead of referring it to the Director under *subsection (1)* or, as the case may be, to the Labour Court under *subsection (2)*.
(4) In this Part, in relation to a case referred under any provision of this section:
(*a*) 'the complainant' means the person by whom it is referred, and
(*b*) 'the respondent' means the person who is alleged to have discriminated against the complainant or, as the case may be, who is responsible for providing the remuneration to which the equal remuneration term relates or who is responsible for providing the benefit under the equality clause or who is alleged to be responsible for the victimisation.[45]

44 Ibid., at Section 44.
45 Ibid., at Section 77.

Crucially, enforcement of determinations, decisions and mediated settlements is outlined under Section 91:

> 91(1) If an employer or any other person who is bound by the terms of:
>
> (*a*) a final determination of the Labour Court under this Part, or
>
> (*b*) a final decision of the Director under this Part,
>
> fails to comply with the terms of the determination or decision then, on an application under this section, the Circuit Court shall make, subject to *section 93,* an order directing the person affected (that is to say, the employer or other person concerned) to carry out the determination or decision in accordance with its terms.
>
> (2) If an employer or the person who is a party to a settlement … fails to give effect, in whole or in part, to the terms of the settlement, then, on an application under this section, the Circuit Court may make an order directing the person affected (that is to say, the employer or the person who is a party to the settlement) to carry out those terms or, as the case may be, the part of those terms to which the application relates; but the Circuit Court shall not, by virtue of this subsection, direct any person to pay any sum or do any other thing which (had the matter been dealt with otherwise than by mediation) could not have been provided for by way of redress … .
>
> (3) An application under this section may not be made before the expiry of:
>
> (*a*) in the case of a determination or decision, the period within which an appeal might be brought against the determination or decision, and
>
> (*b*) in the case of a settlement reached as a result of mediation, 42 days from the date of the written record of the settlement.
>
> (4) An application under this section may be made:
>
> (*a*) by the complainant, or
>
> (*b*) in a case where the Authority is not the complainant, then, by the Authority with the consent of the complainant if the Authority considers that the determination, decision or settlement is unlikely to be implemented without its intervention.
>
> (5) On an application under this section, the Circuit Court shall exercise its functions under *subsection (1)* or *(2)* on being satisfied:
>
> (*a*) of the existence and terms of the determination, decision or settlement, and
>
> (*b*) of the failure by the person affected to comply with those terms.
>
> (6) For the purposes of this section, a determination or decision is final if no appeal lies from it under this Part or if the time for bringing an appeal has expired and either:
>
> (*a*) no appeal has been brought, or
>
> (*b*) any appeal which was brought has been abandoned.
>
> (7) Without prejudice to the power of the Circuit Court to make an order for costs in favor of the complainant or the person affected, where an application is

made by the Authority by virtue of *subsection (4)(b),* the costs of the Authority may be awarded by the Circuit Court.
(8) The jurisdiction conferred on the Circuit Court by this section shall be exercised by the judge for the time being assigned to the circuit where the respondent ordinarily resides or carries on any profession, business or occupation.[46]

Equal Status Act

Important for equal rights and class discrimination cases, discrimination is outlined in Section 3 of the Equal Status Act (2000):

3(1) For the purposes of this Act, discrimination shall be taken to occur where:
(*a*) on any of the grounds specified in *subsection (2)* (in this Act referred to as 'the discriminatory grounds') which exists at present or previously existed but no longer exists or may exist in the future, or which is imputed to the person concerned, a person is treated less favourably than another person is, has been or would be treated,
(*b*) (i) a person who is associated with another person is treated, by virtue of that association, less favourably than a person who is not so associated is, has been or would be treated, and
(ii) similar treatment of that person on any of the discriminatory grounds would, by virtue of *paragraph (a)*, constitute discrimination,
or
(*c*) (i) a person is in a category of persons who share a common characteristic by reason of which discrimination may, by virtue of *paragraph (a)*, occur in respect of those persons,
(ii) the person is obliged by the provider of a service … to comply with a condition (whether in the nature of a requirement, practice or otherwise) but is unable to do so,
(iii) substantially more people outside the category than within it are able to comply with the condition, and
(iv) the obligation to comply with the condition cannot be justified as being reasonable in all the circumstances of the case.
(2) As between any two persons, the discriminatory grounds (and the descriptions of those grounds for the purposes of this Act) are:
(*a*) that one is male and the other is female (the 'gender ground'),
(*b*) that they are of different marital status (the 'marital status ground'),
(*c*) that one has family status and the other does not or that one has a different family status from the other (the 'family status ground'),
(*d*) that they are of different sexual orientation (the 'sexual orientation ground'),

46 Ibid., at Section 91.

> (*e*) that one has a different religious belief from the other, or that one has a religious belief and the other has not (the 'religion ground'),
> (*f*) … that they are of different ages (the 'age ground'),
> (*g*) that one is a person with a disability and the other either is not or is a person with a different disability (the 'disability ground'),
> (*h*) that they are of different race, colour, nationality or ethnic or national origins (the 'ground of race'),
> (*i*) that one is a member of the Traveller community and the other is not (the 'Traveller community ground'),
> (*j*) that one:
> (i) has in good faith applied for any determination or redress provided for in *Part II* or *III*,
> (ii) has attended as a witness before the Authority, the Director or a court in connection with any inquiry or proceedings under this Act,
> (iii) has given evidence in any criminal proceedings under this Act,
> (iv) has opposed by lawful means an act which is unlawful under this Act, or
> (v) has given notice of an intention to take any of the actions specified in *subparagraphs (i)* to *(iv)*,
> and the other has not (the 'victimisation ground').[47]

Further, Section 5 provides for non-discrimination in the disposal of goods and provision of services:

> 5(1) A person shall not discriminate in disposing of goods to the public generally or a section of the public or in providing a service, whether the disposal or provision is for consideration or otherwise and whether the service provided can be availed of only by a section of the public.
> (2) *Subsection (1)* does not apply in respect of:
> (*c*) differences in the treatment of persons on the gender ground in relation to services of an aesthetic, cosmetic or similar nature, where the services require physical contact between the service provider and the recipient,
> (*d*) differences in the treatment of persons in relation to annuities, pensions, insurance policies or any other matters related to the assessment of risk where the treatment:
> (i) is effected by reference to:
> (I) actuarial or statistical data obtained from a source on which it is reasonable to rely, or
> (II) other relevant underwriting or commercial factors,
> and
> (ii) is reasonable having regard to the data or other relevant factors,

47 Equal Status Act, Ireland, at Section 3.

> (*e*) differences in the treatment of person on the religion ground in relation to goods or services provided for a religious purpose,
> (*f*) differences in the treatment of persons on the gender, age or disability ground or on the basis of nationality or national origin in relation to the provision or organisation of a sporting facility or sporting event to the extent that the differences are reasonably necessary having regard to the nature of the facility or event and are relevant to the purpose of the facility or event,
> (*h*) differences in the treatment of persons in a category of persons in respect of services that are provided for the principal purpose of promoting, for a *bona fide* purpose and in a *bona fide* manner, the special interests of persons in that category to the extent that the differences in treatment are reasonably necessary to promote those special interests,
> (*i*) differences in the treatment of persons on the gender, age or disability ground or on the ground of race, reasonably required for reasons of authenticity, aesthetics, tradition or custom in connection with a dramatic performance or other entertainment, or
> (*l*) differences, not otherwise specifically provided for in this section, in the treatment of persons in respect of the disposal of goods, or the provision of a service, which can reasonably be regarded as goods or a service suitable only to the needs of certain persons.[48]

Importantly, Section 7 prohibits discrimination in educational institutions, so important as a tool for advancement:

> 7(1) In this section 'educational establishment' means a preschool service within the meaning of Part VII of the Child Care Act, 1991, a primary or post-primary school, an institution providing adult, continuing or further education, or a university or any other third-level or higher-level institution, whether or not supported by public funds.
> (2) An educational establishment shall not discriminate in relation to
> (*a*) the admission or the terms or conditions of admission of a person as a student to the establishment,
> (*b*) the access of a student to any course, facility or benefit provided by the establishment,
> (*c*) any other term or condition of participation in the establishment by a student, or
> (*d*) the expulsion of a student from the establishment or any other sanction against the student.
> (3) An educational establishment does not discriminate under *subsection (2)* by reason only that

48 Ibid., at Section 5.

(*a*) where the establishment is not a third-level institution and admits students of one gender only, it refuses to admit as a student a person who is not of that gender,

(*b*) where the establishment is an institution established for the purpose of providing training to ministers of religion and admits students of only one gender or religious belief, it
refuses to admit as a student a person who is not of that gender or religious belief,

(*c*) where the establishment is a school providing primary or post-primary education to students and the objective of the school is to provide education in an environment which promotes certain religious values, it admits persons of a particular religious denomination in preference to others or it refuses to admit as a student a person who is not of that denomination and, in the case of a refusal, it is proved that the refusal is essential to maintain the ethos of the school,

(*d*) without prejudice to section 3 of the Refugee Act, 1996, where the establishment is an institution providing adult, continuing or further education or a university or other third-level institution

(i) it provides different treatment in relation to

(I) fees for admission or attendance by persons who are nationals of a member state of the European Union and persons who are not, or

(II) the allocation of places at the establishment to those nationals and other nationals,

or

(ii) it offers assistance to particular categories of persons

(I) by way of sponsorships, scholarships, bursaries or other awards, being assistance which is justifiable, having regard to traditional and historical considerations, or

(II) in relation to the allocation of places at the establishment, where the allocation is made pursuant to an agreement concerning the exchange of students made between the establishment and an educational institution or authority in a jurisdiction other than the State, or

(*e*) where the establishment is a university or other third-level institution, it provides different treatment in the allocation of places at the establishment to mature students (within the meaning of the Local Authorities (Higher Education Grants) Acts, 1968 to 1992).

(4) *Subsection (2)* does not apply

(*a*) in respect of differences in the treatment of students on the gender, age or disability ground in relation to the provision or organisation of sporting facilities or sporting events, to the extent that the differences are reasonably necessary having regard to the nature of the facilities or events, or (*b*) to the extent that compliance with any of its provisions in relation to a student with a disability would, by virtue of the disability, make impossible, or have a seriously detrimental effect on, the provision by an educational establishment of its services to other students.[49]

Further, clubs are given special treatment under Section 9:

9(1) … a club shall not be considered to be a discriminating club by reason only that

(*a*) if its principal purpose is to cater only for the needs of

(i) persons of a particular gender, marital status, family status, sexual orientation, religious belief, age, disability, nationality or ethnic or national origin,

(ii) persons who are members of the Traveller community, or

(iii) persons who have no religious belief,

(iv) it refuses membership to other persons.[50]

Certain measures are not prohibited under Section 14:

14. Nothing in this Act shall be construed as prohibiting:

(*a*) the taking of any action that is required by or under:

(i) any enactment or order of a court,

(ii) any act done or measure adopted by the European Union, by the European Communities or institutions thereof or by bodies competent under the Treaties establishing the European Communities, or

(iii) any convention or other instrument imposing an international obligation on the State,

or

(*b*) preferential treatment or the taking of positive measures which are *bona fide* intended to:

(i) promote equality of opportunity for persons who are, in relation to other persons, disadvantaged or who have been or are likely to be unable to avail themselves of the same opportunities as those other persons, or

(ii) cater for the special needs of persons, or a category of persons, who, because of their circumstances, may require facilities, arrangements, services or assistance not required by persons who do not have those special needs. [51]

Further, certain activities are not considered discrimination under Section 15:

49 Ibid., at Section 7.
50 Ibid., at Section 9.
51 Ibid., at Section 14.

> 15(1) For greater certainty, nothing in this Act prohibiting discrimination shall be construed as requiring a person to dispose of goods or premises, or to provide services or accommodation or services and amenities related to accommodation, to another person ('the customer') in circumstances which would lead a reasonable individual having the responsibility, knowledge and experience of the person to the belief, on grounds other than discriminatory grounds, that the disposal of the goods or premises or the provision of the services or accommodation or the services and amenities related to accommodation, as the case may be, to the customer would produce a substantial risk of criminal or disorderly conduct or behaviour or damage to property at or in the vicinity of the place in which the goods or services are sought or the premises or accommodation are located.[52]

Importantly, redress in respect of prohibited grounds is covered under Section 21:

> 21(1) A person who claims that prohibited conduct has been directed against him or her may, subject to this section, seek redress by referring the case to the Director.
> (2) Before seeking redress under this section the complainant:
> (*a*) shall, within 2 months after the prohibited conducted is alleged to have occurred, or, where more than one incident of prohibited conduct is alleged to have occurred, within 2 months after the last such occurrence, notify the respondent in writing of:
> (i) the nature of the allegation,
> (ii) the complainant's intention, if not satisfied with the respondent's response to the allegation, to seek redress by referring the case to the Director,
> and
> (*b*) may in that notification, with a view to assisting the complainant in deciding whether to refer the case to the Director, question the respondent in writing so as to obtain material information and the respondent may, if the respondent so wishes, reply to any such questions.
> (3) If, on application by the complainant, the Director is satisfied:
> (*a*) that exceptional circumstances prevented the complainant from notifying the respondent in accordance with *subsection (2)*, and
> (*b*) that it is just and equitable, having regard to the nature of the alleged conduct and to any other relevant circumstances, that the period for doing so should be extended beyond the period of 2 months provided for in that subsection, the Director may direct that, in relation to that case, *subsection (2)* shall have effect as if for the reference to 2 months there were substituted a reference to such period not exceeding 4 months as is specified in the

52 Ibid., at Section 15.

direction; and where such a direction is given, this Part shall have effect accordingly.

(4) The Director shall not investigate a case unless he or she is satisfied either that the respondent has replied to the notification or that at least one month has elapsed after it was sent to the respondent.

(5) The Minister may by regulations prescribe the form to be used by a complainant and respondent for the purposes of *subsection (2)*.

(6) Subject to *subsection (7)*, a claim for redress in respect of prohibited conduct may not be referred under this section after the end of the period of 6 months from the date of the occurrence of the prohibited conduct to which the case relates or, as the case may be, the date of its most recent occurrence.

(7) If, on application by the complainant, the Director is satisfied that exceptional circumstances prevented the complainant's case from being referred within the time limit specified in *subsection (6)*:

(*a*) the Director may direct that, in relation to that case, *subsection (6)* shall have effect as if for the reference to a period of 6 months there were substituted a reference to such period not exceeding 12 months as is specified in the direction, and

(*b*) where such a direction is given, this Part shall have effect accordingly.[53]

Finally, mediation is provided for under Section 24:

24(1) Subject to *subsection (2)*, if at any time after a case has been referred to the Director under section 21 it appears to the Director that the case is one which could be resolved by mediation, the Director shall refer the case for mediation to an equality mediation officer.

(2) If the complainant or the respondent objects to a case being dealt with by way of mediation, the Director shall not exercise his or her powers under this section … .

(3) Mediation shall be conducted in private.

(4) Where a case referred under section 21 is resolved by mediation

(*a*) the equality mediation officer concerned shall prepare a written record of the terms of the settlement,

(*b*) the written record of the terms of the settlement shall be signed by the complainant and the respondent,

(*c*) the equality mediation officer shall send a copy of the written record, as so signed, to the complainant and the respondent, and

(*d*) a copy of the written record shall be retained by the Director.

(5) If, after a case has been referred to an equality mediation officer, it appears to the equality mediation officer that the case cannot be resolved by

53 Ibid., at Section 21.

mediation, the officer shall issue a notice to that effect to the complainant and the respondent.[54]

Conclusion

Due to the overall legislation, employer behaviour has changed in countries with anti-discrimination laws in that explicit discrimination, especially in recruitment, has reduced. However, society's and employers' attitudes to workers from religious minorities do not yet appear to have shifted as much as towards groups such as women and people from minority ethnic communities, where legislative protection has, generally, operated for longer. Discriminating against workers on the basis of their class is unfair to individuals and harmful to the economy. The principle is that redressing this inequality is a shared responsibility by all aspects of government stakeholders in class analysis, planning and training. The State's accountability for violations committed by private actors has long been an important debate. This will be of critical relevance to Commonwealth governments and the Secretariat as part of their continuing priority work in the area of democracy, rule of law and human rights. The increased participation of all, especially seniors at decision-making levels in conflict prevention, mediation and resolution is vital, in the pursuit of "Class Act".

54 Ibid., at Section 24.

Chapter 9
Class Act in the European Union

Introduction

In the quest for tolerance of class distinctions in *Class Act*, this chapter will examine efforts against class discrimination in the European Union (EU). As well as examining the European Court of Justice, it will review the European Union treaties from their inception, as well as other important legislation, namely the Treaty of Paris, the Treaty of Rome, the Maastricht Treaty, the Treaty of Amsterdam, the Treaty Establishing a Constitution for Europe and the Charter of Fundamental Rights of the European Union, the Treaty of Lisbon, the European Social Charter and the European Convention for the Protection of Human Rights and Fundamental Freedoms (ECHR). Finally, important European Council legislation affecting equal rights will be analyzed, namely Council Decision 2000/750/EC establishing a Community Action Programme to Combat Discrimination (2001 to 2006) and Council Directive 2000/78/EC Establishing a General Framework for Equal Treatment in Employment and Occupation.

Initially, many centuries ago, Europe was united within the Roman Empire. Throughout its history, the European continent has naturally been restless, fragile, contradictory, competitive and pluralistic, divided by ethnicity, language and religion. National ambitions and self-interest have been the predominant political forces throughout the twentieth century. However, with the two World Wars and the threat of the Cold War, European integration by peaceful methods was seriously reconsidered as an alternative to the independent and aggressive nation state. With democratic governments reinstated in liberated Europe in the post-war era, the restructuring of the region began. A Congress of Europe was held in the Hague in 1948, bringing together leading figures from France, Britain, the Netherlands, Belgium, Germany, Italy and elsewhere. Britain's Prime Minister Churchill referred to the idea of a setting up of "a kind of United States of Europe", which made a powerful impact.[1] Political integration is the peaceful creation of a larger political unit out of several separate ones, which voluntarily give up some powers to a central authority and renounce the use of force toward the other units.[2] In Europe, a political structure at a supranational level exists. Only continental-wide superpowers can think of solving their major problems at the national level, but for

1 Nicoll, William and Salmon, Trevor, *Understanding the New European Community*, Exeter, 1994, p. 11.

2 Daltrop, Anne, *Political Realities, Politics and the European Community*, London, 1982, p. 2.

smaller powers like Europe, it requires wider alliance decisions. It is a multi-tiered approach to government and decision-making that is working.

There have been several important legislative instruments in Europe. The Treaty of Paris (1951) created the European Steel and Coal Community (ESCC). The two Treaties of Rome (1957) separately established the European Economic Community (EEC) and the European Atomic Energy Community (EAEC). The Single European Act (1986) introduced measures aimed at achieving an internal market and greater political cooperation. The Maastricht Treaty (1992) established EU citizenship and European Monetary Union (EMU). The Treaty of Amsterdam (1997) introduced measures to reinforce political union and prepare for enlargement toward Eastern Europe. The Nice Treaty (2001) defined the institutional changes necessary for enlargement. Finally, the Treaty Establishing a Constitution for Europe seeks to simplify and synthesize previous treaties within a single, clear, foundational document for the European Union.

Treaty of Paris

The advocates of integration sought to escape from national rivalries. Thus came the flagship of European integration, the European Communities. The first of these was the Coal and Steel Community, also known as the Treaty of Paris signed on 18 April 1951, which entered into force on 23 July 1952 and expired on 23 July 2002. It removed the coal and steel industries from full national control to a supranational stewardship. The High Authority, which it created, was presided over by Jean Monnet and comprised of delegates from the Member States, making decisions in consultation with the Assembly. The Treaty of Paris was regarded only as a starting point, with the success foreseen in this sector expected to spread to others.

The Preamble of the Treaty of Paris states:

> Considering that world peace can be safeguarded only by creative efforts commensurate with the dangers that threaten it,
> Convinced that the contribution which an organised and vital Europe can make to civilisation is indispensable to the maintenance of peaceful relations,
> Recognising that Europe can be built only through practical achievements which will first of all create real solidarity, and through the establishment of common bases for economic development,
> Anxious to help, by expanding their basic production, to raise the standard of living and further the works of peace,
> Resolved to substitute for age old-rivalries the merging of their essential interests; to create by establishing an economic community, the basis for a broader and deeper community among peoples long divided by bloody conflicts;

and to lay the foundations for institutions which will give direction to a destiny henceforward shared.[3]

Treaty of Rome

Monnet, the most influential of the founding fathers of the European Economic Community, insisted on cooperation across national frontiers in a sector by sector approach at the Messina Conference held in 1955, with the foreign ministers of the six countries involved to meet at. They resolved that the moment had come to go a step further towards the construction of Europe by setting up a customs union with no internal tariff barriers, only a common external tariff.

The Treaty of Rome was signed by France, Italy, West Germany, Luxembourg, the Netherlands and Belgium on 25 March 1957, and entered into force on 1 January 1958, creating the European Economic Community (EEC). The European Community was set up by the Treaty of Rome to maintain peace in Europe and to foster prosperity through cooperation. With the Treaty of Rome, the European Economic Community States transferred to the Community the power to conclude treaties with international organizations and with non-member countries.[4] Lord Denning, a leading constitutional expert, stated "the Treaty of Rome is like an incoming tide. It flows into the estuaries and up the rivers. It cannot be held back."[5] The Member States agreed to work together for an integrated multinational economy for the free movement of labor and capital in the Community, while having joint institutions and common policies toward underdeveloped regions of the Community and toward those outside the Community. The Treaty gave the community institutions power to take the necessary steps to adjust national legal rules through harmonization procedures. This was required in order to remove national legal arrangements inhibiting the free movement of products, people and resources. The larger market allowed for a more rational use of resources and provided for higher productivity. By 1 July 1968, all internal tariffs had been abolished among the Member States for a Community-wide production and distribution of products and services,[6] and with the abolition of tariffs encouraging mutual trade, intra-Community trade in manufactured products was about 50% higher than previously. The long-term implications of the Treaty of Rome were a system of majority voting among the representatives of the national governments in the Council, a supranational bureaucracy over which national governments would

3 Treaty of Paris, at the Preamble.

4 Nicoll, William and Salmon, Trevor, *Understanding the New European Community*, Exeter, 1994, p. 20.

5 Ibid., p. 99.

6 Daltrop, Anne (1982), *Political Realities, Politics and the European Community*, Longman, London, 1982, p. 18.

have little control, a directly elected European Parliament and a commitment by the Member States to work for a closer union.

The Preamble of the Treaty of Rome states:

> … Determined to lay the foundations of an ever closer union among the peoples of Europe,
>
> Resolved to ensure the economic and social progress of their countries by common action to eliminate the barriers which divide Europe,
>
> Affirming as the essential objective of their efforts the constant improvement of the living and working conditions of their peoples,
>
> Recognising that the removal of existing obstacles calls for concerted action in order to guarantee steady expansion, balanced trade and fair competition,
>
> Anxious to strengthen the unity of their economies and to ensure their harmonious development by reducing the differences existing between the various regions and the backwardness of the less favoured regions,
>
> Desiring to contribute, by means of a common commercial policy, to the progressive abolition of restrictions on international trade,
>
> Intending to confirm the solidarity which binds Europe and the overseas countries and desiring to ensure the development of their prosperity, in accordance with the principles of the Charter of the United Nations,
>
> Resolved by thus pooling their resources to preserve and strengthen peace and liberty, and calling upon the other peoples of Europe who share their ideal to join in their efforts,
>
> Have decided to create a European Economic Community … .[7]

In accordance with Article 3 of the Treaty of Rome, the activities of the Community include:

> 3(a) the elimination as between Member States, of customs duties and quantitative restrictions on the import and export of goods, and of all other measures having equivalent effect;
>
> (b) a common commercial policy;

7 Treaty of Rome, at the Preamble.

(c) an internal market characterised by the abolition, as between Member States, of obstacles to the free movement of goods, persons, services and capital;
(d) measures concerning the entry and movement of persons in the internal market ...;
(e) a common policy in the sphere of agriculture and fisheries;
(f) a common policy in the sphere of transport;
(g) a system ensuring that competition in the common market is not distorted;
(h) the approximation of the laws of the Member States to the extent required for the functioning of the common market;
(i) a policy in the social sphere comprising a European Social Fund;
(j) the strengthening of economic and social cohesion;
(k) a policy in the sphere of the environment;
(l) the strengthening of the competitiveness of Community industry;
(m) the promotion of research and technological development;
(n) encouragement for the establishment and development of trans-European networks;
(o) a contribution to the attainment of a high level of health protection;
(p) a contribution to education and training of quality and to the flowering of the cultures of the Member States;
(q) a policy in the sphere of development cooperation;
(r) the association of the overseas countries and territories in order to increase trade and promote jointly economic and social development;
(s) a contribution to the strengthening of consumer protection;
(t) measures in the spheres of energy, civil protection and tourism.[8]

Important for equal rights, Article 6(a) prohibits discrimination:

> 6(a) Within the scope of application of this Treaty, and without prejudice to any special provisions contained therein, any discrimination on grounds of nationality shall be prohibited.[9]

Further, in terms of the free movement of persons, services and capital, in particular workers, Article 48 provides:

> 48.1. Freedom of movement for workers shall be secured within the Community by the end of the transitional period at the latest.
> 2. Such freedom of movement shall entail the abolition of any discrimination based on nationality between workers of the Member States as regards employment, remuneration and other conditions of work and employment.

8 Ibid., at Article 3.
9 Ibid., at Article 6(a).

> 3. It shall entail the right, subject to limitations justified on grounds of public policy, public security or public health:
> a. to accept offers of employment actually made;
> b. to move freely within the territory of Member States for this purpose;
> c. to stay in a Member State for the purpose of employment in accordance with the provisions governing the employment of nationals of that State laid down by law, regulation or administrative action;
> d. to remain in the territory of a Member State after having been employed in that State, subject to conditions which shall be embodied in implementing regulations to be drawn up by the Commission.
> 4. The provisions of this Article shall not apply to employment in the public service.[10]

Important in the fight against class discrimination, Article 117 promotes an improved standard of living:

> 117. Member States agree upon the need to promote improved working conditions and an improved standard of living for workers, so as to make possible their harmonisation while the improvement is being maintained.
> They believe that such a development will ensue not only from the functioning of the common market, which will favour the harmonisation of social systems, but also from the procedures provided for in this Treaty and from the approximation of provisions laid down by law, regulation or administrative action.[11]

Further, co-operation among the Member States is envisioned in Article 118 for the betterment of life:

> 118. Without prejudice to the other provisions of this Treaty and in conformity with its general objectives, the Commission shall have the task of promoting close co-operation between Member States in the social field, particularly in matters relating to:
> employment;
> labour law and working conditions;
> basic and advanced vocational training;
> social security;
> prevention of occupational accidents and diseases;
> occupational hygiene; the right of association, and collective bargaining between employers and workers.
> To this end, the Commission shall act in close contact with Member States by making studies, delivering opinions and arranging consultations both on

10 Ibid., at Article 48.
11 Ibid., at Article 117.

problems arising at national level and on those of concern to international organisations.
Before delivering the opinions provided for in this Article, the Commission shall consult the Economic and Social Committee.[12]

Important for women, in terms of equal pay, Article 119 states:

119. Each Member State shall during the first stage ensure and subsequently maintain the application of the principle that men and women should receive equal pay for equal work.
For the purpose of this Article, 'pay' means the ordinary basic or minimum wage or salary and any other consideration, whether in cash or in kind, which the worker receives, directly or indirectly, in respect of his employment from his employer.
Equal pay without discrimination based on sex means:

(a) that pay for the same work at piece rates shall be calculated on the basis of the same unit of measurement;

(b) that pay for work at time rates shall be the same for the same job.[13]

Education as a tool for advancement is safeguarded under Article 126:

126.1. The Community shall contribute to the development of quality education by encouraging cooperation between Member States and, if necessary, by supporting and supplementing their action, while fully respecting the responsibility of the Member States for the content of teaching and the organisation of education systems and their cultural and linguistic diversity.
2. Community action shall be aimed at:
developing the European dimension in education, particularly through the teaching and dissemination of the languages of the Member States;
encouraging mobility of students and teachers, inter alia by encouraging the academic recognition of diplomas and periods of study;
promoting cooperation between educational establishments;
developing exchanges of information and experience on issues common to the education systems of the Member States;
encouraging the development of youth exchanges and of exchanges of socio-educational instructors;
encouraging the development of distance education.
3. The Community and the Member States shall foster co-operation with third countries and the competent international organisations in the sphere of education, in particular the Council of Europe.
4. In order to contribute to the achievement of the objectives referred to in this Article, the Council:

---

12 Ibid., at Article 118.

13 Ibid., at Article 119.

> (a) acting in accordance with the procedure referred to in Article 189b, after consulting the Economic and Social Committee and the Committee of the Regions, shall adopt incentive measures, excluding any harmonisation of the laws and regulations of the Member States;
> (b) acting by qualified majority on a proposal from the Commission, shall adopt recommendations.[14]

Finally, Article 127 covers safeguards vocational programs:

> 127.1. The Community shall implement a vocational training policy which shall support and supplement the action of the Member States, while fully respecting the responsibility of the Member States for the content and organisation of vocational training.
> 2. Community action shall aim to:
> facilitate adaptation to industrial changes, in particular through vocational training and retraining;
> improve initial and continuing vocational training in order to facilitate vocational integration and reintegration into the labour market;
> facilitate access to vocational training and encourage mobility of instructors and trainees and particularly young people;
> stimulate cooperation on training between educational or training establishments and firms;
> develop exchanges of information and experience on issues common to the training systems of the Member States.
> 3. The Community and the Member States shall foster cooperation with third countries and the competent international organisations in the sphere of vocational training.
> 4. The Council, acting in accordance with the procedure referred to in Article 189c and after consulting the Economic and Social Committee, shall adopt measures to contribute to the achievement of the objectives referred to in this Article, excluding any harmonisation of the laws and regulations of the Member States.[15]

Maastricht Treaty

The Maastricht Treaty was signed on 7 February 1992 and entered into force on 1 November 1993, creating the European Union (EU). The EU became an internal market of over 340 million people providing for the free movement of goods, capital, services and citizens of Member States. The Maastricht Treaty affirms that it marks a new stage in the process of European integration undertaken with the establishment of the European Communities. It was designed to create a firm basis

14 Ibid., at Article 126.
15 Ibid., at Article 127.

for the construction of the future of Europe, by deepening the solidarity between peoples while respecting the different histories, cultures and traditions. Further, the Maastricht Treaty espoused the desire to enhance the democracy and efficient functioning of the institutions so as to enable them better to carry out, within a single institutional framework, the tasks entrusted to them. The foundations for a united Europe were laid on fundamental values including peace, unity, equality, freedom, solidarity and security, through intergovernmental cooperation and the creation of the three pillars of EC society. By the Maastricht Treaty, the European Union confirms its "attachment to the principles of liberty, democracy and respect for human rights and fundamental freedoms and of the rule of law".

The Preamble of the Maastricht Treaty states:

> RESOLVED to mark a new stage in the process of European integration undertaken with the establishment of the European Communities,
>
> RECALLING the historic importance of the ending of the division of the European continent and the need to create firm bases for the construction of the future Europe,
>
> CONFIRMING their attachment to the principles of liberty, democracy and respect for human rights and fundamental freedoms and of the rule of law,
>
> DESIRING to deepen the solidarity between their peoples while respecting their history, their culture and their traditions,
>
> DESIRING to enhance further the democratic and efficient functioning of the institutions so as to enable them better to carry out, within a single institutional framework, the tasks entrusted to them,
>
> RESOLVED to achieve the strengthening and the convergence of their economies and to establish an economic and monetary union including, in accordance with the provisions of this Treaty, a single and stable currency,
>
> DETERMINED to promote economic and social progress for their peoples, within the context of the accomplishment of the internal market and of reinforced cohesion and environmental protection, and to implement policies ensuring that advances in economic integration are accompanied by parallel progress in other fields,
>
> RESOLVED to establish a citizenship common to nationals of their countries,
>
> RESOLVED to implement a common foreign and security policy including the eventual framing of a common defence policy, which might in time lead to a

> common defence, thereby reinforcing the European identity and its independence in order to promote peace, security and progress in Europe and in the world,
>
> REAFFIRMING their objective to facilitate the free movement of persons, while ensuring the safety and security of their peoples, by including provisions on justice and home affairs in this Treaty,
>
> RESOLVED to continue the process of creating an ever closer union among the peoples of Europe, in which decisions are taken as closely as possible to the citizen in accordance with the principle of subsidiarity,
>
> IN VIEW of further steps to be taken in order to advance European integration,
>
> HAVE DECIDED to establish a European Union.[16]

Article A of the Maastricht Treaty states:

> A. By this Treaty, the High Contracting Parties establish among themselves a European Union, hereinafter called 'the Union'.
> This Treaty marks a new stage in the process of creating an ever closer union among the peoples of Europe, in which decisions are taken as closely as possible to the citizen.
> The Union shall be founded on the European Communities, supplemented by the policies and forms of co-operation established by this Treaty. Its task shall be to organise, in a manner demonstrating consistency and solidarity, relations between the Member States and between their peoples.[17]

Finally, Article B states:

> B. The Union shall set itself the following objectives:
> to promote economic and social progress which is balanced and sustainable, in particular through the creation of an area without internal frontiers, through the strengthening of economic and social cohesion and through the establishment of economic and monetary union, ultimately including a single currency in accordance with the provisions of this Treaty;
> to assert its identity on the international scene, in particular through the implementation of a common foreign and security policy including the eventual framing of a common defence policy, which might in time lead to a common defence;
> to strengthen the protection of the rights and interests of the nationals of its Member States through the introduction of a citizenship of the Union;

16 Maastricht Treaty, at the Preamble.
17 Ibid., at Article A.

> to develop close co-operation on justice and home affairs;
> to maintain in full the 'acquis communautaire' and build on it with … the aim of ensuring the effectiveness of the mechanisms and the institutions of the Community.[18]

Treaty of Amsterdam

The Treaty of Amsterdam, the treaty establishing the European Community, amending previous Treaties, was signed on 2 October 1997 and entered into force on 1 May 1999. The following was added to the Preamble of the Treaty establishing the European Community:

> DETERMINED to promote the development of the highest possible level of knowledge for their peoples through a wide access to education and through its continuous updating.[19]

Article 2 enumerates some of the principles of the Treaty:

> 2. The Community shall have as its task, by establishing a common market and an economic and monetary union and by implementing common policies or activities … to promote throughout the Community a harmonious, balanced and sustainable development of economic activities, a high level of employment and of social protection, equality between men and women, sustainable and non-inflationary growth, a high degree of competitiveness and convergence of economic performance, a high level of protection and improvement of the quality of the environment, the raising of the standard of living and quality of life, and economic and social cohesion and solidarity among Member States.[20]

Important for all people, in order to combat discrimination, Article 13, amending Article 6(a) of the Treaty of Rome for specificity, states:

> 13. Without prejudice to the other provisions of this Treaty and within the limits of the powers conferred by it upon the Community, the Council, acting unanimously on a proposal from the Commission and after consulting the European Parliament, may take appropriate action to combat discrimination based on sex, racial or ethnic origin, religion or belief, disability, age or sexual orientation.[21]

---

18 Ibid., at Article B.
19 Treaty of Amsterdam, at the Preamble.
20 Ibid., at Article 2.
21 Ibid., at Article 13.

Further, in terms of the free movement of persons, services and capital, in particular workers, Article 39, amending Article 48 of the Treaty of Rome, states:

> 39. 1. Freedom of movement for workers shall be secured within the Community.
> 2. Such freedom of movement shall entail the abolition of any discrimination based on nationality between workers of the Member States as regards employment, remuneration and other conditions of work and employment.
> 3. It shall entail the right, subject to limitations justified on grounds of public policy, public security or public health:
> (a) to accept offers of employment actually made;
> (b) to move freely within the territory of Member States for this purpose;
> (c) to stay in a Member State for the purpose of employment in accordance with the provisions governing the employment of nationals of that State laid down by law, regulation or administrative action;
> (d) to remain in the territory of a Member State after having been employed in that State, subject to conditions which shall be embodied in implementing regulations to be drawn up by the Commission.
> 4. The provisions of this Article shall not apply to employment in the public service.[22]

Important for women, in terms of equal pay, Article 141, amending Article 119 of the Treaty of Rome, states:

> 141.1. Each Member State shall ensure that the principle of equal pay for male and female workers for equal work or work of equal value is applied.
> 2. For the purpose of this Article, 'pay' means the ordinary basic or minimum wage or salary and any other consideration, whether in cash or in kind, which the worker receives directly or indirectly, in respect of his employment, from his employer.
> Equal pay without discrimination based on sex means:
> (a) that pay for the same work at piece rates shall be calculated on the basis of the same unit of measurement;
> (b) that pay for work at time rates shall be the same for the same job.
> 3. The Council, acting in accordance with the procedure referred to in Article 251, and after consulting the Economic and Social Committee, shall adopt measures to ensure the application of the principle of equal opportunities and equal treatment of men and women in matters of employment and occupation, including the principle of equal pay for equal work or work of equal value.
> 4. With a view to ensuring full equality in practice between men and women in working life, the principle of equal treatment shall not prevent any Member State from maintaining or adopting measures providing for specific advantages

22 Ibid., at Article 39.

in order to make it easier for the under-represented sex to pursue a vocational activity or to prevent or compensate for disadvantages in professional careers.[23]

Treaty Establishing a Constitution for Europe and Charter of Fundamental Rights of the European Union

The Heads of State or Government of the then 25 Member States and the candidate countries signed the Treaty establishing a Constitution for Europe on 29 October 2004, but it was not ratified by all Member States of the enlarged Union. It was written in order to enable the European Union to ensure the well-being of citizens, and the defense of values and interests; to assume responsibilities as a leading international player; to fight unemployment and social exclusion more effectively; to promote sustainable economic growth; to respond to the challenges of globalization; to safeguard internal and external security; and to protect the environment. The Charter of Fundamental Rights of the European Union, part of the intended Constitution of Europe, has to be seen in the wider context of the European Union's long-lasting commitment to human rights and fundamental freedoms and of its policy in the areas of justice, freedom, security and social rights.

The Preamble of the Treaty 2004/C 310/01 establishing a Constitution for Europe states:

> DRAWING INSPIRATION from the cultural, religious and humanist inheritance of Europe, from which have developed the universal values of the inviolable and inalienable rights of the human person, freedom, democracy, equality and the rule of law,
>
> BELIEVING that Europe, reunited after bitter experiences, intends to continue along the path of civilisation, progress and prosperity, for the good of all its inhabitants, including the weakest and most deprived; that it wishes to remain a continent open to culture, learning and social progress; and that it wishes to deepen the democratic and transparent nature of its public life, and to strive for peace, justice and solidarity throughout the world,
>
> CONVINCED that, while remaining proud of their own national identities and history, the peoples of Europe are determined to transcend their former divisions and, united ever more closely, to forge a common destiny,
>
> CONVINCED that, thus 'United in diversity', Europe offers them the best chance of pursuing, with due regard for the rights of each individual and in awareness of their responsibilities towards future generations and the Earth, the great venture which makes of it a special area of human hope,

23 Ibid., at Article 141.

> DETERMINED to continue the work accomplished within the framework of the Treaties establishing the European Communities and the Treaty on European Union, by ensuring the continuity of the Community *acquis*,
>
> WHO, having exchanged their full powers, found in good and due form. [24]

Article I-1 on the establishment of the Union states:

> I-1. 1. Reflecting the will of the citizens and States of Europe to build a common future, this Constitution establishes the European Union, on which the Member States confer competences to attain objectives they have in common. The Union shall coordinate the policies by which the Member States aim to achieve these objectives, and shall exercise in the Community way the competences they confer on it.
> 2. The Union shall be open to all European States which respect its values and are committed to promoting them together.[25]

The Union's values are outlined in Article I-2:

> I-2. The Union is founded on the values of respect for human dignity, liberty, democracy, equality, the rule of law and respect for human rights, including the rights of persons belonging to minorities. These values are common to the Member States in a society in which pluralism, non-discrimination, tolerance, justice, solidarity and equality between women and men prevail.[26]

Further, in the fight against class discrimination, the Union's objectives are outlined in Article I-3, including the promotion of social justice and the eradication of poverty:

> I-3. 1. The Union's aim is to promote peace, its values and the well-being of its peoples.
> 2. The Union shall offer its citizens an area of freedom, security and justice without internal frontiers, and an internal market where competition is free and undistorted.
> 3. The Union shall work for the sustainable development of Europe based on balanced economic growth and price stability, a highly competitive social market economy, aiming at full employment and social progress, and a high level of protection and improvement of the quality of the environment. It shall promote scientific and technological advance.

24 Treaty establishing a Constitution for Europe, at the Preamble.
25 Ibid., at Part I, Article I-1.
26 Ibid., at Part I, Article I-2.

> It shall combat social exclusion and discrimination, and shall promote social justice and protection, equality between women and men, solidarity between generations and protection of the rights of the child.
> It shall promote economic, social and territorial cohesion, and solidarity among Member States.
> It shall respect its rich cultural and linguistic diversity, and shall ensure that Europe's cultural heritage is safeguarded and enhanced.
> 4. In its relations with the wider world, the Union shall uphold and promote its values and interests. It shall contribute to peace, security, the sustainable development of the Earth, solidarity and mutual respect among peoples, free and fair trade, eradication of poverty and the protection of human rights, in particular the rights of the child, as well as to the strict observance and the development of international law, including respect for the principles of the United Nations Charter.
> 5. The Union shall pursue its objectives by appropriate means commensurate with the competences which are conferred upon it in the Constitution.[27]

Important for equal rights, fundamental freedoms and non-discrimination are upheld in Article I-4:

> I-4. 1. The free movement of persons, services, goods and capital, and freedom of establishment shall be guaranteed within and by the Union, in accordance with the Constitution.
> 2. Within the scope of the Constitution, and without prejudice to any of its specific provisions, any discrimination on grounds of nationality shall be prohibited.[28]

The primacy of Union law is emphasized in Article I-6:

> I-6. The Constitution and law adopted by the institutions of the Union in exercising competences conferred on it shall have primacy over the law of the Member States.[29]

Further, relations between the Union and Member States are contained in Article I-5:

> I-5. 1. The Union shall respect the equality of Member States before the Constitution as well as their national identities, inherent in their fundamental structures, political and constitutional, inclusive of regional and local self-government. It shall respect their essential State functions, including ensuring

27 Ibid., at Part I, Article I-3.
28 Ibid., at Part I, Article I-4.
29 Ibid., at Part I, Article I-6.

> the territorial integrity of the State, maintaining law and order and safeguarding national security.
> 2. Pursuant to the principle of sincere cooperation, the Union and the Member States shall, in full mutual respect, assist each other in carrying out tasks which flow from the Constitution.
> The Member States shall take any appropriate measure, general or particular, to ensure fulfillment of the obligations arising out of the Constitution or resulting from the acts of the institutions of the Union.
> The Member States shall facilitate the achievement of the Union's tasks and refrain from any measure which could jeopardise the attainment of the Union's objectives.[30]

Important in the fight against class discrimination and education as a tool for advancement, Article I-17 promotes supporting and coordinating complementary action in certain areas including education and vocational training under Article I-17(e):

> I-17. The Union shall have competence to carry out supporting, coordinating or complementary action.
> The areas of such action shall, at European level, be:
> (a) protection and improvement of human health;
> (b) industry;
> (c) culture;
> (d) tourism;
> (e) education, youth, sport and vocational training;
> (f) civil protection;
> (g) administrative cooperation.[31]

The Preamble of the Charter of Fundamental Rights of the European Union, part of the Constitution of Europe, states:

> The peoples of Europe, in creating an ever closer union among them, are resolved to share a peaceful future based on common values.
>
> Conscious of its spiritual and moral heritage, the Union is founded on the indivisible, universal values of human dignity, freedom, equality and solidarity; it is based on the principles of democracy and the rule of law. It places the individual at the heart of its activities, by establishing the citizenship of the Union and by creating an area of freedom, security and justice.

---

30 Ibid., at Part I, Article I-5.
31 Ibid., at Part I, Article I-17.

The Union contributes to the preservation and to the development of these common values while respecting the diversity of the cultures and traditions of the peoples of Europe as well as the national identities of the Member States and the organisation of their public authorities at national, regional and local levels; it seeks to promote balanced and sustainable development and ensures free movement of persons, goods, services and capital, and the freedom of establishment.

To this end, it is necessary to strengthen the protection of fundamental rights in the light of changes in society, social progress and scientific and technological developments by making those rights more visible in a Charter.

This Charter reaffirms, with due regard for the powers and tasks of the Community and the Union and the principle of subsidiarity, the rights as they result, in particular, from the constitutional traditions and international obligations common to the Member States, the Treaty on European Union, the Community Treaties, the European Convention for the Protection of Human Rights and Fundamental Freedoms, the Social Charters adopted by the Community and by the Council of Europe and the case law of the Court of Justice of the European Communities and of the European Court of Human Rights.

Enjoyment of these rights entails responsibilities and duties with regard to other persons, to the human community and to future generations.

The Union therefore recognises the rights, freedoms and principles set out hereafter.[32]

Importantly, equality before the law is contained in Article II-80:

II-80. Everyone is equal before the law.[33]

Further, Article II-81 deals with non-discrimination, which includes social origin and property:

II-81. 1. Any discrimination based on any ground such as sex, race, colour, ethnic or social origin, genetic features, language, religion or belief, political or any other opinion, membership of a national minority, property, birth, disability, age or sexual orientation shall be prohibited.
2. Within the scope of application of the Treaty establishing the European Community and of the Treaty on European Union, and without prejudice to the

32 Treaty establishing a Constitution for Europe, the Charter of Fundamental Rights, at Part II, the Preamble.

33 Ibid., at Part II, Article II-80.

> special provisions of those Treaties, any discrimination on grounds of nationality shall be prohibited.[34]

Continuing on, importantly, Article III-118 states:

> III-118. In defining and implementing the policies and activities referred to in this Part, the Union shall aim to combat discrimination based on sex, racial or ethnic origin, religion or belief, disability, age or sexual orientation.[35]

Finally, Article III-124 provides for measures for combating discrimination:

> III-124. 1. Without prejudice to the other provisions of the Constitution and within the limits of the powers assigned by it to the Union, a European law or framework law of the Council may establish the measures needed to combat discrimination based on sex, racial or ethnic origin, religion or belief, disability, age or sexual orientation. The Council shall act unanimously after obtaining the consent of the European Parliament.
> 2. By way of derogation from paragraph 1, European laws or framework laws may establish basic principles for Union incentive measures and define such measures, to support action taken by Member States in order to contribute to the achievement of the objectives referred to in paragraph 1, excluding any harmonisation of their laws and regulations.[36]

Treaty of Lisbon

Finally, the Treaty of Lisbon amending the Treaty on European Union and the Treaty establishing the European Community was signed at Lisbon on 13 December 2007. The Preamble of the Treaty of Lisbon states:

> DRAWING INSPIRATION from the cultural, religious and humanist inheritance of Europe, from which have developed the universal values of the inviolable and inalienable rights of the human person, freedom, democracy, equality and the rule of law.[37]

Specifically in combating discrimination, Article 5(b) notes:

34 Ibid., at Part II, Article II-81.
35 Ibid., at Part III, Article III-118.
36 Ibid., at Part III, Article III-124.
37 Treaty of Lisbon, at the Preamble.

> 5(b) In defining and implementing its policies and activities, the Union shall aim to combat discrimination based on sex, racial or ethnic origin, religion or belief, disability, age or sexual orientation.[38]

The Treaty of Lisbon hoped to provide for: a more democratic and transparent Europe, with a strengthened role for the European Parliament and national parliaments, more opportunities for citizens to have their voices heard and a clearer sense of who does what at European and national level; a more efficient Europe, with simplified working methods and voting rules, streamlined and modern institutions for a Europe Union of 27 members and an improved ability to act in areas of major priority for today's Union; a Europe of rights and values, freedom, solidarity and security, promoting the Union's values, introducing the Charter of Fundamental Rights into European primary law, providing for new solidarity mechanisms and ensuring better protection of European citizens; and Europe as an actor on the global stage by bringing together Europe's external policy tools, both when developing and deciding new policies, harnessing Europe's economic, humanitarian, political and diplomatic strengths to promote European interests and values worldwide, while respecting the particular interests of the Member States in Foreign Affairs.

European Social Charter

The European Social Charter promotes the right of workers to equal opportunities and equal treatment in matters of employment and occupation without discrimination. It espouses the notion of "equal pay for work of equal value", and also provides for the equal treatment with regard to access to employment, vocational training, promotion and working conditions, aimed at eliminating all discrimination, both direct and indirect, in the world of work, providing for opportunities for positive measures. In the Preamble to the European Social Charter of 18 October 1961, the governments signatory hereto, being members of the Council of Europe, undertake the agreement:

> Considering that the aim of the Council of Europe is the achievement of greater unity between its members for the purpose of safeguarding and realising the ideals and principles which are their common heritage and of facilitating their economic and social progress, in particular by the maintenance and further realisation of human rights and fundamental freedoms;
>
> Considering that in the Convention for the Protection of Human Rights and Fundamental Freedoms signed at Rome on 4th November 1950, and the Protocol thereto signed at Paris on 20th March 1952, the member States of the Council

38 Ibid., at Article 5(b).

> of Europe agreed to secure to their populations the civil and political rights and freedoms therein specified;
>
> Considering that the enjoyment of social rights should be secured without discrimination on grounds of race, colour, sex, religion, political opinion, national extraction or social origin;
>
> Being resolved to make every effort in common to improve the standard of living and to promote the social well-being of both their urban and rural populations by means of appropriate institutions and action.[39]

In the Preamble to the European Social Charter (revised) of 3 May 1996, the governments signatory thereto, being members of the Council of Europe, undertake the agreement:

> Considering that the aim of the Council of Europe is the achievement of greater unity between its members for the purpose of safeguarding and realising the ideals and principles which are their common heritage and of facilitating their economic and social progress, in particular by the maintenance and further realisation of human rights and fundamental freedoms;
>
> Considering that in the Convention for the Protection of Human Rights and Fundamental Freedoms signed at Rome on 4 November 1950, and the Protocols thereto, the member States of the Council of Europe agreed to secure to their populations the civil and political rights and freedoms therein specified;
>
> Considering that in the European Social Charter opened for signature in Turin on 18 October 1961 and the Protocols thereto, the member States of the Council of Europe agreed to secure to their populations the social rights specified therein in order to improve their standard of living and their social well-being;
>
> Recalling that the Ministerial Conference on Human Rights held in Rome on 5 November 1990 stressed the need, on the one hand, to preserve the indivisible nature of all human rights, be they civil, political, economic, social or cultural and, on the other hand, to give the European Social Charter fresh impetus;
>
> Resolved, as was decided during the Ministerial Conference held in Turin on 21 and 22 October 1991, to update and adapt the substantive contents of the Charter in order to take account in particular of the fundamental social changes which have occurred since the text was adopted;

---

39 European Social Charter, 1961, at the Preamble.

> Recognising the advantage of embodying in a Revised Charter, designed progressively to take the place of the European Social Charter, the rights guaranteed by the Charter as amended, the rights guaranteed by the Additional Protocol of 1988 and to add new rights.[40]

Important for all workers, under Part I, several rights and principles are espoused, including in (30) the fight against poverty and social exclusion:

> The Parties accept as the aim of their policy, to be pursued by all appropriate means both national and international in character, the attainment of conditions in which the following rights and principles may be effectively realised:
>
> 1. Everyone shall have the opportunity to earn his living in an occupation freely entered upon.
> 2. All workers have the right to just conditions of work.
> 3. All workers have the right to safe and healthy working conditions.
> 4. All workers have the right to a fair remuneration sufficient for a decent standard of living for themselves and their families.
> 5. All workers and employers have the right to freedom of association in national or international organisations for the protection of their economic and social interests.
> 6. All workers and employers have the right to bargain collectively.
> 7. Children and young persons have the right to a special protection against the physical and moral hazards to which they are exposed.
> 8. Employed women, in case of maternity, have the right to a special protection.
> 9. Everyone has the right to appropriate facilities for vocational guidance with a view to helping him choose an occupation suited to his personal aptitude and interests.
> 10. Everyone has the right to appropriate facilities for vocational training.
> 11. Everyone has the right to benefit from any measures enabling him to enjoy the highest possible standard of health attainable.
> 12. All workers and their dependents have the right to social security.
> 13. Anyone without adequate resources has the right to social and medical assistance.
> 14. Everyone has the right to benefit from social welfare services.
> 15. Disabled persons have the right to independence, social integration and participation in the life of the community.
> 16. The family as a fundamental unit of society has the right to appropriate social, legal and economic protection to ensure its full development.
> 17. Children and young persons have the right to appropriate social, legal and economic protection.

40 European Social Charter (revised), 1996, at the Preamble.

> 18. The nationals of any one of the Parties have the right to engage in any gainful occupation in the territory of any one of the others on a footing of equality with the nationals of the latter, subject to restrictions based on cogent economic or social reasons.
> 19. Migrant workers who are nationals of a Party and their families have the right to protection and assistance in the territory of any other Party.
> 20. All workers have the right to equal opportunities and equal treatment in matters of employment and occupation without discrimination on the grounds of sex.
> 21. Workers have the right to be informed and to be consulted within the undertaking.
> 22. Workers have the right to take part in the determination and improvement of the working conditions and working environment in the undertaking.
> 23. Every elderly person has the right to social protection.
> 24. All workers have the right to protection in cases of termination of employment.
> 25. All workers have the right to protection of their claims in the event of the insolvency of their employer.
> 26. All workers have the right to dignity at work.
> 27. All persons with family responsibilities and who are engaged or wish to engage in employment have a right to do so without being subject to discrimination and as far as possible without conflict between their employment and family responsibilities.
> 28. Workers' representatives in undertakings have the right to protection against acts prejudicial to them and should be afforded appropriate facilities to carry out their functions.
> 29. All workers have the right to be informed and consulted in collective redundancy procedures.
> 30. Everyone has the right to protection against poverty and social exclusion.
> 31. Everyone has the right to housing.[41]

In terms of class discrimination cases, under Part V, Article E is a provision on non-discrimination, which includes social origin or other status:

> The enjoyment of the rights set forth in this Charter shall be secured without discrimination on any ground such as race, colour, sex, language, religion, political or other opinion, national extraction or social origin, health, association with a national minority, birth or other status.[42]

Under Part II, the right to work is provided for in Article 1:

41 Ibid., at Part I.
42 Ibid., at Part V, Article E.

> 1. With a view to ensuring the effective exercise of the right to work, the Parties undertake:
>
> 1. to accept as one of their primary aims and responsibilities the achievement and maintenance of as high and stable a level of employment as possible, with a view to the attainment of full employment;
> 2. to protect effectively the right of the worker to earn his living in an occupation freely entered upon;
> 3. to establish or maintain free employment services for all workers;
> 4. to provide or promote appropriate vocational guidance, training and rehabilitation.[43]

Further, Article 4 guarantees the right to a fair remuneration and equal pay:

> 4. With a view to ensuring the effective exercise of the right to a fair remuneration, the Parties undertake:
>
> 1. to recognise the right of workers to a remuneration such as will give them and their families a decent standard of living;
> 2. to recognise the right of workers to an increased rate of remuneration for overtime work, subject to exceptions in particular cases;
> 3. to recognise the right of men and women workers to equal pay for work of equal value;
> 4. to recognise the right of all workers to a reasonable period of notice for termination of employment;
> 5. to permit deductions from wages only under conditions and to the extent prescribed by national laws or regulations or fixed by collective agreements or arbitration awards. The exercise of these rights shall be achieved by freely concluded collective agreements, by statutory wage-fixing machinery, or by other means appropriate to national conditions.[44]

In addition, Article 24 provides for termination of employment under appropriate means:

> 24. It is understood that for the purposes of this article the terms 'termination of employment' and 'terminated' mean termination of employment at the initiative of the employer.
>
> 1. It is understood that this article covers all workers but that a Party may exclude from some or all of its protection the following categories of employed persons:
>
> a. workers engaged under a contract of employment for a specified period of time or a specified task;

43 Ibid, at Part II, Article 1.

44 Ibid., at Article 4.

> b. workers undergoing a period of probation or a qualifying period of employment, provided that this is determined in advance and is of a reasonable duration;
>
> c. workers engaged on a casual basis for a short period.
>
> 2. For the purpose of this article the following, in particular, shall not constitute valid reasons for termination of employment:
>
> a. trade union membership or participation in union activities outside working hours, or, with the consent of the employer, within working hours;
>
> b. seeking office as, acting or having acted in the capacity of a workers' representative;
>
> c. the filing of a complaint or the participation in proceedings against an employer involving alleged violation of laws or regulations or recourse to competent administrative authorities;
>
> d. race, colour, sex, marital status, family responsibilities, pregnancy, religion, political opinion, national extraction or social origin;
>
> e. maternity or parental leave;
>
> f. temporary absence from work due to illness or injury.
>
> 3. It is understood that compensation or other appropriate relief in case of termination of employment without valid reasons shall be determined by national laws or regulations, collective agreements or other means appropriate to national conditions.[45]

Pursuant to Article 22, the Parties undertake to adopt or encourage measures enabling all workers, in accordance with national legislation and practice, to contribute to the determination and the improvement of the working conditions, work organization and working environment; to the protection of health and safety within the undertaking; to the organization of social and sociocultural services and facilities within the undertaking; and to the supervision of the observance of regulations on these matters.[46]

Importantly, in the fight against class discrimination, Article 7 provides for the right of children and young persons to protection:

> 7. With a view to ensuring the effective exercise of the right of children and young persons to protection, the Parties undertake:
>
> 1. to provide that the minimum age of admission to employment shall be 15 years, subject to exceptions for children employed in prescribed light work without harm to their health, morals or education;
>
> 2. to provide that the minimum age of admission to employment shall be 18 years with respect to prescribed occupations regarded as dangerous or unhealthy;

45 Ibid., at Article 24.

46 Ibid., at Article 22.

3. to provide that persons who are still subject to compulsory education shall not be employed in such work as would deprive them of the full benefit of their education;
4. to provide that the working hours of persons under 18 years of age shall be limited in accordance with the needs of their development, and particularly with their need for vocational training;
5. to recognise the right of young workers and apprentices to a fair wage or other appropriate allowances;
6. to provide that the time spent by young persons in vocational training during the normal working hours with the consent of the employer shall be treated as forming part of the working day;
7. to provide that employed persons of under 18 years of age shall be entitled to a minimum of four weeks' annual holiday with pay;
8. to provide that persons under 18 years of age shall not be employed in night work with the exception of certain occupations provided for by national laws or regulations;
9. to provide that persons under 18 years of age employed in occupations prescribed by national laws or regulations shall be subject to regular medical control;
10. to ensure special protection against physical and moral dangers to which children and young persons are exposed, and particularly against those resulting directly or indirectly from their work.[47]

Further, Article 10 guarantees the right to vocational training, with education a tool for advancement:

> 10. With a view to ensuring the effective exercise of the right to vocational training, the Parties undertake:
>
> 1. to provide or promote, as necessary, the technical and vocational training of all persons, including the handicapped, in consultation with employers' and workers' organisations, and to grant facilities for access to higher technical and university education, based solely on individual aptitude;
> 2. to provide or promote a system of apprenticeship and other systematic arrangements for training young boys and girls in their various employments;
> 3. to provide or promote, as necessary:
>   a. adequate and readily available training facilities for adult workers;
>   b. special facilities for the retraining of adult workers needed as a result of technological development or new trends in employment;
> 4. to provide or promote, as necessary, special measures for the retraining and reintegration of the long-term unemployed;

47 Ibid., at Article 7.

5. to encourage the full utilisation of the facilities provided by appropriate measures such as:
   a. reducing or abolishing any fees or charges;
   b. granting financial assistance in appropriate cases;
   c. including in the normal working hours time spent on supplementary training taken by the worker, at the request of his employer, during employment;
   d. ensuring, through adequate supervision, in consultation with the employers' and workers' organisations, the efficiency of apprenticeship and other training arrangements for young workers, and the adequate protection of young workers generally.[48]

Additionally, Article 17 safeguards the right of children and young persons to social, legal and economic protection:

> 17. With a view to ensuring the effective exercise of the right of children and young persons to grow up in an environment which encourages the full development of their personality and of their physical and mental capacities, the Parties undertake, either directly or in co-operation with public and private organisations, to take all appropriate and necessary measures designed:
> a. to ensure that children and young persons, taking account of the rights and duties of their parents, have the care, the assistance, the education and the training they need, in particular by providing for the establishment or maintenance of institutions and services sufficient and adequate for this purpose;
> b. to protect children and young persons against negligence, violence or exploitation;
> c. to provide protection and special aid from the state for children and young persons temporarily or definitively deprived of their family's support;
> 2. to provide to children and young persons a free primary and secondary education as well as to encourage regular attendance at schools.[49]

Finally, Article 30 safeguards the right to protection against poverty and social exclusion:

> 30. With a view to ensuring the effective exercise of the right to protection against poverty and social exclusion, the Parties undertake:
> a. to take measures within the framework of an overall and co-ordinated approach to promote the effective access of persons who live or risk living in a situation of social exclusion or poverty, as well as their families, to, in

48 Ibid., at Article 10.
49 Ibid., at Article 17.

particular, employment, housing, training, education, culture and social and medical assistance;

b. to review these measures with a view to their adaptation if necessary.[50]

European Law and the European Court of Justice

The extension of civil rights marks another step toward European integration. The concept of citizenship is based on the principle that nationals of Member States have certain rights to move freely across national borders in the common market. Freedom of movement, under the Treaty of Rome, applied only to certain economic categories of workers, the self-employed and service providers. This, however, was expanded by the Treaty of Amsterdam and the European Court of Justice, which had a profound impact on employment.

There are five European Union (EU) institutions, each playing a specific role, namely the European Parliament, which is elected by the citizens of the Member States; the Council of the European Union, which represents the governments of the Member States; the European Commission, which is the executive body; the European Court of Justice, which ensures compliance with the law; and the Court of Auditors, which controls sound and lawful management of the European Union budget. There are five other important bodies, namely the European Economic and Social Committee, which expresses the opinions of organized civil society on economic and social issues; the Committee of the Regions, which expresses the opinions of regional and local authorities; the European Central Bank, which is responsible for monetary policy and managing the euro; the European Ombudsman, who deals with citizens' complaints about maladministration by any European Union institution or body; and the European Investment Bank, which helps achieve European Union objectives by financing investment projects. A number of agencies and other bodies complete the system.[51]

Specifically, the Commission is responsible for making legislative proposals, executing policies and monitoring the compliance of Member States with their obligations. It is the driving force behind European integration by its right of initiative. It is also the guardian of the Treaties by its right to intervene with Member States and to demand compliance with their obligations. If Member States breach their Treaty obligations, they will face Commission action and possible legal proceedings in the European Court of Justice. As assistance to the European Court of Justice, the Commission is the European Union watchdog for the observance of the Treaties, as it originates and administers European Union law. The Council of Ministers is composed of representatives of Member State governments, and decides on Commission proposals. It is the Union's legislator,

---

50 Ibid., at Article 30.

51 Nicoll, William and Salmon, Trevor, *Understanding the New European Community*, Exeter, 1994, p. 97.

with all decisions involving new policies requiring unanimity. The Assembly is charged with proposing, to the Council, arrangements for universal direct elections. In addition, the Council, in turn, commends them to the Member States for adoption under constitutional procedures. The Assembly is consultative and can, if it has a sufficient majority, express its non-confidence in the commission by dismissing it.

The European Court of Justice (ECJ) is the European Union's supreme constitutional authority. It renders judgments on the obligations of the institutions, Member States and citizens. The very existence of the European Union is conditional on the recognition of the binding nature of its rules, by the Member States, by the institutions, and by individuals. European Union law has successfully embedded itself thoroughly in the legal life of the Member States through the supervision of the European Court of Justice. The founding European Treaties are the primary source of European Union law, and therein is found the central jurisdiction of the European Court of Justice. European Union law involves primary law, namely Treaties, and secondary law, namely legislative acts, both of which are binding on national governments and take precedence over national law. The nature of the European Union, its existence and its functions, demand a consistent application of European Union law between Member States.

The ECJ was to provide the legal sanctions for the carrying out of the Treaties. Before the European Community and the European Union, courts operating beyond national boundaries were constrained by international agreement, such as the International Court of Justice. In essence, European Union citizens are affected by two legal systems, national and European Union law. The courts of law must apply both systems of law where relevant, and if there is a conflict, the European Union law takes precedence. The supremacy of European Union law is implicit in the nature of the European Union, since its existence and functioning require its application. European Union law is directly applicable to Member States, and there is no requirement that it be passed into national law for its validity, since the rights and obligations accrue directly to European Union citizens.

The primacy of European Union law and its direct applicability are distinctive features of the European Union, turning freedoms into rights. It is a system of laws, which is directly applicable to people and institutions in Member States, and is invoked in national courts. European Union law touches on many aspects of national life, including immigration, control of foreign workers, and matters relating to equality. Thus, national law has been challenged or influenced by European Union law, which is enforced and overseen by the European Court of Justice. This surrender of sovereignty cannot be reversed by measures taken by national authorities in conflict with European Union law, relinquishing far-reaching powers to an independent legal order, which binds Member States. Points of law and the interpretation of Treaties are decided by the European Court of Justice, the European Union's judicial institution having jurisdiction over disputes concerning the Member States. Often, the national court is faced with issues, such as the interpretation of a Treaty, the validity of acts or the lack of a judicial remedy under national law. If a nation State's court decides that a question of European Union law needs to be answered before it can render a judgment, it can go before the European Court of Justice for a ruling. The European Union Treaties are part of the domestic law of the State, and as such, they impinge on the finality of national court decisions.

Where European Union law has direct effect, it will take precedence over domestic law in such cases as equality in employment. Under national law, the national court of the Member State is within its limits of discretion, when interpreting domestic law. However, domestic law must be in accord with the requirements of European Union law, and if this is not possible, then domestic law is inapplicable. This, therefore, is a strong incentive for national courts to rule against **class** discrimination. The European Union can legislate directly through regulations, which are binding in law and are automatically incorporated into the national legal systems of Member States, without the need for specific individual ratification. It can also work through the legal systems of the Member States, by the use of the Commission, which implements directives with broad objectives. Although directives require some legal action, such as legislation, by the Member States before they become national law, they are laws transposed into Member States' legislation to enforce Treaty principles. Importantly, decisions by the European Court of Justice are binding as force of law, whereas recommendations and opinions by the Council of Ministers or the Commission are not.

European Union legislation establishes that a citizen of the European Union should not be discriminated against in the workplace. In employment, discrimination can occur in two ways: direct discrimination when people are treated differently solely on the basis of a discriminatory ground; and indirect discrimination when people are treated differently because of an apparently neutral provision, criterion or practice determining recruitment, pay, working conditions, dismissal and social security in practice disadvantaging a substantially higher proportion of the members of one group. Such provisions, criteria or practices are prohibited under European Union law, unless it is proven that they are justified by objective reasons in no way related to discrimination such as class. In examining positive action, European Union law allows European Union countries and companies to undertake several initiatives to counter discrimination. While there is no official definition of positive action, it does include all measures which are designed to counter the effects of past disadvantages and existing discrimination, and to promote equality of opportunity in the field of employment. Historically, there have been discriminatory policies directly on their face or indirectly, applied to different groups. Positive action is needed not only to help guarantee equality, but also to combat the perpetuation of traditional discriminatory attitudes so as to ensure access to equal opportunities for all.

The European Court of Justice is at the heart of the legal system, and ensures that European Union law is observed in the interpretation and application of the Treaties. Its judgments are binding on Member States. The court reviews the lawfulness of acts of Council, the Commission, the Member States' governments and citizens. National laws in conflict with European Union law may be declared invalid by the European Court of Justice. Appeals against acts of an institution or a Member State can be lodged by any other institution, government, firm or individual citizen directly affected.

Two types of cases may be brought before the European Court of Justice, namely direct actions, brought directly before the Court by the Commission, other European Union institutions or a Member State, or preliminary rulings, requested by courts or tribunals in the Member States on a question of European Union law. The European Court of Justice may hear a variety of cases involving: annulment of binding legal acts; failure to act; infringement of the European Union Treaties under Article 33, in order to have Commission decisions or recommendations declared void for lack of competence, infringement of an essential procedural requirement, the Treaty or any rule of law relating to its application, or misuse of powers; preliminary rulings, in which national courts petition the Court of Justice for a ruling on a point of European Union law, binding in the case; damages; and application of staff regulations. The Treaties state that the European Union's legal system, which must not be impeded by any State, applies throughout the European Union.

The legal order is called the "originality" of the European Union, which is the jurisdiction of the constitutional court, the European Court of Justice. The Court's decisions are made by majority vote, presented in open court. The judgments are directly applicable to Member States and are enforceable through the national courts. The Court of Justice located in Luxembourg may sit in plenary session, when a Member State or a European Union institution is a party to the proceeding and so requests or when a case is considered complex and important, or may sit in chamber. Since all the official languages of the European Union are used at some point, the Court provides for a large translation and interpretation service. The Court is also assisted by an Advocate General, as amicus curiae acting as an independent judicial observer representing the public interest, who makes a reasoned presentation of the case before the Court, gives a summary of the submissions of the parties, puts forth observations of oral hearings, statute law and previous cases, and offers an opinion, which although published is not binding on the Court. In order to enable the Court of Justice to concentrate its activities on the fundamental task of ensuring uniform interpretation of European Union law, a Court of First Instance was established in 1989, which has jurisdiction over actions brought by individuals and companies against decisions of the European Union institutions and agencies, and these judgments are in turn subject to appeal before the European Court of Justice on a point of law.

As the arbiter of European Union law, the European Court of Justice, with its power, has strengthened the European Union as a political system, and defiance of its rulings has been exceptional. By creating a body of independent European Union law, the European Union has promoted its survival, by requiring harmonization of the laws of the Member States. The national courts are, therefore, responsible for aligning national law with European Union law. The Treaties are a comprehensive code of law, which set out the rights and duties of governments and individuals, and from which rights and remedies can be deduced. Interestingly, for the European Court of Justice, the European Union's common aims count more than a literal construction of legal texts, and in turn, the legal character of the European Union is concerned with influencing, shaping and controlling the legislative output of the European Union. Fundamental rights are part of the bedrock of the European Union's legal order. The European Court of Justice held that the protection of such rights, while inspired by the constitutional traditions common to Member States, must be ensured within the framework of the structure and objectives of the European Union (*Internationale Handelsgesellschaft* [1970] ECR 1125, [1972] CMLR 255).[52] Importantly, in a seminal case, the European Court of Justice stated:

> The integration into the laws of each Member State of provisions which derive from the Community, and more generally the terms and the spirit of the Treaty, make it impossible for the States, as a corollary, to accord precedence to a unilateral and subsequent measure over a legal system accepted by them on a basis of reciprocity … The executive force of Community law cannot vary from one State to another … without jeopardising the attainment of the object of the Treaty ... It follows from all these observations that the law stemming from the treaty, an independent source of law, could not, because of its special and original nature, be overridden by domestic legal provisions, however framed, without being deprived of its character as Community law and without the legal basis of the Community itself being called into question (*Costa v. ENEL* [1964] CMLR 425).[53]

In terms of the burden of proof, in the European Court of Justice, the plaintiff has the burden of showing, in indirect cases, that a neutral policy has a disproportionate impact (*Teuling v. Bredrijfsvereniging*, [1987] ECR 2497).[54] The burden is then shifted to the defendant who must justify this by objective reasons other than discrimination. The plaintiff must then show that the explanation is not effective for the purpose, or that there is an alternative provision to accomplish it in a manner that has a less discriminatory impact. Otherwise, if there is a difference in treatment, it must be justified by objective factors other than discrimination. If a provision is neutral on its terms, but factually disadvantages a particular group, an employer bears the burden of justification. The European Court of Justice requires a showing of objective justification as a defense to discrimination.

52 *Internationale Handelsgesellschaft* [1970] ECR 1125, [1972] CMLR 255.

53 *Costa v. ENEL* [1964] CMLR 425.

54 *Teuling v. Bredrijfsvereniging* [1987] ECR 2497.

European Convention for the Protection of Human Rights and Fundamental Freedoms (ECHR)

Crucially for human rights, the European Convention for the Protection of Human Rights and Fundamental Freedoms, which came into being on 4 November 1950, affords protection against discrimination. In the Preamble of the European Convention for the Protection of Human Rights and Fundamental Freedoms, the Governments signatory hereto, being Members of the Council of Europe, undertake the agreement:

> Considering the Universal Declaration of Human Rights proclaimed by the General Assembly of the United Nations on 10th December 1948;
>
> Considering that this Declaration aims at securing the universal and effective recognition and observance of the Rights therein declared;
>
> Considering that the aim of the Council of Europe is the achievement of greater unity between its Members and that one of the methods by which the aim is to be pursued is the maintenance and further realisation of Human Rights and Fundamental Freedoms;
>
> Reaffirming their profound belief in those Fundamental Freedoms which are the foundation of justice and peace in the world and are best maintained on the one hand by an effective political democracy and on the other by a common understanding and observance of the Human Rights upon which they depend;
>
> Being resolved, as the Governments of European countries which are like-minded and have a common heritage of political traditions, ideals, freedom and the rule of law to take the first steps for the collective enforcement of certain of the Rights stated in the Universal Declaration.[55]

Article 1 guarantees:

> 1. The High Contracting Parties shall secure to everyone within their jurisdiction the rights and freedoms defined.[56]

Important in the fight against class discrimination, the prohibition of discrimination is guaranteed under Article 14, which includes social origin or other status:

55 European Convention for the Protection of Human Rights and Fundamental Freedoms (ECHR), at the Preamble.

56 Ibid., at Article 1.

> 14. The enjoyment of the rights and freedoms set forth in this Convention shall be secured without discrimination on any ground such as sex, race, colour, language, religion, political or other opinion, national or social origin, association with a national minority, property, birth or other status.[57]

The right to an effective remedy is secured by Article 13:

> 13. Everyone whose rights and freedoms as set forth in this Convention are violated shall have an effective remedy before a national authority notwithstanding that the violation has been committed by persons acting in an official capacity.[58]

Further, Article 17 provides for the prohibition of abuse of rights:

> 17. Nothing in this Convention may be interpreted as implying for any State, group or person any right to engage in any activity or perform any act aimed at the destruction of any of the rights and freedoms set forth herein or at their limitation to a greater extent than is provided for in the Convention.[59]

Importantly, the European Court of Human Rights is established under Article 19:

> 19. To ensure the observance of the engagements undertaken by the High Contracting Parties in the Convention and the Protocols thereto, there shall be set up a European Court of Human Rights, hereinafter referred to as 'the Court'. It shall function on a permanent basis.[60]

Article 32 outlines the jurisdiction of the Court:

> 32.1. The jurisdiction of the Court shall extend to all matters concerning the interpretation and application of the Convention and the protocols thereto which are referred to it as provided in Articles 33, 34 and 47.
> 2. In the event of dispute as to whether the Court has jurisdiction, the Court shall decide.[61]

Article 27 outlines the structure of the Committees, the Chambers and the Grand Chamber:

---

57 Ibid., at Article 14.
58 Ibid., at Article 13.
59 Ibid., at Article 17.
60 Ibid., at Article 19.
61 Ibid., at Article 32.

> 27.1. To consider cases brought before it, the Court shall sit in committees of three judges, in Chambers of seven judges and in a Grand Chamber of seventeen judges. The Court's Chambers shall set up committees for a fixed period of time.
> 2. There shall sit as an ex officio member of the Chamber and the Grand Chamber the judge elected in respect of the State Party concerned or, if there is none or if he is unable to sit, a person of its choice who shall sit in the capacity of judge.
> 3. The Grand Chamber shall also include the President of the Court, the Vice-Presidents, the Presidents of the Chambers and other judges chosen in accordance with the rules of the Court. When a case is referred to the Grand Chamber under Article 43, no judge from the Chamber which rendered the judgment shall sit in the Grand Chamber, with the exception of the President of the Chamber and the judge who sat in respect of the State Party concerned.[62]

Inter-State cases are provided for under Article 33:

> 33. Any High Contracting Party may refer to the Court any alleged breach of the provisions of the Convention and the protocols thereto by another High Contracting Party.[63]

Individual applications are provided for under Article 34:

> 34. The Court may receive applications from any person, non-governmental organisation or group of individuals claiming to be the victim of a violation by one of the High Contracting Parties of the rights set forth in the Convention or the protocols thereto. The High Contracting Parties undertake not to hinder in any way the effective exercise of this right.[64]

Further, third-party intervention is provided for under Article 36:

> 36.1. In all cases before a Chamber or the Grand Chamber, a High Contracting Party one of whose nationals is an applicant shall have the right to submit written comments and to take part in hearings.
> 2. The President of the Court may, in the interest of the proper administration of justice, invite any High Contracting Party which is not a party to the proceedings or any person concerned who is not the applicant to submit written comments or take part in hearings.[65]

62 Ibid., at Article 27.
63 Ibid., at Article 33.
64 Ibid., at Article 34.
65 Ibid., at Article 36.

Article 35 contains the admissibility of evidence criteria:

> 35.1. The Court may only deal with the matter after all domestic remedies have been exhausted, according to the generally recognised rules of international law, and within a period of six months from the date on which the final decision was taken.
> 2. The Court shall not deal with any application submitted under Article 34 that:
> (a) is anonymous; or
> (b) is substantially the same as a matter that has already been examined by the Court or has already been submitted to another procedure of international investigation or settlement and contains no relevant new information.
> 3. The Court shall declare inadmissible any individual application submitted under Article 34 which it considers incompatible with the provisions of the Convention or the protocols thereto, manifestly ill-founded, or an abuse of the right of application.
> 4. The Court shall reject any application which it considers inadmissible under this Article. It may do so at any stage of the proceedings.[66]

Further, Article 37 contains the striking out of applications:

> 37.1. The Court may at any stage of the proceedings decide to strike an application out of its list of cases where the circumstances lead to the conclusion that:
> (a) the applicant does not intend to pursue his application; or
> (b) the matter has been resolved; or
> (c) for any other reason established by the Court, it is no longer justified to continue the examination of the application.
> However, the Court shall continue the examination of the application if respect for human rights as defined in the Convention and the protocols thereto so requires.
> 2. The Court may decide to restore an application to its list of cases if it considers that the circumstances justify such a course.[67]

Article 38 outlines the examination of the case and friendly settlement proceedings:

> 38.1. If the Court declares the application admissible, it shall:
> (a) pursue the examination of the case, together with the representatives of the parties, and if need be, undertake an investigation, for the effective conduct of which the States concerned shall furnish all necessary facilities;

66 Ibid., at Article 35.
67 Ibid., at Article 37.

(b) place itself at the disposal of the parties concerned with a view to securing a friendly settlement of the matter on the basis of respect for human rights as defined in the Convention and the protocols thereto.

2. Proceedings conducted under paragraph 1.b shall be confidential.[68]

Further, Article 39 outlines the finding of a friendly settlement:

> 39. If a friendly settlement is effected, the Court shall strike the case out of its list by means of a decision which shall be confined to a brief statement of the facts and of the solution reached.[69]

Public hearings and access to documents are provided for under Article 40:

> 40.1. Hearings shall be in public unless the Court in exceptional circumstances decides otherwise.
> 2. Documents deposited with the Registrar shall be accessible to the public unless the President of the Court decides otherwise.[70]

Further, Article 41 provides for just satisfaction:

> 41. If the Court finds that there has been a violation of the Convention or the protocols thereto, and if the internal law of the High Contracting Party concerned allows only partial reparation to be made, the Court shall, if necessary, afford just satisfaction to the injured party.[71]

Importantly, final judgments are contained in Article 44:

> 44.1. The judgment of the Grand Chamber shall be final.
> 2. The judgment of a Chamber shall become final:
> (a) when the parties declare that they will not request that the case be referred to the Grand Chamber; or
> (b) three months after the date of the judgment, if reference of the case to the Grand Chamber has not been requested; or
> (c) when the panel of the Grand Chamber rejects the request to refer under Article 43.
> 3. The final judgment shall be published.[72]

Further, reasons for judgments and decisions are contained in Article 45:

68 Ibid., at Article 38.
69 Ibid., at Article 39.
70 Ibid., at Article 40.
71 Ibid., at Article 41.
72 Ibid., at Article 44.

> 45.1. Reasons shall be given for judgments as well as for decisions declaring applications admissible or inadmissible.
> 2. If a judgment does not represent, in whole or in part, the unanimous opinion of the judges, any judge shall be entitled to deliver a separate opinion.[73]

In addition, binding force and execution of judgments are contained in Article 46:

> 46.1. The High Contracting Parties undertake to abide by the final judgment of the Court in any case to which they are parties.
> 2. The final judgment of the Court shall be transmitted to the Committee of Ministers, which shall supervise its execution.[74]

Finally, Article 47 provides for advisory opinions:

> 47.1. The Court may, at the request of the Committee of Ministers, give advisory opinions on legal questions concerning the interpretation of the Convention and the protocols thereto.
> 2. Such opinions shall not deal with any question relating to the content or scope of the rights or freedoms defined in Section I of the Convention and the protocols thereto, or with any other question which the Court or the Committee of Ministers might have to consider in consequence of any such proceedings as could be instituted in accordance with the Convention.
> 3. Decisions of the Committee of Ministers to request an advisory opinion of the Court shall require a majority vote of the representatives entitled to sit on the Committee.[75]

In addition, the Preamble of Protocol No.1, entitled Enforcement of Certain Rights and Freedoms not included in Section I of the Convention, states that:

> The Governments signatory hereto, being Members of the Council of Europe,
> Being resolved to take steps to ensure the collective enforcement of certain rights and freedoms other than those already included in Section I of the Convention for the Protection of Human Rights and Fundamental Freedoms signed at Rome on 4th November, 1950 (hereinafter referred to as 'the Convention'),
> Have agreed as follows.[76]

---

73 Ibid., at Article 45.

74 Ibid., at Article 46.

75 Ibid., at Article 47.

76 European Convention for the Protection of Human Rights and Fundamental Freedoms as amended by Protocol No. 1, at the Preamble.

Important for education as a tool for advancement and in the fight against class discrimination, under Protocol No. 11, Article 2 safeguards the right to education:

> 2. No person shall be denied the right to education. In the exercise of any functions which it assumes in relation to education and to teaching, the State shall respect the right of parents to ensure such education and teaching in conformity with their own religious and philosophical convictions.[77]

Further, important for equal rights, in the Preamble of the Protocol No. 12 to the European Convention for the Protection of Human Rights and Fundamental Freedoms, the Member States of the Council of Europe signatory hereto, undertake the agreement:

> Having regard to the fundamental principle according to which all persons are equal before the law and are entitled to the equal protection of the law;
>
> Being resolved to take further steps to promote the equality of all persons through the collective enforcement of a general prohibition of discrimination by means of the Convention for the Protection of Human Rights and Fundamental Freedoms signed at Rome on 4 November 1950 (hereinafter referred to as 'the Convention');
>
> Reaffirming that the principle of non-discrimination does not prevent States Parties from taking measures in order to promote full and effective equality, provided that there is an objective and reasonable justification for those measures.[78]

Article 1 outlines the general prohibition against discrimination, which includes social origin or other status:

> 1(1) The enjoyment of any right set forth by law shall be secured without discrimination on any ground such as sex, race, colour, language, religion, political or other opinion, national or social origin, association with a national minority, property, birth or other status.
> (2) No one shall be discriminated against by any public authority on any ground such as those mentioned in paragraph 1.[79]

---

77 European Convention for the Protection of Human Rights and Fundamental Freedoms as amended by Protocol No. 11, at Article 2.

78 European Convention for the Protection of Human Rights and Fundamental Freedoms as amended by Protocol No. 12, at the Preamble.

79 Ibid., at Article 1.

In addition to the words "social origin", it is noteworthy that the words "other status" in Article 14 of the ECHR should include class, and such a specific inclusion was considered unnecessary from a legal point of view, since the list of non-discrimination grounds is not exhaustive, and since inclusion of any particular additional ground might give rise to unwarranted *a contrario* interpretations as regards discrimination based on grounds not so included. According to the Explanatory Memorandum prepared by the Council of Europe, the expression "any right set forth by law" in Article 1 of Protocol 12 is meant to cover (i) the enjoyment of any right specifically granted to an individual by national law; (ii) the enjoyment of a right which may be inferred from a clear obligation of a public authority under national law, such as where a public authority is obliged under national law to behave in a particular manner; (iii) the exercise of a discretionary power by a public authority; and (iv) any other act or omission by a public authority. The prime objective of Article 1 is to embody a negative obligation on public authorities not to discriminate; it does not impose a general positive obligation to take measures to prevent or prohibit all instances of discrimination between private persons. On the other hand, the duty to "secure" might entail a positive obligation where there is a clear gap in protection from discrimination under domestic law, and would oblige a ratifying State to secure protection against discrimination on all the proscribed grounds, including class.

The right of all individuals to equality before the law and to protection from discrimination is a fundamental right which is essential in order to allow any democratic society to function properly, since it helps to achieve the objectives of promoting economic and social progress, and a high level of employment by increasing economic and social cohesion. Two key instruments were adopted which were intended to prevent and combat discrimination: Directive 2000/78/EC prohibiting discrimination in employment; and Council Decision 2000/750/EC the Community Action Programme to Combat Discrimination, supporting and supplementing efforts at the Community level and in the Member States to promote measures to prevent and to combat direct or indirect discrimination, whether based on one or on multiple factors, aiming at promoting greater public consensus on the extent and impact of discrimination.

Council Decision 2000/750/EC Establishing a Community Action Programme to Combat Discrimination (2001 to 2006)

Important for equal rights, the Preamble of Council Decision 2000/750/EC of 27 November 2000 Establishing a CommunityAction Programme to Combat Discrimination states:

> (1) The European Union is founded on the principles of liberty, democracy, respect for human rights and fundamental freedoms, and the rule of law, principles which are common to all Member States. In accordance with Article

6(2) of the Treaty on European Union, the Union should respect fundamental rights as guaranteed by the European Convention for the Protection of Human Rights and Fundamental Freedoms and as derived from the shared constitutional traditions common to the Member States, as general principles of Community law.

(2) The European Parliament has strongly and repeatedly urged the European Union to develop and strengthen its policy in the field of equal treatment and equal opportunities across all grounds of discrimination.

(3) The European Union rejects theories which attempt to determine the existence of separate human races. The use of the term 'racial origin' in this Decision does not imply an acceptance of such theories.

(4) In the implementation of the programme, the Community will seek, in accordance with the Treaty, to eliminate inequalities and promote equality between men and women, particularly because women are often the victims of multiple discrimination.

(5) The different forms of discrimination cannot be ranked: all are equally intolerable. The programme is intended both to exchange existing good practice in the Member States and to develop new practice and policy for combating discrimination, including multiple discrimination. This Decision may help to put in place a comprehensive strategy for combating all forms of discrimination on different grounds, a strategy which should henceforward be developed in parallel.

(6) Experience of action at Community level, in particular in the field of gender, has shown that combating discrimination in practice calls for a combination of measures and in particular of legislation and of practical action designed to be mutually reinforcing. Similar lessons can be drawn from experience dealing with racial and ethnic origin and disability.

(7) The programme should deal with all grounds of discrimination with the exception of sex, which is dealt with by specific Community action. Discrimination on different grounds can have similar features and can be combated in similar ways. Experience built up over many years in combating discrimination on some grounds, including sex, can be used to the benefit of other grounds. However, the specific features of the diverse forms of discrimination should be accommodated. Therefore, the particular needs of people with disabilities should be taken into account in terms of the accessibility of activities and results.

(8) Access to the programme should be open to all public and/or private bodies and institutions involved in the fight against discrimination. In this connection

account must be taken of the experience and abilities of both local and national non-governmental organisations.

(9) Many non-governmental organisationsat European level have experience and expertise in fighting discrimination, as well as acting at European level as the advocates of people who are exposed to discrimination. They can therefore make an important contribution towards a better understanding of the diverse forms and effects of discrimination and to ensuring that the design, implementation and follow-up of the programme take account of the experience of people exposed to discrimination. The Community has in the past provided core funding for various organisations working in the area of discrimination. The core funding of effective non-governmental organisations may be a valuable asset in combating discrimination.

(10) The measures necessary for the implementation of this Decision should be adopted in accordance with Council Decision 1999/468/EC of 28 June 1999 laying down the procedures for the exercise of implementing powers conferred on the Commission(4).

(11) It is necessary, in order to reinforce the added value of Community action, that the Commission, in cooperation with the Member States, should ensure, at all levels, the coherence and complementarity of actions implemented in the framework of this Decision and other relevant Community policies, instruments and actions, in particular those in the fields of education and training and equal opportunities between men and women under the European Social Fund and those to promote social inclusion. Consistency and complementarity with the relevant activities of the European Monitoring Centre on Racism and Xenophobia should also be ensured.

(12) The Agreement on the European Economic Area (EEA Agreement) provides for greater cooperation in the social field between the European Community and its Member States, on the one hand, and the countries of the European Free Trade Association participating in the European Economic Area (EFTA/EEA), on the other. Provision should be made to open up this programme to participation by the candidate countries of Central and Eastern Europe, in accordance with the conditions established in the Europe Agreements, in their additional protocols and in the decisions of the respective Association Councils, to Cyprus, Malta and Turkey, funded by additional appropriations in accordance with the procedures to be agreed with those countries.

(13) A financial reference amount, within the meaning of point 34 of the Interinstitutional Agreement of 6 May 1999 between the European Parliament, the Council and the Commission(5) is included in this Decision for the entire

duration of the programme, without thereby affecting the powers of the budgetary authority as they are defined by the Treaty.

(14) The Commission and the Member States should make efforts to ensure that all the texts, guidelines and calls for proposals published under this programme are written in clear, simple and accessible language.

(15) It is appropriate that account should be taken of the need to provide special assistance, where appropriate, to enable people to overcome the obstacles to their participation in the programme.

(16) It is necessary for the success of any Community action to monitor and evaluate the results set against the objectives.

(17) In accordance with the principle of subsidiarity as defined in Article 5 of the Treaty, the objectives of the proposed action concerning the contribution of the Community to combating discrimination cannot be sufficiently achieved by the Member States because, inter alia, of the need for multilateral partnerships, the transnational exchange of information and the Community-wide dissemination of good practice. In accordance with the principle of proportionality as defined in the said Article, this Decision does not go beyond what is necessary to achieve those objectives,
HAS DECIDED AS FOLLOWS.[80]

The establishment of the Programme is undertaken under Article 1:

1. This Decision establishes a Community action programme, hereinafter referred to as 'the programme', to promote measures to combat direct or indirect discrimination based on racial or ethnic origin, religion or belief, disability, age or sexual orientation … .[81]

Objectives of the Programme are outlined in Article 2:

2. Within the limits of the Community's powers, the programme shall support and supplement the efforts at Community level and in the Member States to promote measures to prevent and combat discrimination whether based on one or on multiple factors, taking account, where appropriate, of future legislative developments. It shall have the following objectives:

---

80 Council Decision 2000/750/EC of 27 November 2000 establishing a Community Action Programme to Combat Discrimination (2001 to 2006) [OJ L 303, 02/12/2000 P. 0023 – 0028], at the Preamble.

81 Ibid., at Article 1.

> (a) to improve the understanding of issues related to discrimination through improved knowledge of this phenomenon and through evaluation of the effectiveness of policies and practice;
> (b) to develop the capacity to prevent and address discrimination effectively, in particular by strengthening organisations' means of action and through support for the exchange of information and good practice and networking at European level, while taking into account the specific characteristics of the different forms of discrimination;
> (c) to promote and disseminate the values and practices underlying the fight against discrimination, including through the use of awareness-raising campaigns.[82]

Article 3 stipulates the Community actions to be undertaken:

> 3.1. With a view to achieving the objectives set out in Article 2, the following actions may be implemented within a transnational framework:
> (a) analysis of factors related to discrimination, including through studies and the development of qualitative and quantitative indicators and benchmarks, in accordance with national law and practices, and the evaluation of anti-discrimination legislation and practice, with a view to assessing its effectiveness and impact, with effective dissemination of the results;
> (b) transnational cooperation and the promotion of networking at European level between partners active in the prevention of, and the fight against, discrimination, including non-governmental organisations;
> (c) awareness-raising, in particular to emphasise the European dimension of the fight against discrimination and to publicise the results of the programme, in particular through communications, publications, campaigns and events.[83]

Finally, in terms of the implementation of the Programme and cooperation with the Member States, Article 4 states:

> 4.1. The Commission shall:
> (a) ensure the implementation of the Community actions covered by the programme in conformity with the Annex;
> (b) have a regular exchange of views with representatives of non-governmental organisations and the social partners at European level on the design, implementation and follow-up of the programme and on related policy orientations. To that end the Commission shall make the relevant information available to the non-governmental organisations and the social

82 Ibid., at Article 2.
83 Ibid., at Article 3.

partners. The Commission shall inform the committee established under Article 6 of their exchange of views.

2. The Commission, in cooperation with the Member States, shall take the necessary steps to:

(a) promote the involvement in the programme of all the parties concerned, including non-governmental organisations of all sizes;

(b) promote active partnership and dialogue between all the partners involved in the programme, inter alia to encourage an integrated and coordinated approach to the fight against discrimination;

(c) ensure the dissemination of the results of the actions undertaken within the framework of the programme;

(d) provide accessible information and appropriate publicity and follow-up with regard to actions supported by the programme.[84]

Council Directive 2000/78/EC Establishing a General Framework for Equal Treatment in Employment and Occupation

Important for equal rights, the Preamble of Council Directive 2000/78/EC of 27 November 2000 Establishing a General Framework for Equal Treatment in Employment and Occupation states:

(1) In accordance with Article 6 of the Treaty on European Union, the European Union is founded on the principles of liberty, democracy, respect for human rights and fundamental freedoms, and the rule of law, principles which are common to all Member States and it respects fundamental rights, as guaranteed by the European Convention for the Protection of Human Rights and Fundamental Freedoms and as they result from the constitutional traditions common to the Member States, as general principles of Community law.

(2) The principle of equal treatment between women and men is well established by an important body of Community law, in particular in Council Directive 76/207/EEC of 9 February 1976 on the implementation of the principle of equal treatment for men and women as regards access to employment, vocational training and promotion, and working conditions(5).

(3) In implementing the principle of equal treatment, the Community should, in accordance with Article 3(2) of the EC Treaty, aim to eliminate inequalities, and to promote equality between men and women, especially since women are often the victims of multiple discrimination.

84 Ibid., at Article 4.

(4) The right of all persons to equality before the law and protection against discrimination constitutes a universal right recognised by the Universal Declaration of Human Rights, the United Nations Convention on the Elimination of All Forms of Discrimination against Women, United Nations Covenants on Civil and Political Rights and on Economic, Social and Cultural Rights and by the European Convention for the Protection of Human Rights and Fundamental Freedoms, to which all Member States are signatories. Convention No 111 of the International Labour Organisation (ILO) prohibits discrimination in the field of employment and occupation.

(5) It is important to respect such fundamental rights and freedoms. This Directive does not prejudice freedom of association, including the right to establish unions with others and to join unions to defend one's interests.

(6) The Community Charter of the Fundamental Social Rights of Workers recognises the importance of combating every form of discrimination, including the need to take appropriate action for the social and economic integration of elderly and disabled people.

(7) The EC Treaty includes among its objectives the promotion of coordination between employment policies of the Member States. To this end, a new employment chapter was incorporated in the EC Treaty as a means of developing a coordinated European strategy for employment to promote a skilled, trained and adaptable workforce.

(8) The Employment Guidelines for 2000 agreed by the European Council at Helsinki on 10 and 11 December 1999 stress the need to foster a labour market favourable to social integration by formulating a coherent set of policies aimed at combating discrimination against groups such as persons with disability. They also emphasise the need to pay particular attention to supporting older workers, in order to increase their participation in the labour force.

(9) Employment and occupation are key elements in guaranteeing equal opportunities for all and contribute strongly to the full participation of citizens in economic, cultural and social life and to realising their potential.

(10) On 29 June 2000 the Council adopted Directive 2000/43/EC(6) implementing the principle of equal treatment between persons irrespective of racial or ethnic origin. That Directive already provides protection against such discrimination in the field of employment and occupation.

(11) Discrimination based on religion or belief, disability, age or sexual orientation may undermine the achievement of the objectives of the EC Treaty, in particular the attainment of a high level of employment and social protection,

raising the standard of living and the quality of life, economic and social cohesion and solidarity, and the free movement of persons.

(12) To this end, any direct or indirect discrimination based on religion or belief, disability, age or sexual orientation as regards the areas covered by this Directive should be prohibited throughout the Community. This prohibition of discrimination should also apply to nationals of third countries but does not cover differences of treatment based on nationality and is without prejudice to provisions governing the entry and residence of third-country nationals and their access to employment and occupation.

(13) This Directive does not apply to social security and social protection schemes whose benefits are not treated as income within the meaning given to that term for the purpose of applying Article 141 of the EC Treaty, nor to any kind of payment by the State aimed at providing access to employment or maintaining employment.

(14) This Directive shall be without prejudice to national provisions laying down retirement ages.

(15) The appreciation of the facts from which it may be inferred that there has been direct or indirect discrimination is a matter for national judicial or other competent bodies, in accordance with rules of national law or practice. Such rules may provide, in particular, for indirect discrimination to be established by any means including on the basis of statistical evidence.

(16) The provision of measures to accommodate the needs of disabled people at the workplace plays an important role in combating discrimination on grounds of disability.

(17) This Directive does not require the recruitment, promotion, maintenance in employment or training of an individual who is not competent, capable and available to perform the essential functions of the post concerned or to undergo the relevant training, without prejudice to the obligation to provide reasonable accommodation for people with disabilities.

(18) This Directive does not require, in particular, the armed forces and the police, prison or emergency services to recruit or maintain in employment persons who do not have the required capacity to carry out the range of functions that they may be called upon to perform with regard to the legitimate objective of preserving the operational capacity of those services.

(19) Moreover, in order that the Member States may continue to safeguard the combat effectiveness of their armed forces, they may choose not to apply the

provisions of this Directive concerning disability and age to all or part of their armed forces. The Member States which make that choice must define the scope of that derogation.

(20) Appropriate measures should be provided, i.e. effective and practical measures to adapt the workplace to the disability, for example adapting premises and equipment, patterns of working time, the distribution of tasks or the provision of training or integration resources.

(21) To determine whether the measures in question give rise to a disproportionate burden, account should be taken in particular of the financial and other costs entailed, the scale and financial resources of the organisation or undertaking and the possibility of obtaining public funding or any other assistance.

(22) This Directive is without prejudice to national laws on marital status and the benefits dependent thereon.

(23) In very limited circumstances, a difference of treatment may be justified where a characteristic related to religion or belief, disability, age or sexual orientation constitutes a genuine and determining occupational requirement, when the objective is legitimate and the requirement is proportionate. Such circumstances should be included in the information provided by the Member States to the Commission.

(24) The European Union in its Declaration No 11 on the status of churches and non-confessional organisations, annexed to the Final Act of the Amsterdam Treaty, has explicitly recognised that it respects and does not prejudice the status under national law of churches and religious associations or communities in the Member States and that it equally respects the status of philosophical and non-confessional organisations. With this in view, Member States may maintain or lay down specific provisions on genuine, legitimate and justified occupational requirements which might be required for carrying out an occupational activity.

(25) The prohibition of age discrimination is an essential part of meeting the aims set out in the Employment Guidelines and encouraging diversity in the workforce. However, differences in treatment in connection with age may be justified under certain circumstances and therefore require specific provisions which may vary in accordance with the situation in Member States. It is therefore essential to distinguish between differences in treatment which are justified, in particular by legitimate employment policy, labour market and vocational training objectives, and discrimination which must be prohibited.

(26) The prohibition of discrimination should be without prejudice to the maintenance or adoption of measures intended to prevent or compensate for

disadvantages suffered by a group of persons of a particular religion or belief, disability, age or sexual orientation, and such measures may permit organisations of persons of a particular religion or belief, disability, age or sexual orientation where their main object is the promotion of the special needs of those persons.

(27) In its Recommendation 86/379/EEC of 24 July 1986 on the employment of disabled people in the Community(7), the Council established a guideline framework setting out examples of positive action to promote the employment and training of disabled people, and in its Resolution of 17 June 1999 on equal employment opportunities for people with disabilities(8), affirmed the importance of giving specific attention inter alia to recruitment, retention, training and lifelong learning with regard to disabled persons.

(28) This Directive lays down minimum requirements, thus giving the Member States the option of introducing or maintaining more favourable provisions. The implementation of this Directive should not serve to justify any regression in relation to the situation which already prevails in each Member State.

(29) Persons who have been subject to discrimination based on religion or belief, disability, age or sexual orientation should have adequate means of legal protection. To provide a more effective level of protection, associations or legal entities should also be empowered to engage in proceedings, as the Member States so determine, either on behalf or in support of any victim, without prejudice to national rules of procedure concerning representation and defence before the courts.

(30) The effective implementation of the principle of equality requires adequate judicial protection against victimisation.

(31) The rules on the burden of proof must be adapted when there is a prima facie case of discrimination and, for the principle of equal treatment to be applied effectively, the burden of proof must shift back to the respondent when evidence of such discrimination is brought. However, it is not for the respondent to prove that the plaintiff adheres to a particular religion or belief, has a particular disability, is of a particular age or has a particular sexual orientation.

(32) Member States need not apply the rules on the burden of proof to proceedings in which it is for the court or other competent body to investigate the facts of the case. The procedures thus referred to are those in which the plaintiff is not required to prove the facts, which it is for the court or competent body to investigate.

(33) Member States should promote dialogue between the social partners and, within the framework of national practice, with non-governmental organisations

to address different forms of discrimination at the workplace and to combat them.

(34) The need to promote peace and reconciliation between the major communities in Northern Ireland necessitates the incorporation of particular provisions into this Directive.

(35) Member States should provide for effective, proportionate and dissuasive sanctions in case of breaches of the obligations under this Directive.

(36) Member States may entrust the social partners, at their joint request, with the implementation of this Directive, as regards the provisions concerning collective agreements, provided they take any necessary steps to ensure that they are at all times able to guarantee the results required by this Directive.

(37) In accordance with the principle of subsidiarity set out in Article 5 of the EC Treaty, the objective of this Directive, namely the creation within the Community of a level playing-field as regards equality in employment and occupation, cannot be sufficiently achieved by the Member States and can therefore, by reason of the scale and impact of the action, be better achieved at Community level. In accordance with the principle of proportionality, as set out in that Article, this Directive does not go beyond what is necessary in order to achieve that objective,

HAS ADOPTED THIS DIRECTIVE.[85]

Article 1 outlines the purpose of the Council Directive in combating discrimination:

1. The purpose of this Directive is to lay down a general framework for combating discrimination on the grounds of religion or belief, disability, age or sexual orientation as regards employment and occupation, with a view to putting into effect in the Member States the principle of equal treatment.[86]

Further, the scope of the Directive is outlined in Article 3:

3(1) Within the limits of the areas of competence conferred on the Community, this Directive shall apply to all persons, as regards both the public and private sectors, including public bodies, in relation to:

---

85 Council Directive 2000/78/EC Establishing a General Framework for Equal Treatment in Employment and Occupation, at the Preamble.

86 Ibid., at Article 1.

> a. conditions for access to employment, to self-employment or to occupation, including selection criteria and recruitment conditions, whatever the branch of activity and at all levels of the professional hierarchy, including promotion;
> b. access to all types and to all levels of vocational guidance, vocational training, advanced vocational training and retraining, including practical work experience;
> c. employment and working conditions, including dismissals and pay;
> d. membership of, and involvement in, an organisation of workers or employers, or any organisation whose members carry on a particular profession, including the benefits provided for by such organisations.
>
> (2) This Directive does not cover differences of treatment based on nationality and is without prejudice to provisions and conditions relating to the entry into and residence of third-country nationals and stateless persons in the territory of Member States, and to any treatment which arises from the legal status of the third-country nationals and stateless persons concerned.
>
> (3) This Directive does not apply to payments of any kind made by state schemes or similar, including state social security or social protection schemes.[87]

Importantly, the concept of discrimination is defined under Article 2:

> 2(1) For the purposes of this Directive, the 'principle of equal treatment' shall mean that there shall be no direct or indirect discrimination whatsoever on any of the grounds referred to in Article 1.
>
> (2) For the purposes of paragraph 1:
>
> a. direct discrimination shall be taken to occur where one person is treated less favourably than another is, has been or would be treated in a comparable situation, on any of the grounds referred to in Article 1;
>
> b. indirect discrimination shall be taken to occur where an apparently neutral provision, criterion or practice would put persons having a particular religion or belief, a particular disability, a particular age, or a particular sexual orientation at a particular disadvantage compared with other persons unless:
>
> i. that provision, criterion or practice is objectively justified by a legitimate aim and the means of achieving that aim are appropriate and necessary, or
>
> ii. as regards persons with a particular disability, the employer or any person or organisation to whom this Directive applies, is obliged, under national legislation, to take appropriate measures … in order to eliminate disadvantages entailed by such provision, criterion or practice.
>
> (3) Harassment shall be deemed to be a form of discrimination within the meaning of paragraph 1, when unwanted conduct related to any of the grounds

87 Ibid., at Article 3.

> referred to in Article 1 takes place with the purpose or effect of violating the dignity of a person and of creating an intimidating, hostile, degrading, humiliating or offensive environment. In this context, the concept of harassment may be defined in accordance with the national laws and practice of the Member States.
> (4) An instruction to discriminate against persons on any of the grounds referred to in Article 1 shall be deemed to be discrimination within the meaning of paragraph 1.
> (5) This Directive shall be without prejudice to measures laid down by national law which, in a democratic society, are necessary for public security, for the maintenance of public order and the prevention of criminal offences, for the protection of health and for the protection of the rights and freedoms of others.[88]

Further, Article 11 guards against victimization:

> 11. Member States shall introduce into their national legal systems such measures as are necessary to protect employees against dismissal or other adverse treatment by the employer as a reaction to a complaint within the undertaking or to any legal proceedings aimed at enforcing compliance with the principle of equal treatment.[89]

However, Article 4 contains genuine occupational requirements:

> 4(1) … Member States may provide that a difference of treatment which is based on a characteristic related to any of the grounds referred to in Article 1 shall not constitute discrimination where, by reason of the nature of the particular occupational activities concerned or of the context in which they are carried out, such a characteristic constitutes a genuine and determining occupational requirement, provided that the objective is legitimate and the requirement is proportionate.[90]

Further, Article 8 provides for minimum requirements:

> 8(1) Member States may introduce or maintain provisions which are more favourable to the protection of the principle of equal treatment than those laid down in this Directive.
> (2) The implementation of this Directive shall under no circumstances constitute grounds for a reduction in the level of protection against discrimination already afforded by Member States in the fields covered by this Directive.[91]

---

88 Ibid., at Article 2.
89 Ibid., at Article 11.
90 Ibid., at Article 4.
91 Ibid., at Article 8.

Positive action is provided for under Article 7:

> 7(1) With a view to ensuring full equality in practice, the principle of equal treatment shall not prevent any Member State from maintaining or adopting specific measures to prevent or compensate for disadvantages linked to any of the grounds referred to in Article 1.[92]

Importantly, in terms of remedies and enforcement, Article 9 provides for defense of rights:

> 9(1) Member States shall ensure that judicial and/or administrative procedures, including where they deem it appropriate conciliation procedures, for the enforcement of obligations under this Directive are available to all persons who consider themselves wronged by failure to apply the principle of equal treatment to them, even after the relationship in which the discrimination is alleged to have occurred has ended.
> (2) Member States shall ensure that associations, organisations or other legal entities which have, in accordance with the criteria laid down by their national law, a legitimate interest in ensuring that the provisions of this Directive are complied with, may engage, either on behalf or in support of the complainant, with his or her approval, in any judicial and/or administrative procedure provided for the enforcement of obligations under this Directive.[93]

The burden of proof is detailed in Article 10:

> 10(1) Member States shall take such measures as are necessary, in accordance with their national judicial systems, to ensure that, when persons who consider themselves wronged because the principle of equal treatment has not been applied to them establish, before a court or other competent authority, facts from which it may be presumed that there has been direct or indirect discrimination, it shall be for the respondent to prove that there has been no breach of the principle of equal treatment.[94]

Article 16 provides for compliance:

> 16. Member States shall take the necessary measures to ensure that:
> a. any laws, regulations and administrative provisions contrary to the principle of equal treatment are abolished;
> b. any provisions contrary to the principle of equal treatment which are included in contracts or collective agreements, internal rules of undertakings

92 Ibid., at Article 7.
93 Ibid., at Article 9.
94 Ibid., at Article 10.

> or rules governing the independent occupations and professions and workers' and employers' organisations are, or may be, declared null and void or are amended.[95]

Finally, Article 17 deals with sanctions:

> 17. Member States shall lay down the rules on sanctions applicable to infringements of the national provisions adopted pursuant to this Directive and shall take all measures necessary to ensure that they are applied. The sanctions, which may comprise the payment of compensation to the victim, must be effective, proportionate and dissuasive. Member States shall notify those provisions to the Commission by 2 December 2003 at the latest and shall notify it without delay of any subsequent amendment affecting them.[96]

Currently, the Member States of the European Union are: Austria, Belgium, Denmark, Finland, France, Germany, Greece, Ireland, Italy, Luxembourg, the Netherlands, Portugal, Spain, Sweden and the United Kingdom, and since 1 May 2004, Cyprus (Greek part), the Czech Republic, Estonia, Hungary, Latvia, Lithuania, Malta, Poland, Slovakia and Slovenia, expanded it from 15 to 25 Member States, and since 1 January 2007, Bulgaria and Romania bringing the number to 27 Member States. Candidate countries are Croatia, the Former Yugoslave Republic of Macedonia, and Turkey. The remaining European Countries which are not Member States of the European Union are Albania, Andorra, Belarus, Bosnia-Herzegovina, Iceland, Liechtenstein, Moldova, Monaco, Montenegro, Norway, Russia, San Marino, Serbia, Switzerland, Ukraine and Vatican City.

The European Union is at a crossroads challenged to adapt the vision of the "founding fathers" that was first designed for six Member States to a future union of over twenty States. In essence, Europe is now the biggest frontier-free market in the world. The single market removed three types of barriers to free movement, namely physical, technical and fiscal. The four freedoms of the Union, for goods, services, people and capital, have become a reality. Further, the new single currency, the euro was introduced as legal tender on 1 January 1999, and replaced the currencies of those Member States in agreement on 1 January 2002. The criteria used for a nation to secure membership in the ever-growing European Union are: (1) democratic institutions and the rule of law, with respect for human rights and minorities within the borders; (2) a functioning market economy capable of competing within the union's single market; and (3) the acceptance of obligations of membership, signing on to the union's body of rules. The latter is perhaps the most important criterion for equal rights and their enforcement.

European enlargement has increased the population of the European Union by almost 20%, to roughly 500 million inhabitants, the third most populated political

---

95 Ibid., at Article 16.

96 Ibid., at Article 17.

entity in the world after China and India.[97] The European Union's share of the world population is falling though. If current trends for fertility, mortality and migration continue, the European Union population will peak in the year 2025 and revert to its current level in the year 2050. Further, Europe has experienced an increased divorce rate, a falling birth rate, a longer life expectancy and a positive net balance of migration. The trend towards ageing of the European population, a major challenge for the EU-15, is present in the new EU. Immigration, the other driving force behind European Union demographic change, has grown considerably over the last decade. At present, it accounts for three-quarters of the net growth of the EU-15 population. The situation in the new Member States, on the other hand, has changed very little. In some of the Baltic republics, the population has even declined as a result of emigration. With the accession of the ten new Member States in 2004, migratory movements from acceding countries to EU-15 countries, historically **class**ified as immigration flows, have become internal mobility. Previous experience and recent estimates suggest that labor mobility from new to old Member States will be moderate, with specific situations in the border regions. Furthermore, in the light of cultural and historical links, new Member States could become host countries for people emigrating to the European Union from countries of other countries.

The socio-economic conditions in the EU-15 countries have been marked by steady improvements in employment and real income since 1995. Furthermore, significant progress has been recorded in reducing disparities both among countries and among regions within the countries. By contrast, eight of the new Member States, Estonia, Hungary, Latvia, Lithuania, Poland, the Czech Republic, Slovakia and Slovenia, experienced an economic crisis as they emerged from a long period of economic stagnation under the old regime and started on the road towards a market economy. However, the great majority of them have already made up the ground lost during the initial transition period. Moreover, the new Member States are well placed for pursuing faster economic growth after enlargement, thereby making progress in achieving real convergence.

In the area of social cohesion, the differences between the EU-15 countries and the new Member States are particularly pronounced. With enlargement, income disparities increased considerably. Whereas income differentials between the EU-15 countries and regions diminished significantly, they rose among the new Member States, and so the European Union must therefore address the new east–west divide resulting from enlargement. Employment levels in the EU-15 countries, a major determining factor of economic and social inclusion, still show a north–south divide, which has significant implications for the social situation. With enlargement, the lower employment rates in several regions of the south will be mirrored in the east due to the effects of restructuring and job losses in

97 Commission Report on the social situation in the European Union, Report on social protection in Europe 2004 [not published in the Official Journal].

agriculture and industry. This substantial reduction of jobs in these sectors has not yet been compensated for by the growth of services.

As for investing in education, the new Member States are outperforming the majority of the EU-15 countries in upper secondary education. However, the EU-15 countries produce better results when it comes to tertiary education. Disparities as regards life-long learning and familiarity with information and communication technologies (ICT), more current in the EU-15 countries, also exist. Satisfaction with life also differs considerably between the EU-15 countries and the ten new Member States, the latter being significantly less satisfied with their personal safety and social life. The instruments of social protection aim to reduce poverty, promote social and civil dialogue, create jobs and tackle regional and social disparities in a strategic fashion.

As for minimum income and social assistance, almost all the EU-15 Member States provide all legal residents with some form of minimum income guarantee, supplemented by various benefits and allowances in the form of cash or services, which help to reduce the risk of poverty and promote effective integration in the labor market. The impact of social assistance programs in the countries of Central and Eastern Europe show poor targeting, widespread under-coverage and low levels of benefits. Some countries have reinforced schemes intended to ensure adequate minimum levels of income through guaranteed minimum income schemes, social pensions or universal social assistance guarantees.

European societies are witnessing a growing trend towards ethnic, cultural and religious diversity that continues post enlargement due to a combination of factors such as the ageing of the population, labor shortages in certain sectors, and political instability and poverty. Measures to promote the inclusion and participation of ethnic minorities are therefore needed. In the new Member States, immigration is a fairly recent phenomenon and the main focus is on the situation of the historical minorities, including the Roma, who often have lower levels of training and are more likely to live in low income households. It will be necessary to tackle these problems by combining measures for employment, social inclusion and the fight against discrimination.

Importantly, the extent of civic mindedness, trust and participation of the population forms the basis of a civil society that influences the economic, social and political performance of a country. In most of the new Member States of Central and Eastern Europe, civil society is marked by sparse participation in public life and distrust of public institutions, a legacy of the previous centralized regimes. Even if civic participation has improved since the beginning of the transition period, it is still lower than in the EU-15 countries. Collective bargaining at bipartite and tripartite level is fairly limited in the new Member States. Despite sustained efforts to develop industrial relations and social dialogue in the ten new Member States, their social partners still face challenges with a view to fully participating in economic and social governance.

Developments in coordination on policies and employment at the European Union level have broadened the scope of the European Social Agenda. The situation in several acceding countries calls for political efforts to be intensified to prevent disparities in living conditions, and to fight against poverty and social exclusion. To achieve these objectives, it will be important to draw on mutually reinforcing synergies between social and employment policies. The new Member States have a number of achievements and advantages in their favor, such as a relatively high level of training, an ability to tackle difficult reform issues and a good level of social cohesion. With the support of European Union policies, these advantages will become the basis of a powerful driving force of economic growth and social progress within the enlarged Union.[98]

Overall, legislation and education have proven to help overcome some discrimination. The European Union has provided important contributions to the ending of class discrimination in the coming together of people of different nations, and equality in employment is a real commitment for the Member States. The right of all individuals to equality before the law and to protection from discrimination is a fundamental principle of all democratic societies.[99] Establishing an effective set of laws against discrimination is an essential part of stamping out unfair treatment, but laws themselves are not enough. If discrimination is to be eliminated, attitudes and behavior must also change. A European Union-wide action program against discrimination was developed, with its purpose to support activities which combat discrimination and to raise awareness as to measures being taken across the Union to tackle it.

According to the 57th Eurobarometer survey on discrimination 2002, few respondents reported personally experiencing discrimination on any of the six grounds explored, but the most often cited ground for discrimination was age (5%), followed by race or ethnicity (3%), religion or beliefs (2%), physical disability, learning difficulties or mental illness (2%) and sexual orientation (less than 1%).[100] Young people, the better educated and those on the left of the political spectrum were more likely to report having experienced discrimination. Further, those who personally experienced discrimination, young people and respondents with leftist political views were significantly more likely to report witnessing discrimination. The most often cited ground for witnessed discrimination was race or ethnicity (22%), followed by learning difficulties or mental illness (12%), physical disability (11%), religion or beliefs (9%), age (6%) and sexual orientation (6%). The rates of witnessed discrimination are considerably higher than the rates of discrimination experienced, and in general, the longer the time spent in full-time education, the more likely a respondent was to report having witnessed

---

98 Ibid.

99 Eurobarometer 57, *Discrimination in Europe, For Diversity Against Discrimination*, 2003, Alan Marsh and Melahat Sahin-Dikmen, The European Opinion Research Group (EEIG) for the European Commission Directorate General Employment and Social Affairs.

100 Marsh, Alan, and Sahin-Dikmen, Melahat, *Discrimination in Europe*, London, 2002.

discrimination. Professionals and managers and the service sector employees were more likely than the other respondents to report witnessing discrimination on all grounds; compared with manual workers and the self-employed, twice as many professional and managerial employees reported witnessing discrimination on grounds of religion.

The young, better-educated and non-manually-employed women are more likely to oppose discrimination, older male manual workers with little education less so, but there is no clear evidence that the tendency to believe discrimination right or wrong, or to attribute such views to others, is socially determined to any great degree.[101] However, despite widespread legal protection, discrimination continues to exist and further efforts are needed to ensure that the right not to be discriminated against is implemented effectively in an enlarged European Union. Therefore, 2007 was designated as the European Year of Equal Opportunities for All, with the aim to inform people of their rights, to celebrate diversity and to promote equal opportunities for everyone in the European Union.

In the European Employment Strategy, the European Union has set out to combat unemployment and significantly increase the employment rate of Europe on a lasting basis. "Flexicurity" strategies imply political choices between various aspects of flexibility and security. The flexicurity model remains in line with the central elements of the European Union strategy for sustainable economic growth with more jobs, better jobs and greater social cohesion. Policy measures must focus on making the labor market more open to all workers, rather than putting the blame for their exclusion from employment on them. Seen as an integral part of the macroeconomic policy-mix, flexicurity should be an additional tool strengthening the European social model, which promotes strong social protection, gender equalities, high living standards and quality of life, social cohesion and measures to combat exclusion, both from the labor market and within society. The effects of policies related to flexicurity on vulnerable groups must be adequately considered as should the interconnected dimensions of social cohesion, nondiscrimination and equality. The flexicurity approach must draw on a high level of workforce training.

Assuring a flexible approach towards employees not only attracts the best workers, but it also contributes to achieving employment targets and reducing barriers to the labor market by making employment accessible to more people. Flexible and short-term contracts should not lead to increased discrimination in employment by providing a rationale to terminate employment and becoming a substitute for discrimination. Flexicurity policies must make it attractive for employers to employ workers from various minorities, and attractive for workers to remain or re-enter employment. A two-fold responsibility exists: on the employer side, this responsibility lies in the provision of suitable working conditions accommodating diverse practices, of adequate early warning systems, and of the availability of training and support to workers to find future employment; on employee side, there is an individual responsibility to remain continuously

101 Ibid.

employable.[102] Thus, it will be necessary to develop incentives to change people's behavior with regard to class distinctions and to combat discrimination.

Overall, the Union is convinced of the usefulness of international cooperation so that countries can learn and profit from each other's experience. The Organization for Security and Co-operation in Europe (OSCE) is one of the largest regional security organization in the world with 55 participating States from Europe, Central Asia and North America. OSCE was created by the 1975 Helsinki Final Act which contained a provision to "respect ... human rights and fundamental freedoms, including freedom of thought, conscience and religion, and belief", as well as "equal rights and self-determination of peoples".[103] The OSCE's Parliamentary Assembly passed a declaration in Ottawa in 1995 calling on member states to provide equal protection against discrimination for all, social origin being among the grounds specifically protected from discrimination:

> 29. Calls on the participating States to ensure that all persons belonging to different segments of their populations be accorded equal respect and consideration in their constitutions, legislation and administration and that there be no subordination, explicit or implied, on the basis of ethnicity, race, colour, language, religion, sex, sexual orientation, national or social origin or belonging to a minority.[104]

In terms of education as a tool for advancement and to combat class discrimination, the fifth annual "indicators and benchmarks" report, drawn up by the commission's Education Directorate General, along with Eurostat, the CRELL Research Centre and the Eurydice European Unit, examines each country's performances regarding completion of secondary education, early school leaving rate, low achievement in reading literacy, the number of mathematics, science and technology graduates, and the participation of adults in lifelong learning activities.[105] For the EU as a whole, "overall performance is on a par with the best in the world". About 3 million more European students are now in higher education and 1 million more students graduate each year than in 2000, with 13 million more higher education graduates in the EU's working-age population than in 2000. Roughly 60% of 15–29 year-olds are enrolled in schools and higher education, comparable with the US and 18% higher than in Japan, but almost 108 million people in Europe, about a third of the labor force, still have low educational attainment. Six million young people, one in seven of all 18–24 year-olds, obtained only compulsory education or less. Of the 25–64 year-olds, they are three times more likely to participate in lifelong learning if they have completed at least upper secondary education. In general, boys do

102 Eurobarometer 263, *Discrimination in the European Union*, 2007.

103 Helsinki Final Act.

104 OSCE Parliamentary Assembly declaration 1995.

105 Osborn, Alan, "Europe: Raising Education Standards" *University World News*, issue 0037, 20 July 2008.

less well in reading than girls and have more special education needs but girls did less well in mathematics and under-performed in maths, science and technology. Except in low reading achievement where, instead of a 20% decrease, the share of low achievers in the EU has increased by more than 10%, progress has been made. Thus, the number of maths, science and technology graduates has risen and now exceeds the 15% benchmark growth rate. Some progress has been made in reducing the number of early school leavers, increasing upper secondary attainment of young people and increasing adult participation in lifelong learning.

Nine countries, Finland, Denmark, Sweden, the United Kingdom, Ireland, Poland, Slovenia, Norway and Iceland have beaten the five benchmarks on average and are still progressing. Also, lifelong learning is becoming a reality in Sweden, the UK, Denmark, Norway and Iceland, countries that have developed comprehensive and coherent lifelong learning strategies. In reading, the top countries are Finland, Ireland and Estonia, with Romania and Bulgaria at the bottom. In early school leaving, the best were the Czech Republic, Poland and Slovakia plus perhaps Slovenia, and the worst are Malta and Portugal. Countries as a whole have done well in raising graduate numbers in maths, science and technology; the target was a 15% increase whereas the numbers actually rose by 29% over 2000, and the female share rose from 30.7% to 31.6%. Poland, Estonia and Ireland were the best-achieving, with Belgium, Slovenia, Austria, the Netherlands, Cyprus and Malta at the foot of the table. A target of 12.5% of the working-age population engaged in lifelong learning was set and the level has increased from 7.1 % in 2000 to 9.7% in 2006, with Sweden, Denmark and the UK at the top and Bulgaria and Romania at the bottom.[106]

Conclusion

It is important that equality be achieved in securing access to jobs, which are commensurate with skill levels. Some groups are still lagging behind due to horizontal segregation, and vertical segregation, with difficulty acceding to higher positions in the occupational hierarchy. The system has failed to reward skills, and even provides guises for discrimination. The demographic changes on the horizon will bring about a further need for qualified workers. However, some remain under-utilized, considered as reserve labor. This attitude is a barrier to progressive legislation. Although European laws have gone a long way to improving the plight of many in the European Union, in reality, some have yet to enjoy the equality they are entitled to in theory. The European Union is a political structure, which emerged out of a general act of will of heterogeneous States. It is ultimately dependent on statements of general principle. Therefore, European Union law is the motor to enable the European Union to move toward its ultimate aim, the "ever closer union".

106 Ibid.

In terms of tolerance of class distinctions, the European Union's action program has several main components, namely a fair deal in rights at work involving equality legislation and court cases; better opportunities to earn a living involving the promotion of jobs, education and entrepreneurship; getting minorities in positions of power involving equal opportunities in employment; and European Union-wide networks involving training, expanding subjects in school and reinforcing a positive image of all, regardless of class.[107] Relations between the institutions of the European Union are based on partnership, cooperation and mutual dependence. The concern is to enhance the social, economic and cultural welfare of all citizens in an atmosphere of peace. This, thereby, advances the cause of freedom in stamping out discrimination of any kind, including class discrimination, through the effective use of laws and the courts, in the pursuit of "Class Act".

107 Commission of the European Communities, *Equal Opportunity for Women and Men*, Brussels, no date, p. 5.

Chapter 10
Conclusion to Class Act

In the quest for tolerance of class distinctions in *Class Act*, a deep embedded patriarchal authority is still keeping society on the designated track, as *de jure* discrimination has given way to *de facto* discrimination, and in essence, inequality, once obvious and accepted, is now hidden and protected in a most dangerous way. Since within society there is an a-priori assumption of freedom and impartiality, the burden is high on the attackers of this universal opinion. Human inequality both encompasses class discrimination and conceals it, and although other types of discrimination exist apart from class inequality, discrimination which is so blatant and open as to focus on one's class and social origin is most persistent and threatening to society. Therefore, seeking out inequality and bringing it to the forefront of microscopic debate can only serve to advance all quests for equality.

Both legislation and the court system have made inroads into class discrimination. It is important to have adequate legislation to influence conduct and outcomes, as well as an appropriate legal system to achieve favorable and enforceable results. By cooperating and learning from other similarly disadvantaged groups in the fight for equality of opportunity, more advances can be made in the fight for class equality. We will never totally correct the injustices of the past or of the present. However, with a greater appreciation of class and the pursuit of tolerance of class distinctions, as well as a better understanding of the importance of adequate legislation, future endeavors in the field will help to improve the situation for all people.

Countries around the world have made important progress in the development of equal rights. Equality rights legislation and court challenges are required, in order to improve the situation of all in the workplace. The desire is for equal human rights for all. Class discrimination is an equal opportunity discrimination as it cuts across race, ethnicity, gender, language, age, sexual orientation, religion and disability. Therefore, the law needs to be enforced by way of the courts to achieve greater equality in an effort to modify historical attitudes, so that nations conform to certain standards. There should be real freedom to choose one's amount of participation in the work force, in the pursuit of flexibility as to a just remuneration and access to employment.

Further, taking into account the fact that continuing inequalities and noticeable progress coexist, rethinking employment policies is necessary in order to integrate the class neutral perspective, not only to address any negative implications of current patterns of work and employment, but also to draw attention to a wider range of opportunities. Governments and other actors need to promote an active and visible policy of mainstreaming the '*Class Act*' perspective into all policies and programs.

The central importance of equality legislation in order to bring about change is evident and indeed critical. Our very rights as human beings emanate from the word of the law and the interpretation given by the highest courts in the land. Therefore, it is imperative that the struggle for class equality encompass the legal system. The concept of total equality has never truly existed, nor was it ever meant to be anything more than empty promises of change. Absolute equality is not sought in this book, nor is it realistic. However, in a feeling of mutual respect for individual differences, a better equality among humans is possible and desirable through society's laws and legal institutions.

The keys to the future are the implementation and development of the law, the deepening in understanding of specific legal issues relating to employment discrimination, and the raising of the level of awareness of legal rights and obligations. In addition, a continuing exchange of experience and expertise needs to occur on the international front for mutual benefit among all groups in order to best serve the fight for class equality. We must all strive to promote and improve the situation of all humans through networks of awareness, in the raising of initiatives, the dissemination of information and the provision of support for equality. In addition, there needs to be a full employment policy for the integration of all humans into the labor market, the reduction of barriers to access and participation in employment, the improvement in the quality of employment through education, training and management of resources, and the improvement in the status of all in society for a change of attitudes and a lasting progress.[1]

Further, we must learn from other groups' experiences in the fight for equality. As such, like the civil rights' movement, the women's liberation movement and the disability movement, in examining legislation, we should take into account the human rights movement in general, and specifically its advancements in class rights and tolerance for those of all different classes. Therefore, in the struggle to secure equal rights for all, the consultation process must include input from other groups for strategic purposes in order to strengthen the cause. The process must be one of inclusion not exclusion.

It is realistic to say that inequality in general exists, but especially inequality of opportunity within the labor force. This is to be expected, since not all humans have occupied a major role in the employment sphere. In addition to this, laws have been enacted and courts have enforced them in a traditionally younger white male non-disability dominant way. However, all humans too need to be a rallying symbol of political and economic force, so that equality can become a reality. The impact of equality legislation will depend on the legislative provisions as well as the effectiveness of the legislation's enforcement.

The full and equal enjoyment of all human rights and fundamental freedoms should be a priority for all and is essential for the advancement of all. Equal rights are explicitly mentioned in the Preamble to the Charter of the United Nations, and

1 Commission of the European Communities, *Promotion of Positive Action*, Brussels, 1991, p. 4.

all the major international human rights instruments should include class or social origin as one of the grounds upon which States may not discriminate. Unless the human rights of all are fully recognized and effectively protected, applied, implemented and enforced in national and international law as well as in national practice in family, civil, penal, labor and commercial codes and administrative rules and regulations, they will exist in name only.[2]

In the fight against class discrimination, Robert F. Kennedy said it best about the importance of education:

> I suspect there may always be arguments about what constitutes a higher education, but wise men through the ages have at least been able to agree on its purpose. Its purpose is not only to discipline and instruct, but above all to free the mind – to free it from darkness, the narrowness, the groundless fears and self-defeating passions of ignorance. You may sometimes regret it, for a free mind insists on seeking out reality, and reality is often a far and more painful matter than the soft and comfortable illusions of the intellectually poor.[3]

It is evident that we are moving in the right direction, since some change has taken place. However, further change is necessary and plausible. Only by working on the very thing that controls and defines all of our lives, the law, can further progress be made. Once again, the memorable words of the Rev. Martin Luther King Jr. in his struggle for civil rights are most relevant today in the struggle for equality for those who are discriminated against, including for their class and social origin in the pursuit of "Class Act":

> I have a dream that one day every valley shall be exalted, every hill and mountain shall be made low, the rough places shall be made plain, and the crooked places shall be made straight and the glory of the Lord will be revealed and all flesh shall see it together. This is our hope..And when we allow freedom to ring, when we let it ring from every village and hamlet, from every state and city, we will be able to speed up that day when all of God's children..will be able to join hands and to sing in the words of the old Negro spiritual, 'Free at last, free at last; thank God Almighty, we are free at last'.[4]

---

2 United Nations, *Beijing Declaration and Platform for Action*, 1995.

3 Kennedy, Robert F., Speech, Commencement Exercises, Trinity College, Washington, D.C., 2 June 1963

4 King Jr., Martin Luther, *March on Washington*, 28 August 1963.

Bibliography

African Charter on Human and Peoples' Rights, 1981.

American Convention on Human Rights, 1978.

American Declaration of the Rights and Duties of Man, 1948.

American Federation of State, County and Municipal Employees v. Washington, 770 F.2d. 1401 (1985).

American Nurses Association v. State of Illinois, 783 F.2d. 716 (1986).

Anti-Discrimination Act, Australia, 1991.

Australia's Beijing Plus Five Action Plan 2001–2005.

Axworthy, Lloyd (1988), "Free Trade, The Costs for Canada", in A.R. Riggs and Tom Velk, *Canadian-American Free Trade: (The Sequel) Historical, Political and Economic Dimensions*, Montreal: The Institute for Research on Public Policy.

Basi v. Canadian National Railway (1984), 9 CHRR 4. D/5029 (CHRTribunal).

Bill of Rights Act, New Zealand, 1990.

Black, Sandra, Devereux, Paul and Salvanes, Kjell, "Why the Apple Doesn't Fall Far: Understanding Intergenerational Transmission of Human Capital", *American Economic Review*, Vol. 95, No. 1 (Mar. 2005), pp. 437–49.

Blake v. Ministry of Correctional Services and Mimico Correctional Institute (1984), 5 CHRR D/2417 (Ontario).

Board of Trustees of Keene State College v. Sweeney, 439 US 24 (1978).

Brecher, Irving (1987), "The Free Trade Initiative, On Course or Off", in A.R. Riggs and Tom Velk, *Canadian-American Free Trade: Historical, Political and Economic Dimensions*, Montreal: The Institute for Research in Public Policy.

Brennan v. City Stores, 479 F.2d. 235 (1973).

British North America Act, Canada, 1867.

Campbell, Bruce (1993), *Free Trade, Destroyer of Jobs*, Ottawa: Canadian Centre for Policy Alternatives.

Canada Employment Equity Act, Canada, 1995.

Canada–United States Free Trade Agreement, 1989.

Canadian Advisory Council on the Status of Women (1992), *Feminist Guide to the Canadian Constitution*, Ottawa.

Canadian Bill of Rights, Canada, 1960.

Canadian Human Rights Act, Canada, 1978.

Cassin, René (1969), From the Ten Commandments to the Rights of Man, France.

Central Alberta Dairy Pool v. Alberta (Human Rights Commission), [1990] 2 S.C.R. 489.

Charter of the Organization of African Unity, 1963.

Charter of Rights and Freedoms, Quebec.

Civil Rights Act, United States, 1964.

Coleman, Frank (1977), *Hobbes and America*, Toronto: University of Toronto Press.

Commission for Racial Equality (2002), Code of Practice on the Duty to Promote Race Equality, UK.

Commission of the European Communities (no date), *Equal Opportunity for Women and Men*, Brussels.

Commission of the European Communities (1991), *Promotion of Positive Action*, Brussels.

Commission Report on the social situation in the European Union, Report on social protection in Europe, 2004 [not published in the Official Journal].

Constitución Política de los Estados Unidos Mexicanos, Mexico.

Constitution Act of 1867, Canada.

Constitution Act of 1982, Canada.

Constitution of Ireland, 1937.

Constitution of South Africa, 1996.

Copenhagen Declaration on Social Development, 1995

Corning Glass Works v. Brennan, 417 US 188 (1974).

Costa v. ENEL [1964] CMLR 425.

Council Decision 2000/750/EC of 27 November 2000 Establishing a Community Action Programme to Combat Discrimination (2001 to 2006).

Council Directive 2000/78/EC of 27 November 2000 Establishing a General Framework for Equal Treatment in Employment and Occupation.

County of Allegheny v. American Civil Liberties Union Greater Pittsburgh Chapter, 492 U.S. 573 (1989).

Cox, Archibald (1967), *Civil Rights, The Constitution and the Court*, Cambridge, MA: Harvard University Press.

Cox, Archibald (1976), *The Role of the Supreme Court in American Government*, New York: Oxford University Press.

d'Aquino, Thomas (1987), "Truck and Trade with the Yankees, The Case for a Canada-U.S. Comprehensive Trade Agreement", in A.R. Riggs and Tom Velk, *Canadian-American Free Trade: Historical, Political and Economic Dimensions*, Montreal: The Institute for Research on Public Policy.

Daltrop, Anne (1982), *Political Realities, Politics and the European Community*, London: Longman,.

Davis v. Passman, 442 US 228 (1979).

Declaration of Independence, United States, 1776.

DeJong, Peter, Brawer, Milton and Robin, Stanley, "Patterns of Female Intergenerational Occupational Mobility: A Comparison with Male Patterns of Intergenerational Occupational Mobility", *American Sociological Review*, Vol. 36, No. 6 (Dec. 1971), pp. 1033–42.

Discrimination Act, Australia, 1991.

Easterbrook, W.T. and Aitken, Hugh (1976), *Canadian Economic History*, Toronto: Macmillan,.
Economic Commission for Africa (2002), *Economic Report on Africa*.
Ely, J. (1980), *Democracy and Distrust*, Cambridge, MA: Harvard University Press.
Employment Contracts Act, New Zealand, 1991.
Employment Equality Act, Ireland, 1998.
Employment Equity Act, South Africa, 1998.
Employment Relations Act, New Zealand, 2000.
Employment Rights Act, UK, 1996.
Equal Opportunities Commission, *Code of Practice on Equal Pay*, UK.
Equal Pay Act, UK, 1970.
Equal Pay Act, United States, 1963.
Equal Status Act, Ireland, 2000.
Equality Act, UK, 2006.
Equality Act, UK, 2010.
Eurobarometer 57, *Discrimination in Europe, For Diversity Against Discrimination*, 2003, Alan Marsh and Melahat Sahin-Dikmen, The European Opinion Research Group (EEIG) for the European Commission Directorate General Employment and Social Affairs.
Eurobarometer 263, *Discrimination in the European Union*, 2007.
European Convention for the Protection of Human Rights and Fundamental Freedoms, 1950.
European Convention for the Protection of Human Rights and Fundamental Freedoms as amended by Protocol No. 1.
European Convention for the Protection of Human Rights and Fundamental Freedoms as amended by Protocol No. 11.
European Convention for the Protection of Human Rights and Fundamental Freedoms as amended by Protocol No. 12, 2000.
European Social Charter, 1961.
European Social Charter (revised), 1996.
Fair Work Act, Australia, 2009.
Federal Task Force on Disability Issues (1996), *Equal Citizenship for Canadians with Disabilities: The Will to Act*.
Federalist Papers, United States, 1787–88.
Fried, Morton (1967), *The Evolution of Political Society*, New York: Random House.
Fry, Earl (1987), "Trends in Canada-U.S. Free Trade Discussions", in A.R. Riggs and Tom Welk, *Canadian-American Free Trade: Historical, Political and Economic Dimensions*, The Institute for Research in Public Policy, Montreal.
General Agreement on Tariffs and Trade, 1947.
Gillette v. United States, 401 U.S. 437 (1971).
Government of Canada (1993), *The North American Free Trade Agreement at a Glance*, Ottawa.

Government of Canada (2002), *NAFTA at Eight*, Ottawa.
Griffin Cohen, Marjorie (1987), *Free Trade and the Future of Women's Work, Manufacturing and Service Industries*, Toronto: Garamond Press.
Griggs v. Duke Power Co., 401 US 424 (1971).
Grismer: Terry Grismer (Estate) v. The British Columbia Superintendent of Motor Vehicles et al., [1999] 3 S.C.R. 868.
Habermas, Jürgen (1998), *Between Facts and Norms*, Massachusetts: MIT Press,.
Hamelin, Jean (1976), *Histoire du Québec*, Edisem: St. Hyacinthe.
Harris, Diana K. (2005), "Age Norms", in Erdman B. Palmore, Laurence Branch and Diana K. Harris, *Encyclopedia of Ageism*, New York: The Haworth Press, Inc.
Harris, Richard (1988), "Some Observations on the Canada-U.S. Free Trade Deal", in A.R. Riggs and Tom Velk, *Canadian-American Free Trade: (The Sequel) Historical, Political and Economic Dimensions*, Montreal: The Institute for Research on Public Policy.
Hatfield, Robert, "Duty to Accommodate", *Just Labour*, Vol. 5 (Winter 2005), p. 23.
Hayes, Bernadette, "Female Intergenerational Occupational Mobility Within Northern Ireland and the Republic of Ireland", *British Journal of Sociology*, Vol. 38 (May 1987), p. 66.
Helsinki Final Act, 1975.
Hornstein, Zmira (2001), *Outlawing Age Discrimination: Foreign Lessons, UK Choices*, Bristol: The Policy Press.
Human Resources and Social Development Canada (2006), Anti-Discrimination Clauses and Practices.
Human Rights Act, Australia, 2004.
Human Rights Act, New Zealand, 1993.
Human Rights Act, UK, 1998.
Human Rights and Equal Opportunity Commission Act, Australia, 1986.
Hurtig, Mel (1991), *The Betrayal of Canada*, Toronto: Stoddart Publishing.
Inter-American Democratic Charter, 2001.
Interim Constitution of South Africa, Schedule 4.
Internationale Handelsgesellschaft, [1970] ECR 1125, [1972] CMLR 255.
Kennedy, President John F. (1961), Address to the Canadian Parliament, 17 May.
Kennedy, Robert F. (1963) Speech, Commencement Exercises, Trinity College, Washington, D.C., 2 June.
Kimel v. Florida Board of Regents, 528 U.S. 62 (2000).
King Jr., Martin Luther (1963), March on Washington, 28 August.
Labor Canada (1986), *Equal Pay for Work of Equal Value*, Ottawa.
Laun, Louis (1987), "U.S.-Canada Free Trade Negotiations: Historical Opportunities", in A.R. Riggs and Tom Velk, *Canadian-American Free Trade: Historical, Political and Economic Dimensions*, Montreal: The Institute for Research in Public Policy.

Layton, Robert (1987), "Why Canada Needs Free Trade", in A.R. Riggs and Tom Velk, *Canadian-American Free Trade: Historical, Political and Economic Dimensions*, Montreal: The Institute for Research in Public Policy.

Ley del Seguro Social, Mexico.

Ley Federal de Trabajo, Mexico.

Lipsey, Richard (1987), "Canada's Trade Options", in A.R. Riggs and Tom Velk, *Canadian-American Free Trade: Historical, Political and Economic Dimensions*, Montreal: The Institute for Research in Public Policy.

Maastricht Treaty, 1992.

Magna Carta, Great Britain, 1215.

Mandel, Michael (1989), *The Charter of Rights and the Legalization of Politics in Canada*, Toronto: Wall & Thompson.

Marbury v. Madison, 1 Cranch 137 (1803).

Marsh, Alan and Sahin-Dikmen, Mehalat (2002), *Discrimination in Europe*, London: Policy Studies Institute.

McCullough v. Maryland, 4 Wheaton 415 (1819).

McDonnell Douglas Corp. v. Green, 411 US 792 (1973).

McPhail, Brenda (1985), *NAFTA Now*, Lanham: University Press of America.

Meiorin: British Columbia (Public Service Employee Relations Commission) (BCPSERC) v. The British Columbia Government and Service Employees Union (BCGSEU) [1999], 35 C.H.R.R. D/257 (S.C.C.).

Merrett, Christopher (1996), *Free Trade, Neither Free Nor About Trade*, New York: Black Rose Books.

Mexican Investment Board (1994), *Mexico Your Partner for Growth, Regulatory Reform and Competition Policy, Setting the Incentives for an Efficient Economy*, Mexico City.

Minister of Home Affairs and Another v Fourie and Another (Doctors For Life Internationaland Others, Amicus Curiae); Lesbian and Gay Equality Project and Others v. Minister of Home Affairs and Others, (CCT 60/04), (CCT 10/05); 2006 (1) SA 524 (CC); 2006 (3) BCLR 355 (CC) (1 December 2005).

Murphy v. Miller Brewer Co., 307 F.Supp. 829 (1969).

Nader, Ralph (1993), *The Case Against Free Trade*, San Francisco: Earth Island Press.

Neufeld, E.P. (1987), "Financial and Economic Dimensions of Free Trade", in A.R. Riggs and Tom Velk, *Canadian-American Free Trade: Historical, Political and Economic Dimensions*, Montreal: The Institute for Research on Public Policy.

Nicoll, William and Salmon, Trevor (1994), *Understanding the New European Community*, Exeter: Prentice Hall.

North American Agreement on Labor Cooperation, 1993.

North American Free Trade Agreement, 1994.

North, Arthur (1964), *The Supreme Court, Judicial Process and Judicial Politics*, New York: Appleton Century Crofts.

Northern Ireland Act, 1998.

OECD (1998), *Human Capital Investment – An International Comparison*, Paris: OECD, pp. 15–34.
OECD (2004), Education at a Glance.
Ontario Human Rights Commission v. Simpsons-Sears Ltd., [1985] SCR 536.
Osborn, Alan, "Europe: Raising Education Standards", *University World News*, issue 0037, 20 July 2008
OSCE Parliamentary Assembly declaration 1995.
Pope John Paul II (1981), *Laborem Exercens*, Rome.
Pope John XXIII (1963), *Pacem in Terris*, Rome.
Population Council, *Horizons* research summary, "Poverty, Educational Attainment, and Livelihoods: How Well Do Young People Fare in KwaZulu Natal, South Africa?", Washington, D.C., 2004.
Promotion of Equality and Prevention of Unfair Discrimination Act, South Africa, 2000.
Protocol on the Rights of Women in Africa, 2003.
Protocol to the African Charter on Human and Peoples' Rights on the Establishment of an African Court on Human and Peoples' Rights, 2003.
Race Relations Act, New Zealand, 1971.
Race Relations Act, UK, 1976.
Race Relations Act (Amendment) Regulations, UK, 2006.
Race Relations Act (Statutory Duties) Order 2001, 2003, 2004, UK.
Racial Discrimination Act, Australia, 1975.
Racial Hatred Act, Australia, 1995.
Raynauld, André (1987), "Looking Outward Again", in A.R. Riggs and Tom Velk, *Canadian-American Free Trade: Historical, Political and Economic Dimensions*, Montreal: The Institute for Research on Public Policy.
Regina v. Oakes, [1986] 1 S.C.R. 103.
Rosenfeld, Rachel, "Women's Intergenerational Occupational Mobility", *American Sociological Review*, Vol. 43, No. 1 (Feb. 1978), pp. 36–46.
Sex Discrimination Act, Australia, 1984.
Sex Discrimination Act, UK, 1975.
Shakes v. Rex Pak Ltd. (1982), 3 CHRR D/1001.
Soldatos, P (1988), "Canada's Foreign Policy in Search of a Fourth Option: Continuity and Change in Orientation Towards the U.S.", in A.R. Riggs and Tom Velk, *Canadian-American Free Trade: (The Sequel) Historical, Political and Economic Dimensions*, Montreal: The Institute for Research on Public Policy.
Spaulding v. University of Washington, 740 F.2d. 686 (1984).
Statute of the Inter-American Court on Human Rights, 1980.
Stone, Frank (1987), "Removing Barriers to Canada", in A.R. Riggs and Tom Velk, *Canadian-American Free Trade: Historical, Political and Economic Dimensions*, Montreal: The Institute for Research on Public Policy.
Teuling v. Bredrijfsvereniging, [1987] ECR 2497.
Treaty establishing a Constitution for Europe, 2004.
Treaty of Amsterdam, 1997.

Treaty of Lisbon, 2007.
Treaty of Paris, 1951.
Treaty of Rome, 1957.
Treaty of Waitangi, New Zealand, 1840.
United Nations (1945), Charter of the United Nations.
United Nations (1945), Statute of the International Court of Justice.
United Nations (1948), Universal Declaration of Human Rights.
United Nations (1951), Equal Remuneration Convention (ILO No. 100).
United Nations (1958), Discrimination (Employment and Occupation) Convention (ILO No. 111).
United Nations (1960), Convention against Discrimination in Education.
United Nations (1964), Employment Policy Convention (ILO No. 122).
United Nations (1965), International Convention on the Elimination of All Forms of Racial Discrimination.
United Nations (1966), International Covenant on Civil and Political Rights.
United Nations (1966), International Covenant on Economic, Social and Cultural Rights.
United Nations (1966), Optional Protocol to the International Covenant on Civil and Political Rights.
United Nations (1979), Convention on the Elimination of all Forms of Discrimination against Women.
United Nations (1991), Principles for Older Persons.
United Nations (1995), Beijing Declaration and Platform for Action.
United Nations (1999), Optional Protocol to the Convention on the Elimination of All Forms of Discrimination against Women.
United Nations (2002), Second World Assembly on Ageism, International Plan of Action on Ageing
United Nations Development Programme (1994), *Human Development Report*, Oxford: Oxford University Press.
United States Constitution, United States, 1776.
Velk, Tom and Riggs, A.R. (1988), "The Ongoing Debate Over Free Trade", in A.R. Riggs and Tom Velk, *Canadian-American Free Trade: (The Sequel) Historical, Political and Economic Dimensions*, Montreal: The Institute for Research on Public Policy.
Watkins, Mel (1989), "The Political Economy of Growth", in Wallace Clement and Glen Williams, *The New Canadian Political Economy*, Kingston: McGill-Queen's University Press.
Wigle, Randall (1987), "The Received Wisdom of the Canada-U.S. Free Trade Qualifications", in A.R. Riggs and Tom Welk, *Canadian-American Free Trade: Historical, Political and Economic Dimensions*, Montreal: The Institute for Research in Public Policy.
Wirth, L. (1945), "The Problem of Minority Groups", in R. Linton (ed.), *The Science of Man in the World Crisis*, New York: Columbia University Press, pp. 347–72..

Workplace Relations Act, Australia, 1996.
World Declaration on Education for All: Meeting Basic Learning Needs, The Framework for Action to Meet Basic Learning Needs, 1990.
World Summit on Social Development, 1995.

Index

For Product Safety Concerns and Information please contact our EU representative GPSR@taylorandfrancis.com Taylor & Francis Verlag GmbH, Kaufingerstraße 24, 80331 München, Germany